World Musics and Music Education

Facing the Issues

Edited by BENNETT REIMER

Based on a Northwestern University
Music Education Leadership Seminar

 The National Association for Music Education

Production Editor: Carol Anne Jones

Copyright © 2002
MENC—The National Association for Music Education
1806 Robert Fulton Drive
Reston, VA 20191

ISBN 1-56545-145-7

World Musics and Music Education

Facing the Issues

Contents

Preface
The Northwestern University
Music Education Leadership Seminars

The music education profession, like all others, must engage itself in continual efforts to improve its effectiveness and viability. Such efforts need to be made at a variety of levels, reflecting the complexity of this field. One of these levels, often neglected, requires the profession to nurture the expertise of its most influential members.

The Northwestern University Music Education Leadership Seminars (NUMELS) are conceived as a means of elevating all aspects of the music education profession by providing an intensive learning experience for people who are its top-level leaders, thinkers, and activists. A relatively small number of music educators exercise a high degree of influence on the profession's fortunes. These are the professionals who are most visible, productive, active, and well regarded in their respective areas of music education expertise. A great deal of the success of music education, in refining its understandings and reforming its practices, depends on their wisdom.

The continuing education of these national and international leaders occurs through their own, self-directed efforts to keep abreast of the issues most relevant to their work. Seldom, if ever, is there an opportunity available to them to expand their expertise by coming together with people as advanced as they, specifically to serve their needs for continued growth by learning from each other and from experts in related fields. The luxury, intensity, and excitement of being a student rather than a teacher is rare indeed for people at that high level of attainment, but is no less needed if their intellectual horizons and professional efficacy are to continue to expand.

In alternating summers starting in 1996, a small number of people (around a dozen) who are among the leading music educators in the particular aspect of music education on which a particular seminar focuses, have been invited to be participants. They spend five days at Northwestern University in informal discussions (led, in turn, by each participant), in interactions with guest instructors who are identified as being able to add useful dimensions to their expertise, in strategy sessions on needed professional initiatives in which they see themselves playing key roles, and in various other activities they mutually devise.

The 1996 NUMELS focused on the topic "Performance in the Context of the National Standards for Music Education." The 1998 Seminar was on "Issues of Multiculturalism in Music Education." The 2000 seminar dealt with "Composing in the Schools: A New Horizon for Music Education." "Popular Music and Music Education: Determining Our Obligations" is the topic for 2002.

The seminars are not product oriented in the sense of creating a final report, policy recommendation, or consensus document. Their purpose is to deepen and expand the leadership capacities of each attendee in whatever way each chooses to apply the learnings he or she has gained. However, during the first seminar the participants and NUMELS Director Bennett Reimer expressed the desire to share with the wider profession the wealth of experience and insights of the attendees, including those they gained as a result of the seminar. They jointly planned and wrote a book, *Performing with Understanding: The Challenge of the National Standards for Music Education,* published by MENC in 2000.

The present book is the outcome of the same desire by the participants in the second NUMELS. It is presented with the hope that the profession's understandings and practices in regard to world musics will be enhanced by the ideas and proposals these leaders present. Future books by seminar attendees are anticipated.

The seminars could not have occurred without the enthusiastic support of the Dean of Northwestern University's School of Music, Bernard Dobroski, who has supplied the financial wherewithal required and offered an extraordinary level of hospitality, making each NUMELS personally as well as professionally memorable. I am grateful to him for his remarkable generosity. Gratitude is also extended to Margaret A. Senko, MENC's Executive Editor, for her expert editing of the first book and her wise guidance for this second one. Editorial work for the present book was skillfully supplied by MENC's Carol Anne Jones.

I extend my heartfelt thanks to the authors of this volume for their patience and guidance in the arduous process of shepherding the book from conception to completion.

—Bennett Reimer

Introduction

The Need to Face the Issues

Bennett Reimer

Music of all periods, styles, forms, and cultures belongs in the curriculum. The musical repertory should be expanded to involve music of our time in its rich variety, including currently popular teenage music and avant-garde music, American folk music, and the music of other cultures.[1]

This statement, item two of eight in "The Tanglewood Declaration," from the Tanglewood Symposium of 1967, is revealing for what it says about music education in the United States in the late 1960s and for what has been accomplished and remains to be accomplished in the years that have followed. Clearly, there was a need at that time to declare that change was called for in the accepted repertoire of school music. That repertoire tended to be limited, requiring expansion in several directions. It needed to attend to the music of the contemporary world, a musical repertoire previously, and still at that time, largely ignored. Popular musics of young people also needed to be included in the curriculum and were largely absent from it. American folk music was indeed represented in the form of folk songs sung in general music classes, but apparently not sufficiently or in the optimal ways the writers of the Declaration desired. And the music of other cultures needed to be taught—something seldom done in school music beyond token songs of questionable veracity. This document demon-strated refreshing openness to musics beyond the Western classical tradition, as well as a challenge to the profession to liberalize its conception of what was "proper" to teach in classrooms and rehearsal halls.

Since that time, contemporary musics have appeared more frequently in general music classes and performance settings—although, many would argue, not sufficiently. American folk music has perhaps fared somewhat better, given its familiarity in school programs. As to popular musics, progress toward serious inclusion and study has been, I suggest, minimal. Jazz has indeed become commonplace, but jazz is in no conceivable way "popular."[2] The study of popular music in focused, relevant ways remains largely unaddressed in music education to this day.

In the case of "music of other cultures," taken to mean musics from around the world in addition to the music of America's Western heritage, several events have conspired to elevate world musics to high levels in the profession's consciousness and to increasing acceptance as important sources of musical experience and learning (although, as with contemporary musics, especially at their forward edges of development, not as fully as some would wish.) One need only review the publications of MENC—its journals, books, and associated materials—to find ample evidence that world musics beyond Western literature have gained an impressive presence.

3

One significant event effecting the heightened interest has been the ever-increasing presence on American soil of musics that, at one time, existed only in far-off places. As America has become more inhabited by peoples from a great variety of world cultures, previously foreign musics have become increasingly indigenous and therefore harder to ignore, especially when so easily available through the various media. As children of school age bring with them the experience of musics of their increasingly diverse family homelands, that experience calls out for recognition and respect. And when culture-bearers are readily at hand and eager to share their musical knowledge and skills, the obligation of teachers to be expert in and responsible for a variety of musics is somewhat relieved.

Politically, the rise of power among foreign-born peoples and their American-born progeny has added urgency to the need to preserve and honor their cultures, including, inevitably, their musics. Political correctness (in the positive rather than pejorative sense) has called on Americans of diverse heritages to be open to those of others. Cultivating a ubiquitous expression such as music among a particular culture's members is a healthy way to preserve the sense of community that music engenders. Sharing the music with others is also healthy in that it connects communities in mutual respect and enjoyment. All this has added to the rising interest in and acceptance of the need for inclusion of world musics as an integral and important dimension of music education.

As is typical in music education, when an idea becomes prevalent, the profession acts with great energy to implement it. Clinics,

workshops, courses, teaching materials, books and articles, and associated instruments and paraphernalia, all burgeon in response to the demand for accomplishment. As the idea of musical multiculturalism took hold, supported by politically favorable attitudes, implementation did indeed take place rapidly and abundantly, but perhaps with insufficient grounding. Theoretical work establishing a sound basis for practice, probing the complexities and conundrums of the multicultural idea and pointing out possible misunderstandings, impracticalities, abuses, and confusions, was far outstripped by immediately usable materials and methodologies. Admirable as many of these are, a sense has arisen among thoughtful supporters of the multicultural movement that an examination, or re-examination, of its premises, promises, and problems is very much in order. In fact, the continuing viability of the idea of world musics as integral to music education in America may well depend more on building a firmer theoretical foundation for the enterprise than on generating more teaching materials, at least at this point in history. Practice, when it has too far outstripped its supporting base of principles, is likely to become rudderless, the doing separated from a clear grasp of why and how it should be done. Inevitably, teaching begins to lose its point, and energy and interest begin to slacken.

The participants in this Northwestern University Music Education Leadership Seminar were keenly aware of the many unaddressed and unresolved issues awaiting attention and were increasingly uncomfortable with the many ways world musics were being taught, absent a firmly established basis. Far from being complacent about the many successes achieved over the past decade or so, they were, while grateful for progress made, convinced that focused, thoughtful attention to fundamental issues was necessary if that progress were to continue and to avoid possible dissipation, as can easily happen when initial enthusiasms begin to run into difficult questions of purposes and goals. Why, exactly, are we doing all this? Is what we are doing defensible? Can the obligations of developing solid world musics offerings be fulfilled despite a weak infrastructure of support for it in teacher education, research, assessment, philosophical guidance, and curriculum development? The profession has seemed to be enthusiastic about including musics from around the world in school music programs, but uncertainty about the why, what, when, and how issues surrounding the enterprise remained (and remain) rampant.

The professionals who gathered at Northwestern University in the summer of 1998 reflected, in their presentations and discussions, both the seeming health and vitality of the world musics movement and the doubts, reservations, and unresolved dilemmas that face them in their work. All were delighted to learn about the others' successes and hopes, while also being chastened by how many fundamental issues remained far from resolution.

Some of those issues, addressed during the seminar and now in this book, are as follows:

■ The values question: why are we doing this?
■ The problem of defining terms to achieve better clarity in a very confusing field of study.

■ The historical antecedents of the movement and the question of its continuing relevance in today's world and the emerging world.
■ The "us" and "them" dilemma: can world musics be genuinely shared?
■ The authenticity issue: what, exactly, defines a culture's music?
■ Developing bimusicality and/or multimusicality as goals and possibilities.
■ Emphasis on musical learnings/understandings or emphasis on cultural learnings/understandings? What is the relation of the two?
■ Should world musics be "integrated" or "fused" in the total music program or given autonomy as a distinct area of study?
■ What repertoires are properly included in school music programs, and what should be avoided as inappropriate outside of very specific cultural settings?
■ What can or should be specified as curricular goals and objectives? How can learnings be appropriately assessed?
■ Can convincing, respectful materials be made available that reflect and honor the physical/social/political/belief-system environments from which particular musics come?
■ How should educators deal with negative attitudes in various locales toward musics outside cultural mainstreams?
■ What constitutes effective and relevant teaching methodology, given the substantive differences among various cultures in their conceptions of how teaching and learning should be undertaken?
■ How can insights from ethnomusicology—the scholarly study of particular cultures and subcultures—be integrated within teachers' and students' experiences?

■ What partnerships among schools and communities might serve to enhance learnings about various world musics?

■ And, of course, underlying many if not most of the above, how can teachers be best prepared for the daunting challenges that the study of world musics presents?

In the chapters of this book, these and other issues are faced by each author from his or her particular perspective and experience. The seminar did not attempt to forge a consensus on any of these issues. The purpose of the seminars, as explained in the Preface, is to enhance the leadership capacities of the attendees by the sharing of views and ideas that this intensive experience allows, so that they can make better progress toward resolution of issues in mind and practice and also better help the profession at-large make similar progress. Each chapter includes a description of the author's personal history in regard to world music involvements and opens a window on issues that the author sees as central, with reflections on them and, in many cases, suggested solutions.

For Terese Volk, the history and philosophical premises of multiculturalism have been a major concern. She reviews a variety of positions about the value of world musics in education and raises the issue of how or if "outsiders" of a culture can become "insiders." Can a person be "bimusical" in authentic ways? Can teachers be trained, or retrained, to enhance student growth when their own education in world musics and the surrounding issues is scant? The old problems remain unsolved to this day, Volk argues, and need as much attention now as earlier. A philosophy grounding our efforts

is yet to be firmly established, and we will not be as effective as we need to be without it. "Until the day that the entire profession can agree, it will be up to each music educator to find a place for world musics in his or her own working philosophy," she observes.

Anthony Palmer spells out several basic dilemmas underlying the idea of multicultural music education, including word-meaning confusions, our tendency to view the world through our own preconceptions, the relation of music as music to culture as culture, and how music can be properly learned given differences of musical interests in different cultures. His major efforts are focused on forging a philosophical basis sound enough to include musics from all over the world as based on the human imperatives of environment, community, and mind/body. "The music of a people will contain their answers to the fundamental questions of existence, that is, the truths of their experience," Palmer notes. On the basis of this premise, he explores many of the issues listed above, throwing light on them through examples from a variety of cultures, each depending on music as a central way to achieve humanness.

While Peter Dunbar-Hall's perspective is Australian, his experiences with diverse cultures have led him to view many issues relating to multiculturalism as being relevant to music education around the world. He probes the conflicted meanings of the term "multicultural" and then discusses its influences in Australia, especially in its manifestations in the music curriculum of New South Wales. The issues he raises in the examination are applicable far beyond that setting. This leads him to an overview of multiculturalism in Western thought as connected with specific dilemmas he was presented with as a teacher. Approaching music not based on Western thinking as if it were so based, Dunbar-Hall suggests, "could be considered a form of colonialism." That danger deserves serious consideration by all who approach music with Western preconceptions.

As an American music educator who has spent much of her life working in South Africa, Elizabeth Oehrle's perspectives are unusual. She sketches the complex background of South Africa's musical culture and education in light of its political setting—a setting that cannot be ignored in discussions of what multiculturalism can mean in such circumstances. The confusions about language raised by that country's Western and African interactions pervade its educational system, causing uncertainty about what a diverse approach might entail. Oehrle relates the early history of African-Americans to the history of South Africans, traditions being threatened in both places. The curriculum in music at the University of Natal is described as an attempt to redress a Eurocentric approach, as are the African Music Project and another research program focused on African traditions. All contribute to what she calls an "African Renaissance" in that country. But serious obstacles remain, with the arts being largely neglected in schooling. "We ignore the cultural dimension in education at our own peril," Oehrle asserts. Achieving a diverse musical culture in South Africa, as elsewhere, remains a significant challenge.

Robert W. Stephens reflects on musical experience from an African-American perspective. His experiences in school, which ignored the musics of the African tradition, presented him with issues of racism, separatism, and assimilation and the effects that they have had on musical culture and learning. He offers diverse definitions of multiculturalism, stressing that one of its important functions is to address America's enduring problem of race. Music is more than sound, he argues, in that it embodies images and attitudes about what different people are like. If we are to celebrate our diverse culture, he insists, we must "prepare all students for the realities of living in a racially, ethnically, socially, and culturally pluralistic world." Whose musics will be included in our shared memory? Stephens points out that our schools have an obligation to protect and honor our collective accomplishments if we are ever to achieve a just and equitable society. If we continue to ignore musics of African heritage, as the schools did when he was a student, our greatness as a people will be seriously diminished.

Ethnomusicologist Anthony Seeger—grandson of Charles, nephew of Pete, and child of schoolteachers—learned early that music is a powerful force in social conflict and cultural identity. As a child he was immersed in folk musics and world musics, but, becoming disillusioned with the difficult life of the performer as his famous uncle lived it, he decided to become a student and scholar of music instead. He became deeply involved in studies of a Brazilian Indian tribe. He also spent many years as director of the Smithsonian Museum Folkways Recordings and, despite his reservations about performing, has done so for children for many years.

Seeger describes the musical practices of the tribe he studied, leading to reflections about music, schools, and the worlds in which they exist. This leads him to propose three pathways in which world musics can be incorporated into schooling: in music programs, in curricula in the social studies, and in students' own research. Each is explained in rich detail. "We should try to keep up with the world in our teaching," Seeger believes, "because it is in the world that our students will have to apply what they have learned—not only when their education is complete, but every day."

Three questions guide Ellen McCullough-Brabson's work to prepare teachers to offer world music experiences. "What is my culture? What is my musical culture? How can music educators teach music of another culture effectively?" Looking closely at one's own cultural beliefs and premises leads to a more open view of those of others' cultures, allowing a firm foundation for dealing with other musics in valid ways. In her explanation of what culture is, she poses many questions needing to be answered, such as "What music would best represent the world to extraterrestrials?" She gives as one answer the list of musical selections sent on the Voyager space vehicles. This exercise in identifying the world's musical treasures leads to her treatment of how one decides what music is of most worth to teach and learn. With many examples, lists, tables, and stories, she illustrates the specifics of choosing and teaching a wide variety of musics. Helping teachers understand both their own and others' musics allows them to help students "explore the amazing

musical sounds of the world."

Milagros Agostini Quesada raises the issue of the many meanings of multiculturalism in the context of the confusion surrounding its aims. The ethnomusicologist's perceptions can be of great assistance to music educators in the task of achieving clarity; her review of ideas from that field does indeed lead toward a more secure grasp of the issues. Quesada discusses the role of the teacher and how familiarity with a music leads to confidence about teaching it. Teacher expertise is explained and clarified, as are the issues of context and authenticity. Many world music examples are included to apply her suggestions, and many practical guidelines are offered. The need for "reasonable adaptivity" in issues of authenticity is pointed out, recognizing that contextual knowledge, while important, should not prevent widespread enjoyment of musics outside their particular cultural surroundings. Many musical/cultural universals allow crosscultural experiences of power and validity. "Underlying the unfamiliar variety of sounds and timbres that the students hear defined as music, the commonality of music as a human experience comes across," says Quesada. She reminds us here of an important quality of music as music, allowing us to cherish musics from all over the world while retaining our own selfhood and cultural identification.

Is the search for consensus in defining terms such as "multicultural," "ethnic," "folk," "traditional," "world music," "non-Western music," an exercise in futility? Bryan Burton plunges into this political/philosophical minefield as he reflects on the spirited discussions occurring at the

Seminar. He gives his own solutions, recognizing that others will also prove useful. Explanations of the "a-word"—authenticity—and of cultural connections and fusions are followed by his rationale for teaching world musics and his approach to them by teaching "from the inside out," in which the musics are presented as closely as possible to the ways they would exist in their home cultures. He offers an extended and pointed discussion of ways to prepare teachers to do this, with many specifics of course offerings, experiences, and learnings that will accomplish the task effectively, including ways to get world music programs started at both elementary and secondary levels, taking advantage of out-of-school resources. Whatever the complexities of teaching diverse musics of the world, Burton argues, "All of us benefit when music education wholeheartedly accepts, reflects, and enriches this diversity."

Though a native of Hong Kong, Victor Fung has lived in Indiana, Minnesota, Ohio, and Texas, and this gives him an unusual perspective on issues of world musics. Cultural differences, for Fung, are to be treasured, not seen as problems. He posits four fundamental positions relevant to including world musics in American schools: (1) all music is culturally contextual; (2) all musics provide experiences beyond their particularities of sound; (3) every cultural music is fluid and changeable rather than static; and (4) diversity is a valuable resource in every society. Each position is explained with many specific examples of music and of teaching. He then presents a conceptualization of eight types of musical experiences as related to five primary musical parameters, this construct

leading to strategic guidelines teachers can follow if they are to include world musics effectively in their curricula. Specific and pointed teaching ideas are given in abundance. As we succeed in making world musics accessible to more and more people, the term "world musics" may disappear, Fung imagines, because the "boundaries between 'world musics' and 'music' are becoming less clear."

Rita Klinger is a "materials girl," basing her teaching on available materials (as many or most do) and, therefore, being confronted with issues such as what constitutes "quality" or "authenticity" in those materials. She suggests that the term "trustworthiness" is less problematic than "authenticity" and offers a variety of keys to determine whether materials can be considered worthy of trust and, therefore, use. Another dimension of the search for excellent teaching materials is the set of questions that one must ask as one evaluates them: who? what? why? when? and where? Each contributes to the choice of the material that will best serve a particular purpose.

Underlying Klinger's experiences with multiculturalism has been the issue of political correctness and how to navigate safely in its dangerous waters. With many anecdotes, she illustrates the conflicts that teachers must often face, including how to fairly represent those "Dead White Guys." At bottom, she insists that no matter what music we are teaching, "it is our job to make that unfamiliar music not only familiar, but meaningful."

Preparing effective teachers for elementary general music classrooms in which the world of music receives its due is Kathy Robinson's focus. She paints a picture of three exemplary public elementary schools she studied; in each, the teacher struggled to offer richly diverse musical literatures and understandings. Her research identified seven core challenges facing teachers devoted to world musics as essential learnings: (1) the relation of musical form to context, (2) folk and classical traditions, (3) transmission and transformation, (4) in-school and out-of-school settings, (5) making and receiving music, (6) understanding and pleasure, and (7) philosophy and practice. On the basis of her findings, Robinson offers her own goals for the world musics program and definitions that serve to clarify those goals. Issues of lack of time, need for materials, and teacher beliefs, attitudes, and levels of preparation are raised and addressed. She proposes a set of courses that can form the basis for a valid undergraduate teacher education curriculum, each different dimension of the total program including the study of music literatures from around the world. If the teachers she had studied in her research had been offered such an education, Robinson believes, they would have been far more effective in achieving their goals. "Teacher education is the key," she asserts.

Patricia Shehan Campbell's "Life in World Musics" is described and reflected on in her broad-ranging chapter. Both personally revealing and reflectively probing, her many experiences with many musics allow her to offer insights about the challenging issues that all must face if world music education is to occur effectively. We learn a great deal about her as a person, musician, scholar, and, mostly, teacher, all of it relevant to those who have also played these roles. While Campbell has shared her

insights through many publications, we are able to view clearly, through this chapter, the struggles that led her to those insights—struggles that all teachers, in their own ways, must go through as they develop their professionalism. Her successes and failures are likely to have been experienced as well, however individually, by all those who have attempted to expand their expertise into previously unfamiliar territories so that they could expand their students' understandings accordingly. That goal is one that never reaches full attainment, says Campbell: "Developing the musical worlds of students—as well as their worldviews through the musical cultures they encounter—requires teachers who will continue to seek and thrive on new knowledge that they themselves acquire."

This book does not solve all the issues facing our profession in regard to expanding its musical repertoires to include musics of the world. No book could. But it surely raises those issues to higher levels of clarity and, just as surely, offers probing and useful insights that take us further toward viable solutions. The diversity of views and positions represented by these devoted professionals reflects the complexity of the problems they have spent much of their careers addressing. Underneath that diversity are common beliefs about the great value of the enterprise; of the need for continuing study; of respect for diverse musics and the necessity to demonstrate that respect by the way one approaches and teaches them; of the centrality of the knowledgeable, devoted teacher; and of the fascination for both those who teach and those who learn of music as it exists in the multiple imaginations represented by world cultures. That we in music education are willing to face the issues in order to secure more of the musical treasures that the world offers is testament to our growing maturity as a profession.

Notes

1. "The Tanglewood Declaration," *Documentary Report of the Tanglewood Symposium,* ed. Robert A. Choate (Reston, VA: MENC, 1968), 139.

2. In the year 2000, according to the Recording Industry of America's *Recording Industry Releases Consumer Profile,* jazz accounted for 2.9 percent of total sales. (Classical music claimed 2.7 percent). For more information, see www.riaa.com.

BENNETT REIMER, John W. Beattie Professor of Music Emeritus at Northwestern University in Evanston, Illinois, was chair of the music education department and directed the Center for the Study of Education and the Musical Experience, which he founded. The author or editor of over one hundred books and articles, his interests have ranged over diverse topics, including the philosophy of music education, multicultural and international music education issues, interdisciplinary arts principles, curriculum theory, research theory, teacher education, musical intelligences, and the applications of cognitive psychology to music learning.

The Large Picture

1

Multiculturalism: Dynamic Creativity for Music Education

Terese M. Volk

My early musical training was entirely in the classical tradition. Except for Christmas carols and a little popular music, I knew no other styles. I didn't even like jazz. I first became aware of musics from around the world in 1972 as a result of a curriculum course for my master's degree at the Eastman School of Music. While working on my final project, my professor suggested that I read Will Schmid's dissertation, "Introduction to Tribal, Oriental, and Folk Music: A Rationale and Syllabus for a New Course for Undergraduate Music Education Curricula."[1] His research suddenly opened up the whole world of musics to me; I was fascinated!

I began to travel to hear world musics first-hand. I found myself intrigued by new instrumental sounds, by the look and feel of these instruments in my hands, and by new styles of song and dance. I wanted to share my experiences, and so I started arranging songs from around the world for my bands and string orchestras. I finally decided to return to school for a Ph.D. and chose Kent State University, where I could combine music education and ethnomusicology. There I had the privilege of studying Chinese, Thai, African, and Arabic musics with master teachers from those cultures. I began to seek ways to apply these various musics to actual classroom, band, and orchestra situa-

tions. I also found that historical research was the research venue I most enjoyed; I was able to combine my interests in history and multicultural music education in my own dissertation, "A History of Multicultural Music Education in the Public Schools of the United States, 1900–1990,[2] and in continuing research projects.

For 26 years, as an urban instrumental music educator, I taught students from very diverse backgrounds. Today, as an assistant professor, I work with both preservice teachers and graduate students. My students and I share music cultures and explore new musics in order to be able to bring those musics into the classroom. My experience with world musics continues to grow. My students and I are excited by it— and we are all still learning!

Issues and Terminology

The issues involved in multicultural music education have proven to be stimulating, if sometimes challenging, and often controversial. Even the term "multicultural" is a loaded word, with definitions ranging from "many cultures" to inclusiveness for ethnicity, gender, age, and ecological concerns. Political connotations also overlay these definitions. The question of terminology can lead to entire card-catalog entries, among them "multicultural music," "ethnic music," "world music" or "world musics," and "intercultural music." Complicating this, the term "world music" tends to evoke the popular music genre "world beat." There is no consensus as yet, although "world musics"—generally understood to be the music from any culture or ethnicity—appears to be more in usage today. For the purposes of continuing this chapter, I shall use the terms "multicultural" (i.e., "many cultures") and "world musics," although I acknowledge that there are differences in connotations.

Where We've Been: Yesterday's Growth

Historical Development

Multiculturalism has been a part of the United States since its inception, and music education has been trying to come to terms with it for well over a century. Ever since Lowell Mason placed the importance of the European classical tradition above the indigenous folk musics of America or the music of American composers, music educators have been making choices for or against musical diversity in their classrooms. In 1893, music educators had the opportunity to encounter the "exotic other" through live performances of world musics presented on the Midway Plaisance of Chicago's Columbian Exhibition.[3] At the turn of the century, there were also a limited number of songs from many nations that slowly began to be available for school performance in the form of music-rack editions and songbooks.[4] As folk songs and dances began to be more common in the schools, comments by Frances Elliott Clark in 1918 pointed to the connections between music and culture in terms of curriculum correlation, particularly for history and geography classes. In her view, beyond learning about music, learning to understand people from their music was simply a natural extension of music education.[5] In a similar vein, the inclusion of Latin American musics in the music curricula of the 1940s was founded on the principle of intercultural understanding as developed under the federal Good Neighbor policy and implemented in general education.[6] During the 1950s, music educators employed folk songs and dances as singing and movement in the activities-centered methodology of the day.

Changes toward a more multicultural perspective came in the 1970s as music educators began to take seriously the recommendations of the Tanglewood Declaration (1967) and to place all musics in the curriculum. The increasing interest in world musics in the classroom escalated throughout the 1980s and culminated at the 1990 MENC Multicultural Symposium: Multicultural Approaches to Music Education. That symposium passed resolutions calling for the kinds of reform in music education that, if speedily and conscientiously employed, would eventually enable music education to incorporate a world perspective into every aspect of music teaching, from elementary to collegiate levels.

Multiculturalism has proven to be one of the elements of change in each teaching generation. At each stage along the way, some component of world musics (for example, a dance, folk song, "foreign" culture, or timbre) has proven a dynamic element for music education. The inclusion of world musics has directly influenced curricular development and has also fostered some of the most creative teaching in the profession, as educators have come to grips with new musics in their classroom. Music educators, having taken more than 100 years to acknowledge that all musics belong in the curriculum, now face the problems that accompany that acknowledgment—problems of philosophy, teacher training and retraining, repertoire, and bimusicality, to name only a few. It will take all of our creativity to resolve these issues.

Philosophical Development

Before the 1960s, there had been few attempts to articulate philosophical inquiry for music education.[7] Until that time, music education still primarily operated on the original ideals established by Lowell Mason and his contemporaries in the field and, to some extent, still reflected John Dewey's ideas for progressive education and a more child-centered curriculum. Music was healthy for students; it developed them morally, physically, and intellectually. Music classes were still intended to cultivate good taste in the student and that implied teaching the European art music tradition, even though the activity-based music curriculum of the mid-twentieth century included folk musics from many countries. In 1970, Bennett Reimer presented his philosophy of music education based on aesthetics. As important as this step was, there was very little in this philosophy regarding world musics. He did mention that "music of the many ethnic and cultural groups in American society, music of the past and much more music of the present, musics of various types—jazz, pop, folk, as well as concert—all should be considered 'proper' sources for finding expressive music,"[8] but he did not offer any further justification for their serious inclusion in the curriculum. Reimer's acceptance of these music styles as sources of "good music" for the classroom reflects the Tanglewood Declaration published only three years earlier.

Changes toward a more multicultural perspective in the schools began to develop during the 1970s. Researchers such as Margaret Gibson, Geneva Gay, James Banks, and Richard Pratte began to identify concepts underlying multiculturalism in general education and to explore the educational implications of each.[9] In music education, David B. Williams and David Elliott followed their lead.

David B. Williams's early efforts at the Southwest Research Laboratory resulted in "Four Approaches to the Selection of Ethnic Folk Music for Use in Elementary Music Programs."[10] He identified the Traditional approach, the Non-Western approach, the Ethnic-American unidirectional approach, and the Ethnic-American multidirectional approach. Williams rejected the first three approaches because of their narrow focus and lack of teacher training. He felt that the fourth approach would provide the most relevance in the classroom, enabling students to learn many of the musics in America and then broaden to musics around the world.

In 1989, David Elliott followed Pratte's existing model of six concepts of multicultural education (assimilation, amalgamation, open society, insular multiculturalism, modified multiculturalism, and dynamic multiculturalism) and applied them to music education.[11] Elliott found the first four concepts to be either ethnocentric or too limiting. He felt Modified Multiculturalism approached his multicultural ideal, but did not fully achieve it. Dynamic Multiculturalism, on the other hand, provided a means to bring objectivity and interaction into musical encounters, engendering discussions on topics such as tuning systems or the roles of teachers and listeners.

Even with the identification of these approaches, there has been little philosophical investigation of the issues involved with multicultural music education, although it is becoming a topic of interest for both national and international researchers. Abraham Schwadron opened the door to such discourse with his idea of comparative aesthetics. Through comparative aesthetics, Schwadron sought to reconcile musical content and context, to honor both the universality of musical expression and the fact that these expressions are found only within their socio-cultural contexts.[12]

In 1975, following Schwadron's ideas, Anthony Palmer wrote what has since become the linchpin dissertation study for research in the field, providing a philosophical basis for multicultural music education. Like Schwadron, Palmer based his reasoning on accepting the intrinsic value of each music and tried to develop "a music program in world perspective."[13]

Palmer suggested that seeking universals and comparatives across musics would profit the student if taught through a "mode of inquiry into the major questions of global music in both teaching processes and learning outcomes."[14] More recently, Palmer has revisited his thinking and come to the conclusion that "meanings of music must be

sought so that other people's music can form the channel through which we understand life's experiences from their point of view."[15] In a practical curricular application, Palmer has suggested that the learning processes of a music culture must accompany the music when it is transferred to the classroom. He saw this as the most effective way for a "transevaluation of musical values"[16] to take place.

In 1988, Lucy Green, a British music education researcher, found musical meaning to be both musically and culturally bound. She contended that music is perceived both through its inherent musical meanings and its delineated (social) meanings—and that both are important. In fact, these meanings are so intertwined that to emphasize one over the other destroys the music. She further explained musical style as the medium by which we experience music as music and not simply noises or random sounds. According to Green, we experience musical meaning only when we are familiar with the style: "the greater the familiarity with style, the [more] *affirmative* the experience."[17]

As to the role of music education, Green asserted that "anyone of any nationality or race is a perfectly suitable listener to the inherent meanings of any music, so long as they have learnt how to listen, so long as they are familiar with the style: schools are supposedly there to generate such learning."[18] Green also offered as a caution: "It is always valuable to play music, but unless the instruments are authentic and the skill is adequate, it is useless to pretend it is any style, other than a special classroom style."[19]

Bennett Reimer published a second edition of his philosophy in 1989. While not changing his philosophical base in aesthetics, this edition included popular musics, jazz, and world music cultures, not just as sources for "good music" but as viable musics for study in the music curriculum. Reimer sought a balanced music education curriculum: one that would not forget the Western music traditions that form the basis of the music culture in the United States, yet one that included diverse musics from around the world. Reimer founded his reason for studying musics from a variety of cultures on what he called the "level of affective distinctiveness," stating that "each culture has its special shading of affective experience of the world. Music— and all art—is the most powerful way to explore and experience the specificity of how life is felt by each group sharing a communal subjective identity."[20] Reimer felt music education should be leading the student to the "musical veracity" in each piece and that, in so doing, the student would be able to discover the cultural veracity, or truth of our humanity, that it expresses.[21]

Robert Walker, a Canadian researcher, was one of the first to challenge aesthetics as an exclusive philosophical approach for music education. After reasoning out his own approach to musical meaning, defining what he saw as the belief system underscoring Western music and making comparisons with other musical systems around the world, he suggested simply that "humans invent their own meaning for their music and expect listeners to perceive that meaning."[22] In Walker's view, although aesthetics may indeed provide meaning within the Western art tradition, it might not be valid in other music systems. As Walker stated, "in musical acts … the sounds, as well as the actions needed to produce them, are inextricably involved with cultural beliefs."[23] Meaning, therefore, is culture-specific. In the light of this reasoning, he suggested a "pan-cultural approach to music education,"[24] an approach that would both introduce students to the Western music culture and provide for the study of other musics.

Walker based his pan-culturalism on two foundational ideals: first, and perhaps reminiscent of Murray Schafer's "ear-cleaning,"[25] students should experience as wide a variety of "culture-free sounds" as possible, by which Walker meant assorted nontraditional instrumental or environmental sounds. Second, students should experience the music of each culture in the context of its accompanying belief systems, especially through hearing and, if possible, performing the genuine music of the particular culture. Walker presented this as his recommended approach toward acquiring understanding of that culture's music. In this sense, Walker's work hearkens back somewhat to Schwadron's ideas about comparative aesthetics, acknowledging that meaning in music is different from culture to culture.

In 1995, David Elliott presented his philosophy of music education based in praxialism, and the human action of making music within context. Elliott argued that since music is found worldwide, "MUSIC is a diverse human practice consisting in many different musical practices or Musics." He continued, "If MUSIC consists in a diversity of music cultures, then MUSIC is inherently multicultural. And if MUSIC is inherently multicultural, then music education ought to be multicultural in essence."[26] Elliott suggested that students can learn to be bimusical or multimusical through experiences with musics of different cultures.

More recently, June Boyce-Tillman, another British researcher, proposed a model for study in world musics, one that accounts for both musical content and context. Her model, that of a tree with roots, trunk, and branches, provides a visual image for describing any musical culture. The roots established the sound materials, the trunk added expressive elements, and the branches developed into different musical "vernaculars," with further idioms as twigs and leaves. She then overlaid this model with a spiral to represent human progression and development within the culture. Both the tree and spiral represent the dynamic nature of people and their musics.[27]

Where We Are: Today's Issues

Transformations

Among the deeper concerns of multiculturalism are discussions of affect, or feelingfulness, and the intrinsic and extrinsic (cultural) meanings found in music. The music educator's task is to help students encounter meaning in music for themselves. One way to accomplish this is to assist them in understanding both what is happening inside the music itself (e.g., chordal structure or tension/release) and also the cultural context's impact within the music (e.g., timbres or forms) and on the action of making music in that culture (e.g., composing, performing, listening, or improvising)—as ethnomusicologists would say, studying music in, and as, culture.

Though challenging, two researchers in particular have argued that this approach is necessary. Green sees the delineational

(cultural) meaning as an integral part of the musical meaning. Walker, in particular, speaks strongly on the issue of meaning in culture, going so far as to call insensitivity to cultural beliefs and their links with music "ill-educated and musically crude."[28]

Still, the question remains: "How can someone whose knowledge of musical meaning is already culturally formed share feelingfully in another music culture?" Could that be the ultimate transformation/communication? The philosophical thinking so far in our profession has nudged the door open for discussion. Music educators are more fully aware of layers of meaning in music than ever before, but this issue is far from resolved.

A Methodology to Teach about "Us" and "Them"

Prominent among the issues facing multicultural music education today is the question of how to deal with "us" and "them." If teaching another music culture is to enable students to better understand both the music and the people of that culture, then students will be faced with an "insider/outsider" situation. Researchers are concerned with the practical problems of presenting world musics in the classroom. There are those who contend that, while you can become "different," that is, changed somehow because of a musical encounter with another culture, you cannot ever become truly "other." Others have offered various methodologies to help students develop a sense of "other-mindedness."

Schwadron's answer was comparative aesthetics;[29] Palmer employs the learning processes found in the culture along with the music of that culture.[30] Reimer focuses on the "affective distinctiveness" and "musical veracity" in each musical selection and on placing a specific musical culture within the larger picture of music around the world.[31]

Elliott's suggestion is active music making, through which students can be led to a better understanding of others,[32] while Walker employs a three-pronged learning methodology in his pan-culturalism: listen, create, and perform.[33]

Music educators today have tried several of these methods, more or less successfully, depending on their own abilities and familiarity with a second music culture. For example, following Palmer's suggestion, many teachers today are beginning to feel comfortable employing the oral/aural methodology found in nearly every music culture as a means to teach the music of those cultures; teachers have found ways to include this methodology along with the usual note-reading approach for musical literacy in the classroom. Others are starting to teach improvisation by beginning with music cultures, such as Indian or Arabic musics, that are based upon improvisation employing scalar material (*ragas* or *maqamat*). This not only provides for an authentic musical experience in the music from another culture while allowing students to give voice to their own musical expressions, but often has proved a means of branching out to improvisation in Western musics or jazz.

Most music teachers working with world musics support the idea of presenting social context along with the musical experiences. In order to incorporate context in the lesson, teachers often follow one of two approaches. In what might be termed the "Pete Seeger" (named for the folk singer)

approach, some teachers allow students to first sing the songs and enjoy the music, always with the proviso that the students also learn about the original music and listen to it in class. Other teachers follow the "Mike Seeger" (named for Pete's brother) approach. This approach is more research-based and has a structured format. Students first learn about the music and the culture through class projects and then present their understanding of the music in as authentic a performance of the music as possible.

Still other music educators could find Boyce-Tillman's model useful in stimulating musical assessment and promoting critical thinking.[34] Comparisons of different musical styles within one music culture could be traced as the leaves and twigs from one of the branches on her musical "tree." Societal changes in music can be seen spiraling through these styles (for example, when studying jazz styles developing across the twentieth century). Teachers are often faced with the issue of controversial music, either in text or context. This model could help students focus on the inherent social factors or personal struggles of the people in controversial songs. Listening to a recording of Billy Holiday performing the song "Strange Fruit," about the hanging of African-American men, might be one such example.

Repertoire and Authenticity
Another issue is that of repertoire. Teachers are constantly faced with questions such as, "Whose music(s)?" and "Which selections from within that music?" Choices must be made for which musics are to be studied during the school year—

whether controlled by a required state education department or school district curriculum, the specific cultures of classroom students, or even the teacher's personal preferences. Multicultural materials are needed that supplement the existing curriculum in all areas of music education: choral, band, orchestra, and general music. These materials would offer teachers and students a wide variety of choices beyond what is currently available in classroom music texts and expand the more traditional repertoire for large performing groups. However, there is also valid concern that the Western art music tradition not be relegated to a corner in favor of so much diversity.

Connected to this is the issue of authenticity. Music educators tend to agree that repertoire should be representative, authentic, and taught in an authentic manner. Selecting the songs, dances, and instrumental compositions for class use requires discernment, sensitivity, and care. When in doubt, the best recommendation is to contact a culture-bearer (a person from a particular culture who is a practicing musician in that culture) or a researcher known to have expertise in that music culture. On the other hand, there are those who feel that sometimes it is better to teach even one song from one other culture well, rather than to avoid teaching about another culture completely.

Music educators also need to heed Green's warning that school music culture can often be at odds with music in real life. In trying to teach songs from around the world, we do in a sense "capture" them for school use and then bring them into the school music culture. One problem is that if we do not perform the musics as authentically as possible, we have done the original music culture a disservice. On the other hand, we could inadvertently misrepresent a music culture by teaching a selection that may no longer even be performed in that culture. Teachers worry lest, by taking songs and dances out of context, we find out that, for all our efforts, we have created static pieces of music. To find a balance, teachers must always remember that music is dynamic within its culture, growing and changing with its society.

Music educators agree that contextualization may help provide the answer to this issue. Older selections can continue to be presented but from a socio-historical context, much the way we continue to present music from the Baroque period in Western art music. Relatively new or currently popular pieces will also benefit from social (cultural) context, as this enables the student to place the music within a living culture today. Music that is encountered through a combination of contextual and actual musical experiences helps students relate the music to real people in real parts of the world. It can enable students to find meaning in music even more deeply than studying only in one form or the other. By viewing music in and as culture, students can begin to understand how others view themselves—how others think in sound. Today we have the capability to add contextualization more easily than at any other time in history—with access to more information than ever before as a result of both research in ethnomusicology and Internet technology.

Bimusicality

Bimusicality is also connected to the issue of authenticity. Indeed, one of the advantages often cited for including world musics in the music curriculum is that multicultural music education offers the opportunity to foster bimusicality in students. However, exactly how this would be accomplished, and even its practicality in the classroom, remains under discussion. Some favor in-depth exploration of a second music culture across several years of the music curriculum; others feel it would be better to give students a broader view of several different music cultures. Other concerns revolve around what exactly constitutes "bimusicality." Is it the ability to perform, compose, improvise, or listen comfortably in any two music cultures from within the Western tradition, such as rock and the European classical tradition, or must it be a culture from the Western tradition and a culture other than the Western tradition? If bimusicality is to be one of the goals of multicultural music education, what kind of assessments will be necessary? Who determines how well students can function in another music culture if they are not living in that culture?

On the other hand, perhaps the issue isn't bimusicality but rather the development of each individual's musicality? Active involvement (performing, composing, improvising, or listening) in another music culture authentically may be only the beginning. World musics could bring students a fresh perspective on sounds and sound possibilities or teach students about the ways in which other people think in sound. By providing many musical choices, students could succeed in finding their own musical voices—anything from an eclectic blend of many cultural styles to a specific ethnic expression. If this is so, multicultural music education can provide one way for students to begin to express their own musical individuality and creativity. Just as participants experience musical layers of meaning from cultural (what the entire musical event means to the cultural group) to intrinsically musical (what the musical sounds, e.g., instrument choices, vocal timbres, pitch levels or dynamics, mean in that culture) to personal (what the music means to particular performers, listeners, or composers), so students can find new meanings in their own creativity through a range of activities, from inventing simple call-and-response patterns to improvisation to composition. Students could develop their own individual musical style, possibly leading to entirely new music cultures. This is no more far-fetched than the developing subcultures of rock music (e.g., heavy metal or rap). Such multicultural music education could even lead to something beyond the amalgam that forms the basis of today's popular world beat music.

Teacher Training/Retraining

Of course, to properly enhance student growth through any of these approaches, applications, methodologies, and materials requires teacher training and retraining. In spite of developing repertoire, the fact is that until the last thirty years not much effort was made to assist music teachers who must deal daily with multiple cultures—either those within the student body or in the musics being taught. My own research has shown that the addition of various music cultures to the curriculum was not sufficient to bring about substantial changes for the profession in terms of developing a multicultural approach in the classroom.[35] Teachers were given scant information about the authenticity of the transcriptions; they were simply expected to be able to read the music and teach the folk songs in the music texts. There was little acknowledgment that teaching these musics required any different knowledge base or musical training than that obtained through education in the European classical tradition. This European tradition also provided the primary perspective from which to view all other musics.

A fife-and-drum corps played "The World Turned Upside Down" as the British surrendered to the American forces at Yorktown. A popular song of the day, one wonders if the British noticed the irony of the title as the "upstart Colonials" took over. It is possible that American music teachers might have felt similarly—that their world had turned upside down—when they found their classes suddenly overflowing with immigrants at the turn of the nineteenth century or when schools were first desegregated during the 1950s and '60s, or with bi-, tri-, and multilingual curricula during the last part of the twentieth century. What teachers themselves had learned and the ways in which they taught suddenly appeared outmoded, and the retraining necessary to cope with the new situation seemed an impossible feat. The concern remains the same today: there is so much new material to learn.

Yet society has demanded that the profession stay abreast of changing social situations. Today, state mandates, and, in many cases, local music curricula require compliance with multicultural regulations.

However, these requirements are not always fully implemented. Certainly most in-service teachers today did not receive the necessary training to implement all the current multicultural curricular requirements, and they are painfully aware of their inadequate knowledge in this area. It is not uncommon to observe teachers at a workshop hungrily gathering songs from cultures with which they have just become acquainted and discussing plans to teach those songs immediately.

Fortunately, there are many forms of teacher retraining available and many more opportunities for learning various musics from around the world than ever before. For the in-service teachers, the choices include college classes, conference sessions, in-service workshops, and personal encounters with culture-bearers, including the students within their own classrooms.

Equally problematic is the fact that many of the preservice teachers in colleges right now will not receive adequate information to feel confident teaching even one music other than the Western art tradition in the classroom. The state and college requirements for certification are changing to include experiences with diversity, and these are slowly having an effect. More colleges and schools of music are offering methods courses that are taught from a multicultural perspective. However, this needs to be included not just in methods courses, but in classes for repertoire, history, theory, and even chorus, band, and orchestra. There is still a long way to go for complete implementation of a teacher education program that can reasonably be expected to produce teachers who are comfortable dealing with both a diverse student population and a diverse musical curriculum. Only part of that comfort zone will come from contacts with new musics through classes, concerts, and culture-bearers. The rest must come from within each preservice or in-service teacher, as he or she grapples with learning the unfamiliar.

It is important that both preservice and in-service teachers become aware of the process by which they encounter a new music. This process is not unlike visiting another country and not knowing the language. There is initial discomfort, followed by minimum competence, before any kind of fluency takes place. Wonderful experiences can take place at any point along this journey, but often it is not until the last stage that the person encounters any real depth in the experiences, whether in the new country or in a new musical genre. Knowing this process will assist teachers both in their next musical encounter and in understanding what is happening with their students as they work to learn a new music.

Attitudes

The future of music education depends on the creative energy of its teachers. Teaching from a multicultural perspective requires a change in perspective on the part of the music educator. Teachers need to view Western art music within the context of the entire world of music and to be aware that personal prejudices can inadvertently continue to foster stereotypical ideas. Past research on attitudes of teachers toward multicultural music education has shown that most teachers are in favor of it but feel inadequate about teaching it.[36]

They cite the need for training, materials, and experience with assorted musics. More recently, teachers have been asked about their confidence levels or feelings of efficacy with regard to teaching world musics following workshops or formal class instruction.[37] Results indicate that this kind of coursework in particular was helpful, but there has been no study to date as to the long-term effects of this kind of in-service training. If the number of teachers participating in conference sessions on world musics are any indication, music teachers today continue to have a very positive attitude toward learning about world musics. The narrow perspective that viewed European music as somehow "the best" seems to be changing to allow for all kinds of musical expression. It would appear that the many equally valid music systems in the world have been taken seriously for classroom music, at least on the part of in-service teachers. When this is the norm for all music teacher education programs, we will finally have a corps of multicultural music teachers.

What will be special about our future music educators? These new teachers will be open, excited, and dedicated people who will not only be good musicians within the Western European art music tradition, but at least adequate in one other music culture. They will also be excellent teachers who are process oriented but not unmindful of a quality end-product. These future teachers will be able to become facilitators to encourage student learning and, thereby, will often find themselves learning from their students, who could possibly be fine musicians in their own music cultures.

Where We Could Be: Future Possibilities

Educational Policies

Multicultural education in general, and multicultural music education in particular, have been colored by American society and the educational system. Music education for the most part has developed in reaction to demographic changes, government laws, historical events, social demands, and, more recently, educational policies that have begun to address multicultural issues.

Perhaps the most dramatic change in education came in 1954 with the Supreme Court decision Brown v. Board of Education ending segregation in schools. The civil rights movement, with its accompanying legislation—along with several acts mandating bilingual education—also impacted on school curricula. In 1972, the Ethnic Heritage Act declared that all citizens have the right to learn about their own heritage and those of the rest of our society. These laws have had a great effect on multiculturalism in both general and music education.

In order to come into compliance with these various laws, most state regulations for teacher graduation and certification now require multicultural training, either in course work, student teaching, or both. Although school budgets are downsizing in many districts, demands that multicultural topics be included in all subject areas are on the increase. The National Standards for Arts Education officially has incorporated the use of world musics. Most state standards for music education also have a multicultural component. Following both state mandates and music education standards, many school districts are redesigning their music curricula.

Thirty years ago, music education was among the first subject areas to formally recommend teaching a multicultural curriculum to all children. Today, there is a greater acceptance of musics from all styles and cultures in the classroom. If the trend toward more experiences in a diversity of musics continues, music education in the future looks to include encounters with many musics in school as a matter of course, to assist students in exploring these musics, and to help students develop their own musical expressions from a wide range of sounds, styles, and musical cultures.

Predictions

As we enter the new millennium, a paradigm shift is occurring. The only stability may be change itself. Those who desire to maintain the status quo may find it difficult to accept change. The reconstructionist multicultural education advocates are not aware of this resistance. Nonetheless, they would completely restructure all of education to promote equity, justice, and a curriculum that provides for the learning needs of a diverse population.[38]

In thirty years, the current minority population in the United States will become the majority. This is already occurring in our urban areas. Whether we are ready for it, the future is already here. The world is in our classroom, yet the educational establishment is notoriously slow to change. We need a new window for looking out on this changing world. It is just possible that world musics will provide that open window, a way to learn about both the musics and the people who make them. It can help us to enable all students to express themselves musically, to think in music, and

to open up for them the possibilities of sound beyond the worlds of rock or classical European music. It can mean varied performance, composition, and listening opportunities, as well as exciting connections to other disciplines. It can even move teachers into new roles as facilitators and co-learners.

Final Considerations

There is still a long way to go. In 1976, Abraham Schwadron looked to the twenty-first century and predicted a day when music educators would teach a multicultural curriculum. He foresaw music curricula focused on the critical exploration of all musics as a core component, with all students given the opportunity to develop performance skills in a variety of music cultures.[39] However slowly, his vision is beginning to come true. There are world musics taught in some schools—islands of change in a sea of long-held music teaching tradition—and these islands are beginning to have an effect. Indeed, world musics in the curriculum have already begun to change music education in ways only imagined thirty years ago. Would even Schwadron have thought that by the 1990s there would be elementary schools able to boast of having an African drumming ensemble, middle school choruses that would sing Balkan folk songs with the appropriate timbre, high school bands thrilling audiences with an arrangement of Chinese folk songs, and a college Thai ensemble so good it could tour Thailand?

Yet for all these developments, Schwadron's crystal-ball-gazing still poses questions for music educators today: What are the goals for multicultural music educa-

tion? How do we deal with the issue of authenticity? As we begin to select music cultures and materials for classroom presentation, whose cultures and which materials do we choose? Whatever the answers, they will depend on the philosophical approach of the questioner. If multicultural music education is to be fully accepted, a professional, as well as a personal, perspective that rationalizes the presence of world musics in music education is needed. And, until the day that the entire profession can agree, it will be up to each music educator to find a place for world musics in his or her own working philosophy.

Postlude—Personal Ruminations

Multiculturalism in music education has been a dynamic and creative force within our profession, opening our ears and broadening our perspective. Since 1838, visionaries have told us about this world of music. For over a century, we have gradually been adding to the music curriculum musics from around the world and from the cultures within the United States—from European folk songs and African-American spirituals to Hispanic melodies, Indian ragas, and Chinese opera. Each addition took approximately thirty years—or one teaching generation—before it became common curricular material.

Those of us attending this seminar are among the first generation of multicultural music educators, and we hope our students, and their students, will continue our work. The changes that we envision will occur slowly, as narrow-minded attitudes are replaced with a broader view of music making, teaching, and learning throughout the world. It will take another generation of teachers, teachers who will have learned a new openness to and acceptance of other musics, for us to be able to drop the term "multicultural" and speak only of "music educators."

We are on the cusp, as it were, the liaison between ethnomusicological research and the practicality of the classroom. If we have done anything, it is to "raise consciousness," to use an idiom from the 1960s. We have made our profession more aware of what needs to be done. We have tried to show the way, and perhaps in our own classes, we have achieved what we hope can be done in all music classes. What we do *now* will hinder or hasten the development of that true multicultural music educator and the day when we will simply teach *music*. It would be nice to have worked ourselves out of a job because we were no longer needed, having fulfilled our goals.

There is still more out there—more music, more creative ways to teach it, and more ways to help students experience it. If we, who are the leaders, do not follow the vision, does the profession have the time to wait another twenty years for the cycle to regenerate? We must always remember that today is the history of tomorrow.

Children bring their own ears, hearts, and musics to music class. If teachers can learn to step back and become facilitators, students themselves can become teachers as they share their musics.

A philosophical approach or concept that allows for the validity of teaching all musics is one possible way to achieve this. Our profession could use "a philosophic frame that values diversity,"[40] one with a stable system that in itself contains flexibility. Such a system can view world musics as dynamic, representative of the nature of music as a worldwide human expression. This system would see the need for educators to be aware of the changes in culture itself and to allow for creative, alternative answers to problems as they arise.

Notes

1. Will Schmid, "Introduction to Tribal, Oriental, and Folk Music: A Rationale and Syllabus for a New Course for Undergraduate Music Education Curricula" (Ph.D. diss., Eastman School of Music, University of Rochester, 1971).

2. Terese M. Volk, "A History of Multicultural Music Education in the Public Schools of the United States, 1900–1990" (Ph.D. diss., Kent State Univ., 1993).

3. Marie McCarthy, "American Music Education as Reflected in the World's Columbian Exposition in Chicago, 1892–93," *The Bulletin of Historical Research in Music Education* 15, no.2 (1994): 111–42.

4. Volk, "A History," 66–67.

5. Frances Elliott Clark, "Music in Education," *Music Supervisors Journal* 5, no. 1 (1918): 14–18 and no. 2 (1918): 12–18.

6. Volk, "A History," 151.

7. See in particular *Basic Concepts in Music Education* (Chicago, IL: National Society for the Study of Education, 1958).

8. Bennett Reimer, *A Philosophy of Music Education* (Englewood Cliffs, NJ: Prentice Hall, 1970), 40.

9. Margaret A. Gibson, "Approaches to Multicultural Education in the United States: Some Concepts and Assumptions," *Anthropology and Education Quarterly* 7, no. 4 (1976): 7–18; Geneva Gay, "Changing Conceptions of Multicultural Education," *Educational Perspectives* 16, no. 4 (1977): 4–9; James A. Banks, *Multiethnic Education: Theory and Practice,* 2nd ed. (Boston: Allyn and Bacon, 1988); Richard Pratte, *Pluralism in Education: Conflict, Clarity, and Commitment* (Springfield, IL: Charles C. Thomas, pub., 1979).

10. David B. Williams, "Four Approaches to the Selection of Ethnic Folk Music for Use in Elementary Music Programs," in "Southwest Research Laboratory (SWRL) Music Program: Ethnic Song Selection and Distribution," a

report by David P. Williams (SWRL Technical Note, TN-3-72-28, Sept. 3, 1972) CD-ROM, ERIC, ED 109040.

11. David Elliott, "Key Concepts in Multicultural Music Education," *International Journal of Music Education,* No. 13 (1989): 11–18.

12. For an example of Schwadron's thinking on the subject, see Abraham Schwadron, "Comparative Music Aesthetics and Music Education," *Journal of Aesthetic Education* 9, no. 1 (1975): 99–109; "Comparative Music Aesthetics: Toward a Universality of Musicality," *Music and Man* 1, no. 1 (1973): 17–31.

13. Anthony J. Palmer, "World Music in Elementary and Secondary Music Education: A Critical Analysis" (Ph.D. diss., University of California–Los Angeles, 1995), 125.

14. Ibid., 127.

15. Anthony Palmer, "On a Philosophy of World Musics in Music Education," in *Critical Reflections on Music Education,* ed. Lee R. Bartel and David J. Elliott (Toronto: Canadian Music Research Centre, University of Toronto, 1996), 140.

16. Ibid.

17. Lucy Green, *Music on Deaf Ears* (Manchester, UK: Manchester Univ. Press, 1988), 34.

18. Ibid., 67.

19. Ibid., 143.

20. Bennett Reimer, *A Philosophy of Music Education,* 2nd ed. (Englewood Cliffs, NJ: Prentice Hall, 1989), 145–46.

21. Ibid.

22. Robert Walker, *Musical Beliefs* (New York: Teachers College Press, 1990), xv.

23. Ibid., 227.

24. Ibid., 221.

25. Ibid., 221–23, 228; See R. Murray Schafer, *Ear Cleaning: Notes for an Experimental Music Course* (Don Mills, Ontario: BMI, 1967) and *The Thinking Ear: On Music Education* (Indiana River, Ontario: Arcana Editions, 1986).

26. David Elliott, *Music Matters: A New Philosophy of Music Education* (New York: Oxford Univ. Press, 1995), 44, 207. Elliott uses the term "practice" to encompass all musical genres, e.g., the practice of jazz, the practice of Chinese music, or the practice of Baroque music.

27. June Boyce-Tillman, "Conceptual Frameworks for World Musics in Education," *Philosophy of Music Education Review* 5, no. 1 (Spring 1997): 3–13.

28. Walker, *Musical Beliefs,* 227.

29. Schwadron, "Comparative Music Aesthetics and Music Education" and "Comparative Music Aesthetics: Toward a Universality of Musicality."

30. Palmer, "On a Philosphy of World Musics."

31. Bennett Reimer, *A Philosophy of Music Education.*

32. David Elliott, *Music Matters.*

33. Walker, *Musical Beliefs,* 223, 228.

34. June Boyce-Tillman, "Conceptual Frameworks."

35. Volk, "A History," 326.

36. See, for example, Jerrold Moore, "An Assessment of Attitude and Practice of General Music Teachers Regarding Global Awareness and the Teaching of Music from a Multicultural Perspective in American Schools" (Ph.D. diss., Kent State Univ., 1993); Milagros Agostini Quesada, "The Effects of an In-Service Workshop Concerning Puerto Rican Music on Music Teachers' Self-Efficacy and Willingness to Teach Puerto Rican Music" (Ph.D. diss., Kent State Univ., 1992); Terese M. Volk, "Attitudes of Instrumental Music Teachers toward Multicultural Music in the Instrumental Program," *Contributions to Music Education,* no. 18 (1991): 48–56.

37. Terese M. Volk, "Reactions to a 'Teaching World Musics' Course," research in progress.

38. Christine Sleeter, "An Analysis of the Critiques of Multicultural Education," in *Handbook of Research on Multicultural Education,* ed. James A. Banks (New York: Macmillan, 1995), 81–84.

39. Abraham Schwadron, "Comparative Music Aesthetics and Education: Observations in Speculation" in *Music Education for Tomorrow's Society: Selected Topics,* ed. Arthur Motycka (Jamestown, RI: GAMT Music Press, 1976), 21.

40. Boyce-Tillman, "Conceptual Frameworks," 12.

TERESE M. VOLK is assistant professor of instrumental music education at Wayne State University in Detroit, Michigan. She has authored *Music, Education, and Multiculturalism: Foundations and Principles* (New York: Oxford Univ. Press, 1998), and her research has been presented at national and international venues and published in several music education journals.

2
Multicultural Music Education: Pathways and Byways, Purpose and Serendipity

Anthony J. Palmer

*S*ounds of all sorts have always been of interest to me, especially when, in my teens, I developed an active interest in composition. I find intense fascination in the peculiar timbres, modes, and rhythms that I hear in other musics. My first recollection of a transformative nature occurred in 1964. I attended one of my first major conferences, the MENC national meeting in Philadelphia. There I witnessed a performance by Kemio Ito, Japanese koto virtuoso. The music was strange and wonderful at the same time. He was dressed in traditional kimono. Little did I dream that twenty years later I would hear Eto-sensei once again, this time in Tokyo and in Western dress.

Subsequently, I continued to explore but without a strong focus. In 1969, while working for my doctorate at UCLA, I encountered Abraham A. Schwadron. He became my principal mentor, and I began a more purposeful search of the crosscultural area. Mantle Hood, director of the Institute for Ethnomusicology at the time, also became an influence. One quarter term of his seminar focused on Hawaii. Again, I had no idea that I would move to Hawaii and spend nine years there. The various non-Western per-

formances at UCLA, because of the institute, were a delight. Meeting people with interests in other cultures was not only enjoyable but supportive.

I wrote my dissertation on the problems of expanding the music education curriculum to a world base. I investigated the philosophical and practical problems of bringing music from other cultures into the classroom. This led to a series of explorations that are still being pursued. I realized immediately upon completing the dissertation that I knew the problem intimately on an intellectual level, yet I hadn't experienced making music in another culture (referred to as "bimusicality"). This was one of the paramount criteria on which Mantle Hood established the Institute of Ethnomusicology. Steeped in the Western choral tradition, I was determined to fill this deficit with substantial experience.

This led me to the UCLA Gagaku group. I had some private sessions on shō with Suenobu Togi, the director, for several weeks, and then joined the ensemble. I played with the group for about four years before moving out of state, returning a couple of times each year to renew my skills and understanding. In 1983, I was fortunate to receive a Japan-United States Friendship Commission as a Creative Artist Fellow and spent almost a year in Japan, principally in Tokyo, beginning in June 1984. I studied hichiriki with Kanehiko Togi, a member of the Imperial Court Gagaku.

During my stay in Japan, I took advantage of attending several concerts per week, usually of traditional Japanese music. I also became acquainted with the choral musicians and composers and subsequently wrote some articles on Japanese contemporary choral composition. Tokyo was particularly alive with music of all sorts, but I ventured into as many parts of the country as possible to observe the folk and traditional celebrations as well, made a point of attending as many Kabuki and Nō theater performances as possible, and met as many traditional musicians as could be arranged. I voraciously read novels and history books about Japan and that helped enormously to structure a framework in which I could contemplate the differences between east and west, Asian and Euro-American, and take advantage of my residence there.

The Japan experience was intense and enlightening about a great many things besides music. Considering that music is a reflection of a culture in innumerable ways that are difficult to define, I returned to the U.S. a decidedly different person. It was during this period that my basic understanding of human existence, which forms the platform on which I continue to work to this day, matured. I came to realize that, while we are different in style and presentation, we work out of a fundamental quality of humanness that we all share as one species. The differences are exhilarating and worthy of much more positive and constructive attention than we have given them. Rather than fear difference, we should delight in the marvelous, myriad array of ways in which

each group deals with reality and truth.

My subsequent experience in Hawaii confirmed many of my beliefs about life and music, and culture and humanity. There are attributes for crossing cultures that remain the same whatever culture is visited, principally an open mind and insatiable curiosity. I hope my discussion of these issues will be useful to others.

Introduction

The purpose of this chapter is to explore the ramifications of what we generally call multicultural musics when included in an educational program. To keep the text and ideas flowing for the reader, I have dispensed with specific scholarly citations. Nevertheless, the resource list at the end of this chapter will show the type of references called upon and furnish the basis for further study for those who wish to embark on the journey that is suggested by this discussion. Further, while my discussion is intentionally somewhat conversational in tone, this should not be interpreted as less substantive. Finally, because there are considerable materials from several sources that show specific methodologies in presenting various musics, I have dwelled on the philosophical basis and issues for what is known as "multicultural musics" and attempted to support them with concrete examples.

Establishing a Basis for Discussion
Word Problems

Words pick up numerous connotations when used by a variety of people with differing understandings and knowledge. Because of the political climate in the United States over the past few decades, the term "multicultural" has come to represent for some a panacea for the country's social problems. At the same time, it has signaled for others the end of the dominance of Euro-American civilization as it was known in the first half of the twentieth century. However, if we are to evaluate essences rather than appearances, we have to transcend labels. A rose by any other name would smell as sweet.

To find the true values of a culture and the ways in which music is reflective of those values, we must look beneath the surface. Each group, while fundamentally the same as all others, expresses itself in a different musical guise. We have to dispense with our understandings of terms like "music" or "musics," "world," "ethnic," "multicultural, or "non-Western." To become empathic, we must become chameleon-like and adapt to the new environment. A changed disposition allows us to get an inside glimpse of another people and their music. Although labels may help guide us through the array of the various musics of other cultures, ultimately the map is not the territory. The label is neither the music nor its meaning.

Other Barriers

There are other barriers to overcome. We have a tendency to consider everything outside our own experience as other and to accept only that which matches our own ideals. We have mental references (musical representations) that form our views of reality. For example, a scale heard from a foreign culture is matched immediately against our preconceptions of how a musical scale should sound. Because the human mind constantly measures comparisons (e.g., hot/cold, high/low, and near/far),

the scale reference can be used as a measure of difference. The comparisons work best when we use them for guidance rather than rejection.

By beginning with a proper attitude toward humanity, we see that we are one species and, therefore, begin life with identical nervous systems and psyches. Different experiences in the real world then shape us socially, physiologically, and psychically. Yet, we can still only respond within the confines of being human. We can only hear from approximately 20 to 20,000 cycles per second. Despite a use that is amazingly diverse, we still have only two hands with five digits, albeit two wonderful opposable thumbs. Circular breathing and producing two vocal tones simultaneously stagger the Western imagination, yet, with the right training, these actions fall within human capability. We are at once flexible—in using what we have—and limited—to the degree that physical and mental limitations do exist. Additionally, we have a consciousness that is puzzled and perplexed by the world. Many find it necessary to seek guidance from a force greater than ourselves in order to retain equilibrium.

These are boundaries of human existence, but they also bind us together as a single species, which make us much more alike than different. Although fundamentally we are one, as a species we have developed various musical systems whose differences require examination.

Consider the element of pitch and how it is used throughout the world. Even in the Western world, pitch was and is a fluctuating phenomenon. While Westerners adhere to an abstract notion of A equaling 440 cps in a tempered scale, orchestras continue to tune above 440 cps and seldom play in a true tempered scale of 100 cents per half-step. Traveling to Indonesia, our ears are caught by the strangeness of Pelog or Slendro tuning of *gamelan*, which operates quite differently than Western modes. The microtonal fluctuations of Asian Indian music challenge Western ears.

There are numerous examples of pitch variability, but, when adding tone quality to the equation, the possibilities are almost beyond comprehension. Comparing Chinese opera, with its intense use of nasality, to the Western vocal timbre makes that immediately apparent. Even within the narrow confines of human capabilities, then, the possibilities are not easily exhausted when all of the variables—time, tone quality or timbre, musical expression, and form, for example—are brought into play.

So, while music at the expressive level—when human consciousness becomes manifest in sound—is entirely variable within certain boundaries, we have the following in common:

1. We share the species-specific trait of making music.
2. We create practical and theoretical rules by which we organize musical sound.
3. We use musical sound in very specific ways within a defined cultural framework.

Further, music and art do not exist as an aural or visual reality until expressed in a particular time and place. Although the arts in general are easily discussed, ultimately we are forced to look at or listen to an art that is particular. In a *real* sense, especially because of its communicative value, art cannot exist solely as a mental abstraction. Moreover, if we are to understand human existence and its expression through music, we must study all music, not just a portion. Otherwise, we learn only partial truths.

Multicultural Dilemmas

Studying the whole world of music requires thoughtful response. There are at least three dilemmas that must be recognized if we are to initiate a multicultural program:

1. Teaching any and all music from both musical and cultural perspectives. Music can be taught as an isolated phenomenon for its internal values, for example, the way it uses time and pitch, tone and expression, and medium and form. Or, music can be taught as a complex sound structure that has cultural meaning embedded in the musical choices. One has to choose carefully because music without context is isolated from human values and the life of the culture. Conversely, cultural context without sufficient musical content is not music learning.

2. The ways in which music is learned. Two views present opposite choices. Music from other cultures can be learned from our own points of view. That is, we can apply our criteria of what music should be like to the other music. The second choice is to experience other music from the inside, as the cultural members experience it. This latter view requires becoming *other,* a path less easily traveled and taking much more time. It contains more difficulty psychologically, but from educational perspectives, there are also implications for curricular and financial resources beyond the ordinary.

3. The effects that becoming "other" causes. Each time we step outside our own culture, we not only broaden our horizons, but we also develop a new concept of reality. Because it is impossible to be a-cultural, what we experience is our culture whether well-defined, contradictory, or ambiguous. By experiencing two—or more—cultures concurrently, we are different human beings than we would be if one culture were to be experienced in isolation.

To illustrate this point, consider that hearing a musical system other than our own may come as a shock. Suddenly, we have a comparison. However, we are tremendously adaptive, and our sense of reality is forever changed. Comparisons might occur with pitch, time, timbre, form, textures, and musical expression. The object may appear different, foreign, or even questionable in value. Recognizing this process as a facet of human experience requires that we exercise care. It is too easy to reject the other as not worthy to be examined and studied. That barrier will keep us from understanding the other culture. Differences, after all, are not necessarily *better or worse*. Rather, they are often nothing more than dissimilarities. Tracing every system to its roots will lead us to the same place, the species-specific human psyche. We can then achieve an understanding that every expression of human music making has value.

Given the discussion thus far, I would like to take you on a journey of my explorations in the realm of the multicultural. I hope that the dilemmas will be seen not as either-or relationships but as a symbiotic dynamic without identifiable cause-and-effect relationships. Human behavior is much too intricate to allow us to make superficial judgments. It will be seen, also, that there are psychic and spiritual realities permeating music making that must not be ignored.

A Basic Philosophy for the Study of World Musics

Should we study music of the whole world? This is a legitimate question. After all, if we study music from other cultures, do we not have to give it time to the detriment of study of our own? At first thought, the answer seems to be "yes"—unless, of course, there is a different set of assumptions—a reconceptualization of music, of why we study music, and of what benefits can be derived from the time and effort expended.

At an early age, humans develop a concept of the *self*. They become "I" or "me" with the full force of psychic recognition that demands answers to certain questions of existence: Who am I? Why am I here? What is this *here* of which I am aware?

The responses may take a number of directions. We may seek pleasure as a sedative to ward off the anxiety caused by the questions. We may subscribe to one or another religion that offers answers to human dilemmas of ethics and morals. We may strike out on our own psycho-philosophical journey to discover the world beneath appearances.

Whatever path we take, I believe that we create objects and processes that reflect our deepest-held beliefs, our deepest anxieties, and answers to our deepest questions in order to retain a sense of sanity and purpose in the world. We know of no culture that has not directed a significant portion of its energies toward organizing specific kinds of sound for fundamental socio-psychological purposes in the lives of its people. Each culture has decidedly different conceptions of what might be called *beauty*. Yet, there has never been one that has not created objects out of the available materials and *beautified* them in form, color, and texture. The added intricacies do not seem to have any appreciable effect on function. Psychological necessity, not function of the object, is the stimulus to decorate.

Significant decorations are found in the caves at Lascaux, on the burial implements of the Neanderthals, and in the more recent tombs of highly developed Egyptian culture. The fundamental method of responding to daily and extraordinary life is through what we broadly call the arts, so-called "fine" and "practical": music, dance, drama, painting, sculpture, costume, body decoration, burial sites, religious sites, interior and exterior home design, gardens, and automobiles. In short, everything in our lives has important considerations beyond function.

All cultures produce objects and events that can be labeled *artistic*. That is, the object has the qualities of thoughtful, conscious, refined effort to create something distinct, individual, and out of the ordinary, whether the object or event also has practical value. Such embellishments are of practical value only to the extent that they communicate specific ideas, attitudes, and cultural identification. Moreover, the objects or events have form, color, intensity, proportion, and other artistic attributes that necessarily call for *artistic* decisions.

What we call art is the natural expression of human consciousness. At base, these expressions are psychological and spiritual in their widest possible meanings. Our existence is predicated on consciousness. That is the unique quality of being alive. Although the body may exist in a vegetative state, it is not then independent and capable of perceiving and making judgments. That demands consciousness, which, when applied, results in choices being made—choices about our existence.

Human activity, then, is largely concerned with initiating and sustaining—or avoiding—the quest for truth and reality. This is the purpose of life: to find meaning to our existence. And art—what we generally mean by that term—is the process whereby we explore, discover, and answer the basic questions: who am I? why am I here? what is this *here* all about? From these existential questions stem all of life's other questions of being: how we know, what we value, and how to act ethically. Given this premise, then, everything in a multicultural program more easily follows. In fact, any music program rests on these kinds of basic assumptions, whether recognized consciously or not.

Imperatives in Shaping Music

Yes, we are one species, but we respond to life's vicissitudes and joys in different ways because of our experiences in the world. While the fundamental impulse is a species-specific trait to make music, each culture will do so in its own unique way because of the imperatives to which its members respond. I will point to at least three of these imperatives in illustrating how music as an expression of human consciousness must be considered at a multitude of levels. Music is fundamental to the human species, but as it rises to the here-and-now of concrete expression, it is shaped by these imperatives. Nonetheless, in whatever style each piece becomes manifest, it is a singularly unified force from beginning to end and must be viewed in this way if we are to gain access to the questions of why we do what we do. The three imperatives are environmental, communal (including religion, social aspects, cultural qualities, and political organization), and psychophysiological.

1. The Environmental Imperative

Given a particular geographical location and attendant meteorological conditions, there are only certain kinds of materials with which to make music other than with voices. The Inuit are likely to use whale bones and skins from large fish or mammals to make drums, bone whistles, and the like. Conversely, the inhabitants of southern and eastern Asia have bamboo in abundance, and so a Chinese *sheng* or Japanese *shō* is an expected normalcy. While these examples appear obvious, environment must be recognized as a given in any anthropology of music.

Beyond materials, an extension of the environmental imperative is to consider the natural course of events that determine just how much time is available to make music, individually or collectively. A ready food supply may offer more time for making music than where food is scarce and much time needs to be spent in hunting or gathering. Cultivation of food requires more settlement and a different way of life. Weather plays a part in this situation in pro-

found ways, both in how much food is available and how growing and harvesting seasons are determined.

Topography is another consideration; mountains, desert, prairie, and plush valleys interacting with weather all play a role in the response that human groups make to the total environment. Whether a group is stationary or nomadic may well determine the kinds of instruments that are built according to their portability. The settled Javanese built large weighty *gamelan*, which for the Saharan Bedouin nomads, whose music was largely vocal, would have been extremely inappropriate.

The symbiotic relationship between weather, natural environmental phenomena, and the religious- or God-archetype differentiates cultural style in music in yet more profound ways. One propitiates the rain god in one locale, the wind god in another, and an earthquake or fire god in still different places. Frequency of occurrence of natural events may determine the worship calendar. Where the gods live, e.g., Delphi or Mt. Olympus, may well affect how and where the rituals are carried out. Catharsis and similar concepts occupied the attentions of the classical Greek philosophers; their views on music are exemplary in showing how intricately musical style was tied to religious beliefs and cosmological concepts. While natural phenomena form the environment, the stimulus—the obverse side—lies in the response that humans make to the environment, which constitutes the immense variability of musical behavior.

2. The Communal Imperative

Consider at least that food supplies and

other environmental factors may determine the size and density of the group and define areas of habitation. The response in living arrangements that follows on how best the group can survive may influence the pathways in which music develops. The political structure also may play a role in whether a matriarchy or patriarchy exists, and whether rule is by consensus or authoritarian. For example, although music is an integral part of all Sub-Saharan African life, in some Sub-Saharan cultures music is strictly a communal affair while, in others, the king has his few royal drummers.

There is a symbiotic relationship between cultural expression and musical structure and style. Alan Lomax has done considerable work in drawing connections between the two. The organization of the symphony orchestra has been compared to the monarchical political framework in Europe. The practice of Northern Indian music has been described in both musical and cultural terms that suggest the musical structure and the interdependent ensemble relationships mirror the operation of society.

Examples of the interplay between place, cosmogony, and human response can be found throughout the world in the history of culture. A Hawaiian example, concerning the origin of the hula, is typical of these relationships. It is widely believed that the Hawaiians came from Bora-Bora, of the Society Islands (French Polynesia), of which Tahiti is the largest and most influential. The last major wave arrived around 600 A.D., bringing with it sacred dances, drumming, and chants. There are distinctive differences in the style of dance between Tahiti and Hawaii. These could only have occurred through an evolution-

ary process in the Hawaiian Islands group because of the new setting and its presumed isolation for hundreds of years. The obvious surface difference is the speed at which the hips rotate, the Tahitian being rapid and the Hawaiian being a slow undulation. There are more subtle distinctions in the positions of the feet and knees and the way the hands and arms are used to express the meaning of the chant.

The myth of Pele and her sister Hiiaka, in which dance is integral, tells one origin of hula. This myth is basic to Hawaiian cosmogony and stands at the core of Hawaiian story. The islands originated from volcanic activity in the middle of the Pacific; the largest island, Hawaii, still has intense volcanic action. Thus, Pele and volcanoes are at the center of the Hawaiian experience.

Having been born as a flame from the mouth of her mother, Pele made her way down the island chain until she found a place dry and hot enough to settle, the pit of the Kilauea volcano on the southernmost portion of Hawaii. While Pele had a fiery temperament, Hiiaka was calm, kind, a great dancer and poet, and the one to whom most of the chants and songs that come from this myth are attributed. Hopoe was Hiiaka's close friend, who also taught Hiiaka the hula. Together they danced the first hula for Pele on the beach at Nanahuki on the Big Island. The story tells of Pele's love for Chief Lohiau, his subsequent death, and then resurrection by Hiiaka. Pele's jealousy caused her to destroy the trees and Hopoe, both so loved by Hiiaka. The story ends by telling of Hiiaka's anger at Pele and their subsequent reconciliation.

Hula and chant permeate this myth, and

the three hundred or so songs and chants are sacred. Few performances, both commercial and in competitions, fail to include at least some portion of the story and accompanying song and dance.

The Merrie Monarch Festival was begun a few decades ago in honor of King David Kalakaua, whose reign dominated the last quarter of the nineteenth century. He was responsible for revitalizing the Hawaiian people's traditions by frequent sponsorship of dance and music gatherings, hence, the nickname "Merrie Monarch." The dancers competing in the Festival, held on Hawaii each spring, go to the volcanic crater and pay homage to Pele before the competition with offerings of berries, bananas, and gin. They seek blessings from Pele to guide their hearts to purity and their steps to perfection.

3. The Psychophysiological Imperative

The third imperative works in two major ways, the first in terms of the physiology of a people. Their height, length of limbs, lung capacity, shape of mouth, and size of lips may all contain dispositions toward size and style of instruments in very subtle ways. As their instruments are the fruit of materials in the environment, so may they also be reflective of the physiology of their makers.

Secondly, each individual personality has inclinations, leanings, and propensities that make one choice preferable over others. These collective inclinations produce a consensus that characterizes the culture in general ways but manifests itself—because of innumerable variables of socio-cultural interaction—as specific choices of musical elements. The theoretical Chinese traditional music system, for example, contains 360 different pitches, stemming from the rational system of measuring pipes by proportion. Out of the gamut of possibilities, however, the Chinese musicians chose a set of modes composed only of five tones each. The five tones and their various transformations are symbolic of "Universal Harmony," the use of which can be sustaining or destructive of this order. The Chinese belief in the power of music to affect individuals or the universe has always been fundamental to their traditional music system.

Music is reflective and representative of deeper processes than the surface elements in a musical structure. Our choices have meanings of overriding necessity. Each musical system, consequently, will be different and imbued with the cosmogony and spiritual beliefs of each group or subgroup of people. We as a species constantly respond to our environment, both stationary and mobile, including our brothers and sisters in the world. Living is a dynamic process of constant change and interaction.

To conclude, the music of a people will contain their answers to the fundamental questions of existence, that is, the truths of their experience. Each group finds its own truths. This is the crux of the discussion. By studying other music from the inside and learning to respond to a music from the cultural member's point of view, we realize another truth, another dimension, of human existence. Achieving this difficult goal gives us a deeper and broader understanding of what it means to be human. That is, after all, the primary raison d'etre, the search for the "holy grail" of truth and affirmation of our existence. Anything less is inadequate to explain the expense in resources, human and otherwise, and the extraordinary efforts to produce something so seemingly superfluous. Yet, at base, the answer is not complex at all. Like breathing, it simply is.

In closing, there is a constant dynamic of activity and energy that flow from the depths and the need to make music according to the style in which music emerges in a culture. There is no progress in music, only validity. The music either satisfies the inherent and assumed criteria for the culture, or it dies stillborn. To speak to a majority of the people in a culture, the music must have mass appeal. This need not be negative; it's all part of the process of psychic survival. If there is any absolute, it lies not in a musical genre, but in the needs of the human psyche to be musical.

Implementation of a "World Musics" Program

Everything now flows from the foregoing. The implementation of such beliefs must adhere to the tenets of such beliefs. The following elements are offered as the most important in a school music program based on global proportions, (a) authenticity of musical materials, (b) curricular goals and objectives, (c) learning *through* versus learning *about*, (d) qualifications of a multicultural music teacher, and (e) teaching materials and learning environment.

Authenticity of Musical Materials

If, by studying music, truths are revealed about human existence, then the musical experience must be as identical to the original as possible. This principle applies to all music. While Bach's *Brandenburg Concertos* are musically satisfying with contemporary instruments, they lack the sound that Bach and his audience heard, which keeps us

from fully understanding them. It is no good to pose an unanswerable question such as, "Would Bach have used modern instruments had they been available?" They didn't exist and could not even have been imagined. Additionally, we are also saying, falsely, that our music of today is not authentic because there are yet better ways to perform it, especially with instruments that have not yet been developed. We are what we are at any given stage of existence, and we express as fully as we possibly can our innermost passions of that moment.

If it has been altered in some way, the music from another culture begins to lose its ability to carry that culture's messages. While we might be able to respond to any music on a physical basis at least—most music carries an obvious temporal pattern—the music will not carry the same connotations that it needs to in order to reveal a specific set of human values.

Let's be more detailed. Monodic music pitched to diatonic nontempered scales that is suddenly accompanied by a tempered piano with standard Western chords, arranged for a multivoice texture, is immediately not the original music and will mislead the listener. This is a surface way to go about learning another's music. Basal series texts are particularly remiss in presenting music from other cultures, although, in recent years, some series include authentic recordings; that is, they feature performers from the culture. One still finds, however, many folk songs from other cultures that, when performed under present classroom conditions with wrong instrumentation, wrong pronunciation of texts, and so forth, would not be recognized by the cultural members whose music is being reproduced.

This is not learning from the inside.

How does one go about learning from the inside? A very difficult task is now present, but not insurmountable. At the beginning, I stated that music had to be reconceptualized. This is our beginning of knowledge and understanding.

Music exists primarily in time. The time element has an intimate relationship with the human psyche and anatomy: music structures will reflect and symbiotically reconstruct time along the lines of the culture's values as expressed in the way that the body moves. This has implications for musical experience. Moving to music of other cultures is one of the doors through which we must pass to get at the essence of a music. This process cannot be done superficially, however. By having students (and ourselves) take time to move to music frequently, our bodies will discover subtleties that our minds, through an intellectual and analytical approach, will miss. Secondly, by using authentic recordings (i.e., music from the culture made by musicians the culture accepts as representative), other musical factors come into play: scalar structures with their peculiar tuning, color by way of instruments and voices used, textures, language, and so forth. All of these form a totality that cannot be separated in perception of the music but can be pointed to as elements making up the whole.

As to musical instruction, think of this more as a learning than as a teaching process. To obtain an insider's view, the culture's method of transmission must be studied and adopted to the extent possible. The messages contained in the music are also contained in the instruction. Culture is the complete weave, neither woof nor warp alone, but a cloth that envelops, warming

its inhabitants and protecting from exterior forces. To illustrate, cultures that rely on oral transmission not only develop the specific contents of the music but develop the ability to remember long passages of musical substance. This ability improves as more must be committed to memory. Written symbols, on the other hand, have an advantage in being able to be transmitted indirectly. At the same time, writing inhibits the development of memory. The African *griot* can recite generations of history. The Homeric legends are of an age prior to writing. Their structure, once committed to paper, was distinctly different than the forms following based primarily on the written word. "The medium," as McLuhan says, "is [also] the message."

In summary, the authenticity of the musical experience is vital and should be as close to exact replication as possible. If there is too much deviation—only developed sensitivities can determine this—the music containing the culture's truths will be lost.

Curricular Goals and Objectives

If the goal of studying a music is to learn from the inside those truths a culture has discovered, then extensive amounts of time must be spent in such pursuit. Whatever culture is studied, the rules are the same. Keeping an open mind, desiring to learn from the inside, experiencing the culture as the culture's members learn the music, learning from authentic practitioners and materials—all these are important components in a program of music, Western or otherwise.

To spend sufficient time requires that the program begin as early as possible. I would recommend two parallel tracks, one Western, because we are speaking from the viewpoint of American schools, and one from another group or subgroup, each maintaining its own integrity in instruction and materials. These parallel tracks would exist for the full thirteen years (K–12) plus any preschool ages that can be scheduled. The most amazing fact to learn about human beings is their resilience and adaptability; the younger the children, the more they possess these qualities. Humans not only can learn two things concurrently but will keep each pattern—language, music, whatever—distinct and clearly set apart. Millions of people grow up in multilingual and multimusical households and have no difficulty with one expression inhibiting another. Even drawing from the same musical well, styles can differ considerably. A good example is the jazz player who plays so-called legitimate music as well: witness someone like Wynton Marsalis. Calling on more disjunct comparisons, the Japanese Imperial Court musicians have been playing Western music with the proper instruments since the late nineteenth century, when such music was introduced. They are also expert in the traditional Japanese Gagaku repertoire on appropriate instruments, a genre that is also highly evolved and complex.

As to which music, this is a local issue. There is no reason why a large school system might not have a few tracks operating beside the Western music tradition. Parents and students are then free to choose the alternate track according to their own needs and long-range desires. On the surface, this might seem idealistic. But, if learning what being human is all about and learning the *art* of a specific culture will help to answer fundamental questions of existence, is this not what schools are for? If a school is restricted to only two tracks, given limited resources in smaller districts, one being Western, then choices must be made and this should be done with an eye on availability of practitioners, instruments, materials, and other local variables. Usually, the ethnic makeup of the community will play a major role in the choice.

After the student engages in the two tracks for several years (at least to the end of sixth grade), and his or her learning base is solidified in the two cultures, learning the musical expressions of other cultures is now appropriate. The original tracks, however, should not be abandoned lest the student end up with an immature view of the cultures initially studied.

Learning *through* versus Learning *about*

Too much of the curriculum of present-day schools in America is a "learning about." John Dewey's idea of learning through doing and Herbert Read's learning through art have vanished in the rush toward accountability, behaviorism, and other mechanical approaches to education. Except for rare instances, as in Montessori and Waldorf schools or other private venues, public education is largely a factory approach. The idea of doing, making the learning process an authenticating experience, is frequently missing in many programs. And when students in the public schools are doing, it is too frequently the equivalent of painting by numbers.

To focus on this difference more precisely, learning *through* is an active making of music: performing, composing, improvising, moving, listening, and investigating structure, cultural context, and psychological meaning and then reapplying these understandings to the act of making music. These experiences form the basis for empathy. Once the *making* patterns are established in the neuronal pathways of the brain and the muscles develop motive memory, this information, through the proper stimuli, can be recalled anytime during one's life. In addition, there is a basis for continued development.

Conversely, learning *about* is an emphasis on the periphery of music, such as dates of a composer's life, factual information about instruments, how an orchestra is seated, what the instruments look like, and other related data. Listening to music becomes a passive activity that may, but too frequently does not, include focus on musical structure and cultural context. Moreover, it may only have minimal effect on the brain's musical functioning.

The best place to witness an obvious example of learning *about*—although it appears at all levels of education—is the college music appreciation classroom. Students are frequently in large classes where a lecturer explains what the music is about while the students sit passively and listen. Further, there is little context given for the music except in general terms. There is no active engagement of the kinesthetic aspect except as supplied by the student inadvertently. And so, there may even be some students who are adept at recognizing musical style instantly and even understanding something about the structure.

What may be missing is the fundamental premise on which this discussion is based,

which is the holistic learning that integrates all aspects of human existence, allowing us to learn by various human characteristics. Learning music through the body—necessary to any holistic approach and applicable to all ages—is every bit as important as learning with the intellect. Moreover, learning the music from a psychological perspective is an imperative of understanding the people who made the music and those for whom it was made.

Holism needs to be defined further. If we can think of the *I* or *me* as being completely unified, we are more than the organ called brain, even when we think of brain as mind. The brain, while a primary repository of our experiences, does not consciously initiate action. According to numerous neurological studies, we begin to act—which frequently involves movement—and then recognize that we wish to act. In other words, the whole body and being is, in effect, mind; brain is less than mind. Signals are constantly going back and forth between the brain and all parts of our bodies, which add up to the total *me*. I am my thoughts, I am my body, and I am my feelings, all intertwined and working as a completely integrated holistic unit. The *mind* and the *me* are one and the same.

Although consciousness cannot exist without brain, there is now some question about whether thought (i.e., neuronal activity) originates only in the brain. If we think of the mind of each individual as totally encompassing, then there are serious ramifications for learning in all fields, not only in music. The heart of the matter is this: If we are to learn from the inside, we have to replicate as much as possible the culture's processes of learning, for therein lies both the form and content of the culture. We can then understand as the cultural members understand what it means to be human from their point of view. Learning *through,* as contrasted above to learning *about,* is the sure way to engage in the widest range of possible experiences that leads to knowing from within. Until we walk in another's shoes, we don't understand the journey, musically or culturally.

The Qualifications of a Multicultural Music Teacher

The key component of any music program is the teacher. Given the basic qualifications of high levels of musicianship and a personality that is suited for the teaching profession (and all that that entails), only a few additional qualifications for a world musics program would be considered extremely helpful, if not absolutely essential.

Open Mind and Creative Thinking. An open mind, especially about all things human, is critical to crossing cultures successfully. Finding empathy is difficult at times, particularly when another culture is radically different in mores and beliefs, as well as in certain practices in daily events. To learn to think and look at life through the other culture's mindset requires a special step across an invisible divide. Once crossed, the transformation is made and biculturalism can proceed with continued growth commensurate with continued experience. Those with a highly judgmental outlook on life may have a more difficult time bridging the gap. Empathy that allows one to deeply feel and be sensitive to other people and their outlook reveals the kind of personality that will also be

amenable to thinking in new ways. Creative questioning is an indispensable component in the search for truth, which could lead to new avenues of exploration that might otherwise remain dormant.

Music study to a large degree requires convergent behavior. The highly desired quality of ensemble could not exist without it. Divergent thinking patterns, however, are critical to the discovery of new modes of behavior and new ways of thinking and require that one set aside the dicta passed down via teachers, various publications, and other sources of conventional wisdom. To cite one example, definitions of music are sometimes culturally induced and, therefore, do not transfer to other cultures easily.

Philosophical Bent. A person who is somewhat philosophical is also at an advantage in crossing cultures. Presumably one who has this penchant, who has an insatiable curiosity, will more likely be interested in other disciplines just as a matter of keeping informed about the world and human endeavor. Studies from the social, psychological, physical, and biological sciences are important for looking at the human race at both the macro- and micro-levels. An anthropology of music is as important as the technical music studies in which one might engage. The thinking patterns exercised by anthropologists are philosophical in nature and result in the search for the reasons why people do what they do. For example, why do people make music, and what is the reason so much effort and so many resources are expended toward such an activity that seems to produce so little of permanence? Questions like this are at the base of any examination of music around the world and are steeped in philosophical processes to produce reasonable answers.

A related study of aesthetics is paramount because it raises the necessary questions of beauty, value, and a philosophy of art. As shown by their languages, many cultures do not have words for beauty, art, and other areas discussed previously regarding decoration of functional objects. For Westerners, this can be misleading and may suggest that Western artistry is superior. For many cultures, the purpose of an object—music or visual art of some sort—is what it does at a functional level. Yet, all cultures show admiration for artistic achievement and values.

Other Facets. The intangibles that may not have a name are just as important in the ultimate evaluation of someone who wishes to teach in a world musics program. To establish bonds with another requires sincerity and authentic expression of interest in others. Suspicions of exploitation will prohibit exchanges of music, ideas, artifacts, knowledge, and performance expertise.

The willingness to try new things (e.g., food, dress, language, new instruments, new ways of singing, and different ways of moving in dance forms) is an important quality. One learns crossculturally by living in the other person through that person's activities and cultural behavior.

In summary, given an excellent musical ear, mind, sensitivity, and other qualities that make for a good teacher, crossing cultures will demand a certain kind of approach that may inhibit some or make of others a perfect bridge to the other culture. The qualities discussed are not carved in granite but can be learned, as most behavior is. So, essentially, it is the desire to accomplish specific goals that will lead one

through the necessary steps to achieve becoming *other* and gaining insight to another mode of being.

Teaching Materials and Learning Environment

Much of the discussion here is related to factors of authenticity described earlier, that is, models of the music by authentic practitioners and the learning style of the culture being copied as much as possible. Two additional aspects are the resources for materials and the environment where the learning occurs.

There is a wealth of materials now available from libraries, university music departments, community facilities and organizations dedicated to specific cultures, the World Wide Web, record and book stores, and, not least, music practitioners. I will present two examples to illustrate ways of dealing with multicultural materials and their implementation in an effort to make connections with other cultures and to explore the ways in which others value music as a means of expressing their beliefs. The first, from Hawaii, is with practitioners directly from the culture being studied. The second example, from Tennessee, shows what can be done through secondary representatives who have knowledge and experience in the culture.

The Hawaiian Experience. The model described here can be replicated virtually anywhere in the United States. A brief account will show the general picture. In the late 1970s, the Hawaii State Constitution Convention included a provision mandating that Hawaiian culture (e. g. , music, hula, storytelling, and farming techniques) be taught in the schools. The resulting legislation created the means whereby *kūpuna* (elders from the culture, embodiments of the traditions) would be engaged to enter the schools and inculcate Hawaiian values in the students. A formal program was developed and published. The *Hawaiian Studies Program Guide* details the history of the program, the areas of study, how the kūpuna should be used, and overall goals and objectives. Language and *hula* (a single word encompassing music, dance, religion) were major emphases of the program. Several materials were developed, one of which is the *Music Resource Book*. It contains three sections: *Na Mele,* comprising songs or chants used in the program; *Mele,* songs composed expressly by Hawaiian composers, kūpuna, and teachers in the program; and *Na Mele Hoonanea,* simply songs to enjoy that were not part of the formal program but could be used by kūpuna and teachers.

Of the 365 people presently on the list of kūpuna, most are qualified in music and dance, which they regularly teach. Most are used in the elementary grades, with a few working at the secondary level. I studied one particular kupuna, Kelii Chun, who taught at Kalihi Waena, an elementary school in one of the oldest areas of Honolulu. My study incorporated making a video of her work, which was then shown on public access television. Grandmotherly and with a considerable background in Hawaiian music and dance, Kupuna Chun engaged the children in music and dance activities, but also included the all-important Hawaiian "commandments," which exhibit the spirit of *aloha: kokua* (individual help); *laulima* (cooperation, many hands

working together); *alu like* (acting cooperatively); *lokahi* (unity); *kuleana* (individual rights and responsibilities within a group situation); and *hooponopono* (setting trouble to right through group or family discussion/therapy). Although Kelii Chun attended Kalihi Waena School when it was largely of Hawaiian ethnicity, now in the 1990s, most of the students have their origins from southeast Asia and the Pacific Islands. The children benefit greatly by being brought into the Hawaiian culture through the instruction. This is important because the population of Hawaii consists of four-fifths Asian and Polynesian ancestry, and the overall culture is permeated with Hawaiian values.

The outstanding aspects of this experience for our purposes are not the legal and legislative components. The Hawaiian electorate made a decision to follow that path. Of greater significance is that although Hawaii is blessed with a wide variety of ethnicities, including peoples of European origins, every location in the United States has access to at least one group that maintains distinctive customs, music repertoire, unique celebrations, and other cultural values that can be characterized as ethnic. Whether one is talking about the Tambouritza groups that are found in Pennsylvania, the Native American groups found throughout the continent, Latino music in New York City and Los Angeles, the African-American music found throughout most of our cities and towns, or the Cajun music in Louisiana, music outside the Western mainstream can be brought into the schools and studied, learned, and performed to the advantage of the students and their understanding of music and culture. The principle is no less applicable to Western music. Essentially, all music is ethnic music in the sense that it arises out of a specific time and place, from a specific group of people, their beliefs, and their efforts to deal with their interpretations of natural and psychic phenomena.

Japanese Music in Tennessee. I returned to the University of Tennessee, Knoxville, from a year-long study of traditional music in Japan in 1985 and immediately set to work applying my experiences to a school project. My interest lay in how elementary school children could learn Japanese music, specifically gagaku, which was my specialty, and folk music. I engaged a music teacher with an excellent reputation who taught in one of the schools close to the university. We chose two of her fourth-grade classes to run a six-week-long program of Japanese music instruction. This also involved a pilot study to assess achievement and preference. Although the results on achievement were encouraging, they were otherwise inconclusive on preference. The idea of studying preference of *other* music is now being carried out in a full-scale study by a doctoral student at the University of Hawaii at Manoa.

The importance of this story lies in the setup of the instruction and the environment for learning that I tried to create. One class studied gagaku, which I'll describe, and the other folk music. Both classes were structured the same way; an attempt was made to duplicate the trappings of Japanese instruction in traditional music. The room was rearranged by moving out desks and setting up a circle of carpet pads; students entering the room took off their shoes and stood at one of the

pads, waited for *sensei* to enter (I did all the instruction), bowed appropriately, exchanged greetings in Japanese, sat when directed, and proceeded to learn the music by rote. I wore *tabi* (white socks with separated large toe), *hana-o* (straw thongs), and *happi* (a kimono-style short, slip-over jacket). I taught the song in Japanese and the gagaku tune in *shoga* (musical syllables).

Etenraku was the gagaku piece, chosen because I had several recordings of various aspects of its performance: shoga sung by my Japanese teacher; the three woodwind parts of *shō*, an instrument with seventeen upright bamboo pipes set in a cup-like container; *hichiricki*, a short double-reed end-blown instrument; *ryutek*, a transverse flute; and a full gagaku ensemble rendition by the Imperial Court musicians. In addition, *Etenraku*, one of the oldest pieces in the repertoire of some 1,200 years, although not danced to as far as we know, is used at important celebrations like weddings, installation of priests, and other major events. The work is composed of three eight-measure phrases, each divided in half, with those halves each further divided in half. The piece had many commendable attributes, not the least of which is accessibility, because of the well-defined form.

To enhance the memory of the work (rather than have students simply listen), I chose to create a bugaku-type dance with unified but distinguishing patterns that fit each eight-measure phrase. Further, dance at the fourth-grade level needed to be concrete, so I placed the dance in the context of a well-known Japanese folk tale. *Urashima Taro* is the story of a young lad taken to the kingdom at the bottom of the sea, a reward for saving a tortoise. Urashima is further rewarded by being given the princess's hand in marriage, thereby furnishing a perfect opportunity for all of the fish of the undersea kingdom to celebrate and several to perform a dance at the wedding.

The instruction was enhanced by having *happi* made of white muslin, the back of which students decorated with their own crest in design and color. Their *tabi* were simply white gym socks. I utilized numerous adjunct materials in introducing the music and project. I brought in my instruments (*shō* and *hichiriki*) for demonstration, showed slides of the gagaku ensemble, its instruments, and *bugaku,* the dance form that accompanies gagaku. After telling them the story of Urashima, I suggested that they find other Japanese folk tales in their school library, which they did, including the one on Urashima. Maps were brought in to show Japan in relation to other Asia-Pacific nations. A Western feature of instruction was to acquaint the students with the idea of *mode,* the basic pattern from which the tones of the melodies are derived. *Etenraku* is in *hyôjô* mode, a pentatonic arrangement beginning on E.

Further, the students were given parallel instruction in other aspects of Japanese culture with their teachers outside of music. One class chose to investigate *origami* and create several beautiful objects; another began writing *haiku.* The whole project was quite appropriate, even if one were to question Japanese music in east Tennessee. A few years before, Matsushita Electronics built a plant in East Tennessee, so there were just enough Japanese students in the schools and American students' parents who worked for the company to make the Japanese presence known.

After beginning the project, parents heard about it and wanted to see what the children had learned. Even though we did not try to bring the instruction to *performance* level, we did display the students' achievements in a special PTA meeting one day after the instructional period was over. Based on anecdotal evidence, there was much success embodied in the comments of approval made to the principal and teachers by the fact that many younger siblings had learned the music well enough to sing it, and the teachers came away with the sense of having done something worthwhile for their students and community.

In summary, there are many opportunities in our own backyards to initiate programs that will introduce folk, ethnic, and art musics that come from outside the usual Western symphony and related repertoire. Moreover, it is my view that all music should be learned within cultural contexts because it is the context that guides the music making and its structure. Any separations we assign to various types should be for the purpose of insight rather than to assign hierarchies of value. Value, it must be kept in mind, is a relative assessment, not an absolute.

Concluding Thoughts

Given the foregoing discussion of possibilities and problems, issues and arguments, traveled pathways, and new explorations that lie ahead, what can the teacher do to ensure that students understand the multicultural perspective? One assurance that your students may weather the storms of constant change is to teach principles. For example, because of the ability of the mind to handle limited amounts of data at a given time, the information is coded in patterns that are understood and able to be recalled. What underlies a melodic phrase in a Western folk song, for example, is no different than that underlying a motif in Javanese *gamelan* music: small chunks that have meaning within the parameters of a musical system and that can be recalled as necessary for reapplication to the ensuing instances. Memorizing extended amounts of musical material requires a certain amount of repetition of patterns with related contrasting units. Consequently, music the world over, because of peculiar human mental processes, is going to have some kind of perceivable form that befits the culture. This is an underlying principle.

Music taught solely as principle or in the abstract, however, is also problematic, for art is specific. Whatever underlies the particular piece of music in terms of principle, structural cohesiveness, and so forth, we are drawn to it also because of its artistic qualities of tone, pitch, time organizations, and rhythms within the cultural matrix and what those excite in our psychophysiological makeup. These two seeming polarities form the tension that whets our interest. Music does represent the deepest feelings and experiences of a particular group in time and place, yet is tied to the underlying psycho-neuronal structure of the human species. On the one hand, music appears to be quite different in style and structure. On the other hand, all is related to the inexplicable imperative to make music and for that music to have meaning for the individual as he or she gropes to make sense of the phenomenal and psychic encounters that life affords.

So, in the process of creating specific musical and cultural experiences, a time for reflection is always appropriate. Putting matters into contexts of larger and longer-range considerations will begin to help the student build a network of knowledge and understandings. Thus, the questions of what it means to be human is constantly present as a subtext to our lives. The questions of life are at the basis of all psychic interactions.

There is a caveat here, however. It would be a mistake to conclude that music is solely to serve this greater need and that there is only functional value in the act itself. This is another way of saying that we do not yet understand the symbiosis between the things we do and the reason we do them. In expressing human nature, music (and the other arts) is both means and ends. It serves to deepen our understanding at the same time that it becomes the means to be human—doing the ultimate human thing, as in singing, dancing, painting, sculpting, and acting. When we are at our best, in an effort to express our joy of being alive in this unfathomable consciousness of ourselves, we both express and search for meaning as a unified and cohesive venture.

Resource List

Ethnomusicology

Bebey, Francis. *African Music, A People's Art.* Trans. by Josephine Bennett. New York: Lawrence Hill, 1975.

Blacking, John. *How Musical Is Man?* Seattle: University of Washington Press, 1973.

Chailley, Jacques. *40,000 Years of Music; Man in Search of Music.* Trans. from the French by Rollo Myers. London: Macdonald, 1964.

Ellis, Alexander J. "On the Musical Scales of Various Nations," *Journal of the Society of Arts* [London] 33, no. 1688 (1885).

Herndon, Marcia, and Norma McLeod. *Music as Culture.* Darby, PA: Norwood, 1982.

Hood, Mantle. "The Challenge of 'Bi-musicality,'" *Ethnomusicology* 4 (May 1960): 55–59.

Hopkins, Jerry. *The Hula*. Hong Kong: Apa Productions, 1982.

Kanahele, George S., ed. *Hawaiian Music and Musicians, An Illustrated History*. Honolulu, HI: University of Hawaii Press, 1979.

Lomax, Alan. *Folk Song Style and Culture*. Washington, DC: American Association for the Advancement of Science, 1968.

Malm, William P. *Japanese Music and Musical Instruments*. Rutland, VT: Charles E. Tuttle Co., 1959.

Merriam, Alan P. *The Anthropology of Music*. Evanston, IL: Northwestern Univ. Press, 1964.

Nettl, Bruno. *The Western Impact on World Music: Change, Adaptation, and Survival*. New York: Schirmer Books, 1985.

Neuman, Daniel M. *The Life of Music in North India: The Organization of an Artistic Tradition*. Detroit, MI: Wayne State Univ. Press, 1980.

Palmer, Anthony J. "To Fuse or Not to Fuse: Directions of Two Japanese Composers, Miki and Takemitsu." In *Proceedings of the Fourth Symposium* (July, 1990). Osaka, Japan: International Musicological Society, 1991.

Palmer, Anthony J. "Leonard B. Meyer and a Cross-Cultural Aesthetics," *Journal of Aesthetic Education* 26, no. 3 (Fall).

Palmer, Anthony J. "Music as an Archetype in the 'Collective Unconscious' and Implications for a World Aesthetic." In *Dialogue and Universalism*. Poland: Institute of Philosophy, Warsaw Univ., 1995.

Palmer, Anthony J. "Music." In *Multicultural Hawaii: The Fabric of a Multiethnic Society*. Edited by Michael Haas. New York: Garland Publishing, 1998.

Rahn, Jay. *A Theory for All Music: Problems and Solutions in the Analysis of Non-Western Forms*. Toronto: University of Toronto Press, 1983.

Sachs, Curt. *The Rise of Music in the Ancient World East and West*. New York: W. W. Norton, 1943.

Sachs, Curt. *The Wellsprings of Music*. The Hague: Martinus Nijhoff, 1962.

Wellesz, Egon, ed. *Ancient and Oriental Music*. London: Oxford Univ. Press, 1957.

Music

Chen, Whey-Fen. "History and Development of Theory of 'Lu': A Translation of Selected Chapters of Huang Ti-Pei's 'Perspectives of Chinese Music." Master's thesis, North Texas State Univ., 1985.

Deva, B. Chaintanya. *Indian Music*. New Delhi: Indian Council for Cultural Relations, 1974.

Portnoy, Julius. *Music in the Life of Man*, New York: Holt, Rinehart and Winston, 1963.

Stein, Leonard, ed. *Style and Idea: Selected Writings of Arnold Schoenberg*. New York: St. Martin's Press, 1975.

Westrup, J. A. *An Introduction to Musical History*. London: Hutchinson's Univ. Library, 1955.

Music Education

Palmer, Anthony J. "World Musics in Elementary and Secondary Music Education: A Critical Analysis." PhD. diss., UCLA, 1975.

Palmer, Anthony J. "World Musics in Music Education: The Matter of Authenticity," *International Journal of Music Education* 19 (1992): 32–40.

Palmer, Anthony J. "Toward an Integrated Aesthetic and the Implications for Music Education," *Philosophy of Music Education Review* 2, no. 1 (spring 1994).

Palmer, Anthony J. "A Perspective on Cross-Cultural Music Education: The Personal Dimension," *Journal of Music Teacher Education* 4, no. 1 (fall 1994): 19–24.

Palmer, Anthony J. "Spirituality and Music Education: A Philosophical Exploration," *Philosophy of Music Education Review* 3, no. 1 (1995).

Palmer, Anthony J. "On a Philosophy of World Musics in Music Education." In *Critical Reflections on Music Education: Proceedings of the Second International Symposium on the Philosophy of Music Education*. Edited by Lee R. Bartel and David J. Elliott. Toronto: University of Toronto, 1996.

Palmer, Anthony J. "Multicultural Music Education: Antipodes and Complementarities," *Philosophy of Music Education* 5, no. 2 (Fall 1997).

Schwadron, Abraham A. *Aesthetics: Dimensions for Music Education*. Washington, DC: MENC, 1967.

Music Psychology

Backus, John. *The Acoustical Foundations of Music*. 2nd ed. New York: W. W. Norton, 1977.

Bamberger, Jeanne. *The Mind behind the Musical Ear: How Children Develop Musical Intelligence*. Cambridge, MA: Harvard Univ. Press, 1991.

Sloboda, John A. *The Musical Mind: The Cognitive Psychology of Music.* Oxford: Clarendon Press, 1985.

Sloboda, John A., ed. *Generative Processes in Music: The Psychology of Performance, Improvisation, and Composition.* Oxford: Clarendon Press, 1988.

Radocy, Rudolf E., and J. David Boyle. *Psychological Foundations of Musical Behavior.* 2nd ed. Springfield, IL: Charles C. Thomas, 1988.

Storr, Anthony. *Music and the Mind.* New York: Free Press, 1992.

Tame, David. *The Secret Power of Music.* Rochester, VT: Destiny Books, 1984.

Tomatis, Alfred A. *The Conscious Ear.* Barrytown, NY: Station Hill Press, 1991.

General and Educational Psychology

Csikszentmihalyi, Mihaly. *The Evolving Self: A Psychology for the Third Millennium.* New York: HarperCollins, 1993.

Gardner, Howard. *Art, Mind, and Brain: A Cognitive Approach to Creativity.* New York: Basic Books, 1982.

Gardner, Howard. *Frames of Mind.* New York: Basic Books, 1985.

Gardner, Howard. *The Unschooled Mind: How Children Think and How Schools Should Teach.* New York: Basic Books, 1991.

Gould, Stephen Jay. *The Mismeasure of Man.* Rev. and enl. New York: Norton, 1996.

Goleman, Daniel. *Emotional Intelligence.* New York: Bantam Books, 1995.

Jung, Carl G. *Symbols of Transformation.* Bollengen Series XX, Vol. 5. Princeton, NJ: Princeton Univ. Press, 1956.

Jung, Carl G. *Psychology and Religion: West and East.* Bollengen Series XX, Vol. 11. Princeton, NJ: Princeton Univ. Press, 1958.

Jung, Carl G. *The Archetypes and the Collective Unconscious.* Bollengen Series XX, Vol. 9, Part I. Princeton, NJ: Princeton Univ. Press, 1959.

Jung, Carl G. *The Structure and Dynamics of the Psyche.* Bollengen Series XX, Vol. 8. Princeton, NJ: Princeton Univ. Press, 1960.

Jung, Carl G. *Civilization in Transition.* Bollengen Series XX, Vol. 10. Princeton, NJ: Princeton Univ. Press, 1964.

Jung, Carl G. *Man and His Symbols.* Garden City, NY: Doubleday, 1964.

Jung, Carl G. *The Spirit in Man, Art, and Literature.* Bollengen Series XX, Vol. 15. Princeton, NJ: Princeton Univ. Press, 1966.

Jung, Carl G. *Psychological Types.* Bollengen Series XX, Vol. 6. Princeton, NJ: Princeton Univ. Press, 1976.

Jung, Carl G. *Psychology and the East.* From *The Collected Works of C. G. Jung,* Vol. 10, 11, 13, 18. Princeton, NJ: Princeton Univ. Press, 1978.

Kozol, Jonathan. *On Being a Teacher.* New York: Continuum, 1981.

Maslow, Abraham H. *The Farther Reaches of Human Nature.* New York: Viking Press, 1971.

Montessori, Maria. *To Educate the Human Potential.* Adyar, Madras 20, India: Kalakshetra Publications, 1948.

Montessori, Maria. *Education for a New World.* With an introduction by J. McV. Hunt. Adyar, Madras 20, India: Kalakshetra Publications, 1963.

Montessori, Maria. *The Montessori Method.* Trans. Anne E. George. 1912; rpt. New York: Schocken Books, 1964.

Neumann, Erich. *The Origins and History of Consciousness.* Bollengen Series XLII. Princeton, NJ: Princeton Univ. Press, 1954.

Neumann, Erich. *Art and the Creative Unconscious.* Bollengen Series LXI. New York: Pantheon Books, 1959.

Ostrander, Sheila, and Lynn Schroeder. *Superlearning.* New York: Laurel Books, 1982.

Pinker, Steven. *The Language Instinct.* New York: Wm. Morrow, 1994.

Progoff, Era. *Jung's Psychology and its Social Meaning.* New York: Grove Press, 1953.

Storr, Anthony. *The Dynamics of Creation.* New York: Ballantine Books, 1993.

Medical/Biological/Neurological

Caplan, Frank, gen. ed. *The First Twelve Months of Life: Your Baby's Growth Month by Month.* New York: Grosset & Dunlap, 1971.

Dennett, Daniel C. *Kinds of Minds.* New York: Basic Books, 1996.

Denton, Derek. *The Pinnacle of Life: Consciousness and Self-Awareness in Humans and Animals.* New York: HarperCollins, 1994.

Diamond, Jared. *The Third Chimpanzee: The Evolution and Future of the Human Animal.* New York: HarperPerennial, 1992.

Elgin, Duane. *Awakening Earth: Exploring the Evolution of Human Culture and Consciousness.* New York: Wm. Morrow, 1993.

Ferris, Timothy. *The Mind's Sky: Human Intelligence in Cosmic Context.* New York: Bantam, 1992.

Greenfield, Susan A. *Journey to the Centers of the Mind: Toward a Science of Consciousness.* New York: W. H. Freeman, 1995.

Jaynes, Julian. *The Origin of Consciousness in the Breakdown of the Bicameral Mind.* Boston: Houghton Mifflin, 1976.

Journal of Consciousness Studies, Controversies in Science and the Humanities 1, no. 1 (1994) through 6, no. 1 (1999) [UK and USA: Imprint Academic].

Lewis, Michael, ed. *Origins of Intelligence, Infancy and Early Childhood.* New York: Plenum Press, 1976.

Merrell-Wolff, Franklin. *Transformations in Consciousness: The Metaphysics and Epistemology.* Albany, NY: SUNY Press, 1994.

Minsky, Marvin. *The Society of Mind.* New York: Simon and Schuster, 1986.

Murphy, Michael. *The Future of the Body: Explorations into the Further Evolution of Human Nature.* New York: G. P. Putnam's Sons, 1992.

Musès, Charles, and Arthur M. Young, eds. *Consciousness and Reality.* New York: Outerbridge and Lazard, 1972.

Neumann, Erich. *The Origins and History of Consciousness.* Bollingen Series XLII. New York: Pantheon, 1954.

Ornstein, Robert. *Multimind.* Boston: Houghton Mifflin, 1986.

Ornstein, Robert. *The Evolution of Consciousness: Of Darwin, Freud, and Cranial—The Origins of the Way We Think.* New York: Prentice Hall, 1991.

Ornstein, Robert. *The Right Mind: Making Sense of the Hemispheres.* New York: Harcourt Brace, 1997.

Ornstein, Robert, and Paul Ehrlich. *New World, New Mind: Moving toward Conscious Evolution.* New York: Simon & Schuster, 1989.

Pearce, Joseph Chilton. *Evolution's End: Claiming the Potential of Our Intelligence.* San Francisco: HarperSanFrancisco, 1992.

Perkins, David N., Jack Lochhead, and John C. Bishop, eds. *Knowledge as Design.* Hillsdale, NJ: Lawrence Erlbaum Associates, Publishers, 1986.

Restak, Richard. *The Brain Has a Mind of Its Own: Insights from a Practicing Neurologist.* New York: Harmony Books, 1991.

Richardson, Frederick, ed. *Brain and Intelligence:*

The Ecology of Child Development. Hyattsville, MD: National Educational Press, 1973.

Philosophy, Aesthetics, and Worldview

Abraham, Ralph. *Chaos, Gaia, Eros: A Chaos Pioneer Uncovers the Three Great Streams of History.* San Francisco, CA: HarperSanFrancisco, 1994.

Barrow, John D. *The Artful Universe.* Oxford: Clarendon Press, 1995.

Briggs, John, and F. David Peat. *Turbulent Mirror: An Illustrated Guide to Chaos Theory and the Science of Wholeness.* New York: Harper and Row, 1989.

Buber, Martin. *I and Thou.* 2nd ed. Trans. by Ronald Gregor Smith. New York: Charles Scribner's Sons, 1958.

Campbell, Joseph. *The Masks of God*, Vols. I–IV. New York: Penguin Books, 1959.

Campbell, Joseph. *Transformations of Myth through Time.* New York: Harper and Row, 1990.

Coles, Robert. *The Spiritual Life of Children.* Boston: Houghton Mifflin, 1990.

Damasio, Antonio R. *Descartes' Error: Emotion, Reason, and the Human Brain.* New York: G. P. Putnam's Sons, 1994.

Dewey, John. *Art as Experience.* New York: Capricorn Books, 1958.

Grant, Michael. *The Founders of the Western World: A History of Greece and Rome.* New York: Charles Scribner's Sons, 1991.

Hall, Edward T. *The Silent Language.* New York: Fawcett World Library, 1959.

Hall, Edward T. *The Hidden Dimension.* Garden City, NY: Doubleday, 1966.

Hall, Edward T. *The Dance of Life: The Other Dimension of Time.* Garden City, NY: Anchor Press/Doubleday, 1983.

Jackson, John G. *Man, God, and Civilization.* New Hyde Park, NY: University Books, 1972.

Johanson, Donald C., and Maitland A. Edey. *Lucy: The Beginnings of Humankind.* New York: Simon and Schuster, 1981.

Kafatos, M., and R. Nadeau. *The Conscious Universe.* New York: Springer-Verlag, 1995.

Kaku, Michio. *Hyperspace: A Scientific Odyssey through Parallel Universes, Time Warps, and the Tenth Dimension.* New York: Oxford Univ. Press, 1994.

Kandinsky, Wassily. *Concerning the Spiritual in Art.* Trans. by M. T. H. Sadler. New York: Dover Publications, 1977.

Kuhn, Thomas S. *The Structure of Scientific*

Revolutions. 2nd ed., enl. International Encyclopedia of Unified Science: vol. II, no. 2, Foundations of the Unity of Science. Chicago: University of Chicago Press, 1970.

Küng, Hans. *Theology for the Third Millennium: An Ecumenical View.* Trans. by Peter Heinegg. New York: Doubleday, 1988.

McLuhan, Marshall, and Quentin Fiore. *The Medium Is the Message.* New York: Bantam Books, 1967.

Munro, Thomas, and Herbert Read. *The Creative Arts in American Education.* Cambridge, MA: Harvard Univ. Press, 1960.

Noel, Daniel C., ed. *Paths to the Power of Myth: Joseph Campbell and the Study of Religion.* New York: Crossroad, 1990.

Northrop, F. S. C. *The Meeting of East and West.* New York: Collier Books, 1946.

Parabola Magazine:, Myth, Tradition, and the Search for Meaning 1, no. 1–24, no. 1(1976–1999); published by the Society for the Study of Myth and Tradition.

Parkinson, C. Northcote. *East and West.* Boston: Houghton Mifflin, 1963.

Portnoy, Julius. *The Philosopher and Music: A Historical Outline.* New York: Humanities Press, 1954.

Read, Herbert. *Education through Art.* New York: Pantheon Books, 1956.

Reimer, Bennett, and Ralph A. Smith, eds. *The Arts, Education, and Aesthetic Knowing.* Chicago: National Society for the Study of Education, University of Chicago Press, 1992.

Ross, Malcolm. *The Aesthetic Impulse.* Oxford: Pergamon Press, 1984.

Sartwell, Crispin. *The Art of Living: Aesthetics of the Ordinary in World Spiritual Traditions.* Albany, NY: State University of New York Press, 1995.

Wilber, Ken. *Sex, Ecology, Spirituality.* Boston: Shambhala, 1995.

Wilson, Edward O. *Consilience: The Unity of Knowledge.* New York: Alfred A. Knopf, 1998.

ANTHONY J. PALMER, recently retired as professor of music from the University of Hawaii, now teaches occasional courses at Boston University as adjunct professor of music education, while continuing his research, composition, and conducting in the Boston area. His credits include numerous articles and workshops on music education, choral music, and aesethetics (particularly crosscultural) at the local, national, and international levels.

Particular Perspectives

3

The Ambiguous Nature of Multicultural Music Education: Learning Music through Multicultural Content, or Learning Multiculturalism through Music?

Peter Dunbar-Hall

*E*ven though Sydney is a culturally diverse city, my experience of multiculturalism did not commence until I began teaching music in secondary schools in the mid-1970s. At that time, training music educators in issues of multiculturalism was not a priority in Australia. The initial shock I experienced when working with students and staff from many cultural, ethnic, and religious backgrounds was immediately replaced by being intrigued by the relationships between music, culture, and education. I maintained and developed this interest by seeking experience in a range of music cultures, among them, performing in a jazz band, studying with a Senegalese master drummer, working for a brief period with jazz and rock bands, playing in a Balinese gamelan, and researching the contemporary music cultures of Australian Aborigines.

These experiences have served to heighten my awareness of the issues involved when music educators teach music from cultures outside their own experiences and those of their students.

These experiences also uncover topics for philosophical consideration and provide insights into what music education is and how and why it occurs. As a form of professional development and enrichment, these experiences provide the basis for publications on the philosophy and practice of music education and shed light on attempts to widen the scope of methods through which we attempt to train music educators in preservice programs.

One of the most significant results of these experiences, and of my ongoing participation in crosscultural settings, has been the realization that multicultural music education acts as a means of crystallizing issues that affect music education as a whole.

Introduction: Multiculturalism, Education, and Music

"Multicultural music education" is a term used worldwide to refer to a specific aspect of music teaching and learning. Despite its global use, the term is confusing because each of its three words has its own sets of contexts, implications, and agendas. The result is that, when all three are combined, they produce another hybrid set of meanings. One of the main problems with the phrase multicultural music education, then, is that, because its three levels of reference are rarely separated, subsequent discussion tends to lack clarity, agreement on definition, and direction in educational philosophy, teaching strategies, and expected outcomes.

"Multicultural," one of the most abused terms of politics, sociology, and cultural studies, is a political descriptor. As such, it signifies party political platforms, decides government spending patterns, and influences national definition and direction.[1] In combination with "education," it produces the construct "multicultural education" as a way of thinking about the rationales, content, and methodologies of teaching and learning that acknowledges "diverse racial, ethnic, social-class, and cultural groups" of students.[2] Multicultural education is recognized internationally as an issue of the late twentieth century and can be linked to the accrued results of migratory patterns since the late nineteenth century, the study of subcultures, and the acknowledgment of post-colonialism as a way of analyzing the relationships between countries and peoples. In these ways, the character of multicultural education as a product and problematic issue of its time must be recognized. Its existence as a response to continually changing societal landscapes draws attention to its origins, its dynamism, and its ongoing processual nature.[3]

The use of the term "multicultural" in combination with "music education" has its own fields of reference. There seems to be tacit agreement that, in this context, the "cultural" in "multicultural" refers to musics foreign to Western-based ones. However, as the increasing literature on cultural studies demonstrates, this narrow definition of the term is at odds with the reality of the diversities of everyday living, where many more factors than ethnic background or geographic provenance decide to which cultures individuals belong or aspire to belong.[4] For example, different levels of socio-economic class,[5] and gay and lesbian,[6] gender-based,[7] and popular music-centered cultures[8] are increasingly discussed as forms of the "multi" that qualifies "culture" in the construction "multicultural." However, as these cultures have their own literatures and increasingly exist in music education as discrete topics of study, most music education literature on the topic of multiculturalism refers to the problems of including non-Western music in music curricula derived from Western-based models, which, to help focus the present discussion, is the meaning employed here, although it must be noted that the problems discussed in this context should be seen as representative of the broader enterprise of teaching musics from different types of cultural sources and as representative of ways in which this enterprise may be handled and conceptualized.

In this chapter, issues of the nature and practice of multicultural music education are problematized from an Australian perspective. Like many other countries, Australia owes much of its sense of nation to the input and coexistence of different cultures. Australian education and, by implication, Australian music education are a response to this cultural diversity. This response can be readily identified in a trail from the definition of Australia as a nation at the federal level, through state government policies, into educational and music education expectations. In this way, analysis of Australian music education can be used to expose and debate issues that affect multicultural music education as an element of music teaching and learning worldwide.

To achieve this, my discussion is organized into the following areas: the background of Australian multiculturalism; multiculturalism in Australian music education; different types of educational multiculturalism; and problems arising from attempts to incorporate multicultural perspectives into music teaching and learning. Through these focus areas, discontinuities between the aims of music education and of multicultural music education are investigated, and questions over the propriety of teaching methods are raised. Possible solutions to these problems are posed, but these solutions only lead to the posing of further, more complex problems. This inability to offer final solutions to the problems of multicultural music education may be the significant outcome of this discussion—it is not the finding of solutions that is important, but the ability to identify issues of concern and thus to raise awareness of potential pitfalls in the undertaking.

Australian Multiculturalism

In common with other colonized countries, such as Canada and the United States of America, Australia has been and continues to be a multicultural country, both *de facto* and *de jure*. For at least 40,000 years, different indigenous nations, each with its own language, music, and lore, have occupied the Australian continent. Of an estimated two hundred and fifty at the time of the white invasion in the late eighteenth century, approximately ninety of these cultures remain.[9] With European colonization in 1788, layers of European-derived cultures were added to this multicultural mix. Migration from Asia, Europe, and South America has continued to strengthen the multicultural nature of Australia, so that currently, of a population of approximately 18 million, 41 percent of Australians were born overseas or have a parent born outside Australia.[10]

While Australia's multicultural nature can be traced through consideration of its indigenous past and migration patterns, the situation has not always been as felicitous as this might imply. Since 1788, treatment of Aborigines and Torres Strait Islanders has been a matter of continued public shame,[11] and for many years a government immigration policy known as the "White Australia Policy" was in force. Passed in 1901, the Immigration Restriction Act stated that "after 1901, non-Whites could only enter Australia on a temporary basis under a permit."[12] By this policy, only suitable, white immigrants were permitted into Australia in an attempt to replicate a British/European-based society, and, in the rarely discussed area of cultural politics, the Anglophile Australian middle-class defined itself as an Anglo-Australian elite, believing that culture came to Australia on a P & O ocean liner.[13]

Awareness of the discriminatory nature of such policies (i.e., that international perceptions of Australia were of a racist nation, that nations with similar migratory patterns were moving toward acceptance of cultural diversity, and that Australia's cultural mix necessitated specific policies and strategies) led successive Australian governments to address this aspect of Australian society.[14]

Since the 1970s, multiculturalism, defined in government documents as "a term which describes the cultural and ethnic diversity of contemporary Australia" and a perspective that attempts to "manage the consequences of this diversity in the interests of the individual and society as a whole,"[15] has been an aspect of the official definition of Australia as a nation. A *zeitgeist* of the 1970s and 1980s,[16] multiculturalism received recognition in a government report on the problems of handling migrant intake in the period up to the mid-1970s[17] and became official government policy in 1989 with the release of the *National Agenda for a Multicultural Australia.* Much of the background to such policy direction lies in postcolonialism, moves toward establishment of Australia as a republic, redefinition of relationships to indigenous Australians, and intense analysis of Australia's world position, especially in relation to the economic nexus of Southeast Asia rather than of Britain and the USA.[18]

Multiculturalism in Australian Music Education

Definition of Australia as a multicultural nation at the federal level is mirrored at state levels as policy, and, following that, in the documents that govern education. At a more specific level, such as syllabus expectations in music, multiculturalism exists in principle in music teaching and learning in a number of ways in the different states of

Australia. Through these increasingly more specific levels, multiculturalism can be shown to flow from national ethos to classroom applications. However, the intentions of multiculturalism alter as this process occurs, so that, by the time policies have reached the level of music classrooms, ambiguity is injected into the reasons for adopting them, into the ways that they are implemented, and into the ways that music is studied. What passes for multiculturalism in music classrooms might not be the result of these policies, but of teaching practices that pre-existed the labeling and adoption of the multicultural ethos theoretically directing Australian educational objectives. Therefore, despite the inclusion of amounts of music from non-Western cultures in music lessons, such teaching might not really be "multicultural" in nature. Rather, it may be the result of assigning the multicultural label to a situation similar in appearance to multiculturalism, but one without the adoption of the philosophies that this label carries with it. Moreover, the overriding approach to music education in Australia, which relies on analysis of musical concepts (pitch, duration, etc.), can be shown to be often antithetical to the aesthetic stances of the music under examination. This creates a serious disjuncture between classroom musical content, educational intention, and methodology. This disjuncture only serves to magnify the problems of multicultural music education. To explain this situation, music syllabi in New South Wales (NSW) will be examined.

Multiculturalism in NSW Music Education

The multicultural character of education in NSW was officially established in the

1983 *Multicultural Education Policy Statement*[19] and a series of support documents.[20] The policy statement sets out how multiculturalism takes effect in NSW schools. Its aims are to develop the following:

■ an understanding and appreciation that Australia has been multicultural in nature throughout its history, both before and after European colonization

■ an awareness of contributions that people of different cultural backgrounds have made and make to Australia

■ intercultural understanding through the consideration of attitudes, beliefs, and values related to multiculturalism

■ behavior that fosters interethnic harmony

■ an enhanced sense of personal worth through acceptance and appreciation, not only of Australian national identity, but also of specific Australian ethnic identities in the context of a multicultural society.[21]

In 1992, approximately a decade after the 1983 *Multicultural Education Policy Statement,* the NSW Department of School Education released its *Multicultural Education Plan,* which sets out the implementation of the principles of multiculturalism in schools. Introductory comments such as the following:

> Schools ... play an important role in forming and informing attitudes and values as well as imparting skills relevant to multicultural ideals. Multicultural education ... enables schools to fulfill their roles in building a cohesive multicultural society.[22]

reinforce the department's support of mul-

ticulturalism, after which strategies for developing crosscultural awareness, viable resources, relevant teaching programs, community awareness, and research that identifies good practice and ensures the success of multicultural education are set out.

In common with music syllabi in other Australian states, those in NSW can be shown to acknowledge these principles of multiculturalism both in intent, expressed in general objectives, and in content, though the latter varies in degree from state to state. Multiculturalism can be found in NSW music education in three forms. First, although not mentioned by name, it is offered as a platform in the rationale for music as a subject in schools: "Music pervades contemporary society and plays an important part in everyday life. Music is a significant part of every culture."[23]

Second, it can be identified in mandated and suggested content for music classes in topics such as "traditional and contemporary music of Aborigines and Torres Strait Islanders," "music from Australia's diverse cultural backgrounds," and "traditional music of a culture."[24]

Third, it has an effect in the development of generic cultural understanding. This is encouraged through pupil experiences in a number of activities through which knowledge of culture as a concept can be acquired. Specifically, music teachers are reminded that "some music exists in its new culture without much change, whereas much music is transformed by its interaction with a new culture and by cross-fertilization of music from various cultures."[25]

This statement is followed by suggested

teaching strategies that reflect multicultural ideologies:

- transcribing and using different methods of notating music
- discussing the role of music in a particular society in its Australian context (festivals, dance, community events, and entertainment)
- gaining an understanding of music in its historical and cultural contexts
- listening to music that has been influenced by music of another culture
- aurally identifying and describing the similarities and distinguishing characteristics in works by composers working in cultural contexts and historical periods
- studying changes in music when it is transported between cultural settings
- describing the different processes used to share and preserve musical expressions in past and present cultures
- describing the technical and musical considerations in realizing and presenting music/dance from a particular culture
- discussing how context can change the acceptance of a musical work.[26]

While these three applications of multiculturalism can be interpreted as implementations of current government policies, reference to syllabi from the period prior to the mandating of multiculturalism demonstrates that, in the teaching of music, such considerations have always been present. For example, in the *Syllabus in Music* issued in 1956, while the majority of content prescribed is Western art music, "folk-songs of various nations" and "folk-music of various nations, with some reference to national characteristics and instru-

ments" are included for study.[27] NSW music syllabi since the late 1950s all contain such topics and encourage the study of non-Western music as a means of widening students' awareness of music, both as applications of universal musical principles and as a collection of differences. Clearly, some aspects of current NSW syllabi that can be defined as multicultural are not the result of the relatively recent introduction of multicultural thinking, but the continuation of philosophical considerations and methods of teaching music that have been in place since the late 1950s. They are also reflections of a characteristic of music study in general—the continued examination of musics from cultures outside that of a student's educational context.

Pluralist and Equitable Multicultural Music Education

Multicultural perspectives can readily be extrapolated from and imputed to NSW music syllabi. At the same time, reference to syllabi from as early as the 1950s shows that current multicultural music education may be a continuation of earlier practices and, therefore, the result of factors external to multicultural ideology. Such deconstruction of "multicultural" music education reveals ambiguity over the reasons for the inclusion of music from diverse cultural origins in NSW music classrooms; this ambiguity results from confusion between the musical and the multicultural aims of syllabi.

There are two ways in which musical material of a non-Western nature is used in NSW music education: (1) in discrete topics (e.g., "traditional music of a culture"), and (2) to provide demonstrations of musical concepts and processes across a range of styles, periods, and genres. This dichotomy of musical use mirrors a two-tiered model of multicultural teaching practices, suggested by Kalantzis and Cope,[28] to critically evaluate educational applications of multiculturalism in Australian education: the pluralist and the equitable.

Pluralist strategies are defined by these writers as those through which cultural differences are emphasized. These include displays of "music, dance, clothes, food and drink,"[29] what the authors of *Mistaken Identity* call a "spaghetti-and-polka" interpretation of multiculturalism.[30] Such an interpretation favors a preservationist approach to cultures from non-Anglo-Celtic Australia, links ethnicity and the concept of culture to either Indigenous Australians or migrants from non-English speaking backgrounds, and emphasizes racial difference. Here culture, evidenced in the outward trappings of foreign "dress, food and dance,"[31] is ossified in a condition in which it may have existed when the parents, grandparents, and great-grandparents of present-day practitioners left their homes to journey to Australia; it may have little to do with the present state of cultural artifact in their countries of origin. The results of this superficial style of multicultural thinking include increased marginalization of those students involved, reinforcing of concepts of racial stereotypes, implications that culture is something of the past and from "somewhere else," and, consequently, strengthening of racist attitudes among students.

In contrast to this, equitable multiculturalism seeks to investigate what culture is and its processual nature, as it emphasizes that culture is common to all people, that it is a dynamic, that "we are all ethnic," and that comprehension of these factors can lead to "empowerment through skills of social literacy."[32] It is not difficult to see which of the two types of multiculturalism is favored by the writers and which is more in line with the aims of multicultural policy at government levels.

The two methods of handling music from non-Western sources in NSW syllabi align with the pluralist and equitable interpretations of multiculturalism and, thus, demonstrate an ideological ambiguity over multiculturalism in NSW music education. Is music education multicultural because it includes music from non-Western sources, or is it multicultural because it seeks to foster positive attitudes to intercultural understanding? In short, is it a case of learning music through multicultural examples or learning multicultural principles through music?

Music studies have the potential, on the one hand, to reinforce racially defined differences, and, on the other, to lead students to comprehension of the processes of culture and the construction of the individual through cultural membership. The discrete study of "traditional music of a culture" is a pluralist approach through which musical differences are learned (usually scales, rhythmic practices, tuning systems, ways of structuring music, types of instruments, and the roles and uses of music). Study of music by means of a concept-based approach (in which pitch, duration, texture, etc., are to be comprehended in all musics) is in line with the equitable approach. While the primary aim of the pluralist approach is to gain an understanding of a "foreign" musical system, that of the equitable approach is to understand music as a system. While the equitable/concept-based approach is closer to the aims of federally expressed multiculturalism, neither of these approaches in music education has as its aim the understanding of culture as a concept, one of the objectives of multiculturalism listed at federal and state levels. Neither approach results from multicultural philosophies introduced into music education after the government-policy decisions defining Australia as a multicultural nation. Rather, both approaches can be shown to result from musicological and educational trends that have informed music syllabi in NSW for some decades. Moreover, the equitable/concept approach, with its imposition of a Western taxonomy of music onto music from non-Western sources, can be shown to be seriously flawed when considered from the perspective of the acknowledgment of cultures—which is a basic tenet of multiculturalism. How can music educators acknowledge and thus affirm cultural difference, while at the same time superimposing their own culture's musical aesthetic as the "correct" way to study music?

Studies of the music of "a culture," "a non-Western culture," or "another culture" have been common in NSW school-based music education through a series of syllabus developments since the late 1950s. This mirrors developments in the university study of ethnomusicology, recalling its beginnings as "comparative musicology," itself the outcome of late nineteenth-century imperialist and orientalist premises through which Western notions of cultural superiority were furthered by their use as the bases of academic studies.[33] The concept-based approach of music education derives from movements in the 1960s, both in Australia and elsewhere, where the study of process replaced the study of content as the focus of school education. This can be readily observed in NSW music syllabi. These syllabi provide information on how music is to be taught and also list topic areas for study. They have not, since the mid-1970s, listed any musical works or the music of specific composers for study. Concomitantly, with the change from content-based education to that based on concepts, Western, historical, male-dominated art music, which had formed the majority of repertoire for study in schools, was gradually replaced through the inclusion of other forms of music. Challenges to the Western historical canon over the past decades have resulted in the wide-ranging sources of music now used for music education.[34]

The replacement of content-based music education with concept-oriented music education can also be read as reflective of trends in late twentieth-century thinking, such as post-modernism and post-structuralism, through which acceptance of diversity, focus on methods rather than subject matter, and predilection for investigations of the (formerly) marginalized have been standardized.[35] Interpreted in this way, "multicultural" music education in Australia is at the intersection of independent educational, musical, historical, and political trajectories, rather than being the outcome of multiculturalism as a new philosophy introduced subsequent to moves at federal government levels in the early 1970s. Its current philosophical and pedagogical confusions are the results of agendas derived from these trajectories. Two examples of attempts to apply the types of teaching resulting from this confusion can be used to illustrate the lack of true multiculturalism in NSW music education and, in this way, to highlight where the problems lie. The first example raises issues of cultural propriety, essentialism, and the faults of a preservationist approach. The second addresses issues of the inappropriateness of Western musical training for the examination of music from other sources.

Multiculturalism and the Thinking behind Western Music Education

The first school in which I taught comprised students from a large number of ethnic and geographic backgrounds. Egyptian, Fijian, Greek, Italian, Lebanese, Maltese, Maori, Spanish, Turkish, Yugoslav, and Vietnamese were among the main groupings. The predominant group was Greek. In an attempt to make teaching pupil-centered and relevant, I introduced topics based around the music of each ethnic group in the school. I began with Greek music. I had read Gail Holst's *Road to Rembetika*[36] and had listened to and enjoyed recordings of *rembetika*, a style of popular music originating in the 1920s among the working classes in Greek port cities. I taught some of the songs, and the students and I observed the instruments used to accompany them. Within a week, a deputation of Greek parents accompanied by the priest of the local Greek Orthodox church called me to the principal's office. They demanded that I stop teaching this music: it wasn't Greek; it was Turkish and offensive.

This music, reminiscent of the *megali ithea* and various early twentieth-century acts of political violence, reminded these immigrant Greeks of the reasons why they had left Greece. It represented a low socio-economic class in Greece; its lyrics were in demotic Greek and utilized slang terms and Turkish expressions—all linguistic practices that had the potential to offend Australian Greeks seeking to divorce themselves from what they considered unacceptable Greek language. My mistake in trying to teach *rembetika* was to assume that, because it was "Greek," it represented all Greek music. Ignorance of issues of class, geographic origin, language, ethnic allegiance, and even morals (the majority of songs concerned drugs, prostitution, jail, and even homosexuality) had been added to musical essentialism. In addition, I had taught from recordings made in the 1920s and 1930s, without properly making explicit that this music was historically situated. Thus, I had used a "museum exhibit" as representative of an ongoing culture, committing an error in history to go along with errors regarding culture.

My second anecdote concerns research into contemporary, Australian-indigenous, popular music. As part of this project, I interviewed a number of Aboriginal rock groups and musicians. One issue that I was particularly keen to investigate was the possibility of links between Aboriginal traditional music and Aboriginal rock music. I had found a rock song by one group that I thought contained strong traditional musical elements, but I needed the group to agree that the melody was derived from a traditional song. To my question, "Can you tell me about the melody?" I received an answer that referred to the words of the text. My second attempt at getting a specific comment on the melodic shape produced a response about the meanings of the lyrics. My third attempt later in the interview produced yet another response about everything but the melody itself. The members of the group could not separate melody from text, and it was only after much more research that the indivisibility of components within Aboriginal musical aesthetics became apparent.

The point of both anecdotes is that, while the research was guided by good intentions both educationally and ethically, it was multiculturally problematic. Designing lessons around *rembetika* was in line with the educational precept that teaching should be relevant to students; the purpose of interviewing Aboriginal rock musicians was to make sure that indigenous artists were properly represented in material written about their music. In relation to Greek *rembetika,* the teaching was a form of essentialism: that is, one type of Greek music had been put forward as representative of all Greek music, of all styles, all sources, and all times. The contingencies of class, morals, and ethnic origin of the music of a discrete culture (actually a subculture) were made clearly obvious in this experience. The presentation of a historical style had not been considered, and the ramifications of presenting music that had strong implications for migrants had not been recognized. In researching Aboriginal music, an attempt had been made to investigate a non-Western system of musical thinking with the conceptual tools of Western music—principally, an approach based on the belief that all music could be analyzed through consideration of musical concepts and processes in isolation from each other. Aboriginal thinking about

music, if that exists in the way Western-trained music scholars theorize about it, does not function in the same way; there is no reason that it should.

These experiences highlight differing cultural perspectives of music and, consequently, differing ways that it can be studied. In the mainstream of Western music studies, analyzing the components of music to show how it is constructed provides much information on the manipulation of sound to produce music and often reveals cultural "rules" or expectations of how music is to sound. Often this approach is used comparatively to arrive at an understanding of varying methods for creating music from a pool of common components, such as pitch, duration, and so forth. Deeper levels of understanding about the ways in which sound is organized rely, on the other hand, on cultural factors that often lie beyond the grasp of those from outside the musical tradition under consideration. Would music education, which to the present has favored the objective-components approach, be better if a balance between that approach and one which acknowledged culturally specific ways of thinking about music was achieved? Would such a balance lead to a more comprehensive understanding of music, while at the same time emphasizing culture and cultural difference?

Conclusion

This chapter began by outlining confusion over the term "multicultural music education" as an aspect of music education on a global level. To indicate this confusion, it was demonstrated that, as a *gestalt*, this set of terms references the implications of its three component words, individually and in various combinations. Above all, differences between the expectations of multicultural education (which Banks and Banks define as education that acknowledges the cultural diversity of students[37]) and multicultural music education (which fluctuates from teaching musical understanding through content from a range of sources to teaching that responds to students' needs and interests) were put forward. In addition, ambiguity over the aims of multicultural music education itself could be shown to result from the coincident use of teaching material from international sources with the introduction of the concept of multiculturalism into Australian music education since the late 1970s. Reference to historical documents of music education in NSW, analyzed as an example of a music education system with the potential to raise issues of international relevance, also demonstrates that what might be seen as current applications of multicultural policy are continuations of earlier music education practices in which music from sources outside Western music was selected for study. In these practices, experience of music from a variety of sources was considered necessary to give students a wide view of musical styles. Due to the fact that no investigation of these issues produced certainty over the definition or intention of multicultural music education, the issues accrue to create an impression of multicultural music education as a site of ambiguous purpose.

To these issues can be added another, more complex problem—the implications of the application of a teaching method developed for and applicable to Western music in the study of music from non-Western origins. This conceptual approach, in which music is atomized into constituent parts as Western analysts perceive it, could be shown to lead to real problems in understanding the music of non-Western cultures. Its use implies that the musical aesthetic stance of one culture can be applied to the music of others. Experience in teaching in multi-ethnic classrooms and in researching Australian Aboriginal music demonstrates that the thinking behind Western music education need not be applicable to music from these sources; in this sense, its use could be considered a form of colonialism.

On a third level, that of the history of music teaching and learning, multicultural music education can be shown to have undergone change over time. Comparison of the 1956 NSW music syllabus with current syllabi shows a move away from a focus on Western art music to inclusion of types of music from many sources. This is an important development in the history of music teaching and learning. In this context, acceptance of diverse teaching content in music classrooms is construed here as the first stage in the development of multicultural music education. However, agreement on the acceptability of multicultural content points to the expectations of a subsequent stage. In this next stage of multicultural music education, the potential for existing methods of study to imply a Western educational hegemony and thus to negate the basis of multiculturalism requires serious consideration.

Notes

1. See Stephen M. Castles, Mary Kalantzis, Bill Cope, and Michael Morrisey, *Mistaken Identity: Multiculturalism and the Demise of Nationalism in Australia* (Sydney: Pluto Press, 1988); Andrew Theophanous, *Understanding Multiculturalism and Australian Identity*

(Melbourne: Elikia Books, 1995), 5; Bligh Grant, *Pauline Hanson: One Nation and Australian Politics* (Armidale: University of New England Press, 1997); Mary Kalantzis and Bill Cope, "No Way to Go Forward," *Sydney Morning Herald*, 31 December 1997, p. 9; National Multicultural Advisory Council, *Multicultural Australia: The Way Forward* (Canberra: author, 1997).

2. James Banks, and Cherry Banks, eds., *Handbook of Research on Multicultural Education* (New York: Macmillan, 1995), xi.

3. Bill Ashcroft, Gareth Griffiths, and Helen Tiffin, eds., *The Post-Colonial Studies Reader* (London: Routledge, 1995); Banks and Banks, *Handbook of Research on Multicultural Education*; Brian Bullivant, *The Pluralist Dilemma in Education: Six Case Studies* (Sydney, Australia: Allen & Unwin, 1981); Bill Cope, *Culture: By Whom and for Whom? The Arts in a Multicultural Society* (paper presented at the Multicultural Arts Conference, Adelaide, Australia, 1988); Ken Gelder and Sarah Thornton, eds., *The Subcultures Reader* (London: Routledge, 1997); Joe Kincheloe and Shirley Steinberg, *Changing Multiculturism* (Buckingham, UK: Open Univ. Press, 1997); New South Wales Department of Education, *Multicultural Education Policy Statement*; Edward Said, *Culture and Imperialism* (London: Vintage Books, 1994); Anthony Welch, *Australia Education: Reform or Crisis?* (Sydney, Australia: Allen & Unwin, 1996).

4. Peter Dunbar-Hall, "Towards a Definition of Multiculturalism in Music Education," in H. Lees, ed., *Music Education: Sharing Musics of the World* (ISME 20th World Conference, Seoul, Korea, July 1992), 186–192; Fred Inglis, *Cultural Studies* (Oxford, UK: Blackwell Pubs., 1993); Carlos Cortés, "Knowledge Construction and Popular Culture: The Media as Multicultural Educator," in Banks and Banks, *Handbook of Research on Multicultural Education*, 169–83; John Shepherd and Peter Wicke, *Music and Cultural Theory* (Oxford: Polity Press, 1997).

5. Kincheloe and Steinberg, *Changing Multiculturalism*.

6. Philip Brett, Elizabeth Wood, and Gary Thomas, eds., *Queering the Pitch: The New Gay and Lesbian Musicology* (London: Routledge, 1994).

7. Lucy Green, *Music, Gender, Education* (Cambridge: Cambridge Univ. Press, 1997); Kincheloe and Steinberg, *Changing Multiculturalism*.

8. Green, *Music, Gender, Education*; John Docker, *Postmodernism and Popular Culture* (Cambridge: Cambridge Univ. Press, 1994).

9. Annette Schmidt, *The Loss of Australia's Aboriginal Language Heritage* (Canberra: Aboriginal Studies Press, 1993).

10. Australian Bureau of Statistics, *Census of Population and Housing: Selected Social and Housing Characteristics—Australia* (Canberra: author, 1997); National Multicultural Advisory Council, *Multicultural Australia*.

11. Charles Rowley, *The Destruction of Aboriginal Society* (Ringwood, Victoria: Penguin, 1972); Lorna Lippmann, *Generations of Resistance: Aborigines Demand Justice* (Melbourne, Australia: Longman Cheshire, 1981); Michael Krygier, *Between Fear and Hope: Hybrid Thoughts on Public Values* (Sydney, Australia: ABC Books, 1997); Galarwuy Yunupingu, *Our Land Is Our Life: Land Rights—Past, Present and Future* (St. Lucia, Queensland: University of Queensland Press, 1997); Gough Whitlam, 1998) "Dragging the Chain: 1897–1997," in *Bringing Australia Together: The Structure and Experience of Racism in Australia,* ed. Foundation for Aboriginal and Islander Research Action (Woolloongabba, Queensland: editor, 1998), 19–33; Peter Dunbar-Hall, "Problems and Solutions in the Teaching of Aboriginal and Torres Strait Islander Music in NSW Secondary Schools" (paper presented at the Australian Society for Music Education national conference, Brisbane, Australia, 1997).

12. Welch, *Australian Education*, 107.

13. Stephen Alomes, *A Nation at Last? The Changing Character of Australian Nationalism, 1880–1988* (Sydney, Australia: Angus and Robertson, 1988), 76.

14. Frank Galbally, F. Merenda, N. Polites, and C. Stransky, *Migrant Services and Programs: Report of the Review of Post-Arrival Programs and Services for Migrants* (Canberra: Commonwealth of Australia, 1978); Alomes, *A Nation at Last*; Freda Hawkins, *Critical Years in Immigration: Canada and Australia Compared* (Sydney, Australia: New South Wales Univ. Press, 1989); Brian Murphy, *The Other Australia: Experiences of Migration* (Cambridge: Cambridge Univ. Press, 1993).

15. National Multicultural Advisory Council, *Multicultural Australia*, 6.

16. See Galbally et al., *Migrant Services and Programs*; Castles et al., *Mistaken Identity*; Sneja Gunew and Fazal Rizvi, eds., *Culture, Difference and the Arts* (Sydney, Australia: Allen & Unwin,

1994); Theophanous, *Understanding Multiculturalism and Australian Identity*; Welch, *Australian Education*; NSW Department of Education, *Taking Stock: Assessing Teaching-Learning Materials for Cultural Bias—Some Guidelines and Strategies* (Sydney: author, 1984b).

17. Galbally et al., *Migrant Services and Programs*.

18. See Alomes, *A Nation at Last* for the history of this development and Mark Ryan, ed., *Advancing Australia: The Speeches of Paul Keating, Prime Minister* (Sydney, Australia: Big Picture Publications, 1995) for the political contexts of these factors.

19. NSW Department of Education, *Multicultural Education Policy Statement*.

20. NSW Department of Education, *Community Language Education: A Support Document to the Multicultural Education Policy 1983* (Sydney: author, 1983a); *Curriculum Implementation: Multicultural Education, Aboriginal Education* (Sydney: author, 1983b); *English as a Second Language Education: A Support Document to the Multicultural Education Policy 1983* (Sydney: author, 1983c); *Ethnic Studies: A Support Document to the Multicultural Education Policy 1983* (Sydney: author, 1983d); *Intercultural Education: A Support Document to the Multicultural Education Policy 1983* (Sydney: author, 1983e); and *Multicultural Perspectives to Curriculum: A Support Document to the Multicultural Education Policy 1983* (Sydney: author, 1983g).

21. NSW Department of Education, *Multicultural Education Policy Statement*, 2.

22. NSW Department of School Education, *Multicultural Education Plan: 1993–97* (Sydney: author, 1992), 3 passim.

23. NSW Department of Education, *Music K–6* (Sydney: author, 1984).

24. NSW Board of Studies, *Music 2/3 Unit* (Sydney: author, 1984).

25. NSW Board of Studies (1994a) Music Support Document, Part 1. (Sydney: author, 1994a), 14.

26. NSW Board of Studies, 1994a, passim.

27. NSW Department of Education, *Syllabus in Music* (Sydney: author, 1956), passim.

28. Mary Kalantzis and Bill Cope, *Pluralism and Equitability: Multicultural Curriculum Strategies for Schools* (Sydney, Australia: Common Ground, 1985).

29. Ibid., 9.

30. Castles et al., *Mistaken Identity*.

31. Kalantzis and Cope, *Pluralism and Equitability*, 12.

32. Ibid., passim.

33. Edward Said, *Orientalism* (London: Routledge & Kegan Paul, 1978; rpt. 1994).

34. See Bill Cope, *Traditional Versus Progressivist Pedagogy* (Sydney, Australia: Common Ground, 1986); Phillipa Roylance, "Transgressing the Official: A Critique of the Affiliations between Musical Representations of Culture and Curriculum," *Research Studies in Music Education*, No. 4 (June 1995): 39–47.

35. David Harvey, *The Condition of Postmodernity: An Enquiry into the Origins of Cultural Change* (Oxford: Basil Blackwell, 1989).

36. Gail Holst, *Road to Rembetika: Music from a Greek Sub-Culture—Songs of Love, Sorrow and Hashish* (Athens: Anglo-Hellenic Publishing, 1975).

37. Banks and Banks, *Handbook of Research on Multicultural Education*, x.

PETER DUNBAR-HALL, chair of music education at Sydney Conservatorium of Music at the University of Sydney in Australia, is widely published on issues of Australian cultural history, Aboriginal music, multiculturalism, and music education in *Australian Aboriginal Studies, British Journal of Music Education, Ethnomusicology, International Journal of Music Education, Journal of Intercultural Studies, Popular Music and Society, Music Education Research, Research Studies in Music Education,* and *The International Review of Aesthetics and Sociology of Music.*

4

A Diverse Approach to Music in Education from a South African Perspective

Elizabeth Oehrle

*M*y experiences with world music began some thirty-five years ago when I made a life-changing decision to take a four-week holiday to South Africa with a friend who was native to that country. I was then associate dean of students at the Eastman School of Music in Rochester, New York, while completing my bachelor's of music. Prior to this, I had majored in history at Hood College and had a master's in education/ personnel from Syracuse University, but music courses had always been my electives. Though I had wished to major in music initially, I dared not. Only those who studied music seriously from a young age had that option, I thought.

My initial exposure to music lessons as a very young child temporarily extinguished my inherent love of music. Solitary practice of uninteresting piano scales did not suit my personality. Fortunately, my deanship at Eastman afforded me rich Western musical experiences and the opportunity to complete my music degree. Having heard so much about South Africa from my friend, I accompanied her when she returned home. Losing my heart to a South African architect shortly after my arrival is my reason for staying these many years.

Though my Alan passed on, I linger because I am still fascinated with both the African and Indian cultures. On arrival, I befriended a penny-whistler, and we spent many hours sitting under a tree by the side of the road while he taught me a little of what he knew. I attended festivals and celebrations and quickly became aware that in South Africa everyone sings and/or plays instruments, dances, and tells stories. It is part of this life. When visiting Vendaland, I discovered their belief that everyone can make music; some simply work harder at it than others. The communal approach to music making and the inherent value of the arts in living spoke to me.

As a music teacher and lecturer in South Africa, I grapple to introduce the musics of Africa and ways of making music into the schools along with Western music, which still dominates formal education. Recently, I established a network for the propagation of intercultural education through music in southern Africa. The Talking Drum *is a publication that aims to promote intercultural education through music. Experiencing both African and Indian musics has deepened my appreciation not only of these musics and of the people who make them, but also of Western music. While the realization that there is so much more to experience is stimulating and keeps me in this part of the world, the urge to return home is strong. Currently, I am developing a cultural-tourism business in South Africa, primarily for Americans. Hopefully, this will enable me to spend time in both South Africa and the United States.*

Background

South Africa is in a state of dramatic changes. Segregated education is being replaced. We have a dual crisis in education—the inherited inequalities of the education system arising from apartheid policies and the magnitude of problems remaining to be surmounted in order to put the education of all on an equal footing.

Both crises offer concerned educators the opportunity not only to rethink the nature and purpose of music/arts education, but also to raise desires and hope for those who wish to take seriously the issues of the education struggle and of social justice in the future. It is important to find ways of developing a praxis of education that opens the spaces necessary for the initiation and development of a democratic community.

One assumption is that schools are places where possibilities exist for teachers and students to be involved in critical thinking and to develop an interest in, tolerance for, and appreciation of diversity. To examine this assumption, we rely on the work of an American educator internationally renowned for his work in critical pedagogy—Henry A. Giroux.[1]

Giroux is critical of the fact that radical educators often tear down but provide nothing in the wake of their truthful, but destructive, comments about education. He attempts to define a positive notion of social control and responsibility upon which to build. To do this, he redefines power and social control. Giroux writes that power has both positive and negative force. Power is dialectic in character, possessing two modes of operation—one constraining and one enabling. Assuming that social control is made to serve social justice, then the notion of power is to empower teachers and students to question and to make sense of music from a grounded vantage point in a way that sheds light on their own worlds—in a way that offers perspective and is therefore always open and never complete.

Social control has both positive and negative possibilities. He sees positive aspects when linked to interests that promote social- and self-empowerment: "Social control speaks to the forms of practice necessary for the demanding task of designing curricula that give students an active and critical voice, providing them with the skills that are basic for analysis and leadership in the modern world."[2]

This leads to the relationship Giroux makes between schooling and what he calls "cultural power." He is critical of the fact that emphasis has been given to so-called high culture, the dominant culture in schools, and is also critical of radical educators who promote only the culture of the oppressed or subordinate culture. He criticizes both for failing "to develop a critical method and pedagogy for dealing with both dominant and subordinate cultures." He sees the notion of cultural power as being "referent for examining what students and others need to learn outside of their own experiences. This points to the need to redefine the role of knowledge within the context of cultural and curriculum studies."[3]

Giroux argues that curriculum should not be based only on matters of self-cultivation or, as he puts it, "the mimicry of specific forms of … knowledge." Curriculum "would be developed around knowledge forms that challenge and critically appropriate dominant ideologies, … and it would also take the historical and social particularities of students' experiences as a starting point for developing a critical classroom pedagogy."[4] Such a curriculum is worthy of consideration in South Africa today. A diverse approach to music in education is one means of facilitating these ideas.

Issues

Toward a Relevant Terminology

Writings in music education in support of various terms such as "multicultural," "multi-ethnic," "world music," "crosscultural," and "intercultural" are numerous. Until very recently, the term "intercultural," rather than "multicultural," music education was more appropriate for South Africa, because the concept of multicultural education formed the basis for separate development under apartheid. During the forty-eight years of apartheid, cultural differences were used to keep people apart. Today, however, we aim to develop respect for cultural differences. Previous negative connotations attached to the term "multicultural" are beginning to fall away; thus, the use of "multicultural" is becoming more acceptable. Following the lead given by J. H. Kwabena Nketia, current director of the International Centre of African

Music & Dance at the University of Ghana in Legon, who used the term "intercultural" at an International Music Educators conference many years ago (and because of the need to build bridges between cultures), I preferred for some time to use that term.

Recently, however, I encountered "a diverse approach to music in education" when I read an article by Elliot Eisner. In this article, he aims to "broaden the ways in which we think about the meaning of research."[5] I suggest that a diverse approach to music in education also aims to broaden the ways in which we think about the meaning of music and the context in which the music is created. Further, I suggest that the premises he presents with respect to research [slightly altered] also hold for music:

1. There are multiple ways in which the world can be known. Artists, dancers, and writers, as well as scientists, have important things to tell us about the world.
2. Human knowledge is a constructed form of experience and, therefore, a reflection of mind as well as nature. Knowledge is made, not merely discovered.
3. The forms through which humans represent their conception of the world not only have a major influence on what humans are able to say; they also influence what they are able to see [and hear].
4. The effective use of any form through which the world is known and represented requires the use of intelligence.
5. [Music] educational inquiry will be more complete and informative as we increase the ways in which we describe, interpret, and evaluate the [world of music]. Which forms of representation become acceptable is as much a political matter as an epistemological one."[6]

We need to realize, accept, and enjoy diversity; thus, it is important to introduce and work with and through this concept. One way is through a diverse approach to music education.

Consider one specific idea of relevance—a "cross-cultural music dictionary."[7] At the Tenth Symposium on Ethnomusicology in South Africa, Maria Smit proposed a new multilingual and crosscultural music dictionary "which could facilitate intercultural communication and understanding within the teaching of all the musics of our country." She points out that "music dictionaries in our country are either biased towards, or concentrate solely on Western music."[8]

Smit states that a major communication problem is the fact that similar objects, phenomena, or practices exist in different cultures but are perceived in different ways. The following is a classic example. Music and dance are clearly distinguished in the English language. However, "Hugh Tracey remarks that in different African music cultures, people do not necessarily agree as to what constitutes music within their experience and comprehension. For example the word *kuvina* or *kusina* in some languages means 'to make music' and 'to dance,' but it does not include the playing of instruments." Rommelaere adds: "In most African music there is an inextricable relationship between music and dance. Among the Xhosa, for example, little distinction is made between the two, and dancing is in fact so much part of the music that it would not even be mentioned."[9]

Teachers and students, not only in South Africa but elsewhere, need to obtain information on terminology in order to be able to appreciate the different musics, understand the different music systems, and perform music from the various music cultures. Smit suggests that there is "a need for a dictionary which explains (i) something about the objects, phenomena or practices to which the terms refer; (ii) the meanings of the terms; and (iii) the way in which these terms are used within the different musical practices."[10] Promoting a more diverse approach to music in education requires the clarity that a crosscultural music dictionary will provide.

At the many conferences I have attended, only twice have I experienced a discussion or proposal relative to the idea of crosscultural music dictionaries. Perhaps one reason is because the majority of such conferences have been situated or organized in the United States, where the need for this new type of dictionary is only now being entertained. For music educators in the new South Africa, as well as for other scholars actively supporting a diverse approach to music education, the need is urgent.

Consequences of a Diverse Approach to Music in Education

Significant consequences of a diverse approach to music education were suggested to me in two encounters I had with university students—first South African students and then American students.

The first (1992) occurred at the University of Natal music department, where students were (and are) exposed to many musics. A questionnaire was distributed to ascertain to what extent eighty music students' attitudes were being altered because they came into contact with new musics. Forty-six students responded. The first question asked which musics were familiar to the student before coming to the university. The second asked which musics were new or were introduced to the student either for the first time or in greater depth since coming to the department. The next three questions and responses are of particular interest:

To what extent have your experiences with new musics given you increased knowledge and understanding? 19–great extent; 21–moderate extent = 40 of 46 replies.

To what extent has your increased knowledge and understanding resulted in changing your attitude or behavior? 13–great extent; 24–moderate = 37 of 46 replies.

To what extent has your change of attitude or behavior resulted in:

a. crossing cultural barriers? 16–great extent; 16–moderate extent = 32 of 46 replies.

b. crossing class barriers? 11–great extent; 16–moderate extent = 27 of 46 replies.

c. greater awareness of our interconnectedness? 15–great extent; 17–moderate extent = 32 of 46 replies.

Of the 57% who responded, more than half said that their change of attitude resulted in crossing cultural and class barriers and discerning a greater awareness of our interconnectedness.

The second encounter (1998) was with responses to an assignment given to American students enrolled in the program "Semester at Sea." Six hundred students from various universities in the United States were on board the SS *Universe Explorer,* a floating university. Eighty-eight students elected to take the course "Music in Africa." At the end of

the course, one assignment was to argue for or against the notion that intercultural music/arts education promotes an interest in, tolerance for, and appreciation of diversity. All agreed with this notion. Here are excerpts from students' responses:

■ I write about my personal experience as an example for this. While I may not be making a formal argument, I do hope that one can realize the new interest in, tolerance for, and appreciation that learning about musical traditions around the world has sparked in me.

Humans are notorious for fearing or shying away from the things they do not understand. Ignorance is bliss in many ways, I suppose. But having been exposed to such wonderful diversity of sounds during this voyage, while at the same time learning the basics of how to appreciate those new musics—I have come to welcome and indeed to *like* new, exotic things.

I have always had a liking for African-influenced music. Perhaps it is the intense focus on rhythmic perfection that first drew me, because I love just about anything with a good beat. By learning a little about the inner workings of music making in Africa, I have taken that step from mere appreciation without understanding to a point where not only does it sound good, but it also *makes sense.* It is like the first time something clicks when learning a foreign language—when you actually begin to read and think and feel in that language.

This course has given me new insights and unlocked new doors that I am only beginning to realize. What is more, I want to learn more now. Intercultural music/arts education is a self-perpetuating odyssey that will last a lifetime once set in motion. I can attest to that.

■ Teaching intercultural art/music is very important for promoting an interest in, tolerance for and appreciation for diversity. It is difficult to imagine someone having an appreciation for something they have never been exposed to

I am a perfect example to illustrate this. Before taking this class, I only knew of or had heard a little African music. I thought that African music was all percussion and never really tried to find out more about it until it was offered on this voyage. Now my eyes have been opened to a whole world of sounds and sights I never knew existed.

In learning about other countries and their people and cultures, especially their music, one gets an appreciation for diversity. An appreciation for diversity is essential in the development of peaceful, productive relationships between countries. I think intercultural music teaching is a step in the direction of ensuring global harmony.

■ I can guarantee that the study of intercultural music and/or arts education promotes an interest and appreciation of diversity. I feel safe with this because of my experience over the past three months. I have never taken a music course prior to this semester. My understanding of music now has expanded, but more importantly, my understanding of other cultures has grown as well.

Learning about the music of Africa has brought me closer to understanding some people and cultures of Africa. Actually being in Africa before and after this new learning, of course, has also made my knowledge much greater, particularly with respect to the Xhosa people and the peoples of Ghana.

By studying world music, one can better understand the culture and appreciate the diversity of the world. From taking an African music course, I have had the opportunity to appreciate the diversity of African cultures as well as hear some amazing instruments developed by some people of Africa.

■ Through the study of other cultures/arts, we begin to break a link in the chain of ethnocentrism. Finding beauty in the music of other cultures, for instance, can lead to further discovery about the people responsible for the music's creation. When we learn that Asia and Africa have art and music traditions possibly thousands of years older than those of Europe, it puts our "great civilization" in perspective.

■ Cultural sensitivity is increasingly necessary in America. Rather than viewing other people and their music as inferior to our own, we should become educated about the new members of our society. By embracing facets of art and musics of the world, we enrich our own lives, broaden respect for the lives of others, and create greater harmony in our country.

The fact is that our world is one of extreme diversity geographically, ethnically, racially, musically, etc.

■ An intercultural approach to music should begin to develop an awareness of diversity at an early age. Children will develop respect for differences.

Both encounters with respect to a diverse approach to music in education realized positive consequences for the great majority of students. Not only did they become more knowledgeable about the world of musics and develop an interest in sounds and people different from themselves; all of the American students went further to support the notion that intercultural music/arts education promotes a tolerance for and appreciation of diversity. Finally, and perhaps of greatest value, is the fact that there was a change of student attitudes that resulted in a deepening awareness of the interconnectedness of the diverse cultures and classes of societies. Music educators should take note of such consequences and realize their particular importance for education.

The Situation with Respect to a Diverse Approach to Music in South African Education

Although my formal education took place in the United States, the greater part of my life as a teacher has been spent in South Africa. One might think that a person with a background in Western music and education would have difficulty obtaining a teaching position in South Africa, but this is not so. A totally Western bias toward music in formal education has been propagated at the southernmost tip of Africa, in spite of the fact that there are many different African, Indian, and Cape Malay musics as well. One result of the situation was described explicitly by Matthew Sgatya at the first National Music Educators Conference in 1985. "By the time the black child reaches the age of five, he is a fully capable musician. The present school method of music soon knocks this potential out of him."[11]

As a lecturer at the University of Natal, one of my tasks was to supervise student teachers. I visited a Zulu student who was teaching in a mission school and had an unforgettable experience. I was taken to a dimly lit classroom where 160 children sat. My student was teaching music to half the children facing one way, and a second person was teaching English to the other half facing the opposite direction. My student was diligently following the prescribed syllabus and attempting to teach notation using chalk and blackboard. I suggested that he take the children outside for the remainder of their music lesson. The children were happy to move. Without any instruction, they immediately formed into groups of five or six and sang and danced

with clicks and claps in a manner that would have made any Orff teacher ecstatic. In the hope that music making like this will remain the rule and not the exception, research and programs have been established at the University of Natal. These will be discussed further on.

The philosophies and processes of music education used in South Africa have come mainly from England, originally introduced by the colonists, and from the United States, introduced by the missionaries and teachers. These same ideas have been continually propagated by the availability of books, records, and articles with a Western bias. Even South African music educators as recently as 1990 elected to use generous funding to bring not just one, but three, keynote speakers from the United States to their National Music Educators Conference in Pretoria. Not one keynote address, however, focused on aspects of music from South Africa.

In a previous article, I suggested that the infusion of American music education ideas into Africa came as a result of certain circumstances.[12] A brief historical sojourn, beginning on the west coast of Africa, moving to the United States, and ending in Southern Africa, will illustrate my point. This excursion may lead us to wonder about what possibilities there might have been for American music education to have developed in other ways, had attitudes of tolerance and genuine interest been exercised with regard to the music practices that the West Africans brought with them to the United States.

Three-and-one-half centuries ago, West Africans came to the United States as slaves. They brought with them virtually nothing other than their music and musical practices. This naturally influenced aspects of their lives in the new world. The different festivals that early Afro-Americans organized for themselves provide but one example. Two such festivals were "'Lection Day" and "Pinkster Day." On "'Lection Day," along with parades, there were games and "singing and dancing to the fiddle, tambourine, banjo and drum;" missionaries described events like these and others as having "heathenish and savage manners."[13] They strove to bring a stop to such practices.

Farmers sometimes looked with suspicion on the use of musical instruments by Afro-American workers because they feared that messages were being sent to long distances when certain drums were played. This resulted in legislation that not only made it illegal for slaves to assemble without being supervised by whites but "also banned the making and playing of drums."[14]

In the 1800s, Protestant missionaries intensified their efforts to convert African slaves. The increased number of blacks in congregations injected more spontaneous and emotional responses into church services. This generated critical comments from missionaries like Charles Colcock Jones, who said "the public worship of God should be conducted with reverence and stillness on the part of the congregation." Jones also advocated that one way to make Afro-Americans "lay aside the extravagant and nonsensical chants and catches and hallelujah songs of their own composing"[15] was to teach them the proper way to sing hymns and psalms. One must assume, then, that dancing and other body movements, foot-stamping, clapping, shouting, interjections, and antiphonal singing were considered improper in those days. These parts of Afro-American church music stemmed from traditional ways of making music in West Africa.

What type of music education was Jones suggesting for the early Afro-Americans? In the eighteenth century, Protestant ministers were particularly concerned with the need to improve the standard of singing at public worship services; thus, singing schools came into existence, and music literacy became of primary importance. Allen Britton's article, "The How and Why of Teaching Singing Schools in Eighteenth Century America," gives vivid descriptions about the manner in which the schools were to be run. Billings, one of the masters, advocated rules not unlike those of other singing masters or ministers of the day. To cite two: all must be punctual or a fine would be imposed, and the singing master's musical decisions are not to be questioned.[16] Thus the type of music education that Jones said that the early Afro-Americans should receive was instruction in singing and music notational literacy. Both the rationale behind the schools and the manner in which they were run were totally foreign to the ways and musical customs of people from West Africa.

The Protestant church not only influenced the music making of the early Afro-American, but it also had an unprecedented effect on American music education. The need for churches to improve both the singing and music literacy of their people gave birth to music education in the United States. It was from these beginnings that music notational literacy has continued to assume a place of primary importance in American music education. This notion, and having a higher regard for Western music than for other musics, were transmitted to Africa.

I cite but a few results. One concerns replies given by three Zulu students at Natal University in Durban. Three questions were put to them: What music did you listen to at home on the radio? What music do you prefer to listen to? What music do you prefer to perform? In each case, they answered—Western music. Another concerns a statement made by Professor Khabi Mngoma when he was at Zululand University. In 1985, he said that "the present emphasis is unfortunately on literacy only."[17] Finally, in conversation with a Zulu student in his final year at university, he said that making music used to be part of his way of life before coming to the university and he used to spend many hours playing the piano. Now, having spent nearly four years at university, he had come to realize that he was not good enough to play the piano any more.

Thus we have swung full circle. We brought Africans to America and discouraged their traditional ways of making music. We initiated a process of music education based on singing and music notational literacy, and then these notions and others were transmitted back to parts of Africa. Music making in parts of Africa stands to lose more than it could hope to gain, because today these notions are incorporated into music education.

In the late 1980s, I corresponded with educators/musicians in approximately twenty-six countries in Africa in an endeavor to discover the extent to which Western music and/or methods and

African music and/or methods are being used. Findings were that Western music and methods are of primary importance in the educational systems of Ghana, Kenya, Uganda, Zimbabwe, and Nigeria. But change is occurring. Traditional music is encouraged in Kenya, Ghana, and Zimbabwe. Indications are, however, that city youth react negatively to the more traditional music. Their preference is for their popular music. Gabon is also concerned with traditional methods of teaching, and new music schools are urged to adopt the type of teaching of traditional music teachers. Kenya, Nigeria, and Uganda give a clear indication of the importance of considering African concepts of music making.[18]

One of the major challenges in South Africa is to bring to the fore the musics of the country at all formal levels of education. This does not mean that non-African musics will be ignored. It means that a balance must be found between the musics of South Africa, Western musics, and other musics. It also means bringing the process of music making, such as the incorporation of oral transmission and the employment of skilled performers from the informal sector, into schools and universities.

Efforts are being made to address the issues mentioned. We shall focus on three, related to the University of Natal in Durban, South Africa—the required music history courses, the newly formed African Music Project, and my research project called NETIEM (Network for Promoting Intercultural Education through Music). Each meets the issues mentioned in a different way.

Moves toward a More Diverse Approach to Music in Education at the University of Natal at Durban

Music History Courses

In 1974 and 1975, three years after the department's inception, this department began to move away from a Western-centered approach to music. This transformation was directed by a young visionary department head, Christopher Ballantine, and initially affected the collection of library resources and the structure of music history courses.

With respect to music history (part of the core courses that students are required to take for three years), some changes were made and the current program followed. Beverly Parker classified the contents of syllabi for these courses from 1976 to 1987.

Note the decrease in time spent on lectures in Western classical music and the increase in time spent with Non-Western, African-American, and Western popular music (see Table 1, Classified Contents of University of Natal Music History Syllabi).

The 1999 music history course appears in the catalogue as follows: the first-year courseload is divided between the first half of the year, "Popular and Traditional Music: Africa and Beyond" (a historical and stylistic overview of many popular and traditional musics of Africa by region, including a more detailed focus on music of southern Africa and an introduction to jazz), and the second half of the year, "Western Classical Music: An Introduction."

During the next two years, students take "Music, Culture, and History." Special top-

Table 1. Classified Contents of University of Natal Music History Syllabi[a]

Subject	Years Studied	Contact Hours as a Percentage of Total Number of Contact Hours in 3-yr. Sequence	
		1976	1987
Western Classical Music	I–III	68.3	41.7
Non-Western, Afro-American, and Western Popular Music	I–III	8.9	24.6
General Topics	II–III	0	4
Seminars (content varies)	II–III	22.8	29.7

In addition to the three-year sequence of music history courses, students also take seminars of their choice. A comparison of topics offered in 1976 with those offered in 1987 indicates some transformation:

- **1976:** Messiaen; Musical Criticism; Experimental Music; Dufay; Dramatic Music of Berlioz; Church Music circa 1670–1750.

- **1987:** Cantus Prius Factus; Music Criticism; Political Dimension of Music; Looking at Lieder; Continuity and Change in South African Music Today; Black Jazz in South Africa.[b]

Notes. [a]B. L. Parker, "Providing an Integrative Factor within the Multi-Cultural University Music Curriculum," *South African Journal of Musicology* 7 (1987): 69. [b]Ibid., 71.

ics concerning classical, popular, or traditional musics of the world are offered, with a particular focus on Western, African, and Indian music and jazz. These topics are approached in lectures and seminars from musicological, ethnomusicological, or other vantage points. Students are offered some flexibility in their topical choices.

In 1999, the Popular Music Studies program was introduced, the first in South Africa and almost certainly the first on the continent. This is in keeping with the fact that the study of popular music has recently gained widespread respectability in the academic world. Increasing numbers of universities around the world are teaching and researching popular music. The visionary Christopher Ballantine, who set our department on the path of a diverse approach to music education twenty-five years ago, initiated this program.

With respect to the library, a major concern was that resources be progressive, comprehensive, and in touch with developments. Today the library is well-stocked with Western classical resources (approximately 60 percent books and scores) and a broad selection relative to many other aspects of music (approximately 40 percent). There are as many recordings of other musics as of Western classical music. The following illustrates the diversity of resources available. In 1998, I had only a few months to prepare to teach on board the SS *Universe Explorer*, the floating university known as Semester-at-Sea. I boarded the ship in Cape Town and sailed for Seattle. My task was to introduce students to the music of the countries we visited en route—Kenya, India, Malaysia, Vietnam, Hong Kong, and Japan. All the resources I

needed were immediately available in the Music Library of the University of Natal. No other library in South Africa could provide this.

Finally, with respect to departmental concerts of various musics for students and the public throughout the year, a continually evolving policy forms the basis for decision making. Currently an equal amount of time goes to the following categories of musics: African traditional, African neo-traditional, Jazz and Popular, Indian, pre-1900 Western classical, and post-1900 Western classical. Naturally, a high quality of performance is also a major criterion with respect to selecting various groups or individuals. One of the most interesting concerts a few years ago was "Flutes for Africa." Performers presented a wide range of different types of flutes and music found in South Africa. The concert opened with a sonata by Ravel for flute and piano and ended with music played by the master of the penny whistle, Spokes Mashiyane. Interspersed was a classical Indian flute player, a jazz flute player, and Pedro Espi-Sanchis performing on the branch of a paw-paw tree. Pedro's duo with Darius Brubeck on piano was unique. The audience included people from all walks of life. There were those who would normally only attend a Western classical concert and those who would normally only attend a jazz concert. I recall the music critic, who had a very strong bias toward Western music, remaining attentive long enough to hear the Ravel. Staff and students from the department were thrilled with the event, as was the audience in general.

The majority of the students look upon these changes positively. The student body is extremely diverse; thus, the syllabus content and the availability of books, journals, and recordings enable the students to delve deeper into the musics with which they are familiar. These same students are also being extended when their ears hear and minds meet new musics that expand their musical knowledge, musicianship, and creative potential.

An African Music Project (AMP)

Music departments in South Africa should have an African music faculty position, one naturally assumes; however, this was not the case at any South African university until 1996. When the idea of having an African music faculty position was first raised at the University of Natal in Durban, the authorities said that funds for such a position were not available. We were told to find funds if we thought such a position was necessary; thus, I took it upon myself to canvass potential donors. After several years, the South African Sugar Association agreed to provide seed funding for the first three years, and the African Music Project (AMP) was born.

Patricia Opondo was hired from 1996–1998 as the AMP Coordinator and was reappointed for the next three years. The following are Opondo's own words about the project:

VISION AND MISSION

The African Music Project is a program of the University of Natal music department, whose mission is to focus on music education, research, performance, and community development. The project has a strong community outreach program which extends the Department's involvement and impact on artistic life in general. The African

Music Project will be an important vehicle for community reconstruction by advocating for African music to occupy a central space in institutions and developing strong relations with the communities in which we live.

AIMS OF THE AFRICAN MUSIC PROJECT

■ to promote the study, practice and appreciation of African music

■ to use music as a tool for empowerment, to bring about change in line with recommendations set by the Reconstruction and Development Program

■ to enhance music of the region by fostering local forms and bridging them with other traditions in the region and beyond

■ to bring existing talent in KwaZulu Natal Province to the forefront and make artists accessible to the wider public

■ to establish links between community organizations; to promote cooperation for wider community involvement via public performances and community residences

■ to encourage musicians and performers to form organizations to enable them to develop and market their talent

■ to develop a mentoring project in community development, to incorporate graduate assistants in campus projects, and to use field assistants linked with community centres to assist with administering community-based projects.[19]

Aware of the vision and aims of the project, portions of Opondo's *Progress Report II, 1996–1997,* spell out the structure and content.[20] Looking first at education, she used a workshop format and local musicians to introduce practical courses in African music and dance. Students experienced *gumboot* dance, *ngoma* dance, *amadinda* xylophone music from Uganda, *maskanda* guitar, and zulu chordophones (*makhweyana* and *ugubhu* gourd bows). Opondo also taught courses such as "Popular Music of

East Africa," "African Rituals," and "Black Vocal Traditions of South Africa and America."

Teacher-training programs in African music and dance were set up for students from two colleges of education with twenty-five experienced teachers. The hope was that the practical skills acquired by these students in genre such as *gumboot* dance or *maskanda* would then be taken to their classrooms. This program also acted as a bridging course for those wishing to register for music at a tertiary institution.

In regard to research training, Opondo's vision includes a research and documentation unit. Initially, she selected six people from varied backgrounds to take part in her documentation training program. Those selected had an interest in community development and a desire to acquire skills in data collection. The aim of this program was to enable participants to engage in research in music and dance performance practices in the Durban Functional Region.

Opondo originated special events, festival, concerts and workshops, including two memorable events: the dance and drumming workshop with members of the National Theatre of Ghana's Dance Factory at the University of Natal and the trip to Ghana by a performing group from the Durban area to take part in the Third Pan-African Historical Theatre Festival (PAN-FEST '97). She reports that artists from forty countries in Africa, the Americas, and Europe took part.

The following needed instruments were acquired: four *power marimbas,* ten pairs of *gumboots,* fifteen tin guitars, six *makweyana* and two *ugubhgu* gourd bows. From Ghana came fifteen drums, one xylophone, four harps, four rattles, and three bells. Two *timbila* xylophones were sent to Mozambique for repair. Opondo's focus for the project is "to use music as an empowerment tool to bring about change" and to "provide practical assistance and ideas to aid the Africanisation of the curriculum."[21]

The 1999 *Undergraduate Handbook* provides more recent developments of the African Music Project:

> *African Music and Dance (three-year course).* Examination of theories of performance practice and development of performance ability. Practical study in various genres of African music and dance, including *isicathula* (*gumboot* dance), *maskanda* guitar, *ingoma* dance (*isihameni, isibacha*), African xylophones (*amadinda, timbila*), South-African chordophones, and African storytelling and theatre.
>
> *African Music Outreach: Music Education.* Introduction to current issues in curriculum development and the development of pedagogical materials for teaching African music and dance. A practical component requires students to teach in a community center or educational institution.
>
> *African Music Outreach: Community Development.* Introduction to the fields of public-sector ethnomusicology and arts administration. The module provides students with skills needed for running community programs. The focus is on proposal writing, fund-raising, and project development. Students will do work in a community centre for the duration of the semester.
>
> *African Music Outreach: Documentation.* Students will acquire practical skill in data collection and analysis and in the production of short ethnographies.[22]

Realizing Opondo's vision and aims and seeing the positive results of her program, I cannot help but be dismayed by how long it took to rectify the lamentable lack of fore-sight with respect to offering African musics at the University of Natal in Durban. There is no doubt that the AMP is an essential part of the program at the university. Other universities in South Africa have yet to follow this lead. They need to better represent and respond to the music needs of the varied African cultures of the country.

Network for Promoting Intercultural Education through Music (NETIEM)

NETIEM is my research project, which began in 1992, when, you may recall, I preferred the term "intercultural." In the context of education and music in Africa, I also prefer the phrase "education through music" rather than "music education" for several reasons: (1) to provide support for the efforts of African countries to move away from the colonial structures of music education imposed upon them—there is a broader view emanating from Africa, and (2) to encourage exploration and development of ideas relative to music making in Africa. John Miller Chernoff writes: "Music is essential to life in Africa .... The development of musical awareness in Africa constitutes a process of education."[23]

At several Ethnomusicology Conferences in South Africa prior to 1991, an appeal was made to ethnomusicologists to become involved in the process of making available materials from the musics of Southern Africa for use in the classroom. You recall that South Africa is only one of many countries in Africa where Western music is of primary importance in the education system.

Existing formal music education philosophies, processes, and the development of a philosophy of music education that takes

into account views of music and music making in South Africa need critical appraisal. We must turn not only to books, because widely distributed and accessible music education texts are generally based on a Western approach.[24] We must turn to local music makers and their music and to researchers. To initiate a process of meeting some of these needs, a network for promoting intercultural education through music was inaugurated (NETIEM). Delegates from the Tenth Symposium on Ethnomusicology in South Africa unanimously supported its purpose, which is to facilitate the propagation of intercultural education through music in South Africa. Requests from Ghana, Namibia, and Zambia to be included in NETIEM and, in order to reflect their inclusion to have the name changed to "Southern Africa," were heeded. Notice was taken of a concern by some that "academic emphasis could put it out of the reach of most people." Finding a relevant balance between the theoretical and practical is important. We began by leaning toward the practical, and this will continue for the next few years.

NETIEM first established an ongoing database of interested people, publishing names and addresses in the first issue of *The Talking Drum*. In the second issue (April 1993), objectives were set out: (1) to facilitate contacts between those working to promote intercultural education through music; (2) to stimulate teachers' cultural awareness and promote the sharing of musics of various cultures or groups; (3) to discover composers, performers, researchers, and teachers active in the field; and (4) to discover places and/or programs where the musics of Southern Africa are taught and performed. The first three issues of *The Talking Drum* disseminated this information, along with lists of relevant dissertations, theses, essays, scores, and cassettes (e.g., a master's thesis by Pessa Weinberg became *Hlabelela Mntwanami* or *Sing, My Child,* her book of Zulu children's songs).

The fourth issue (February 1995) added videos to the list of available resources, ten of which are relevant to African music and one to Indian music. A few titles are "Rhythms of the Tabla," "Maskanda Competition" (maskanda comes from the Afrikaans *musikant* and means "music-maker"), and "Ritual Dancers: Shangaan, Makishi, and Nyau from Zimbabwe."[25]

In addition to various illuminating articles relative to the musics of Southern Africa, such as those about Xhosa Music, individuals with expertise and experience provide materials for use in the classroom. Songs and dances from the Xhosa, Zulu, Tshivenda, and seSotho in South Africa, plus Namibia, Zambia, and Uganda, are prevalent.

In the northern part of South Africa, movement and song are one. Movement does not simply accompany the song; it is an integral part of the process as the irregular rhythmic melody combines with the regular beat of the feet. A basic belief of the Venda is that everyone has the ability to make music. Some simply work harder at it than others. As the children are close to nature, many of their songs relate to creatures of nature. The Tshivenda Action Song in figure 1 is an example. Ronald Netshifhefhe led performers from Mafharalala Primary School in Tsianda, Venda; this music was recorded and transcribed by Jaco Kruger of the Department of Music, Potchefstroom

University, Bloemfontein, South Africa. He explains that

> this song introduces pupils to certain basic aspects of African rhythm. The irregular rhythmic arrangement of the melody contrasts with regular footbeats (indicated by "X") occurring on the first and third crotchets. The footbeats change in bars 5 and 6, illustrating the irregular movement of the crab.
>
> Pupils should stand with their feet slightly apart. "L" and "R" indicate left and right feet, while the black footprint and the arrow indicate which foot moves and in which direction. The foot movements should be small, while the body sways from side to side.[26]

To teach this song, the person must be able to perform the song well. This enables the children to learn by imitation; thus, they must listen carefully to learn the melody and sharpen their powers of observation to pick up the movement. It may be helpful to begin with the movement. Once the children are moving, the leader sings the song and the experience continues.

The tenth issue (December 1998) includes a further innovation—material from "African Music in the Schools" by Sandra Bonnett. The Music Library at Natal University has a store of valuable research materials, reworked for classroom use in subsequent issues. The following, from Bonnett's chapter on "Rhythm," presents a characteristic rhythmic device found in the music of Africa—the interlinking, or interlocking, of two rhythms. To realize this characteristic is to begin to understand that the concept of rhythm varies from culture to culture.

Bonnett writes: "A basic concept is the combination of duple and triple meters.

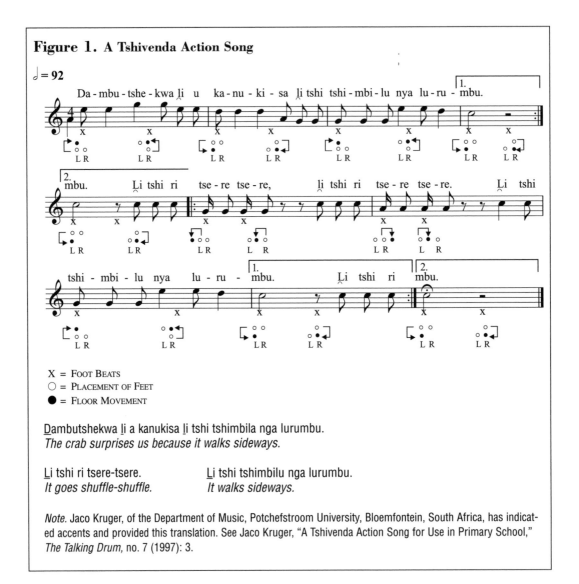

Figure 1. A Tshivenda Action Song

♩ = 92

Da - mbu - tshe - kwa ḽi u ka - nu - ki - sa ḽi tshi tshi - mbi - lu nya lu - ru - mbu.

2.
mbu. Li tshi ri tse - re tse - re, ḽi tshi ri tse - re tse - re. Li tshi

tshi - mbi - lu nya lu - ru - mbu. Li tshi ri mbu.

X = FOOT BEATS
○ = PLACEMENT OF FEET
● = FLOOR MOVEMENT

Ḓambutshekwa ḽi a kanukisa ḽi tshi tshimbila nga lurumbu.
The crab surprises us because it walks sideways.

Li tshi ri tsere-tsere.   Ḽi tshi tshimbilu nga lurumbu.
It goes shuffle-shuffle.   *It walks sideways.*

Note. Jaco Kruger, of the Department of Music, Potchefstroom University, Bloemfontein, South Africa, has indicated accents and provided this translation. See Jaco Kruger, "A Tshivenda Action Song for Use in Primary School," *The Talking Drum,* no. 7 (1997): 3.

When Westerners see a time-signature such as 6/8, we immediately clap the rhythm as shown in figure 2.

Figure 2. Six/Eight Rhythm

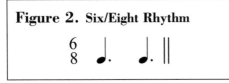

Usually the rhythm would also reflect the melodic accent of the tune and, if a song accompanied it, the verbal accent of the words. An African, if confronted with the same tune, would respond with a duple or triple clap. This clap is purely a time factor, completely neutral, and exists as a metrical foundation on which the time values of the song are built. This is known as "externalizing the beat" and can be seen in a more elaborate form in the music of drum ensembles, where the gong usually functions as a point of reference for the other instruments. Figure 3 shows how a Westerner and an African might approach the same tune."[27]

Once the teacher is comfortable with these concepts, it is possible to experience the grouping of pulses into "2, 3, 4 and 6 and changing at will from one grouping to another. Basically, this is developing the ability to hear duple and triple meters emerging from the same set of pulses.... The class is asked to clap groups of 2, 3, 4 and then 6 pulses. Once this has been mastered, they should practice switching rapidly from one grouping to another."[28] Following this, the teacher arranges the class into one group clapping three pulses = twelve, and one group clapping four pulses = twelve as shown below:

123412341234 123412341234 etc.
123123123123 123123123123 etc.

Because children with a Western musical background usually have trouble keeping a strict metronomic beat, the teacher and children should count out loud one, two three, four or one, two, three at the begin-

ning of each group of pulses. In this exercise, you hear four interlocked with three pulses. You should attempt to shift your listening back and forth from four pulses to three pulses once you have established your own pattern. When you are able to shift your listening from one pattern to another, you are on the road to becoming African in your listening. This simply means that you are able to hear the various rhythmic patterns found in one piece of music.

The interlocking rhythmic principle of three pulses with four pulses or two pulses with three pulses is a fundamental device in the musics of Africa. To experience the latter, Bonnett suggests that the class be divided "in two: one section groups the pulses in twos and the other in threes as previously, but they then combine the rhythms."[29] In other words, one group claps two pulses (1–4–), and the other group claps three pulses (1–3–5–). From these two rhythms arises a third called the "resultant rhythm" (1–345–). Encourage listeners to shift their listening once again and hear three rhythms.

In figure 4, Bonnett gives a visual illustration of the combined rhythms, without the use of Western music notational values. Each vertical line can be represented by the tick of the metronome. To feel and

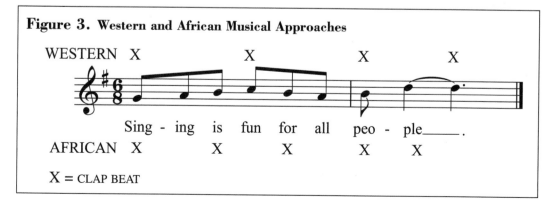

Figure 3. Western and African Musical Approaches

WESTERN X   X   X   X

Sing - ing is fun for all peo - ple_____.

AFRICAN X   X   X   X   X

X = CLAP BEAT

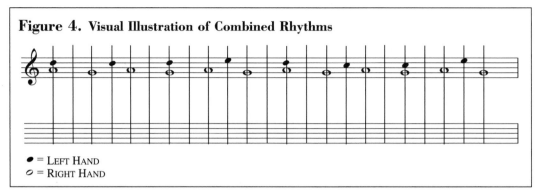

Figure 4. Visual Illustration of Combined Rhythms

● = LEFT HAND
○ = RIGHT HAND

hear each part independently, the class should use two sounds of different qualities and tap the rhythms on their desks, emphasizing one hand and then the other.[30]

Teachers must play with interlocking rhythms before introducing them to children, and they may also explain that they, too, are learning with the children. The present situation in South Africa is such that many teachers are learning new musics with and from their students. NETIEM strives to redress the ethnocentric approach to culture and education, which has been and still is prevalent in South Africa. NETIEM also aims to develop greater understanding, appreciation, and respect for the value of diversity and commonality within the rich and dynamic cultural heritage of South Africa. This project is based on the assumption that it is possible to nurture positive attitudes concerning the value of all musics and all people, thus enriching and improving the human condition.

Conclusion

The courses and programs discussed in this chapter develop materials around knowledge forms that critically appropriate what has been the dominant musical force in formal education in South Africa— Western music. The African Music Project incorporates the historical and social particularities of students and community musicians. Both *The Talking Drum* and music history courses bring to the fore the many musics and processes of music making and dancing that have been overlooked in formal education these many years. Western music remains an essential part of music history courses, but it no longer dominates.

Courses and programs like these are enhancing and expanding the consciousness of the people of South Africa. They also empower and uplift. The phrase "African Renaissance" is prevalent in South Africa. The music and dances of South Africa, a most valuable export, are gaining more and more recognition not only at home, but also abroad. Musicians from overseas are anxious to perform in South Africa and to learn about the diverse processes of music making and dancing in this part of the world. The London Philharmonic visited South Africa around 1994. An article written on their return to London revealed that their experiences with the music of South Africa gave them new perspectives on music and music making. Western music educators are beginning to turn to the musics and musical practices of other cultures. Efforts of this nature will help to eradicate the false notion of the superiority of one music, and, by implication, one people, and kindle a greater awareness and understanding of cultural diversity.

Javier Perez de Cuellar from UNESCO writes:

> For groups and societies, culture is energy, inspiration and empowerment, as well as the knowledge and acknowledgment of diversity: If cultural diversity is "behind us, around us and before us" as Claude Levi-Strauss put it, we must learn how to let it lead not to the clash of cultures, but to the fruitful coexistence and to intercultural harmony.[31]

This is one aim of a diverse approach to music in education in South Africa.

South Africa, because of the legacy of apartheid, will struggle for a long while to assert basic human rights and equal educational opportunities for all. Education through music/arts is part of a way of life for many Africans. For this reason, I naively thought that the inclusion of music/arts in the formal system of education was assured when the new democratic government came to power in 1994. This has not been the case. Though educators are trying to find ways of incorporating a diverse approach to music/arts, a struggle of even greater proportions involves including, or simply maintaining, music/arts as part of the core of formal education. South Africa's dire financial situation causes government planners and educators to rationalize that they can afford to do away with the arts because these subjects make little or no difference to the economic welfare of the country. Education for humanness calls for critical reasoning, imaginative understanding, and cultural exchange.

Education through music/arts utilizes and develops these facilities. We ignore the cultural dimension in education to our own peril.

Notes

1. Henry A. Giroux, *Teachers as Intellectuals: Toward a Critical Pedagogy of Learning* (New York: Bergin & Garvey, 1988).
2. Ibid., 183.
3. Ibid., 184.
4. Ibid.
5. Elliot W. Eisner, "Qualitative Research in Music Education: Past, Present, Perils, Promise," *Bulletin of the Council for Research in Music Education,* No. 130 (Fall 1996): 11.
6. Ibid.
7. Maria Smit, "A Theoretical Framework for a Multilingual and Cross-Cultural Music Education Dictionary: Herbert E. Wiegand's Meta-Lexicography," *Papers Presented at the Tenth Symposium on Ethnomusicology,* ed. Carol Muller (Grahamstown, South Africa: International Library of African Music, 1991), 157.
8. Ibid.
9. Ibid.
10. Ibid.
11. Matthew Sgatya, "Final Session," ed. Christine Lucia, *Proceedings of the First National Music Educators Conference* (Durban: University of Natal Press, 1986), 197.
12. Elizabeth Oehrle, "An Introduction to African Views of Music Making," *Philosopher, Teacher, Musician: Perspectives on Music Education,* ed. E. R. Jorgensen (Chicago: University of Illinois Press, 1993).
13. Portia L. Maultsby, "West African Influences and Retentions in United States Black Music: A Sociocultural Study," *More than Dancing: Essays in Afro-American Music and Musicians,* ed. Irene V. Jackson (Westport, CN: Greenwood Press, 1985), 29.
14. Ibid.
15. Ibid., 31.
16. Allen P. Britton, "The How and Why of Teaching Singing Schools in Eighteenth Century America," *Bulletin of the Council for Research in Music Education,* No. 99 (1989): 23–42.
17. Khabi Mngoma, "Making Music Education Relevant in Africa South," *Proceedings of the Second National Music Educators Conference,*

(Durban: University of Natal Press, 1988): 1–17.

18. Elizabeth Oehrle, "Emerging Music Education Trends in Africa," in *International Journal of Music Education* 18 (1991): 23–25.

19. Patricia Opondo, *Progress Report: African Music Project, University of Natal*. September 30, 1996.

20. Patricia Opondo, "African Music Project Report 11: 1996–1997," unpublished, 1997.

21. Peta Lee, "The African Music Project: Sounds of Success" in *University of Natal Focus* 10, no. 1 (1999): 26.

22. Michael J. F. Chapman, Faculty of Human Sciences, *Undergraduate Studies Handbook for 1999* (Durban: University of Natal, 1999): F99–F100.

23. John Miller Chernoff, *African Rhythm and African Sensibility: Aesthetics and Social Action in African Musical Idioms* (Chicago, IL: University of Chicago Press, 1979): 154.

24. Christopher Small, "Whose Music Do We Teach Anyway?" *Muse Letter #2*, ed. Charlie Keil (n.d.) [81 Crescent Ave., Buffalo, NY, USA].

25. Videos relative to aspects of music making in Africa are available solely for educational purposes; contact Prof. Elizabeth Oehrle, Music Dept., University of Natal–Durban, Dalbridge 4041, South Africa, or oehrle@nu.ac.za.

26. Jaco Kruger, "A Tshivenda Action Song for Use in Primary School," *The Talking Drum*, no. 7 (1997): 3.

27. Sandra Bonnett, "African Music in the Schools," *The Talking Drum*, no. 10 (1997): 15–16.

28. Ibid.

29. Ibid.

30. Ibid.

31. Javier Perez de Cuellar, *Our Creative Diversity: Report of the World Commission on Culture and Development*, 2nd ed. (Paris: UNESCO Publication, 1996).

ELIZABETH OEHRLE, honorary research associate in music at the University of Natal in Durban, South Africa, has published in the *British Journal of Music Education* and the *International Journal of Music Education,* and in the book *Multicultural Perspectives in Music Education* (2nd ed.). With her newsletter *The Talking Drum,* she is currently working to establish a network for promoting intercultural education through music.

5

Memory, Multiculturism, and Music: An African-American Perspective

Robert W. Stephens

Cultural musics are born in the experiences of the people who create them. My experiences growing up in Georgia during America's version of apartheid is a case in point. It was in this setting that I came to understand the meaning of race and the fact that race matters in music and culture. This understanding was made dramatically clear to me when shopping with my grandmother in a local Sears and Roebuck store in the late 1950s. Youthful ignorance gave me license to walk over to a water fountain for a drink. My grandmother, without ceremony but with authority, grabbed my arm with a strength that was equal in intensity only to a stare so firmly focused that it signaled that I had committed a major transgression. Then, so that there would be no doubt, she leaned over and, in a voice riddled with fear and anger, whispered, "Boy, what are you trying to do, get us killed? That's white folks' water. We can't drink from there." This was the wisdom of a woman who was passing on the shared memory, or legacy, if you will, of one of the defining events of the modern world, the largest forced migration of the world, the enslavement of Africans in the Americas.

The "Whites Only" sign did not make sense to me then, but the fear I heard in my grandmother's voice did. That and subsequent experiences made clear to me that the color of my skin both-

ered some people. From that point on, I gradually came to recognize that I would be required to lead a dual existence—one that was acceptable to people who could drink "white folks' water" and one for those who could not.

My early musical training, too, may be characterized by dualism. Generally, it was acknowledged that everyone in my community would, in the vernacular of the old folks, "take up music of some sorts." I did not know at the time that "taking up music" was more than learning to sing a song or play an instrument. It was an essential part of my cultural memory, affirming the indispensable role that music played in the lives of African-Americans. At that time, music in the black community was a form of communication that encouraged the selective retention and passing on of shared memories. Sometimes we refer to these memories as values, attitudes, ways of knowing, or culture, but we agree—individually and collectively—that they are important. This was a music that was a testament to resilience of spirit, affirmation of spirituality, and determination to survive.

For some, taking up "music of some sorts" would mean private lessons with well-known local musicians in addition to school music experiences. For others, it would mean music lessons in public school or participation in a church band, dance band, or religious or secular vocal group.[1] At this point in my development, I had no idea, of course, that the sum total of these religious, blues, jazz, and popular music experiences came together in ways that reflect the aesthetic, social, economic, and political values embedded in the "sound" identity of the African-American musical experience.

My other musical training was interesting as well. While learning to play the clarinet in the school band, it became apparent early on that the struggle between player and instrument and musical notation (and the interaction between the three) was going to be formidable. There was little doubt that it was also going to take some time to get to play music that I liked. And yet, I persisted. Something also happened during the experience of hearing, for the first time, Brahms' Symphony no. 1. That something helped to open the door to a new "embrace space" created in unfamiliar territory. All of these things were life transforming in ways that I did not fully understand at the time. The Belwin Band Builder, Brahms' Symphony no. 1, Randy's Record Mart, and other musical experiences were part of my music education.

This essay, then, is about musical experiences and cultural truths from an African-American perspective: truths that encompass a musical and cultural complex through personal and public meanings and ways that they contribute to the growth of understanding. While this approach is present in all complex human societies, each story is characterized by different ways of thinking. This story is about reconciling differences in musics as personal experience; examining what we do in the academy; defining what we call multiculturalism and why it should have a place at the table, with all the implications that spring forth from the what and why; and determining what this means for the teacher as learner and the learner as teacher.

Some may be concerned with my focus on issues of African-Americans and Whites as our schools and country become more multi-racial. Polarization between African-Americans and Whites has long been a source of contention regionally and nationally. The very nature of the relationship between these two groups played a unique, distinct role in the making of American society. Evidence suggests that these two groups live in very different cultural worlds, which deserve special examination. Much research is needed on the ways in which the interaction between these two groups is shaped and, indeed, shapes relationships in American culture, including race, ethnicity, gender, and religion. For now, I will leave that research to those who wish to examine those issues in future efforts.

Music as a Personal and Cultural Experience

Early in my graduate studies, I came across the term *Gullah* during a class discussion about the retentive African elements in African-American vernacular English. I quickly realized that the discussion was about an aspect of language that was common in the area of Georgia where I grew up. Suddenly, I found myself caught up in an academic exchange about a linguistic feature from which I had been taught to disassociate myself, a linguistic feature that now had a different name for me but still carried the same meanings. That discussion, which was the tip of an iceberg that capped a wealth of cultural and musical traditions, referenced a Creolized language steeped in African culture and practice.

This language of African words, folk narratives, songs, dances, folk religions, prayer rituals, river baptisms, sermons, material culture, folk architecture, and culinary arts provided both continuity and change in African-American culture.[2] These things were not taught in school—not the language, music, religion, or art. Of course, these cultural artifacts formed a complex that gave birth to musical styles and traditions dating back to the seventeeth century that include work songs, field- and street-calls, game songs, songs of social significance, and dance music. These forms, in turn, provided the foundation for folk spirituals, arranged spirituals, and a variety of country and, later, urban blues forms.[3] Like so many others, I felt conflict because what we were taught in school often ignored important things we learned at home, in church, and on the playground. We felt conflict in our commitment to the music program in school, which we enjoyed, because we were unsure why our school program did not recognize the integral role the community music programs played in affirming local values and beliefs. Unfortunately, many school music programs fail to recognize that musical activities in so-called minority communities and school music programs can be mutually supportive.

These are all differences that call for discussion. But there is some common ground. First, and perhaps most importantly, music is stuff that people do. Music education involves much more than performance; it allows us to re-evaluate our ideas about composition, performance, listening, studying, and teaching; it speaks to us on several levels of meaning at once; it marks liturgical moments; it is "an elaborate system of cultural conditioning [that] forms our expressive outburst … of music into different molds. We all have tongues and

vocal cords, and we say the same things, but we speak different languages."[4] These are just some of the features of my early experiences that helped to shape and mold my sense of music and music-making. This was a music education that allowed for musical conversations between myself—as a listener and performer—and other listeners and performers, all of which helped to make sense of what I was hearing and experiencing musically.

My early musical sensibilities were born of performing and listening to a vast array of musical styles, including playing organ and piano in a rhythm-and-blues band and attending church services where hand-clapping and foot-stomping were more the rule than the exception. In these latter venues, I learned to focus my musical attention less on melody and more on rhythm, less on the role of the individual and more on the group, less on highly structured schemas and more on spontaneity. During this process, it was understood that any number of people were permitted to make changes that, in effect, "re-created the song." Nettl calls this "communal re-creation,"[5] a tradition in which songs were learned by hearing; instrument playing was learned by watching and imitating.[6] These principles and qualities—standards, if you will—came to be valued by those of us who shared similar experiences. Our culture included socially transmitted beliefs, behavior patterns, products of our community's endeavors, and a style of social and artistic expression peculiar to our community. For the most part, these are things that I did not learn in school.

Our values and experiences determine who we are and what we do. We make musical decisions and form perceptions according to learned concepts. We make judgments and evaluate creative and expressive acts on the basis of our values and past experiences. These issues are at the core of what we now call multiculturalism. Music education, like society at-large, is struggling with the notion of multiculturalism in a way that reflects a much older debate over issues of race, separatism, and assimilation: a debate in which some claim that "mine is better than yours."

The Academy

Debates about what people value also create drama; that drama is frequently heightened as dialogue unfolds, often confounding those it purports to serve. For example, someone once confided to me that she was taken aback by the vehemence, anger, and hostility that greeted her efforts to discuss issues of multiculturalism with music education majors. One can speculate that the issue for these students may well be the confounding question: "Can there really be multiple musical cultures, all self-created, and all essential?" The larger issue, which is frequently overlooked, is that these "musics" and their attendant benefits come with heavy histories. Those who have benefitted from the historical dominance of their forbears argue that they should not be held responsible for the transgressions of their forebears, and contend that, if there are difficulties in reconciling racial and cultural matters, it is the fault of those who continue to press these uncomfortable issues. I have no doubt that these students are well-meaning. However, all of us are taught to not recognize White privilege. As a result, many of these students see racism,

for example, only in individual acts of meanness and not in the invisible systems that confer dominance on one group.

If university students have difficulty, so too do those who teach them. Terry Miller's wonderfully insightful article in the College Music Society newsletter correctly notes that "the music academy faces its own Y2K problem in the form of a nation now oriented more toward Latin America, Africa, and the Pacific and less so toward Europe. As the U.S. population has become internationalized, the music curriculum continues to emphasize European musical traditions conceived and taught historically, with focus mostly on structure and style and little on cultural context and meaning."[7]

Miller's point raises difficult questions, not the least of which is "How do we begin to think logically and fairmindedly about our own beliefs and viewpoints and the beliefs and viewpoints of those diametrically opposed to ours?"—not just think about them, but explore their adequacy, cohesion, and reasonableness compared to our own. Most importantly, "How do we get our students to do the same?" There are also the matters of implementation and the questions that those matters raise—difficult and vexing, yes, but inevitably these will have to be addressed.

What Is Multiculturalism?

Today's discussion about multiculturalism seems to many to be new. Yet, an examination of American education in its earliest forms argues otherwise. Debates concerning how to address the diverse backgrounds of American students existed during the "great school wars" of the 1840s, as Diane Ravitch calls them, because of demands by Catholic leaders for equal treatment for Catholic students in public schools. Among other things, they objected to having their children read from the Protestant Bible. Dissatisfied with the response they received concerning this objection, Catholics established their own schools.[8] In the 1880s and 1890s, German immigrants demanded the right to have German students taught in the German language. In fact, teaching in German was an established norm in Cincinnati and St Louis, in both public and private schools. But, by the time of the First World War, the practice of teaching German as a foreign language in both public and private schools had fallen on hard times.[9]

In 1915, Horace Kallen advanced the first notion of multiculturalism by coining the phrase "cultural pluralism." Kallen, along with his mentor John Dewey, called for a new public education that would allow a broad range of cultures to reside in American public education.[10] By the 1920s, Kallen's idea of a pluralistic society ran up against the spirited objections of many, including the Ku Klux Klan, which had gained considerable credibility during this era. "Americanization" became, and remained, the watchword throughout much of the 1930s and 1940s.

From 1915, when Kallen's idea of a pluralistic society was presented, through the late 1950s, America not only failed to assimilate African-Americans, it paid very little attention to them. This failure—resulting in continued separation, the rejection of African-American cultural values, and anger—contributed to the rise of a new sense of self-determinacy and worth according to the tenets of a free and pluralistic

society. By the 1960s, White moderates had begun their retreat from liberalism and race issues, a benchmark of the post-civil-rights era, a retreat fueled in large part by school desegregation in the Northern cities and by the rise of Black Nationalism, a development that frightened some Blacks and many White liberals.

Historically, this chain of events tells us that, as it evolved, multiculturalism came to mean many things to many people, being defined by whoever used it for whatever purpose. How this could lead to confusion in understanding the term is easy to see. When applied to educational settings, it is not surprising that people involved in a discipline over a period of time come to understand and talk about it differently from those who are not so involved or to whom the term is new. Similarly, educators, researchers, philosophers, and pedagogues who look at teaching, schools, and society from the vantage point of sociology, psychology, economics, history, anthropology, and the arts, for example, will have differing views of multiculturalism's key concerns.

That said, it is important to clearly define what we are talking about in our discussion of multiculturalism in music teaching and learning. Some scholars, for example, talk about what the expected outcomes should be, while others consider the major determining factor to be the group being studied, with the arena of the school serving as a primary focus.[11] Others choose a different focus when they concern themselves with distinctions between theory and practice.[12] Despite this range of focus, most concepts of multiculturalism as it relates to teaching and learning have some degree of commonality, grow from common and acknowledged concerns, offer guidelines or plans for positive action, and strive to make cultural pluralism and ethnic diversity an integral part of the educational process.

Definitions vary. Some rely on the cultural characteristics of diverse groups (i.e., people of color); others emphasize social problems like oppression, political power, and the re-allocation of economic resources,[13] and still others include all major groups that are different in any way from mainstream society.[14] Here, for example, are some summaries that are used in the broader definition of multiculturalism:

- an ongoing process that requires long-term investment of time and effort, as well as carefully planned, monitored action[15]
- a structure of educational priorities, commitments, and processes to reflect the cultural pluralism of the United States and to ensure the survival of group heritages that make up society, following American democratic ideals[16]
- an education free of inherited biases, with freedom to explore other perspectives and cultures, inspired by the goal of making children sensitive to various ways of life, different modes of analyzing experiences and ideas, and perspectives on history found throughout the world[17]
- a concept advocating diversity, human rights, social justice, and alternative lifestyles for all people as necessary for a quality education[18]
- an approach to teaching and learning based on democratic values that foster cultural pluralism; in its most comprehensive form, a commitment to educational equali-

ty and the development of curricula that build understanding about ethnic groups[19]
- a type of education concerned with various groups in American society who are victims of discrimination because of their unique cultural characteristics (ethnic, racial, linguistic, gender, etc.)[20]
- a comprehensive reform of basic education for all students that challenges all forms of discrimination, permeates instruction and interpersonal relations in the classroom, and advances the democratic principles of social justice.[21]

In the end, multiculturalism, from an African-American perspective, is an attempt to address one of America's most enduring problems, the socially defined concept of race. Racism in this sense embodied "the doctrine that a man's behavior is determined by stable, inherited characters deriving from separate racial stocks and usually considered to stand to one another in relations of superiority and inferiority."[22] This helps explain why Africans who identified themselves as Ejagham, Ibo, Yoruba, or Congolese, when brought to the Americas, were reclassified as "Black." This new distinction, based on social racism, permitted an ideology of exploitation and produced the contrasting category "White." This definition, however, should not be confused—as it often is—with prejudice, which is matter of attitude or feeling linked to discrimination. Multiculturalism, then, calls for the legitimatization of just and equal social institutions, including schools and their curricula, so that we are no longer "Black and White, separate, hostile, and unequal."[23]

Why Multiculturalism?

As music educators, we have become comfortable, I fear, in our beliefs that by singing some songs, dancing some dances, and occasionally making some ethnic instruments, we will somehow bring about positive transformations in our students, schools, and the ways in which we relate to each other. Unfortunately, this belief flies in the face of some harsh realities. If multiculturalism is to be meaningful and lasting, then it must include a much broader agenda and context.

Often, as we search for answers to perplexing issues, our minds need to match an action with a reason; when we can find no reason, only the unreasonable remains. What can be more unreasonable than the following examples? A member of the World Church of the Creator shoots dead a former basketball coach at Northwestern University because he is an African-American. In Texas, an African-American is chained and dragged to pieces behind a truck for a thrill. A Senegalese man is shot to death at a Denver bus stop for being in "White territory." Julius Streicher, a Nazi propagandist, calls for a "racial holy war," offering children coloring books depicting White supremacist themes.

The recent activities of groups and individuals motivated by hate and racial hostility, for example, cross burnings in African-American neighborhoods and cases of blatant police brutality against African-Americans in Los Angeles and Detroit, are symptoms of an inherent social racism that still exists in the United States today. When combined with persistent stereotypical attitudes toward ethnic groups, especially negative perceptions of African-Americans and Latinos, it is painfully obvious that this society does not fully understand, respect, and value its diversity.

Negative perceptions and stereotypical attitudes, when examined in the context of musical style, can also be revealing. For example, when asked if "rap" is music, some students and many colleagues will say "no."[24] Indeed, it is often quite difficult to generate a discussion that acknowledges the influence of the first post-civil-rights, post-"soul-generation" of music. Yet, little doubt remains that rap's influence permeates American music, consumer culture, and politics and represents "the central cultural vehicle for open social reflection on poverty, fear of adulthood, the desire for absent fathers, frustrations about black male sexism, female sexual desires, daily rituals of life as an unemployed teen hustler, safe sex, raw anger, violence, and childhood memories."[25]

Musically, rap attaches high priority to musical elements and their order of importance as it captures the listener's attention. For example, when we listen to music that represents the "classical" tradition, we assign the highest musical preference to melody, then harmony, and finally rhythm. Rap, on the other hand (indeed, much Black popular and religious music), places a higher musical premium on rhythm, then harmony, and finally melody. As both a cultural and musical vehicle, it is easy to see why it generates controversy and attracts detractors.[26]

Music is more than sound; it is also about image. Our society is bombarded with images daily. The current image of "gangsta rappers," both real and imagined, is wide-ranging in impact and perception.

Some view these rappers with disdain; others argue that their music reflects the day-to-day realities that many face in urban America; most view them as menacing and threatening. This negative connotation is true of most media images in general and African-Americans in particular. These images, created by others for public consumption and carried through time, shape and reinforce stereotypical opinions, and opinions inform attitudes.[27] These attitudes transfer quite easily to communities, personal relationships, and musical values. Musically, evidence of stereotypical images varies throughout American history. Throughout the historical development of African music, powerful negative images have persisted. For example, the most popular form of entertainment in the nineteenth century featured white men masquerading as blacks.[28] In the 1920s, jazz was viewed as a "caricature ... its effects are made by exaggeration, distortion and vulgarisms ... the self expression of a primitive race.[29] If we as a society are to change, we must modify the negative racial and ethnic attitudes we hold toward each other; this can only be done through deliberate intervention over a long period of time.

Implications

There is much to do, including school reform at all levels, in order to recognize, accept, and celebrate diversity as a fact of life in the United States and the world at large. These reforms are necessary if schools are to prepare all students for the realities of living in a racially, ethnically, socially, and culturally pluralistic world. And diverse we are. To illustrate, let's look at our schools. In 1997, forty-eight million

students were enrolled in U.S. elementary and secondary schools, just shy of the baby boomers' 1970 all-time high of 48.7 million,[30] but with one difference, however: today's students are more racially and ethnically diverse. In 1972, 85 percent of the students enrolled in elementary and secondary schools were White, 14 percent were African-American, and one percent were Asian. By 1997, 78 percent were White, 17 percent African-American, and 4 percent Asian. The proportion of Hispanics, who can be members of any race, increased from 6 percent in 1972 to 14 percent in 1997.[31]

As numbers change, so too have expectations for who and what is to be included in the content taught. These expectations and changes reflect who we are and help to clarify our understanding of and responsibilities to the past and the future. None of this is done in isolation. The process cannot begin while disregarding the past. Expectations, change, and understanding remain important obligations, if we are to move forward. Strong evidence suggests that many African-American students feel that their school environment is alien and hostile toward them or does not affirm and value who they are. As a consequence, they are not motivated to concentrate or attend to academic tasks with any dedication. Instead, they find themselves in situations where stress and anxiety cause shifts between protecting their psyches (i.e., the sense of who they are) from attack and attending to academic tasks. Thus, stress "adversely affects students' daily academic performances by reducing their willingness to persist at academic tasks and interfering with the cognitive processes involved in learning."[32]

Maintaining and Transmitting Values

Superficial raids on numbers and percentages, however persuasive, don't tell the complete story. They do not address the moral and ethical responsibilities that are vital to maintaining and transmitting the important things we value. Consider this: most animals care for their young, just as we do. However, our young are totally dependent upon their elders in order to survive—for longer periods of time than other animals. When we compare ourselves to "other animals," we measure poorly. We can't run as fast as a squirrel or lion and we can't climb as well as a monkey or gorilla, so we have developed clever ways of communicating with each other to compensate for these shortcomings and to perpetuate the things that we value.

Communication allows us to compensate for our numerous physical shortcomings. We have developed a system of sophisticated codes organized into "grunts and sounds"—speech—which allows us to do many things. We use it to make requests that are practical and functional, such as "Please remember to bring some butter back from the supermarket," or to express feelings and emotions, like "I love you, too, but not in that way."

Our systematized communications extend to music as well. We identify sounds based on the acoustics of an instrument. Our perception of sounds, whether Western or non-Western, is universal; that is, we place stimuli into categories rather than treat them as discrete or isolated events. Everything that happens to us, it seems, needs to be placed into some sort of context in order to have meaning. In this way, we are allowed to prepare our experiences for long-term storage and retrieval.

Effective communication encourages selective retention and passing on of shared memories. Sometimes we refer to these memories as values, attitudes, ways of knowing, or culture, but we agree—individually and collectively—that they are important. The United States has a shared memory that has been communicated one to many and many to one. It is a memory that is shared by people of all the world's heritages; yet, while they are shared memories, they are *different* memories. These collective memories have contributed much to our becoming a great nation. As the twenty-first century begins, we continue the process of deciding who and what will become a part of the shared memory that will be passed on to our young.

In the case of music, decisions about what will be passed to our young have not been shared. More than a few African-Americans would tend to agree with Jorgensen's view that "in a multicultural society in which various spheres of musical validity coexist, the question of whose music is to be taught in state-supported schools has political and musical ramifications and important policy implications .... The tendency to exclude or de-emphasize musics of ethnic minorities and some forms of popular music in favor of Western classical music in Western school curricula illustrates how music teaching tends to ensure the social and cultural reproduction of the establishment and maintain the status quo insofar as ethnic and social stratification is concerned."[33]

As we continue to refine who and what will become a part of the shared memory that will be passed on, the question of who is to be included looms large. Will it include Duke Ellington, B. B. King, Aretha Franklin, Charlie Parker, Public Enemy, William Grant Still, Erykah Badu, Marian Anderson, Jay-Z, or Sun Ra? Will it chronicle hip-hop culture that devolved from deejays like Grand Master Flash, highlighting the West-Indian tradition of elegant, sardonic toasting, and putting down the powerful, a tradition derived from West African griots, people who made a handsome living by not insulting those who paid tribute? Will any or all of these become a part of our sacred shared treasures? Will they become a part of the shared memory that includes others from different times and different places? The answer to these questions will help us answer "What is a nation?" and "What makes a people great?"

Our schools can and must become the curators of our collective accomplishments. Of all the things we enjoy musically or culturally, none was invented today. Those who came before us, both royalty and slaves, invented all of it. Maya Angelou eloquently reminds us that we stand on the shoulders of our elders: we have been paid for by their suffering. Their treasures have been passed to us, and we are required to do the same for those who follow us.[34] These sacred treasures must be inclusive—multicultural, if you will—as thanks to our predecessors and as foundations for a just and equitable society not yet achieved.

Notes

1. Here it should be noted that distinctions in style and performance between religious and secular music were blurred to such an extent that the context did not conform to the more traditional separation of sacred and secular.

2. Charles Joyner offers splendid descriptions taken from the observations of members of the Writers project during their interviews for *Drums and Shadows: Survival Studies among the Georgia Coastal Negroes* (Athens, GA: University of Georgia Press, 1940), xi–xii. Joyner presents a great deal of information on folk speech and naming patterns, including the use of day names and the folk etymology of *Gullah*. Other examples include a broad assortment of African words; folk narratives of "Buh Rabbit," mysterious spiders, and supernatural spirits; African songs; instrumental music on banjos, bones, drums, and gourds used in coastal Georgia; popular dances such as the Buzzard Lope, the Camel Walk, the Fish Tail, and the Snake Hip; vivid descriptions of Moslem ancestors and African prayer rituals that were a part of contemporary religious practices.

3. Dena Epstein, *Sinful Tunes and Spirituals: Black Folk Music to the Civil War* (Urbana, IL: University of Illinois Press, 1977), and Lawrence W. Levine, *Black Culture and Black Consciousness: Afro-American Folk Thought from Slavery to Freedom* (New York: Oxford Univ. Press, 1977), provide insightful and scholarly documentation of African-American music and culture during the years of slavery and beyond.

4. David Reck, *Music of the Whole Earth* (New York: Charles Scribner's Sons, 1977).

5. Bruno Nettl with Melinda Russell, *In the Course of Performance: Studies in the World of Musical Improvisation* (Chicago: University of Chicago Press, 1998), 1–23.

6. Bruno Nettl, *Folk and Traditional Music of the Western Continents* (Upper Saddle River, NJ: Prentice Hall, 1965).

7. Terry Miller, "Beyond Ethnomusicology and Cultural Diversity: Normalizing World Music in the Curriculum," *The College Music Society Newsletter* (October, 1999).

8. Diane Ravitch, *The Great School Wars: New York City, 1805–1973* (New York: W. W. Norton, 1973).

9. David Tyack, *The One Best System: A History of American Education* (Cambridge, MA: Harvard Univ. Press, 1974).

10. Horace Mayer Kallen, "Democracy Versus the Melting Pot," *The Nation* (February 18, 1915); reprinted in Kallen, *Culture and Democracy in the United States* (New York: Boni and Liveright, 1924), 190–92.

11. See, for example, Joseph Polisi, "Balancing the Elements of Arts Literacy," and Arturo Madrid, "Arts Literacy across American Culture," in *The Vision for Arts Education in the 21st Century: The Ideas and Ideals behind the Development of the National Standards for Education in the Arts* (Reston, VA: MENC, 1994)—materials for this book were derived from the Symposium on National Standards for Education in the Arts, Washington, D.C., March 7–9, 1993; Patricia Shehan Campbell, *Music in Cultural Context: Eight Views on World Music Education* (Reston, VA: MENC, 1996); William Anderson, ed., *Teaching Music with a Multicultural Approach* (Reston, VA: MENC, 1991); Charles Fowler, *Music: Its Role and Importance in our Lives* (New York: Glencoe/McGraw-Hill, 1994).

12. See John Sheperd, Philip Virden, Graham Vulliamy, and Trevor Wishart, *Whose Music? A Sociology of Musical Languages* (New Brunswick, NJ: Transaction Inc., 1977); Keith Swanwick, *Music, Mind, and Education* (New York: Routledge, 1988), 15; Michael Mark, *Contemporary Music Education* (New York: Schirmer Books, 1996), 188; and Wayne Bowman, "A Plea for Pluralism: On a Theme by George McKay," in *Basic Concepts in Music Education*, ed. Richard Colwell (Niwot, CO: University of Colorado Press, 1991), 94–110.

13. See Molefi Asante, *Afrocentricity: The Theory of Social Change* (Buffalo, NY: Amulefi Publishing., 1980); Otto Lindenmeyer, *Black History: Lost, Stolen, or Strayed* (New York: Avon Books, 1970); Manning Marable, *Beyond Black and White: Transforming African-American Politics* (New York: Vesco, 1995); Craig Werner, *A Change Is Gonna Come: Music, Race, and the Soul of America* (New York: Plume, 1999); Frank Kofsky, *Black Music, White Business: Illuminating the History and Political Economy of Jazz* (New York: Pathfinder, 1998).

14. See Wanda Ward and Mary M. Cross, eds., *Key Issues in Minority Education: Research Directions and Practical Implications* (Norman, OK: Center for Research on Minority Education, University of Oklahoma, 1989).

15. James A. Banks, *Multicultural Education: Issues and Perspectives* (Boston, MA: Allyn and Bacon, 1993) and H. P. Baptiste, *Multicultural Education: A Synopsis* (Washington, DC: University Press of America, 1979).

16. W. A. Hunter, ed., *Multicultural Education through Competency-Based Teacher Education* (Washington, DC: American Association of Colleges for Teacher Education, 1974).

17. B. Parekh, "The Concept of Multicultural Education," in S. Modgil, G. K. Verma, K. Mallick, and C. Modgil, eds., *Multicultural Education: The Interminable Debate* (Philadelphia, PA: Falmer, 1986), 19–31.

18. Carl A. Grant, *Multicultural Education: Commitments, Issues, and Applications* (Washington, DC: Association for Supervision and Curriculum Development, 1977).

19. Christine I. Bennett, *Comprehensive Multicultural Education: Theory and Practice* (Boston, MA: Allyn and Bacon, 1990).

20. James A. Banks, "Clarification Pluralism and Educational Concepts," *Peabody Journal of Education* 54 (1977): 73–78.

21. Sonia Nieto, *Affirming Diversity: The Sociopolitical Context of Multicultural Education* (New York : Longman, 1996). For a definitive look at and review of multiculturalism, see Geneva Gay, *NCREL Monograph: A Synthesis of Scholarship in Multicultural Education* (Oak Brook, IL: North Central Regional Educational Laboratory, 1994) published by North Central Regional Education Urban Education Program as part of its Urban Education Monograph Series.

22. George M. Fredrickson, *The Arrogance of Race: Historical Perspectives of Slavery, Racism, and Social Inequality* (Middletown, CT: Wesleyan University, 1988), 189.

23. For a compelling analysis of a divided society, see Andrew Hacker, *Two Nations: Black and White, Separate, Hostile, and Unequal* (New York: Ballantine Books, 1993).

24. Tricia Rose defines rap in *Black Noise* (Hanover, PA: Wesleyan Univ. Press, 1994) as "a black cultural expression that prioritizes black voices from the margins of urban America. Rap music is a form of rhymed storytelling accompanied by highly rhythmic, electronically based music."

25. Ibid., 18.

26. See Adolph Reed, "The Allure of Malcolm X," *Malcolm X: In Our Own Image*, ed. Joe Wood (New York: St. Martins Press, 1992); Reed argues that rap is little more than Afrocentric drivel and cracker-barrel wisdom.

27. In a related discussion, T. W. Smith, *Ethnic Images* (Chicago, IL: University of Chicago, National Opinion Research Center, 1990), provides a comprehensive overview and

examination of issues relating to the question of stereotypical images of people of color.

28. Robert C. Toll, *Blacking Up: The Minstrel Show in Nineteenth-Century America* (New York: Oxford Univ. Press, 1974).

29. Rudi Blesh, *Shining Trumpets: A History of Jazz* (New York: da Capo Press, 1958).

30. Tamara Henry, "90s See Boom in School Enrollment," *USA Today,* 2–5 July 1999.

31. Ibid.

32. Ibid.

33. Jorgensen, *In Search of Music Education* (Urbana, IL: University of Illinois, 1997).

34. Maya Angelou, "The Distinguished Annie Clark Tanner Lecture" (lecture presented at the Annual Families Alive Conference, Weber State University, May 8, 1997), www.weber.edu/chfam/html/ angelouspeech.html.

ROBERT W. STEPHENS, professor of music and interim director of the Institute for African-American Studies at the University of Connecticut in Storrs, has written and taught on a broad array of African-American music and culture and is currently researching and developing materials on the African diasporic experience, with special emphasis on Afro-Cuban music and culture.

6

Catching Up with the Rest of the World: Music Education and Musical Experience

Anthony Seeger

*I*t would be nice to say that my journey to world musics began in a dugout canoe, paddled by Amazon Indians and wending its way for days up the tortuous curves of the Suiá Missu river, as I listened to jaguars' grunt as they prowled the sandy beaches in search of turtle eggs. But, in fact, that's the middle of the story.

My journey actually began when I was born into the musically gifted Seeger family. My parents, who would both become elementary school teachers, met at summer camp, sang at summer camps, and ran their own summer camp for over fifty years in Hancock, Vermont. Summer camp music varies from place to place, but the camps that I grew up in sang songs of many kinds and from many parts of the world—African songs, Zionist songs, topical songs, spirituals, contemporary show tunes, and just plain "kids' songs" ("B-I-N-G-O," for example). Inspired by visions of social equality, the potential for a United Nations, and the need to avoid further wars, my young repertoire unselfconsciously merged traditional children's music with idealistic songs from many places. My uncle Pete Seeger, who was then (in the late 1940s) forming the Weavers, was famous for his high falsetto part in their popular

recording of the South African song "Wimoweh." Listening to the Weavers added an Indonesian lullaby and other songs to my childhood repertoire. My grandfather, Charles Seeger, was head of the music division of the Pan-American Union and an expert in the "classical" or "concert" music of Latin America. My parents sang all kinds of songs, sometimes harmonizing for hours in the car on our annual migration to Vermont—until the day I stood up between them and declared, "I want to sing my own songs."

I was not much older when I learned that music is more than pleasing sounds—it has repercussions in the real world. I learned that being a musician—or even an audience member—can be dangerous. In 1952, I was seven when my grandfather, who was refused a passport to attend international conferences, retired from the Pan-American Union. That same year, the Weavers were blacklisted, their performances canceled, and their music no longer played on the radio; they practically disbanded. At the age of eight, I also learned that I had to shut the windows when I played union songs on my little 78 rpm "juke box" record player, because people outside might be listening; people could be questioned before the United States Congress regarding where they had sung what songs and for whom. I wasn't at the infamous Paul Robeson concert in Peekskill, N.Y., where thugs threw rocks at audience members after the show while police stood by, but I learned early that music and politics not only mix but can become different facets of the same process.

Mostly, I was just a little boy with doting parents and a big song repertoire, going to the private school where my parents taught in the winter (they ran the camp in the summer) along with the children of immigrants who had fled the Spanish Civil War or the Holocaust or who were rich and liberal. Like many of my friends, I started to play the alto recorder in third grade, adding the violin in fourth grade (my father's mother was a concert violinist; it was thought I might take after her). At summer camp after fifth grade, I added the five-string banjo to the list; by seventh grade, I was performing for the whole school and, by eighth grade, I had a young fan club. During one concert, an educational program for my fellow students, I performed Civil War songs that I had learned from a 10-inch LP produced by Folkways Records, which my parents had given me. In my case, music and education were combined and never stopped being interrelated.

The critical point for me, however, was a paper I wrote in sixth grade on the music of India. Our school curriculum devoted a considerable amount of time to studying other cultures; for India, we were given a chance to write on any topic we chose. I decided to write on music and obtained another Folkways release, the Folk and Classical Music of India (FW 4422). Most of it left me curious but fairly unmoved; still, the album notes provided useful information for my paper. However, one long track was devoted to a rag for shenai and tabla, by which I was completely transfixed. It was spectacular,

and even an untrained child could hear how the free-rhythm shenai explored the notes of the rag, then moved into rhythmic relationship with the remarkably long cycles of the tabla, and sped the whole thing up to double time. I played that track so often in my room next to the kitchen that my mother called it "Indian water torture" and wondered if I couldn't find something else to play? (In talking with other people who have been converted by a musical performance, both the musical experience itself and parental alienation seem to be part of the story.)

The paper and the experience were each a success. I wrote a paper on African music in eighth grade, based on another Folkways Record, and a ninth-grade paper on Japanese music. I learned where to purchase inexpensive "cut-out" copies of Folkways Records and prowled the bins looking for new kinds of world musics, as well as anything else that looked interesting. I was well set on the journey.

In high school, I attended a boarding school that banned record players and radios because they would bother the other students—in the era before headphones became common. We had to make all of our own music or do without, so I learned new songs on the banjo, roomed with friends who also played, continued to play the violin, sang in the madrigal group, and kept returning to the record store on vacations to stockpile records at home. I listened to the music of the Civil Rights movement and subscribed to journals filled with new topical songs of the 1960s. My repertoire grew to over 150 songs that I could perform before audiences.

In college, I encountered two obstacles. First, even though I had taken harmony courses in high school using the guitar, I had to take piano in order to take music theory courses. Secondly, I saw my uncle Mike Seeger and his group, The New Lost City Ramblers, play to an indifferent audience at the end of a long tour. They were tired, the club manager wasn't nice to them, and I thought, "There must be something more fun I can do with music without this kind of hassle." Fascinated by the writings of Claude Levi-Strauss on Brazilian Indians and of Albert Lord on southern European epics, I decided to become an anthropologist who studied music (rather than either a musicologist or a musician). I married a guitar player with a fine voice and kept the music mostly domestic, for our own enjoyment and that of our friends.

That's how I came to be in the motor boat, sputtering along, carrying my wife, a guitar, a banjo, and 60 kilos of baggage to spend two years with the Suyá Indians of Mato Grosso, Brazil. There I planned to study their social organization, their cosmology, their music, and the relationships between them.

The Suyá were kind but wanted us to contribute something to their lives as well. So we sang for them whenever they asked. It was the only thing we were good at. Otherwise, we were like infants, not speaking the language or knowing how to walk in the forest, unable to avoid the commonest dangers or do anything else useful. Night after night, we took our instruments to the center of the beaten dirt plaza, tuned up, and taught the Suyá such songs as "Michael, Row the Boat Ashore," "Oh, Freedom," "Guantanamera," "Day-O," and "Pretty Polly," among many others. With gestures and wild dancing, I would tell the story of the giant Abiyoyo (I learned it from my Uncle Pete) to delighted adults and terrified children, and the Suyá went to their hammocks satisfied that "their White men" were good people and worth putting up with. We "grew up" eventually, by Suyá terms. I felt that, at my best, I was like a 12-year-old boy for the Suyá. I learned how to speak their language but without an adult's mastery; I

learned how to sing songs appropriate for teenagers; I was in a way a model "Suyá boy" because I wanted to learn everything, to sing all the time, had a good sense of humor, but wasn't terribly good at anything particular yet. My wife's progress paralleled my own, and, after fifteen months in the village, we left and returned to the United States, where I wrote my dissertation on Suyá social organization and cosmology. I felt it was long enough without taking on music, which I didn't think I really understood anyway.

But one year later, in 1975, we went back to Brazil, where I had accepted a job as Associate Professor in the fine Graduate Program in Social Anthropology at the National Museum in Rio de Janeiro. For the next seven years, I learned from my colleagues and students, visited the Suyá often, and readied myself to take on the complex and difficult job of writing about Suyá music. By 1981, I was writing and thinking a lot about music, but there were few ethnomusicologists in Brazil and my wife had finished her research on Brazilian ballad singing, so I accepted a job at Indiana University, in Bloomington, Indiana, to teach Anthropology and Ethnomusicology and to become Director of the Indiana University Archives of Traditional Music.

The word "archive" for most people conjures up visions of dusty old things that nobody needs or wants anymore, kept for reasons obscure to everyone and guarded by fierce archivists who scare off anyone who might want to use them anyway. In reality, musical archives can be places of delightful discovery, intense pleasure, and high excitement. Oral traditions can disappear in a single generation—but they can also be revived if recordings have been preserved. I found that some American Indian communities turned to the Archives to learn songs their grandfathers had sung to researchers; though their parents hadn't wanted to learn them, these grandchildren wanted to sing them again. The same is true for the children of immigrants. Some musicians came to listen to performance styles. Some students were transfixed by the sounds found in the archives, as I had been many years before. I spent seven years learning about archiving, about preserving old tape, and about capturing the attention and interest of students and colleagues alike so that they would use the amazing resource at their own university.

It is difficult to run world-class archives (or any small unit in a large university or museum), because you are often not given nearly as much respect and credit within your own institution as you are given by those outside it. In addition to their own relative fragility in institutions with other interests, archives also face certain problems they cannot avoid: copyright law prevents them from providing copies of published material and contracts with depositors or musicians often restrict their use of unpublished collections. After six years at the Archives, I was ready for a sabbatical, and the family was prepared to head back to the twisting course of the Suiá Missu for more research and music in the Amazon.

Instead, I moved to the Smithsonian Institution to run a record company it had just acquired from the founder—Folkways, with all accompanying rights to make and sell copies and obligations to pay royalties and operate in an ethical, legal fashion. The Smithsonian wanted someone to run the company who was a scholar, knew the folk music scene, was able to work with bureaucracies, knew about preservation on the one hand and copyright on the other, and cared about the company. It seemed that my musical journey had an obvious port-of-call at the Smithsonian. Having listened to Folkways records since I was a child and remembering my transformative experience with the Indian rag, I

agreed that I was a logical candidate and so we moved to the Potomac River instead of the Suiá Missu.

The challenge at the Smithsonian was to move Folkways from the status of a fiercely independent small company to being part of a large bureaucratic institution, while keeping all its titles in print in some form, and using its more than two thousand LP records to further the Smithsonian's mission, which is "the increase and diffusion of knowledge" (according to the will of John Smithson, who gave his fortune to found it)—all without losing money.

My recent involvement in music education is thus partly the result of my responsibility for Folkways Records, which has always emphasized the educational aspect of music. Its best-selling artist is Ella Jenkins, a children's artist; it has dozens of recordings designed for schoolroom use, such as the Civil War volume from which I had learned the songs for my school concert. Folkways had been publishing "world music" since 1950 and was probably the main publisher of ethnomusicological albums through the 1980s.

What a job! I think of it as a bit like the fishing that I spent so many weeks struggling to learn on the Suiá Missu. My job is to hook people on music. Each recording is like a baited hook, and the public are the fish that take the bait and, I hope, swallow it deeply and get hooked on music. Less metaphorically, I hope that people will hear the sounds, and be amazed, transfixed, delighted, or whatever; use the bibliographies to read more and the discographies to listen more; attend live concerts; and learn to play a new instrument. People can be transformed by music, and so the Folkways I have tried to perpetuate by keeping Folkways and other labels in print through Smithsonian Folkways Recordings is a means of sharing knowledge and providing direct experience about music through *recordings. Unlike most record companies, our real goal is not to sell product but to capture imaginations and educate people in the broadest possible sense. I don't care if people purchase the recordings, borrow them, take them out of libraries, hear them on the radio, or download them from the Internet—the real purpose is not the purchase but the process of educating and transfixing and its results. (I do want someone to pay for the music, though, because artists and songwriters live on their royalties, and the staff need to be paid each month—but that is another topic altogether.)*

So, I grew from a child in Manhattan listening to Folkways Records to an adult running Smithsonian Folkways Recordings in Washington, D.C. The Amazon was in the middle, though, and it is to the Amazon and to the lessons I learned there that I will direct your thoughts for the rest of this discussion.

Catching Up to the Suyá Indians: Bringing Multiple Cultures into the Classroom

It would be presumptuous for me to be too specific in my recommendations to teachers. I feel qualified to write at some length on what university teachers could do. Elementary and secondary education, however, has become highly specialized and directed toward meeting certain benchmarks on standardized tests that may not leave much room for experimentation. There has been considerable centralization in the musical arena as well, with statewide committees sometimes selecting textbooks and defining most aspects of curriculum. The points made below are meant more for reflection than for implementation. They grow out of the experiences along the "journey" described above, tempered by my

experience working at Smithsonian Folkways Recordings and performing for groups of children over the decades.

The Suyá Indians live on an affluent to the Amazon called the Xingu River.[1] Until 1959, they lived precariously, warring with most of their neighbors, hunting, fishing, and gathering largely with the help of bamboo, wood, and stone implements. Their language is of the Ge language family, and today they live in a single village of about 200 residents, dealing with the complex forces of the frontier society of which they are today a part. They have never been missionized (until recently they had no school), and they continue to value their collective life over life outside the village, to perform many of the ceremonies their grandfathers performed, and to be proud of their own musical traditions as well as the traditions of other peoples whom they have met and from whom they have learned.

They describe their history as one of acquiring good things from enemies, monsters, and other powerful foreign beings. In music and in myths, an individual usually brings something good to the village and shares it with everyone. Fire they acquired from the jaguar, garden crops from a rodent, names from enemy Indians, new manioc varieties through trade with other Indians, fermented drink from yet others, and music from all of them. All of their music comes from outside the community. They do not have the same concept of "composer" as we do—what we might call a Suyá "composer" they see as an intermediary between the natural world (all parts of which have music) and the human world (which learns and performs the music of the natural world and foreign humans).

They sing in at least eight different languages and are proud of their ability to learn new vocal performance styles and teach the one they have evolved. They are relatively uninterested in instrumental music or in musical instruments—like most original inhabitants of the Americas, their principal interest is in song. When the Suyá decide to sing, the question is "What shall we sing? whose songs? which ceremonies?" This is an area of controversy among them, just as it is in American schools. A large part of the community moved away after an argument over which ceremonies to perform. Although they later moved back, music is a complex cultural arena for them, too. Nevertheless, everyone participates, and everyone knows songs in several languages and styles.

Adult Suyá want their children to learn the traditional ceremonies and songs, which they sing to their children when young while swinging in hammocks and telling stories associated with the songs. They encourage their children to sing as they get older and insist on it when they are adolescents. The whole community evaluates a youth's performances and tries to instill in him or her a respect for and pride in the songs performed by the ancestors as well as by foreign contemporaries.

The Suyá thus have a culturally based enthusiasm for learning music from other societies. When I was with them, they sang songs from five other Indian societies and three European societies—eight different languages! They asked us to sing our songs over and over until they had learned at least part of them. They added evenings or even entire ceremonies of "foreign" songs to their ritual calendar. They were multicul-

tural in other deep and significant ways—in terms of food and material culture.

Of course, there are different ways to become multicultural. The Suyá sometimes traded with people from whom they learned songs (or allowed them to learn to be anthropologists). They also captured women and children from other Indian societies, after clubbing their husbands or parents over the head, and then raised these captives in their village. From these captives, they would learn songs and many other cultural traditions. Such a method is not recommended for classroom instruction, but the results were musically interesting. After all, the United States has incorporated many immigrants within its boundaries, but our schools rarely include their music in the classroom, and the national calendar only sparsely represents their ceremonies among its holidays. In fact, one could argue that the Suyá, living in an isolated village on a bend in a remote river in northern Mato Grosso, are more enthusiastically multicultural and more culturally sophisticated than most people living in the United States.

The Suyá are probably not unique in their understanding and inspiration from multiple cultures. While most ethnomusicologists have studied "the" music of a community, members of communities probably often know a lot of different kinds of music and switch from one genre to another according to the place, the time, and the people participating.

Looking at American music education from the banks of the Potomac, at a midpoint (perhaps) on my journey, I see some odd things about our music education, as well as some directions I think we should be moving in and some steps we should be taking in those directions. In a sense, powerful though the United States economy is and as enviable as its educational system is, we have a lot to do in our music education to begin to catch up with the world as it has become today.

Music, Schools, and the World

Music. Children are bombarded by music every day, only some of which comes from school.[2] They hear music from their parents, their siblings, their friends, their churches, their shopping malls, their television sets, the films they watch, and their computers. In little over 100 years, we have gone from a single recording Thomas Edison created on tinfoil to a world where recorded performances far outnumber live performances and where most of the world's populations can, at least in principle, listen to the music of most of the rest of the world's populations. When I first visited the Suyá, in 1971, the only way they could capture music was to learn it by heart and to perform it; today we (and to a degree the Suyá as well) can capture music on a variety of media and store it in our living rooms, libraries, schools, and universities in a way unthinkable only a short time ago.

Most preschool children are interested in music and have a curiosity that exceeds that of even the Suyá. Every year or so, I give a concert to preschool children, and each time I am interested to see that the same old songs continue to delight new audiences. Young children's music serves as the vehicle for the transmission of some very old songs. For example, "Ring around the Rosie," innocently passed on by children who think it is just an enjoyable circle game, is widely held to refer to plague epidemics that devastated London's population in the seventeenth century. Also, Chicago schoolchildren in the 1950s sang a jump-rope rhyme about Benjamin Franklin turning his back on the "dirty old king."[3] Of course, not everything enjoyed is old: purple dinosaurs on television introduce new repertoire, as do an army of songwriters and very large corporations. But the tasks of life—learning to speak, move in rhythm, count, and remember things—maintain a role for music that has been around for a long time. "One, two, buckle my shoe"—how long has it been since shoes had buckles? A long time indeed, but we still count from one to ten.

Schools. Schools are social institutions, and, as such, they and everything in them are part of social and political processes that are complex, having a great deal do with things other than teaching children. What is music like in schools? It varies by school district and classroom, but I think it fair to say that most of the music taught in schools is based on European traditions, is related very little to what children listen to outside school, and is taught as a subject distinct from, and unrelated to, social studies, English, mathematics, and physical education, even though all of these subjects are integrally interrelated.

Schools are not ideologically neutral, as anyone who has followed the heated debate on "multiculturalism" can attest to. Many of them continue to have the ideology of a melting pot—everyone must attend, and they must all learn the same thing in the same way and come out the same—equal citizens with equal preparation. What else could one expect of a generally isolationist, xenophobic country that has repeatedly looked at education as a means of civilizing the uncivilized?

The American school system is not unique. Schools in most countries are exercises in social engineering. The question really is, what kind of social engineering should we be doing in the United States today? The phrase "social engineering" highlights the ideological nature of education and exposes the reason music curricula are the hotly debated arenas they have become. We are not arguing about what children should learn in sixth grade but about the nature of the country, its self-image, and its future. In those terms, one can understand why Congress investigates artists, and why children have to shut their doors to play certain kinds of music aloud.

The World. We live in a world being radically transformed by economic processes, communications technology, and possibly a post-colonial shift of political and cultural power. The world, and the United States' participation in it, is not what it was in the nineteenth century, when schools were "civilizing savages" or even in the early twentieth century, when much of the current educational philosophy was transformed into curricula. Music is one of the experiences that reveal these transformations—children are experiencing a greater variety of musics than views of history, types of literature, or visions of their own country. Textbooks, journalistic traditions, and national self-involvement may disguise the transformed world, but music reveals it. Because it is part of the experienced world, why shouldn't we study the world as it exists?

Three Paths to Music from Many Cultures in the Schools

I see three ways in which music from other cultures and times can be fruitfully introduced into schools. There may well be others, of course, but these seem to me to be particularly effective:

1. Introduce music from a variety of cultures into music curricula in order to better present, understand, and increase musical enjoyment and creativity.
2. Introduce music from a variety of cultures into curricula in other fields (e.g., social studies) to better present and understand history and the social sciences.
3. Introduce students to their own and each another's musical and cultural heritages by encouraging research into those heritages within their own communities, in order to better understand their community, nation, and world.

Introducing Music from Various Cultures into Music Curricula

Music is a set of sonic and temporal structures that composers arrange, performers adapt, and to which audiences respond in a variety of ways, thus influencing composers' new efforts and performers' subsequent performances. No single culture in the world exploits all the possible tones, timbres, rhythms, and instruments; rather, each tradition selects a finite number of these musical attributes, and "creativity" within any given tradition involves the subtle rearrangement of that culture's musical parameters.

To take a stereotypical example (which is not really fair to the subtlety and richness of musical traditions), one could say that one of the most highly developed sonic resources in European music is harmony—harmonic structures and progressions. While many "European" instruments came from Islamic civilizations, the music played on them differs greatly from that played by their originators. Quite different from the exploration of harmonic structures is an exploration of different tonal relationships found in Maqam and Indian rags (to name just two of a large number of tonal systems devised by people living in a different part of the world—generally east of Europe and west of China and Southeast Asia). In parts of Africa, the subtleties of rhythm have been explored, and complex rhythms are part of the musical traditions, as well as religious beliefs, of a number of African cultures. Complex rhythms, augmented by the interaction of several contributing sub-rhythms, create a sound that is characteristic of the region. American Indians, from the Canadian Arctic to Tierra del Fuego in Argentina, have focused on vocal timbre, repetition, and song as their areas of greatest elaboration. I could go on describing more areas of sonic development, but the point to be demonstrated is that there are many aspects to musical experience and creativity that the forms and traditions of European music do not explore fully.

The reasons for introducing music from other cultures into our music curricula are to better understand music as a structure of sounds, to appreciate music as a widely varied phenomenon, and to stimulate creativity. In so doing, we teach the lesson of music history. Influence from the musics of other cultures on music is not new. Looking at the Americas, one sees clear evidence of a creative mixture of European and African sonic specialization. In other traditions, melismatic singing within harmonic structures speaks to a combination of Arab influence and European influences. Rock music today builds on earlier genres that themselves drew from several traditions, and world beat music does so even more. Musicians of all kinds, from avant-garde to pop, are creating "fusion" music. Classrooms can explore what fusion means, what is easily fused and what is not. They can explore what music is today by exploring some of its influences. Such study encourages appreciation for diversity but also teaches an analytic approach to sound that is not confined to a single sound system. Students can use these processes every day to encounter the world's musics at home, on the street, and in cyberspace.

How this might be done. Can a person who is not an expert in a musical tradition present it to the class? How many musical traditions should be introduced? How long should one spend on them?

Do you need to be an expert? I don't think so. Teachers who teach Shakespeare are neither Elizabethans nor necessarily poets, and the cultural distance between Elizabethan England and the North side of Chicago is great indeed. The Sumerian epic *Gilgamesh* cannot be taught by Sumerians—there aren't any. If schools can teach other subjects without being either experts or practitioners, why not music? The key word to me is "respectful." Neither the works of Shakespeare nor *Gilgamesh* are taught to belittle them or their originators—and the same must be true of music. One needs to respect traditions, admit that one is not an expert in them, and introduce children to them as well as one can—transmitting the excitement of discovery. Additional listening and opportunities for viewing performances on television or on film can supplement. A person can get "hooked" by a fairly approximate presentation—as long as that person can pursue his or her interests through recordings and other sources. I would tend to start with the sounds of music—because no translation is needed. Of course, some kind of introduction and framing may be required, but children can be exposed to music directly.

How many different traditions should you teach? I have no single good answer to this. But starting with the presupposition that music curricula should teach children about sounds and their structures and uses, I would recommend teaching enough traditions to enable students to develop good ears and creative musical minds. One might teach from the music of Europe for harmonic structures, Africa for rhythmic structures, and India for tonal relationships and improvisation. One could explore traditions that build on these, including, for example, African-American gospel music, rock music, or Indian film music. Another method would be to start with the great gong orchestras of Indonesia and analyze time, and then work with several other traditions and times—tabla drumming and jazz drumming, perhaps.

How "authentic" must the music be? Authenticity is a tricky word, and we need to avoid declaring that a given style or performance is "authentic." With that said, there are different opinions regarding the degree of authenticity that is desirable, even within my family. My uncle Pete Seeger has introduced millions of people to musical traditions by creating easily learned adaptations. How many of those who learned "Wimoweh" sought out the song "Mbube" from which it came? My uncle Mike Seeger painstakingly learns the styles of traditional performers and tries to bring them to new audiences, as an early music performer does. Both approaches can inspire others to pursue their own musical journeys. The key issue for me is that there must be a reason for choosing one or another and that the audience is given a means to learn more about the original. Among the considerations might be the children's age, the existence (or lack) of social context being given in social science or history courses, and the intention of the teacher. For example, for sing-along or play-along participation, adaptations might be more successful; for music related to a place whose history and culture are being studied elsewhere, performances by members of the culture might be preferred.

Part of the solution might lie with the community in which one is teaching. One of the great failures of curricula, it seems to me, is that they all too often leave the rest of the world at the gate to the school, rather than bringing it in as an object of reflection. If one were teaching in a school with strong representation of African-American and Southeast-Asian traditions, one could work with the resources at hand—as long as one used the musics to address general musical issues that fit into the curricular goals of the subject, as well as any other possible use to which they might be put.

One of the more imaginative and creative educational experiments in which I have been peripherally involved is the practice of using the elder members of small rural communities to provide the inspiration for musical creativity, as well as strengthening community pride and intergenerational respect. The University of Alabama's Program for Rural Services and Research (PACERS) Small Schools Cooperative organized a program for a facilitator to go to eleven different small rural public schools for a week or so at each. Early in the week, several elders were invited to talk to the children about growing up and working in their community. During the week, the children would discuss what they had learned, and each classroom would write a song about the experiences of one of the elders. At the end of the week, the elders and members of the community were invited back to listen to the songs the children had written.[4] The program was considered a great success by all, and it had the advantage of involving the communities in the schools, using the community as a source for creative work by the students.

Music and the Other Subjects

Music is a good way to add perspective in other parts of the school curriculum. One need not stop using music after children have learned to count to ten by singing "One, two, buckle my shoe." Students may not have an immediate way to encounter original sources because history can seem dry and abstract, but the songs of different historical periods are lively windows on events—actual pieces of history that students can make their own. The founder of Folkways Records, Moses Asch, knew this and created dozens of educational recordings that were designed for use in

school curricula. He produced collections of songs about specific wars, presidential campaigns, westward migration, and the historical experiences of different peoples. The whole enterprise would have been called "multicultural," had that been a word in the 1950s.

One of my favorite recent releases on Smithsonian Folkways is a collection of campaign songs, one used by each elected United States president[5]—historical curiosities, one might think, until one listens to them. Suddenly, the continuities of American politics come to life: scare campaigns and morality charges in the 1800s that make our own pale by comparison. Consider the implications of this song— one that probably helped John Quincy Adams to the White House in 1837:

> Little know ye who's comin'
> Little know ye who's comin'
> Little know ye who's comin'
> If John QUINCY not be comin'
> Knives are coming
> Guns are coming
> Wars are coming, etc.

The song ends announcing that plagues, pestilence, and the Devil himself will be coming if John Quincy Adams is not elected. That's strong wording and puts "spin doctors" and "attack advertising" into the perspective of hundreds of years of presidential elections.

My own "musical journey" was launched when my sixth-grade class was studying India. I was the only one to study Indian music—others took other subjects—but the discoveries were important to me. The teacher knew nothing about Indian music and didn't need to. I had a library, a record store, and some relatives to ask.

I mentioned music and physical education. Music and sports are often linked. A lot of people jog, pedal, and do other exercises to music, and some interesting new music could be introduced to students in some of these activities. A clever music teacher might introduce Brazilian percussion orchestras to soccer games (adding diversity to the brass bands often played at football games, teaching something about both Brazil and about sounds in the process). Exposure to other people's music does not always mean it has to be the object of study in itself—it can be an adjunct to some other part of the curriculum.

Music Collection and Cultural Experience

The Center for Folklife and Cultural Heritage at the Smithsonian has been working with various communities and school systems on projects that encourage children to learn to do research and collection on the cultural traditions of their own school. Working together with teachers and community scholars, curators have developed small pilot projects that involve children in making collections from their family and then setting up various forms of dissemination at their schools—exhibits, performances, and the like.

This kind of local research was pioneered by the *Foxfire* manuals and projects and continues to offer opportunities for classroom development. The diversity of school populations can be turned to advantage and be made the object of reflection and learning. The real challenge is to establish educational parameters that teachers and school boards can understand and

work within.

With children teaching each other about the cultural traditions that they are uncovering, multicultural experience is an outgrowth of a creative, active, learning process rather than the subject matter of it. I think that the most successful form for multicultural education will be when it is demonstrated in all facets of learning—that one learns more and understands better if the contributions growing out of differences are included in the learning process rather than excluded by it or even eliminated through it. The schools of the next century will have to deal with the increasingly diverse school populations. Every war, famine, or natural disaster sends waves of immigrants from around the world. Pooling our cultural understanding can strengthen our understanding of the world we inhabit—and also our school curricula.

Conclusion

Global transformations brought about by changing communications, worldwide economic processes, and cultural interactions have already begun to shape a world that is richer and more diverse in musical forms and experience. Contemporary composers and performers in virtually every culture are already experimenting with the musical resources (styles, instruments, and effects) of other cultures. This is not a new phenomenon; it has been happening for a very long time. Even before audio recording, local traditions were transformed by new musical ideas and instruments. Earlier "world-music trends" were sparked by a genre (religious hymns, for example, spread rapidly around the world and were adapted by many communities to create new musical forms), or by a new musical instrument (the accordion transformed the ensembles used to play local music in many places around the world), or by a new use of music (the social acceptance of nonreligious dance music opened the way for the exploration of dance music genres).

In the face of all this diversity, what should schools be teaching? Just as American schools teach about the history of different parts of the world because not everything important happened in the United States, so music teaching should include the music of other places because not everything musical happens in the European-derived music that largely makes up the canon of American school music. We should try to keep up with the world in our teaching, because it is in the world that our students will have to apply what they have learned—not only when their education is complete, but every day.

Some of the most effective programs I have seen combine very local research and exploration with globally oriented direction. Bringing the resources of communities into the schools can be very stimulating and effective, and exposing children to the sonic and cultural wealth and diversity around them is a very good preparation for exploring the entire world of sound and of experience. Everyone's musical experience is a journey—for some, it is longer and richer than for others, but these fascinating journeys can begin in our schools, allowing our students to travel in directions we can only imagine.

Acknowledgments

My research on the Suyá Indians has been funded by many organizations in the United States and Brazil, including NIMH, FINEP, Wenner-Gren Foundation, Federal University of Rio de Janeiro, Ford Foundation of Brazil, the John Simon Guggenheim Memorial Foundation, and the Smithsonian Institution. I am grateful to all for their trust and support. This paper was influenced by some enjoyable discussions over the years with Patricia Shehan Campbell, Larry Long, Ella Jenkins, and, most recently, Bennett Reimer and the participants in the seminar at Northwestern University where it was originally presented. The errors and excesses, of course, are all my own.

Notes

1. For a brief ethnographic summary of the Suyá, see Anthony Seeger's essay in *Encyclopedia of World Cultures*, Vol. 7: *South America* (Boston: G. K. Hall & Co., 1991), 314–17, and Patricia Shehan Campbell, "Anthony Seeger on Music of Amazonian Indians," in *Music in Cultural Context: Eight Views on World Music Education* (Reston, VA: MENC, 1992), 26–33; for a brief musical ethnography, see *The Garland Encyclopedia of World Music*, Vol. 2: *South America, Mexico, Central America, and the Caribbean*, ed. Dale A. Olsen and Daniel E. Sheehy (New York: Garland Publishing, 1998), 143–49; for an extensive musical ethnography, see Anthony Seeger, *Why Suyá Sing: A Musical Anthropology of an Amazonian People*, with audiocassette tape of examples (Cambridge: Cambridge Univ. Press, 1987). More general works by Anthony Seeger on Suyá music and society, treating topics raised in this article, include "Oratory Is Spoken, Myth Is Told, and Song Is Sung, but They Are All Music to My Ears," in *Native South American Discourse*, ed. Joel Sherzer and Greg Urban (Berlin: Mouton de Gruyter, 1986), 59–82; "Styles of Musical Ethnography," in *Comparative Musicology and Anthropology of Music: Essays in the History of Ethnomusicology*, ed. Bruno Nettl and Philip Bohlman (Chicago: University of Chicago Press, 1991), 342–55; and "Ethnography of Music," in *Ethnomusicology: An Introduction, New Grove Handbook in Music,* ed. Helen Myers (New York: Macmillan, 1992), 88–109.

2. Nicely described in Patricia Shehan Campbell, *Songs in Their Heads: Music and Its Meaning in Children's Lives* (Oxford: Oxford Univ. Press, 1998).

3. *Smithsonian Folkways Children's Music Collection* (Washington, DC: Smithsonian Folkways Recordings, 1998), SF 45043, track 13.

4. The full description of the methodology and some of the songs can be found on Smithsonian Folkways SF 45050 and also in the song book and teacher's guide by Larry Long, *Guidebook, Elders' Wisdom, Children's Song* (Bethlehem PA: SingOut! Publications, 1999).

5. Oscar Brand, arranger, *Presidential Campaign Songs 1789–1996* (Washington, DC: Smithsonian Folkways Recordings, 1999), CD, SF 45051.

ANTHONY SEEGER, former director of Smithsonian Folkways Recordings and curator of the Folkways Collection at the Smithsonian Institution, has taught anthropology and ethnomusicology at the Museu Nacional in Rio de Janeiro and Indiana University at Bloomington. In 2000, he resumed his academic career as professor of ethnomusicology at UCLA in Los Angeles, California.

Issues Applications and Practices: Diverse Perspectives

7

Passing the Cultural Baton of Music

Ellen McCullough-Brabson

*T*he scintillating tunes of the Beatles from England, the exotic timbres of Ravi Shankar's sitar from India, the protest songs about the Vietnam War in Southeast Asia, and the stirring music of the Civil Rights movement in the United States all had a profound effect on my perception of multiculturalism as a young adult attending college in the late 1960s and early 70s. Nonetheless, I must confess that I did not spend a great deal of time contemplating and examining the issue of cultural diversity. I spent the majority of my free time practicing in a safe and secure conservatory practice room as I tried to master the literature written by Western music composers for my instrument. Not until graduate school did I have a "life-changing" experience that challenged my assumptions about my former narrow and exclusive definition of music.

One of my first graduate classes was taught by a music education professor who was well-traveled, well-read, and well-exposed to music from around the world. During his first lecture, he played a collage of excerpts of music that I had never heard before, representing cultures from all over the globe. He asked us to identify the instruments that we had heard, as well as the geographic location where each was played. Much to my dismay, I was totally clueless regarding the answers. His listening exercise demonstrated that it is probably more accurate to say that music is a human creation that elicits an immediate response from the specific listener, rather than a universal language that assumes instant understanding. His compelling message was that to truly comprehend the music of another culture requires study and exposure.

This first "academic" exposure to world musics was a powerful catalyst for changing how I perceived and defined music. I started to actively seek out and discover new songs, dances, recordings, and instruments from around the world. My graduate work served as a springboard for my desire to travel internationally and hear the sounds of instruments live and in their cultural context. And most importantly, I desired to meet the people who made the music. I owe a great deal of thanks to the graduate professor who taught me to listen to music in multiple ways and seek the meaning behind the sounds. He was the first of many scholars who challenged me to continually examine the Hindu expression "One fire burns in many forms" (Rig Veda, India, c. 3000–2000 B.C.).

Magic Carpet

You have a magic carpet
That will whiz you through the air,
To Spain or Maine or Africa
If you just tell it where.
So will you let it take you
Where you've never been before,
Or will you buy some drapes to match
And use it
On your
Floor?
　　　　—Shel Silverstein, *A Light in the Attic*

119

With the mandate for including world musics in the music education curriculum ringing loud and clear, perhaps there are music educators who wish for a "magic carpet" that can easily transport them and their programs to other places in order to reflect and embrace cultural diversity through music. As this poem suggests, it is much easier to continue doing what we know than to take risks and explore new horizons. However, by examining some pertinent questions and carefully considering their answers, there are ways to discover and create workable methods for including music from around the world in any music education curriculum. Music educators may creatively design and weave the warps and woofs in their magic carpet according to their personal definition of their music culture. Their magic carpet can then act as a springboard for examining the music of other cultures. Three critical questions for this curricular template are (1) what is my culture? (2) what is my musical culture? and (3) how can music educators teach music of another culture effectively?

At first glance, music educators may consider the issue of defining their culture and their musical culture as "givens." However, are the answers to these questions really that simple? Should assumptions about culture and musical culture be taken for granted? Have you ever had to define your culture or your musical culture to a cultural outsider? If you sing a song that represents your culture to a foreigner, will his or her understanding of the song increase if you also explain the cultural context for the song? For example, is the emotional import of "The Battle Hymn of the Republic" heightened if you describe the song in rela-

tion to its context of the American Civil War?

What about exploring the music of another culture? Is an understanding of the music and its cultural context also relevant? A personal story illuminates this point. When traveling in Thailand and Burma, my husband and I saw many hugh bells, often referred to as gongs, hanging in Buddhist temples. We observed people randomly striking these instruments. When we asked our guide about this, he replied that when a person performs a good deed, he or she strikes the gong and is blessed. In addition, anyone in the radius of hearing the tone also receives part of the blessing. Our understanding of this instrument greatly increased when we knew the cultural context. We ended up standing around bells a lot. This is not to say that our response of just listening to the bell was not as good or was diminished if we did not know the context of the instrument performance; it only suggests that the meaning of music is often enhanced when the contextual connection is given.

The close relationship of music and culture is a fundamental principle in ethnomusicology, the study of world musics. The premise is that the more you know about the culture of other people and how music connects to that culture, the more your understanding and appreciation for that culture increases. The same principle is true for ourselves. The more we know about our own culture and musical culture, the more sensitive we will be when exploring the music of others.

By examining questions of culture, musical culture, and those cultures' connections with teaching world musics, educators build a firm foundation that provides a springboard for using multicultural music more effectively. The ordering of these three questions is critical; music educators must start their plan of action, their template design for using world music, with themselves. Once teachers contemplate, analyze, and define their own cultural heritage and musical culture, the pathway to understanding and teaching about other cultures and their musics is made much clearer. This chapter explores these three questions in detail to illustrate this point.

What Is Culture?

Culture is the way we do things.
—*Anonymous*

A fundamental issue at the nucleus of a music education curricular scheme that includes world musics is the question "What is culture?" The word *culture* is a key ingredient in the vocabulary of terms used to promote world musics in the classroom, such as *multiculturalism, cultural diversity,* and *intercultural understanding.* Culture has a myriad of definitions that include descriptions from high platitudes to prosaic explanations—for example, according to *Webster's Third New International Dictionary,* culture is

> the total pattern of human behavior and its products embodied in thought, speech, action, and artifacts and dependent upon man's capacity for learning and transmitting knowledge to succeeding generations through the use of tools, language, and systems of abstract thought … the body of customary beliefs, social forms, and material traits constituting a distinct complex of tradition of a racial, religious, or social group … that complex whole that includes

knowledge, belief, morals, law, customs, opinions, religion, superstition, and art.[1]

Other definitions of culture include "A people's culture is the sum total of their thoughts and actions, learned and transmitted through the centuries of adapting to the natural and human world."[2] And Seelye suggests, "The most widely accepted usage now regards culture as a broad concept that embraces all aspects of the life of man, from folktales to carved whales."[3] In other words, as stated in the most simple and prosaic terms, "culture is the way we do things." But why must music educators first define the term culture? The premise is simple. Before we explore and present facts and figures about other cultures, we must first thoughtfully consider and outline the parameters and idiosyncrasies of our own culture.

A true anecdote illustrates this point. My students were assigned to create their own personal "cultural collages" using the dictionary definition of culture. One of them attempted to define herself via a kaleidoscope of pictures that represented her life story through her family heritage, food, holidays, traditions, celebrations, language, stories, music, sports, and proverbs of her culture. When she saw me on campus one afternoon before the project was due, she exclaimed, "What am I going to do? How can I ever complete this assignment? I do not have a culture! If I were a Native American student in the class, like my Navajo friend is, I could do the project! Then I would have the Navajo language and traditional Navajo customs, regalia, and artifacts to share! I am only an Anglo-American! I wish that I had a culture, too!" I was aghast and calmly replied, "But you really do have a culture! If you have never thought about the issue of culture, you may have to dig deeply to find the answer, but everyone has a culture, even if you are a white, main-streamed American who eats Mexican tortillas, Chinese eggrolls, Greek baklava, and Japanese sushi with equal gusto."

As with the attempt by the student described above, defining one's own culture can be a challenging endeavor. This is true especially for those who live in a multicultural society (such as the United States) and who embrace many diverse aspects of their culture, including cultural icons associated with various ethnic groups. Because this issue is a complex one, the use of the dictionary's definition is an effective tool in analyzing and exploring the definition of culture. For example, the last part of the dictionary's definition, "that complex whole that includes knowledge, belief, morals, law, customs, opinions, religion, superstition, and art" provides an excellent springboard for an in-depth look at the make-up of culture. Table 1 provides a detailed series of questions based on this definition for teachers to examine as they try to identify their own culture and create their own cultural "collage" or anthology.

The questions outlined in Table 1 serve as a beginner's guide to explore the concept of culture from several different perspectives. For example, does the definition reflect one's nationality or is it more individualistic? One university student who completed this assignment, Suzan Stowe, explained her idea of American cultural identity, as well as general ideas about culture, through haiku poetry. She wrote,

I have one question:
What is an American?
Look in the mirror ...

This is my culture:
—Generic-American—
A work in progress ...

What makes a culture?
The people, places, and things
that anchor our lives.

The process of making a list of documents, ideas, and items that represent our culture or a collage or cultural anthology that clarifies our personal identity is an intriguing and, perhaps, complex task. Nonetheless, it reinforces the idea that we all really do have a culture.

The complexity of creating a cultural anthology, in this case on a global scale, was illustrated in the 1970s by Carl Sagan. With his colleagues, he initiated a project in tandem with the Voyager spacecraft program designed to communicate selected aspects of our human world to other entities. The idea of sharing artifacts, ideas, and philosophies of a culture with future generations on Earth is not new. But in the Voyager example, the intent was to share selected parts of Earth's culture with extraterrestrials as well. Sagan describes this endeavor:

On August 20, and September 5, 1977, two extraordinary spacecraft called Voyager were launched to the stars. After what promises to be a detailed and thoroughly dramatic exploration of the outer solar system from Jupiter to Uranus between 1979 and 1986, these space vehicles will slowly leave the solar system—emissaries of Earth to the realm of the stars. Affixed to each Voyager craft is a gold-coated copper phonograph record as a message to possible extraterrestrial civilizations that might encounter

Table 1. Culture Questions

I. Knowledge
   A. What are some of the basic tenets that form the foundation of knowledge of your culture? More specifically, what are the basic tenets of knowledge of your profession?
   B. What cultural artifacts contain the knowledge of your culture? (e.g., the library? an encyclopedia? dictionary? globe? a collection of books? novels? the Internet? television? movies? newspapers? magazines?)
   C. Is knowledge, as used in this context, specific to your culture?
   D. Is the knowledge of your culture universal?

II. Beliefs
   A. What are some of the central beliefs of your culture?
   B. What sources describe or represent the beliefs of your culture? (e.g., the Bible? the Torah? the Koran? the Druid Chronicles? the Pledge of Allegiance? Confucius? Proverbs such as: "Early to bed, early to rise, makes a man healthy, wealthy, and wise"? "The early bird catches the worm"? "Slow and steady wins the race"? "Laugh and the world laughs with you; cry and you cry alone"? "If you live in a glass house, don't throw stones"?)

III. Morals
   A. What are some of the morals that form the central core of your culture?
   B. What sources serve as your guides for the development of morals? (e.g., the Bible? the Torah? talk shows on the radio or television, such as Dr. Laura? *Aesop's Fables,* such as"The Hare and the Tortoise"? movies? books?)

IV. Laws
   A. What are some of the basic laws that guide human behavior in your culture? (e.g., the right to a fair trial? the idea that a person cannot be tried twice for the same crime? the right to free speech?)
   B. What sources depict and describe the laws? (e.g., the Constitution? the Declaration of Independence? traffic laws?)

V. Customs
   A. What are some of the customs of your culture?
      I. Holidays (e.g., what rituals are associated with holidays? do you always watch football games on nationally proclaimed holy days? do you fly the American flag on the Fourth of July? do you have cultural-specific rituals that you perform on selected holidays?)
      2. Celebrations (e.g., do you always sing "Happy Birthday" when you celebrate a birthday?)
      3. Foods (e.g.,do you eat specific foods for certain holidays?)
      4. Clothing (e.g., is there specific clothing worn for various rituals, such as a bridal dress or tuxedo for a wedding? is there a specific outfit prescribed for attending meetings, such as Boy Scout or Girl Scout uniforms? is there a specific time of year to wear the color white, such as after Memorial Day or before Labor Day? are sports clubs associated with specific attire and colors? are marching bands required to wear a prescribed uniform? do symphony musicians always wear formal black?)
      5. Sports (e.g., are there specific customs associated with sporting events, such as spectators standing for the National Anthem?)

VI. Opinions
   A. What are some of the widespread opinions of your culture?
   B. Where are these opinions found? (e.g., the editorial page of a newspaper? from fiction or nonfiction books? from weekly magazines? from the media? nightly news? daily talk shows? the radio?)

VII. Religion
   A. What are some of the religions of your culture? (e.g., Buddhism, Christianity, Judaism, Islam, or others?)
   B. Does your culture support religious freedom?

VIII. Superstitions
   A. What are some of the superstitions of your culture? (e.g., is it bad luck to open an umbrella in the house? is it bad luck when a black cat crosses the path in front of you? is it bad luck to walk under a ladder?)

IX. Art
   A. What are the arts of your culture? (e.g., visual arts, music, dance, drama?)
   B. Are the arts valued in your culture?
   C. Are the arts included as subjects in schools?
   D. Is there a social stratification regarding the status of artists, dancers, musicians, and actors?

Note. This outline is not meant to be inclusive, but serves as a springboard for other questions and ideas. Many questions are intentionally rhetorical.

the spacecraft in some distant space and time. Each record contains 118 photographs of our planet, ourselves and our civilization; almost 90 minutes of the world's greatest music; an evolutionary audio essay on "the sounds of earth;" and greetings in almost sixty human languages (and one whale language), including salutations from the President of the United States and the Secretary General of the United Nations.[4]

Sagan wanted to include unique messages on the recording from our planet that represent human emotions from the perspective of many different cultures; music was his answer:

> There is much more to human beings than perceiving and thinking. We are feeling creatures. However, our emotional life is more difficult to communicate, particularly to beings of very different biological make-up. Music, it seemed to me, was at least a creditable attempt to convey human emotions.[5]

If you were part of Carl Sagan's team on this project, what musical selections would you include for an anthology of "90 minutes of the world's greatest music?" Sagan recounts asking a similar question to Lewis Thomas, biologist and president of the Sloan-Kettering Institute. Thomas replied, "I would send the complete works of Johann Sebastian Bach. But that, 'he added as an aside,' would be boasting."[6] Needless to say, the assignment was quite challenging. Sagan invited several consultants to assist with the task. They included Robert E. Brown, executive director for the Center for World Music in Berkeley; Alan Lomax, director of the Cantometrics Project of Columbia University; Jon Lomberg at the

Canadian Broadcasting Corporation, and Murry Sidlin, then the conductor of the National Symphony Orchestra in Washington, D.C., among others. According to Timothy Farris, co-author of the book, *Murmurs of Earth: The Voyager Interstellar Record,* inclusion of music on the Voyager was based on two criteria: "First, contributions from a wide range of cultures should be included, not just music familiar to the society that launched the spacecraft. Second, nothing should be included out of merely dutiful concerns; every selection should touch the heart as well as the mind."[7] Their selections for the Voyager recording include excerpts from music of Western art music composers such as Bach, Mozart, and Beethoven and American musicians Louis Armstrong and Chuck Berry, as well as the music of the Indonesian *gamelan,* the Japanese *shakuhachi,* and Navajo night chant. (For a complete listing of the record excerpts, please refer to table 2.) One can imagine what a formidable and daunting assignment it was to make decisions regarding the "world's greatest music."

But what if you were asked to complete a similar task—to make an imaginary time capsule as a means of thoroughly describing and defining your own culture, with the intent of sharing your perception of your culture with future generations? What items would you include? Would music be a significant part of your collection? What if you could include only ten artifacts in a time capsule that your progeny would open one hundred years from now? What cultural icons and artifacts would you choose that would best represent you and your culture? It is an intriguing assignment that clarifies and crystallizes the

Table 2. List of Musical Selections on Voyager Record

Bagpipes from the Azerbaijan S.S.R., recorded by Radio Moscow (#15).

Brandenburg Concerto no. 2 in F, first movement, composed by Johann S. Bach, performed by the Munich Bach Orchestra, Karl Richter, conductor (#1).

"Cranes in Their Nest," shakuhachi from Japan, performed by Coro Yamaguchi (#9).

"Dark Was the Night," composed and performed by Blind Willie Johnson (#26).

"El Cascabel," Mexican song performed by Lorenzo Barcelata and the Mariachi México (#6).

"The Fairie Round," from *Paueans, Galliards, Almains and Other Short Aeirs,* composed by Anthony Holborne, performed by David Munrow and the Early Music Consort of London (#21).

Symphony no. 5, first movement, composed by Ludwig van Beethoven, performed by the Philharmonia Orchestra, Otto Klemperer, conductor (#18).

"Flowing Streams," ch'in from China, performed by Kuan P'ing-hu (#24).

"Gavotte en rondeaux" from the Partita no. 3 in E major for Violin, composed by Johann S. Bach, performed by Arthur Grumiaux (#10).

"Izlel je Delyo Hagdutin," Bulgarian folk song, performed by Valya Balkanska (#19).

"Jaat Kahan Ho," raga from India, sung by Surshri Kesar Bai Kerkar (#25).

"Johnny B. Goode," composed and performed by Chuck Berry (#7).

"Kinds of Flowers," court gamelan from Java, recorded by Robert Brown (#2).

"Melancholy Blues," performed by Louis Armstrong and His Hot Seven (#14).

Men's house song from New Guinea, recorded by Robert MacLennan (#8).

"Morning Star" and **"Devil Bird,"** Australian Aborigine songs, recorded by Sandra LeBrun Holmes (#5).

Night chant of the Navajo Indians, recorded by Willard Rhodes (#20).

Panpipes and drum from Peru, collected by Casa de la Cultura, Lima (#13).

Panpipes from the Solomon Islands, collected by the Solomon Islands Broadcasting Service (#22).

Percussion from Senegal, recorded by Charles Duvelle (#3).

Prelude and Fugue in C, **no. 1** from *The Well-Tempered Clavier, Book 2,* composed by Johann S. Bach, performed by Glenn Gould, piano (#17).

Pygmy girls' initiation song from Zaire, recorded by Colin Turnbull (#4).

"Queen of the Night" aria, no. 14, from *The Magic Flute,* composed by Wolfgang A. Mozart, performed by soprano Edda Moser and the Bavarian State Opera, Munich, Wolfgang Saivallish, conductor (#11).

"Sacrificial Dance" from *The Rite of Spring* composed by Igor Stravinsky, performed by the Columbia Symphony Orchestra, Igor Stravinsky, conductor (#16).

String Quartet no. 13 in B flat, Opus 130, "Cavatina," composed by Ludwig van Beethoven, performed by the Budapest String Quartet (#27).

"Tchakrulo," chorus from the Georgian S.S.R., collected by Radio Moscow (#12).

Wedding song from Peru, recorded by John Cohen (#23).

Note. This list was reported in Carl Sagan, E. D. Drake, Ann Druyan, Timothy Ferris, Jon Lombert, and Linda Saltzman Sagan, *Murmurs of Earth: The Voyager Interstellar* (New York: Random House, 1978), 204–05. Parenthetical numbers signify the sequence in which the musics were placed on the original Voyager Record.

parameters of culture. Admittedly, there are many definitions of culture. However, this exercise builds a firm foundation for answering the second and more personal question in the template sequence design for including world musics in the curriculum: what is your musical culture?

What is your musical culture?

Know thyself.
—Inscription at the Temple of Apollo at the
Oracle at Delphi, as quoted
in Plutarch, *Morals*

Ethnomusicologists examine and study music as a part of culture, not as an isolated part of life. Indeed, according to Bruno Nettl, "Music can be understood only in its cultural context."[8] This paradigm is often in marked contrast to the role music plays in the school curriculum. Educators often label music as a separate class and treat it as an subject isolated from the "real world," an "out-of-context experience." Indeed, many other subjects are treated in the same way. Therefore, music educators may easily come to view music in the same manner—as a subject to be taught in isolation from any context.

A plethora of stimulating and enriching publications that effectively outline how to teach the music of other cultures takes exception to this approach. These materials carefully discuss and examine world musics in their cultural contexts and the situated meaning of the music. By using these texts, music educators may embrace world musics and more successfully teach music from other cultures. However, herein lies the problem; when asked about their own musical cultures, these same music educators are often stymied. They have never

carefully examined who they are musically because they have never considered their own musical cultures in context and meaning. In fact, they may often respond with great humbleness that their musical cultures may not be "exotic" enough nor even worthy of notice—especially if they identify with the mainstreamed musical culture that is the cultural "given."

Nonetheless, the second part of the template design for including world musics in the curriculum hinges on the idea that the recognition and definition of one's own musical culture enhances and prepares the way for understanding music from other people. As stated earlier, some educators view "cultural context" as an abstract precept or a process that only applies to other musics. However, when teachers explore and examine the idea of cultural context on a personal level—from their own unique perspectives—new insights are gained. For example, what is the cultural context behind the songs "The Star-Spangled Banner," "Happy Birthday," or "We Shall Overcome"? Is your understanding of the connection between culture and musical culture increased by examining these songs and your own life experiences as they relate to them? The answer suggested in this chapter is a resounding "Yes!" Knowing yourself and your own musical culture is a fundamental part of the sequence and process of establishing a music program using world musics. Therefore, we must again ask the question: what is your musical culture?

Many questions stem from this basic query: Does your musical culture include music from the past as well as the present? Does it include music from around the world and other ethnic groups because you value it and feel a personal connection to it? Does it only include music that you really like to sing, listen to, or perform? Would the selection criteria established for the Voyager be your guide (music that "should touch the heart as well as the mind")? If not, what are your criteria for inclusion? For example, would you choose music that represents different decades of your culture? Or, would you choose music from different genres, such as classical, pop, country, rap, rock, or music written only by composers from your own country? And further, if you are a citizen of the United States, do you agree that there is a common American musical culture? If so, how would you define it? Would cultural "outsiders" describe a country's musical culture in the same way? Is defining your country's musical culture the same as describing your own? These are complex issues. The following true story illustrates the challenge of understanding a national musical culture from an outsider's perspective.

A group of American tourists were staying at a hotel in southwestern Turkey in early June. As the hotel employees were preparing dinner, they put on a cassette tape of what they perceived to be "American music." They were sure that their guests would enjoy their entertainment effort. Much to their surprise, the guests laughed heartily as they heard a collage of Christmas carols and tunes that ranged from "Silent Night" to "Feliz Navidad." Convinced that their guests were enjoying the music, the Turkish hosts played it again and again the entire night. They were unaware of the traditional and appropriate cultural context for the per-

formance of Christmas music. Citizens from the United States expect to hear Christmas music in December, not as background music in June. Suffice it to say, cultural insiders usually have the upper hand with regard to music that is representative of their culture. But who speaks for a musical culture? What is American music? What music authentically represents the citizens of the United States of America? No doubt each music educator would define American music differently.

The Music Educators National Conference (MENC) tried to identify one aspect of the musical culture of the United States when it published a list of forty-three songs that all Americans can know and sing. As illustrated in table 3, the majority of these songs reflect the Anglo-European American heritage. To MENC's credit, it includes such diverse songs as the "Battle Hymn of the Republic," "Havah Nagilah," "Sakura," and "Zip-a-Dee-Doo-Dah." But who decided that these songs were the most representative? Would all music educators agree with the song selections? If not, what songs should be added or deleted?

Music educators need to have the opportunity to examine, ponder, and describe their own musical cultures. However, as one begins to identify all the different types of music that bombard a person—even in one day, much less all of the music one has ever heard—defining a musical culture becomes quite challenging. Should one's "musical fingerprint" or "musical DNA" include music from the past and the present? What is a logical starting place for this process? Jeff Titon, editor of *Worlds of Music,* suggests an organizational strategy for outlining and discovering a musical culture. He recom-

Table 3. Forty-Three Songs for All Americans to Know and Sing

"Amazing Grace"
"America (My Country, 'Tis of Thee)"
"America, the Beautiful"
"Battle Hymn of the Republic"
"Blue Skies"
"Danny Boy"
"De Colores"
"Dona Nobis Pacem"
"Do-Re-Mi"
"Down by the Riverside"
"Frère Jacques"
"Give My Regards to Broadway"
"God Bless America"
"God Bless the U.S.A."
"Green, Green Grass of Home"

"Havah Nagilah"
"He's Got the Whole World in His Hands"
"Home on the Range"
"I've Been Working on the Railroad"
"If I Had a Hammer"
"Let There Be Peace on Earth"
"Lift Ev'ry Voice and Sing"
"Michael, Row the Boat Ashore"
"Music Alone Shall Live"
"My Bonnie Lies over the Ocean"
"Oh! Susanna"
"Oh, What a Beautiful Mornin' "
"Over My Head"
"Puff the Magic Dragon"
"Rock-a-My Soul"

"Sakura"
"Shalom Chaverim"
"She'll Be Comin' 'round the Mountain"
"Shenandoah"
"Simple Gifts"
"Sometimes I Feel Like a Motherless Child"
"The Star-Spangled Banner"
"Swing Low, Sweet Chariot"
"Take Me Out to the Ballgame"
"This Land Is Your Land"
"This Little Light of Mine"
"Yesterday"
"Zip-a-Dee-Doo-Dah"

Note. Compiled by MENC: The National Association for Music Education; published in *Get American Singing ... Again* (Milwaukee, WI: Hal Leonard, 1996).

mends exploring a musical culture by examining (1) ideas about music (e.g., belief system, aesthetics, contexts, and history of music), (2) the social organization of music, (3) the repertoire of music (e.g., styles, genres, texts, composition, transmission, and movement), and (4) the material culture.[9] These ideas provide an excellent framework for describing and defining any musical culture, whether one's own or another's.

In order to illustrate this point in the design of world musics curricula suggested here, I put myself in the role of a culture-bearer. The inclusion of this brief musical ethnography should reinforce a simple but profound idea: each music educator has a musical culture to share, explore, and celebrate. By asking yourself similar questions, as illustrated in this musical ethnography, you may find a wealth of information about

yourself and your musical culture. When you start with yourself, there is an immediacy to understanding all the ideas Titon lists (see above) as critical points to consider in examining another musical culture. Because you have "lived" the music, the questions asked are not abstract concepts applied to cultural "others." Your personal musical ethnography resonates with meaning because you have made the effort to explore, examine, and relate these ideas to your past and present musical experiences. Although I could have followed the complete outline as described by Titon for my musical ethnography, I chose to focus on three ideas that appear frequently in texts and materials for teaching multicultural music education. These questions are: what is the music repertoire of the culture? what is the context for the performance of the music repertoire? and what does the music mean? Due to space considerations, I have focused only on a few musical experiences of my early childhood.

Musical Ethnography

Question: Please describe your culture. I am a white American, a product of the culture of the United States of America. When I complete forms that say "Indicate your race," I check Anglo-American or European-American. Sometimes I have to check the box that says, 'other.' I identify with contemporary cultural icons that include the Internet, McDonald's hamburgers, Disneyland, the Super Bowl, and Beanie Babies. Although my roots are from Scotland, Ireland, and Germany, my family is so many generations removed from these countries that I do not identify with them. We never heard Scottish bagpipes in my home, nor did we perform an Irish jig or celebrate German Oktoberfest. The only vestiges of my distant roots that connect me to them are my mother's insistence that we eat sauerkraut and pork for New Year's Day (to bring good luck in the new year) and the theology of Martin Luther, a German, and his profound impact on Lutheranism. Of course, the holiday traditions of decorating a Christmas tree, hanging a stocking for Santa Claus to fill, and hiding Easter eggs at Easter are still time-honored family traditions. And I do say the word "Gesundheit!" when I hear someone sneeze.

Question: Describe your earliest childhood musical memories. Focus on the music repertoire, the context of the musical experience, and what the music meant to you. I was born in the early 1950s in a medium-sized, Midwestern city in north-central Ohio. My earliest musi-

cal memories are from early childhood, before kindergarten; I remember with great fondness my mother affectionately singing a lullaby to me. Phrases filled with the vocables, "Bye–o–bye–o–bye–…," still linger in my ear. The meaning behind the song is the expression of human love that resonates from mother to child. When I asked my mother how she learned this song, she replied that her mother probably sang it to her. She can remember my grandmother singing it to other children in the family, too. I sang this song for my daughter and son when they were babies and hope that they will sing this song and pass the 'cultural baton of music' to their children as well.

I also remember singing in the Cherub Choir at the cavernous Lutheran Church we attended downtown. We sang with a huge group of children and literally filled the front steps that led to the altar in the sanctuary. Pictures documenting this event are adorable. We wore shiny white robes with brightly colored red ribbons tied around our necks. As one parent put it, "When you look that cute, who cares what you sound like?" I can still sing all of the words to a variety of songs that our choir directors taught us, such as "The B-I-B-L-E," "Jesus Loves Me," and "There Were Three Jolly Fishermen." The meaning of these songs, as illustrated in the lyrics, was to teach us about our religion and faith. We learned most of the tunes by rote and repetition, even though we had songsheets with the words printed on them. Because we liked singing these catchy tunes, we sang these songs other times than at church, too.

We joyfully sang in the car as my family and I rode back and forth to family reunions or vacations. Since our car did not have a radio, my sisters and I, and sometimes my mother and father, supplied the music. My mother usually saved her favorite song, "Tell Me Why," for when it was dark outside. When she sang it, it was as if she had spun a cocoon of security around our car as it sped toward home. I believe that she captured the spirit of the song quite beautifully.

Question: Please give a summary of your early childhood musical experiences. If I had to select a word that describes my early childhood musical experiences, it would be that of joy. The songs that I sang and the instrumental pieces I played are associated with warm, special memories of the people who shared the gift of music with me. I learned songs in many contexts: my family sang them in the car, my friends shared them at school, I heard them on television, or a classroom teacher taught them to me. Because I did not have a radio at the time, the world of pop music was alien to me until I attended junior high. With the exception of church choir rehearsals and piano and viola lessons, most of my musical knowledge was learned by rote.

The music of my early childhood clearly represents part of my culture and my heritage. Most of my song repertoire is labeled Anglo-American or European-American. Since multiculturalism was not in vogue when I was a young child, I did not learn any songs in other languages or from different cultures that I can recall. An exception may be "Kumbayah," although I do not remember it ever being identified as a song from South Africa. Every year in elementary school, we sang Christmas carols, and Santa Claus came to hand out candy. I did not know about Chanukah or Kwanzaa until I started teach-

ing. There is no doubt that I was raised in a culture where Anglo-American music, customs, and traditions dominated.

In summary, my musical culture reflects my family traditions and customs, as well as the contemporary "outside culture" of the United States. It also mirrors my classical training in Western music. Since music is such an integral part of my daily life, my cultural collage of music is complex. I embrace all different types of music. If I chose ten songs or musical works that described my musical culture to share with future generations, I would select representative music from my past and present. My list of music resonates and celebrates my individual heritage, as well as my national culture.

Table 4 gives a brief overview and analysis of information gleaned from this autobiographical musical ethnography. As table 4 illustrates, a self-examination of your personal musical culture allows you to consider the concepts of music repertoire, context, and meaning in a personal way. You could even include more detail, if you use the model given by Titon as the basis for your analysis of your musical culture.

Conducting your own musical ethnography illuminates the way for the presentation of world musics because an understanding of culture and music increases as you learn to define your musical self. This process heightens awareness of the timeline between a person's musical past and present, sensitizes us to the importance of cultural context, allows us to explore and examine the meaning of music in our own lives, challenges us to question assumptions about how we learn music, and compels us to know that each of us—even white, mainstreamed Anglo-Americans—has a musical

Table 4. Personal Musical Ethnography—Selected Repertoire, Context, and Meaning

Repertoire	Context	Meaning
"Bye–o–bye–o"	Lullaby sung by a mother to her child	Taught familial love; lulled child to sleep
"B-I-B-L-E" and "Jesus Loves Me"	Lutheran Church Children's Choir	Taught faith, religion
"Tell Me Why"	A song sung in the car when travelling	Shared a song via oral tradition from one generation to the next … Made the time pass

culture to share and celebrate.

An intriguing exercise to consider next is to compare your musical ethnography with the musical ethnography of someone in your own culture. There is no doubt that they are different, a fact that dramatically illustrates how difficult it is to define a common music culture and how complex each culture can be. But perhaps the most compelling reason to conduct your own musical ethnography is to create a series of questions that unlock information about your musical culture. The series of questions that you design then serves as the basis for interviewing someone else from your own or another culture. Once you, as a music educator, can "know thyself," the path to the exploration of teaching world musics is easier to follow.

Teaching Music of Another Culture

As the traveler who has once been from home is wiser than he who has never left his own doorstep, so a knowledge of one other culture should sharpen our ability to scrutinize more steadily, to appreciate more lovingly, our own.

—Margaret Mead,
Coming of Age in Samoa, 1928

Once music educators have gone through the process of examining their own culture and musical culture, the stage is set to explore the culture and music of others. Although there are many ways, the two most common approaches are (1) to examine, evaluate, and select published multicultural materials that are specifically designed to teach world musics (many of these resources provide excellent strategies with accompanying recordings for use in the classroom at a variety of grade levels, including elementary, middle school, and high school), and (2) to connect with a person from another culture in order to learn first-hand the culture and music of the "cultural insider." Although very time-consuming, the latter method is often the most enriching and personally fulfilling. Each of these approaches offers insight into teaching music from a global perspective.

Evaluating and Selecting Teaching Materials

Many years ago, it was not uncommon to find a song or singing game in an elementary music series that had a label like "Song from Africa." The song may have had

African words, but did not include a translation, any information about the song's cultural context, an explanation as to whether the singing game was traditional, or instructions as to whether boys and girls could participate. In addition, the recording that accompanied the song often sounded as if it used Western instruments and singers, rather than African musicians. Music educators were often stymied by this. What did the label "Song from Africa" really mean? Did it represent African musical culture, and, if so, which one?

Another example of what has confounded music educators involves translation. Even though translation of words from one language to another is very subjective, music educators deserve to have some consistency about the message of the song. For instance, three resources have three completely different interpretations of the song, "Che Che Koolay," a singing game from Ghana, Africa. It is fair to note, however, that the language of the song is not codified, making the many different spellings of the title understandable. Nonetheless, the variance in translation of the words is mystifying.

One source indicates that the words of "Che Che Koolay" are most probably vocables (i.e., meaningful sounds that have no translation).[10] Another source states that the words mean: "I give thanks for good thoughts, for clothes for my shoulders, and food for my stomach. I will dance for you."[11] And the third source gives two contradictory views. The recording notes for the song indicate that the words are vocables and have no translation. However, in the text of the accompanying music book, the words are translated, "If you're out in the ocean on your boat, return quickly, rain is

coming.[12] What is a music educator to do? What source do you believe? Which translations and interpretations are accurate?

These two examples support the need for authors and publishers to supply materials for music educators that accurately represent the music of the culture. Fortunately, multicultural music education materials improved tremendously during the last quarter of the twentieth century. Resources that explore the cultural context and meaning of the music, give detailed information regarding the pronunciation of the words and their translation, provide appropriate accompaniment, and make personal connections with members of the culture are exemplary models. A thorough set of criteria for evaluating multicultural music materials, published in Campbell and Scott-Kassner's book, *Music in Childhood,* outlines critical questions.[13]

The guide in table 5 provides important questions to consider as music educators prepare multicultural music materials for their curriculum, whether they teach elementary, middle school, or high school music. Although each point listed merits its own discussion, space limitations allow only for a brief discussion of the issue that music educators raise most frequently: authenticity.

Authenticity

What is authenticity? Why are music educators concerned about it? Several years ago, Bruno Nettl, renowned ethnomusicologist, led a seminar for ethnomusicology students and music educators at the University of Washington. The music educators in attendance quizzed him frequently regarding the issue of authenticity—especially in the context of evaluating music

Table 5. Guide to Authenticity in the Selection of Music

1. Is the recorded music performed by a musician from within the culture? Is the printed music notated, transcribed, and/or attributed to a musician from within the culture? Is a scholar with training and experience within the culture involved in the recording or notating of the score?

2. Are notated instrumental pieces characteristic of the musical style, rather than arrangements for instruments outside the tradition?

3. If a song contains lyrics, are they in the original language? Are they accompanied by a guide to pronunciation? Is an English translation provided? Is it literal, or amended to "fit" the melodic rhythm?

4. If a song involves a game, dance, or movement, are the instructions clear for how to perform it? Is there a photograph, a diagram, an illustration, and/or a clear outline of how to perform the game, dance, or movement?

5. Is there a recorded version of the song or instrumental piece to be performed, so that the "real" music can be heard, used as a model, and later compared to the children's version?

6. Is a cultural context provided for the music? Are there accompanying notes or a book to offer a description of the culture—values; customs; and historical, geographic, and economic issues—that may add to an understanding of the music? What is known of the function and meaning of the music to the people who make it?

Note. This table, which is itself adapted from Judith Cook Tucker, appears in Patricia Shehan Campbell and Carol Scott-Kassner, "Table 13. 1, Guide to Authenticity in the Selection of Music," *Music in Childhood* (New York: Schirmer Books, 1995), 321.

education materials. One day, he finally exclaimed that, to paraphrase his thoughts, ethnomusicologists defined authenticity out of existence in the 1950s. He reminded the participants that the only constant in life is change. There will always be interaction between people of one culture and another and the music that they make. There will always be new and different interpretations of traditional and contemporary music.

Nonetheless, music educators have raised an outcry for music materials that are "authentic," that accurately represent the music of another culture. But what does "authentic" mean? What is the ulti-mate factor that determines whether a music is truly "authentic"? Is music authentic if a culture-bearer contributes it? Do all members of the culture need to agree that the music is, indeed, representative of the culture? Or, should the musicians and performers of the music of the culture, the "music-makers," ultimately decide what music is authentic? To further explore this, consider the authenticity issue with regard to the most bona fide title for the famous early childhood song, "The Eency Weency Spider." The columnist Dave Barry addresses this topic in his column entitled, "Name That Spider:"

The No. 1 issue facing us right now, of course, is the issue of exactly what we, as a nation, should call the spider in the song about the spider who went up the water spout…. I always thought the correct name was the "Inky Dinky" spider, but, recently, when I conducted a scientific survey on this in my newspaper office, I was shocked at the wide variety of responses people gave, such as: the "Hinky Dinky" spider; the "Eency Beensy" spider; the "Eency Weensy" spider; the "Itty Bitty" spider; the "Itsy Bitsy" spider …. So I had my large research staff call Directory Assistance, and they told him it was the (for heaven's sake) "Hokey Dokey" spider.[14]

What do you think? What is the most "authentic" title for this well-known early childhood song? Does it really matter? Further, let us consider the multiple recordings of the song. Which is the most authentic? Is it a recording of a young child singing the song by herself? Or, is it the Sharon, Lois, and Bram version of the song that humorously portrays three different interpretations of the spider singing the song? Or, is it the Carole King or Little Richard rendition? No doubt, the responses to these questions vary greatly. Could it be that each version is "authentic" in its own context? Perhaps there is no "right" answer to these questions because the issue of authenticity interconnects so closely with cultural context.

The topic of authenticity is a big issue with many parameters, definitions, and interpretations. Perhaps the most valuable lesson for music educators to remember is to constantly, consistently, ask the question "Is this music authentic?" and then consider the guidelines for evaluating authenticity that are outlined in table 5.

Cultural Connections

The second approach to teaching the music of another culture is to make a cultural connection with a "cultural insider," someone who is willing to share the music of his or her culture with you. The questions "what is your culture?" and "what is your musical culture?" are directed to someone other than one's self, offering the perspective of looking outward, rather than inward. These two questions are standard queries in ethnomusicological research and serve as a solid framework for exploring multicultural music.

The first essential step in this design is to compile basic background information, as suggested in table 1, about a selected culture. Because this is a time-intensive task, one may question the relevance of this activity. However, preparing an "insider's guide" to the makeup of another culture is critical in understanding music and its cultural context. It is impossible to know what questions to ask about the music of another culture until you know something about that culture and its cultural values. Even though there are many excellent resources that skillfully illustrate this model and that are practical and workable for use in the classroom, the process of preparing at least one cultural study on your own is invaluable. Exploring the background of a culture provides a firm foundation for the examination of the culture's music from an outsider's perspective.

After gathering the research, the next step is to interview a "cultural insider," someone who knows the culture and its music from the inside out. This is the most challenging part. What if you cannot find such a person? Keep in mind that no one person will know all the cultural context for even a single song (unless he or she wrote it!). Selecting a culture for study for which you know you can find a cultural insider to interview is better than arbitrarily choosing a culture with no consideration made for personal contacts. Even though it is not always possible to find a person from the culture whose input will make the culture come to life, personal contact with another human being is by far the most powerful connection in the process of sharing the music of another culture. For example, only when I had the opportunity to meet and develop friendships with Navajo elders and students in my classes did the culture and music of the Diné (Navajo) rise to a higher level of understanding for me. Granted, expecting this connection to occur when studying every culture in the multicultural curriculum is unrealistic. Nonetheless, even if it only happens once, it is a life-changing experience. A brief account of my friendship with Ruth Roessel, a Navajo elder and culture-bearer, illustrates many lessons that I learned while sharing a culture's music from a cultural insider's perspective.

Ruth Roessel

I first met Ruth Roessel many years ago at the Navajo Nation Inn in Window Rock, Arizona, capital city of the Navajo Nation. One of my Navajo students, Leroy Morgan, arranged the interview for me. I was in search of Navajo children's songs that were appropriate for "cultural outsiders" to sing. Leroy informed me that an excellent resource was Ruth Roessel, whom he

described as a "Navajo Nation treasure." His analysis was correct. From that first encounter to the present, Ruth has willingly shared music from her culture. In addition, she has taught me a rich variety of information about her traditions, her customs, her philosophy, and her people, the Diné.

Ruth has lived her whole life in Round Rock, Arizona, a tiny community just outside of Chinle, Arizona, home of the spectacular Canyon de Chelly. She is "born of" (maternal clan) Kiiyaé' ą́ą́nii anii (Towering House Clan) and "born for" (paternal clan) TóDích'íi'nii (Bitter Water Clan). Her father was a medicine man and raised her and her siblings to live the Diné way, to follow "the corn pollen rule," to live the traditional life of the Navajo. She is an authority on many traditional Navajo customs, like raising sheep and rug-weaving. In fact, her son, Monty Roessel, a photojournalist, wrote a book entitled *Songs from the Loom,* in honor of his mother and her craft.[15] Ruth has also authored a book describing the traditional life of a Navajo woman, *Women in Navajo Society,* in which she proclaims her philosophy: "I believe in my culture. I am a Navajo and I am proud of it; therefore, it makes me who I am and what I am."[16]

I had the great pleasure to interview Ruth many times and to attend all the classes that she has taught on Navajo culture, music, and dance at my university. She makes the research data and books written about Navajo culture come to life. Ruth gracefully and beautifully shares her thoughts, feelings, and wisdom about the Navajo creation story; the Holy People; Changing Woman and her twin sons

Monster-Slayer and Child-Born-of-Water; clans; hogans; sheep herding; the Long Walk; the Sheep Reduction Program; Navajo code-talkers; and a myriad of other topics.

My husband and I had the honor of attending the traditional wedding of Ruth's son in her hogan at Round Rock, which was beautiful and profoundly moving. Along with the other family members of the bride, I helped prepare and serve the customary meal for the guests. Nothing that I have read about in a book comes close to participating in the actual experience. Ruth has taught me many things about the traditional Diné way of life by giving me the opportunity to experience her culture on-site, in its cultural context. However, the most significant idea that she shared with me is one that impacts her daily life: she firmly believes in, respects, and honors the Holy People. These deities gave the Navajo everything in their lives, including music, song, and dance. Ruth strives to live her life in beauty and harmony; she personifies the word *hózhó*, which refers to "an all-encompassing philosophy that supplies the underlying framework for the Diné value system and way of life."[17] Her unselfish sharing of her culture provides a firm foundation when I use traditional Navajo music in the classroom.

Teaching Navajo Music

My friendship with Ruth Roessel has given me many insights into ways to use Navajo music in the classroom:

■ Since all Navajo music is ultimately a gift from the Holy People, music educators must respect both sacred and secular genres of their music.

■ It is inappropriate to perform ceremonial music of the Diné out of context.

■ Although non-Navajos can sing and dance during certain social music, there are strictures regarding the correct time to perform even this music that should be honored.

■ Navajo games and Navajo stories also involve time strictures that should be adhered to. The Diné tell coyote tales only between the first frost of winter and the first thunder of spring. Navajos respect the same time frame when playing string- and shoe-games.

■ Be flexible when using terminology. Navajos may refer to the same traditional dances in different ways. For example, the "two-step" may also be called the "skip" dance step. It is best to watch the dancers and follow their lead.

■ Celebrate the Navajo culture, but do not romanticize it. As the adage goes, "People are people." Most of the cultural problems that plague the broader outside culture exist in the Navajo Nation, too.

■ Listen and learn. Try your best to sing Navajo music using Navajo words. If the music uses a traditional nasalized singing style, try to model it.

■ Consider Navajo clan relationships when asking students to dance with each other. It is inappropriate for Navajo men or boys to dance with women or girls of the same clan.

■ Be a risk-taker. If you sincerely want to learn about the music of another culture to include in your curriculum, be willing to make mistakes, pick up the pieces, and make adjustments. The rewards of sharing multicultural music with your students are well worth your efforts.

Whether using published music resources or music materials collected from a cultural insider, the ultimate goal is to use multicultural music in the curriculum with sensitivity, integrity, and respect.

Conclusion

The answers to the three questions—(1) what is my culture? (2) what is my musical culture? and (3) how can music educators teach music of another culture effectively?—lay a firm foundation for a curricular design that includes world musics. The examination and exploration of our own culture and musical culture, as well as the music of others, provide us with rich, vibrant, and colorful fabrics as we weave our own magic carpet, transporting us "to where we've never been before," as we explore the amazing musical sounds of the world.

Notes

1. *Webster's Third New International Dictionary* (Springfield, MA: G. & C. Merriam Company, 1976).

2. Jeff Todd Titon, *Worlds of Music: An Introduction to the Music of the World's People*, 2nd ed. (New York: Schirmer, 1992), xxi.

3. H. Ned Seelye, *Teaching Culture: Strategies for Intercultural Record* (Lincolnwood, IL: National Textbook Co., 1987), 26.

4. Carl Sagan, F. D. Drake, Ann Druyan, Timothy Ferris, Jon Lombert, and Linda Saltzman Sagan, *Murmurs of Earth: The Voyager Interstellar* (New York: Random House, 1978), preface.

5. Ibid., 13.

6. Ibid.

7. Ibid., 162.

8. Bruno Nettl, "Ethnomusicology: Definitions, Directions, and Problems," *Musics of Many Cultures*, ed. Elizabeth May (Berkeley, CA: University of California Press, 1980), 7.

9. Titon, *Worlds of Music*, 6.

10. Abraham Kobena Adzinyah, Dumisani Maraire, and Judith Cook Tucker, *Let Your Voice Be Heard! Songs from Ghana and Zimbabwe* (Danbury, CT: World Music Press, 1986), 12.

11. Barbara Staton, Merrill Staton, Marilyn Davidson, and Susan Snyder, *Music and You: Grade K* (New York: Macmillan, 1988), 217.

12. Sharon, Lois, and Bram, *Elephant Jam* (Toronto: McGraw-Hill Ryerson, Ltd., 1980). Recording: Sharon, Lois, and Bram, *Smorgasbord*, Elephant Records, 1979.

13. Patricia Shehan Campbell and Carol Scott-Kassner, *Music in Childhood* (New York: Schirmer Books, 1995). This guideline is adapted from an earlier publication by Judith Cook Tucker.

14. Dave Barry, "Name that Spider," *IMPACT: Albuquerque Journal Magazine,* January 20, 1987, p. 2.

15. Monty Roessel, *Songs from the Loom,* (Minneapolis, MN: Lerner Publications, 1995).

16. Ruth Roessel, *Women in Navajo Society* (Rough Rock, AZ: Navajo Resource Center, 1981).

17. Ellen McCullough-Brabson and Marilyn Help, *We'll Be in Your Mountains, We'll Be in Your Songs: A Navajo Woman Sings* (Albuquerque, MN: University of New Mexico Press, 2001), 37.

ELLEN MCCULLOUGH-BRABSON, professor of music education at the University of New Mexico, has presented workshops on multicultural music education nationally and internationally and has co-authored *Roots and Branches: A Legacy of Multicultural Music for Children* with Patricia Shehan Campbell and Judith Cook Tucker and *We'll Be in Your Mountains, We'll Be in Your Songs: A Navajo Woman Sings* with Marilyn Help.

8

Teaching Unfamiliar Styles of Music

Milagros Agostini Quesada

As a piano student in my childhood years, I was trained in the European art music tradition. True to the approach to music teaching that prevailed among the conservatory-trained instructors in my native Puerto Rico, I was discouraged from playing by ear or studying any music that was not from the "classical" repertoire. My attempts at those musics, which faithfully continued through my school years in spite of my teachers' admonitions, included popular and traditional Hispanic music styles. The styles that I enthusiastically tried ranged from boleros, Cuban rumbas and guarachas, Puerto Rican plenas and aguinaldos, Dominican merengues, Trinidadian calypsos, and Peruvian waltzes to other styles and rhythms of African, Indian, Spanish, or mixed origins. I liked these musics, but I never played them for my teachers.

Later, as a classically trained music teacher in the city of Ponce, my hometown, I was assigned to a middle school located at the center of a "barrio" where Afro-Puerto-Rican styles were the heart and soul of the community's musical expression. In a desperate attempt to reach the students, who seemed unreachable at the time, I began to utilize in my classes those styles from my unacknowledged musical past. Thus began a process of validation that eventually led to a minor in ethnomusicology and a deep commitment to the teaching of world musics. In addition, I expanded my area of interest to include the formal study of the music of Thailand, playing in a Thai ensemble for nine years. Not only did I finally legitimize a part of my musical past, but in the process I realized that one never learns as much about one's own music as when one studies another's.

Introduction

As a field of study, music education has kept close partnerships with other disciplines such as education, psychology, aesthetics, and areas related to physiology, computer technology, or any field bearing a relationship to music performance as well as teaching and learning. Issues in general education particularly have traditionally crossed over to our field, with the subsequent adaptation of terminology to the profession's needs. Concurrently, concerns have been raised regarding how this borrowing of terms has affected issues idiosyncratic to our field. Such has been the case with the use of the term "multiculturalism" in music education. Many meanings ascribed to this term have been scrutinized and re-interpreted so extensively that it has become, as Terese Volk points out, among the most discussed topics in twentieth-century American education. The original concept has been expanded from a reference to the diverse cultural components in the

United States, along with the intent to teach an enhanced understanding of the world, to an all-encompassing complex of ideas that include differences in religion, gender, socioeconomic status, and exceptionality.[1]

With the use of the term "multiculturalism" in music education, the variety of interpretations that has characterized this concept has inevitably been transferred to our profession. In music education, the word's meaning is generally understood to be more applicable to differences in ethnicity than to differences among cultural subgroups (or subcultural groups). However, in a characteristically kaleidoscopic approach, a variety of competing terms are used within the profession to designate musics from different ethnocultural groups in the United States or from different geographical areas in the world. "World musics," "multiethnic," "ethnic," "folk," and, of course, "multicultural" are some of the designations that have been used for musics that convey ethnocultural identities.[2]

The meeting of minds in tune with "multicultural" music education, which took place at the Northwestern University Music Education Leadership Seminar during June 1998, highlighted not only the kaleidoscopic nature of the term, but also innumerable issues that arise from the problems encountered when teaching musics outside the Western art music tradition. Regardless of the labels we choose, these issues remain difficult to address, but lack of clarity and consistency in our use of terminology only magnifies the problems.

Areas of concern range from a lack of knowledge of the musics to the use of methodology more in tune with traditional European art music education than approaches specifically geared to world musics. The logistic, practical, and philosophical difficulties involved in "transferring" firsthand experiences with these musics which are created in a variety of contexts and for a variety of venues to the public-school classroom, are themselves a major issue. Moreover, because concerns about the teaching of musics from the world can be addressed from different perspectives (i.e., those of the teacher, student, music, and culture), there are endless possibilities for discussion. The problems seem complex enough to make us throw up our hands in frustration and declare the situation hopeless.

However, from my distinguished colleagues at the Symposium, I learned that there need be no chaos in this situation. Indeed, clearly articulated sets of questions dealing with different aspects of the topic consistently emerged during Symposium discussions. Raising good questions is as important as giving good answers—some even argue that the questions are more important in setting new directions within areas of human knowledge and in keeping the old ones fresh and vital. In this important dimension and the subsequent intellectual introspection that it caused in its participants, the Symposium was fully successful.

Questions raised were related to issues that are always present: what terminology to use, which musics to teach, how to train teachers for this, who are the experts in these styles, and how much of an expert the teacher needs to be. In addition, questions dealing with authenticity, context of the music, and teaching methodologies were considered.

Faced with such a vast array of questions, we need to be discriminating with regard to the type of problems that we choose to address. Some issues are unavoidably more urgent because of restrictions imposed by our current situation; the fact that most universities in the nation do not offer courses in musics other than those derived from the European art tradition imposes priorities. Moreover, before taking on the questions that we choose to address, we need to independently accept the fact that we can only hope to resolve complex issues partially and temporarily. The implicit and explicit references to the inclusion of musics from different cultural and ethnic backgrounds in Standards 1, 2, and 9 of the National Standards for Music Education ensure that these musics will become a standard feature in the music curriculum.[3] As the study of musics from different cultures and ethnic backgrounds is implemented by succeeding generations of music educators, some of the same problems will most likely resurface. These will need to be addressed again; new interpretations will replace or add meanings to the old ones. Future generations will need to redefine terms and answer questions according to their own times. Now it is our turn to interpret these issues.

As both an outsider to Thai musics and culture and as a Hispanic American, I have chosen to discuss issues I consider basic to the teaching of music styles outside the European art tradition. In my own experience as a music educator working on curricular adaptations of both of these musics, in my role in teacher training, and in my work with public school students, the same issues have resurfaced at different times,

with varying degrees of relevance. My interest and experiences in ethnomusicology have helped me to identify what I consider the basic questions that our generation needs to address.

Perceptions on Ethnomusicology and Music Education: Preliminary Concepts

Adopting an anthropological perspective, the ethnomusicologist's ultimate object of study is humanity itself, with music as the medium through which humanity emerges.[4] In ethnomusicology, the notion is well-accepted that, although music is a universal phenomenon, different cultures may define music differently. Through the study of people's interactions within a given cultural context, then, musical expression acquires its proper meaning by reflecting the values of those who created it. For this reason—although ethnomusicologists may be outsiders to the music cultures that they study—the methods and approaches utilized in the field dictate as essential the immersion of the ethno-student in the culture being studied. One of the salient methods used to achieve this immersion is field experience, where the student lives among the peoples whose music is being studied. In this way, knowledge about the culture is acquired by direct interaction with the people, by participating in their customs and traditions, by experiencing how they feel and think, and by getting the full impact of this people's collective being. The ethno-student also studies the music under the guidance of a native musician, who, in many cultures, is also a teacher or master, thus learning through the method of music transmission traditional to that culture.

While acknowledging the obvious limitations of replicating this ideal situation with music teachers, ethnomusicological methods and approaches provide logical models for immersing preservice music education students and in-service music teachers in diverse, unfamiliar musics. Undoubtedly, compromises will be required.

In the United States, the study of diverse musics includes musics from around the world, musics from those cultures that have been transplanted to the United States, and indigenous musics. For the music education student or in-service teacher, the field-experience aspect of the ethnomusicological approach would be difficult to reproduce in all these cases. Strategies that provide such experiences are not completely out-of-reach, however, when dealing with indigenous musics or the music from ethnic groups living in the United States. Notwithstanding the inherent limitations, interaction as much as possible with members of a particular ethnocultural group, training by authentic practitioners of a given style and experts in the field, and playing in native performance groups constitute ways of approximating the "immersion" of field experience. The insider of a culture and the native musician, as well as the scholar and ethnomusicologist, are key figures in these strategies and are appropriate resources to be consulted by preservice and in-service music teachers in matters of diverse musics.

However, questions may crop up—such as, in which specific areas native musicians may best offer expert information, how reliable a cultural insider's view may be if this person has lived many years away from his or her cultural homeland, and what particular kinds of expertise the ethnomusicologist should offer? The implied concern in these questions involves deciding who is the true "expert" in a given music culture, and this can cause much confusion.

In ethnomusicology, the ultimate expert in a musical style and its performance practices is generally thought to be the native musician. Non-ethnomusicologists, however, tend to equate knowledge *of* a style with knowledge *about* a style. Depending on the mode of transmission within a given musical culture, the degree of complexity of the music system, and the amount of knowledge the musician can articulate about the style, the native musician may not be able to answer some questions. For example, a traditional musician, who has internalized the music by oral transmission, may not be able to discuss issues that involve theoretical relationships in the music nor understand any inherent need to articulate them in that culture's musical context; in such cases, the performance itself, rather than a verbal discourse, constitutes the native musician's knowledge. Notable exceptions are master musicians of classical traditions from such countries as India, China, and Thailand, among others. Clear theoretical structures have been abstracted from some of these musics and written or oral pedagogical approaches have been articulated.

Another instance in which the practitioner may not be the best source of information involves questions related to the origin and development of a style or musical instrument. Questions concerning changes in performance practices over a period of time or in different areas of the country of origin may be beyond the native musician's knowledge or experience, which may be very localized.

Cultural insiders, even if they are not musicians, are generally considered a reliable source of information for the culture's customs and traditions. In areas of the United States that are heavily populated by members of a specific ethnic group, community members can be a rich source of information. As a result of my own experiences, however, I suggest that some issues concerning the nature of the information provided by these persons be evaluated in light of the following: When different ethnocultural groups live in close proximity, some degree of change is likely. Constant interactions may bring about changes in the traditions of the different groups and in their musics. For immigrants who have lived in this country for many years, perhaps among people of different yet similar ethnic backgrounds, the line between their own traditions and others' may become blurred. In addition, acquired meanings in the musics may be more representative of the immigrant population from a particular country than of the country of origin. For example, particular musical styles from the old country may become a symbol of identity for the immigrant group in the new country. Also, a certain group may preserve musics, customs, and traditions in such pure forms that these differ from the current forms in their country of origin; that is, the musical forms may have evolved and acquired characteristics reflecting new and different values from the society at the time of emigration. Both of these situations are natural occurrences; their implications should be clear. Information provided by

cultural insiders in the United States should be interpreted with caution by avoiding undue generalizations about the musics, customs, and traditions of the country of origin, and vice-versa.

Differences between the insider's and the outsider's views are also acknowledged in the field of ethnomusicology. Insiders from a culture offer what is labeled as the "emic" view, while the outsider ethnomusicologist or scholar provides the "etic" view. The ethnomusicologist has obtained both specific and general knowledge about a style and also a broad cultural perspective from which to draw conclusions. As an outsider, the scholar has an element of objectivity and distance, which the insider may lack. But this objectivity may distort the scholar's perception of meanings within the music because the outsider can never perceive of the music as an insider. For instance, when listening to specific musics, the scholar may be able to perceive stylistic traits that are common to other similar musics or to a parental music culture. Distance allows the outsider to isolate and objectively process and interpret information. The insider, conversely, perceives the same musical elements as a unit that expresses the music's own cultural identity; that is, the insider perceives a "belongingness" that defies analysis. In view of the contrasting messages that these two views may convey (the emic and the etic) and the validity of both, ethnomusicologists are currently abandoning a strict doctrine of differentiation.[5] To this effect, the ethnomusicologist Gerhard Kubik has stated that no one is a total outsider to another's culture or a total insider to his or her own.[6] The implication of these views for the music educator's understanding of "expertise" is clear: when questions about musics arise or consultation is needed, both the scholar and the insider can give complementary, expert answers.

Music Education and World Musics: In Search of Approaches

The methods and approaches used in musicology—mainly from the historical and theoretical-analytical perspectives, which have European art music at their center— have provided the core around which college and university music curricula essentially have been designed. Music educators include this music history as part of what they teach in schools. For expertise and knowledge in this area, we turn to musicologists and musicological findings. In addition, because we are all musicians, we share a common terminology when dealing with teaching methodologies and approaches.

Only for a relatively short time period has there been an interchange on ethnomusicology issues, similar to the the established interchange that exists with regard to traditional musicology issues, perhaps because only recently has the interest in world musics been acknowledged as a serious movement within music education. Moreover, ethnomusicology is a relatively new field, with methods and approaches that may differ from those utilized in traditional musicological inquiry.[7] For example, ethnomusicologists study music as an aspect of culture, using "live" music as the object of their investigation. Ethnomusicological inquiry also includes comparative study of world musics and of all types of music in a particular society, including its

classical and folk traditions. But the emphasis is on the role that music plays in people's lives rather than on the study of music as an object of contemplation in the Western sense, as a "work of art." Consequently, the ethnomusicological view is that all musics are good if they fulfill the purpose for which they were created. This approach may alter held notions of aesthetic judgment and, therefore, establish as crucial the importance of music for what it can communicate about the people who created it.

For music education, the "official" endorsement of musics of all styles and cultures by the Tanglewood Symposium in 1967 increased awareness of the issues involved in teaching musics of other world cultures and reaffirmed the inclusion of all styles of music in the school curriculum.[8] Various music education organizations and prominent professionals issued statements and reports dealing with the increasing need to deal with these issues. At this point, the problems of authenticity, context, and expertise in the different musics became evident because training for the field had been structured largely or entirely around the European music system. This served to highlight the need for thorough, systematic training (including training in transcription of world musics) in the teaching of world musics. Concurrently, a serious preoccupation with preservice and in-service teacher training emerged and remains today. But the rate at which institutions of higher learning have implemented courses on musics other than Western art styles has remained quite slow.[9] Consequently, course offerings in ethnomusicology have remained a limited option for music education students, as well as for those music teachers already in the public school system who express an interest in further training.

At present, institutions of higher education with music programs still do not typically offer world musics courses. Some offer independent studies in these musics at the graduate level. A few music appreciation texts have begun to include chapters on world musics. Training in these musics seems to have progressed only to this extent.

Workshops, published materials, and lesson plans have been the most popular medium for reaching in-service teachers and music education students who do not have access to ethnomusicology-oriented institutions. In the twenty-first century, however, formal training in musics outside the Western classical traditions must become as strong and insistent as that which has been offered in traditional Western-oriented literature. I see no alternative but to work more closely with ethnomusicologists and adapt terminology, methods, approaches, and concepts from that field.

Ethnomusicologists' insights are an invaluable help in dealing with the practical implementation of the teaching of musics created within contexts or in venues difficult to re-create in a classroom setting, as well as in developing appropriate teaching models and strategies. Opportunities to interact with ethnomusicologists on other levels, such as at conventions and professional meetings, are particularly useful in developing teaching approaches. Special projects designed around particular teaching problems, workshops, theoretical models of instruction, discussions of successful practices and programs, and the generation of teaching materials that are circulated

among participating music educators are standard features that have been incorporated into ethnomusicology conventions.

Interacting with ethnomusicologists is particularly important at this point in time because offerings in the study of ethnomusicology are still not standard for undergraduate music programs. While final decisions ultimately depend on the individual music educator, professional integrity urges that the same respect and zealousness for accuracy conceded to the study of Western art music be extended to the study of musics outside the Western tradition as well. This may involve consulting "the experts" and using common terminology to strengthen the communication between music educators and ethnomusicologists.

For the rest of this discussion, the term "world musics," which is commonly used in ethnomusicology, will signify any music from any country, including the United States, that expresses any ethnicity, including those represented in the United States. The use of the word "American" following the national designation of the musics, as in "Chinese American" or "Mexican American," properly identifies musics expressing particular ethnicities as they have developed in the United States. It is to this that the label "multicultural" usually refers.

Which Musics to Teach: The Role of the Teacher

When addressing the question of which world musics to include in the school curriculum, a primary concern should be how confident the teacher feels in teaching a specific style. The following considerations should clarify this assertion.

In general education, research efforts

that explore the effectiveness of method-ologies and new curricula have traditionally centered on the use of teaching processes that are most effective in promoting student achievement. Concurrently, empirical evidence in the area of educational psychology points to the fact that implementation and dissemination of recommendations and methods for teaching have depended to a large extent on their adoption by teachers (i.e., effective methodologies and strategies are useless if teachers do not implement them). If this is so, the crucial factors are those that affect teachers' adoption of pedagogical practices.

Research in the different disciplines, including studies in art and music, suggests that adoption and implementation of practices and teaching strategies depend on the teacher's acceptance of them on philosophical ground—that is, within the context of the studies, a recognition of the worth of what should be taught—as well as on the teacher's perceptions of his or her ability to deal successfully with these practices and strategies.[10] If successful implementation of suggested practices depends on these two factors, the implications for the teaching of world musics styles (or any style, for that matter) become clear: Teachers will be drawn to teach those styles of musics that they perceive to be valuable experiences and in which they feel themselves most likely to be knowledgeable and confident. It follows, then, that a teacher's levels of familiarity with and training to teach specific styles will determine in large measure the degree of implementation of world musics programs.

As discussed previously, college introductory courses in ethnomusicology, profes-sional interchange with ethnomusicologists, and courses dealing with different world musics should be part of every music teacher's training. Performing experiences and direct personal experience with a music tradition should constitute essential parts of that training. At this point in time, however, it is more realistic to expect that not many preservice or in-service school music teachers will have access to such training. For these teachers, the in-service workshop, seminar, or short-term course provides viable alternatives for the acquisition of knowledge and self-confidence in teaching a style.

The organizers of national conventions and workshop offerings should bear some responsibility here in providing a variety of in-service experiences concerning different world musics interests. These offerings should include programs that reflect not only current interest in particular styles but generate interest in other, less "popular" styles—for which there may be less demand. Less familiar styles, such as those based on music systems outside Western traditions, are often underrepresented. Ironically, these are the tuning systems to which Western ears need much more exposure, because they represent conceptualizations of music that are different and, therefore, more difficult to understand. Exciting workshops representing an extensive variety of musics offered by specialists have the potential to arouse music educators' interests and entice them to acquire knowledge about these styles and will eventually lead to a more balanced representation of music styles taught in the schools.

Philosophical acceptance was another factor identified as important in determining the implementation of educational practices. Teachers need to be receptive to the inherent value of a practice if they are to engage in its implementation. As music teachers, we are all familiar with the notion that a teacher's interest in a specific world music style can be awakened by a particularly captivating experience; in fact, that experience in itself may be the most important generator of philosophical acceptance. To be "captivated" by music, regardless of its style, is indeed a necessary condition for the entire profession.

The question remains, however, whether it is a sufficient condition. While the initial philosophical conviction must be there or be awakened, the feeling of self-confidence, that feeling which enables a teacher to successfully deal with the material at hand, is also a necessary condition. World musics teachers who develop workshops, therefore, should include both captivating experiences that inspire and practical activities that generate the feeling in teachers that they are prepared to teach the musics. Besides the required performance experiences, detailed information about the cultural context within which the music was created must be included, so that its significance to those who created it becomes apparent.

What Constitutes Teacher Expertise?

By definition, an "expert" is a person who is highly knowledgeable and skillful in a specific area. This person is assumed to be thoroughly trained. When considering teacher training or expertise in world music styles, I have consistently alluded to the realities of our times. Unlike other aca-

demic disciplines in which areas of study have not been necessarily limited by geographical boundaries, ours has been a European-centered profession. Music teachers, therefore, need to develop expertise in styles far removed from their training and experiences. In my perception, this is perhaps one of the great challenges of our times and one that needs to be confronted by our generation of music educators.

It is apparent that until undergraduate training in music education includes world musics on a regular basis and specialization in this area is possible, some compromise will be necessary regarding teachers' "expertise" in world musics. Establishing to what degree this compromise extends involves careful consideration of the alternatives and an honest, realistic stance.

We are well aware by now that total immersion in a specific culture and its music, which occurs in the ethnomusicological field experience, is largely impossible to reproduce. In view of this limitation, interactions with musicians and cultural insiders are necessary both in teacher training and classroom presentation. Live performances by native musicians provide direct experiences with the music, as well as models for performance practices. Videos, films, experiences with authentic instruments, workshops by experts, and other short-term presentations constitute the typical in-service training for those teachers with limited access to course offerings. In addition, lesson plans, with specific instructions for implementation, and various materials, such as films and recordings, are constantly being developed for music teachers' use.

Whether limited exposure to the style of another music culture is sufficient to give outsiders an adequate amount of familiarity with the music (I will no longer refer to the product of this limited exposure as "expertise") should be of concern. Nevertheless, consideration of all the factors, including existing limitations in training opportunities, helps provide an honest, realistic stance: The thorough training in world musics that teachers need is often inaccessible; limited exposure is currently the only option for many teachers.

The style of music itself is important when considering how effective short-term training may be in preparing a music educator to teach unfamiliar music. In a controlled experimental setting in which I was involved, one group of teachers attended a nine-hour workshop featuring traditional Puerto Rican styles. The workshop included all the elements recommended for this type of training, including information about the culture and context of the music, performances and interactions with a native musician, direct experience with authentic instruments, and a variety of dance, listening, and performance experiences with the styles. Lesson plans with tapes of authentic music examples, background information about the music and its cultural context, and very detailed instructions for implementation were also distributed to participants. In another group, teachers were given only lesson plan packets. Lesson plan packets were identical for both groups. Philosophical acceptance was presupposed because music teachers in both groups willingly participated in the study.

The workshop was highly successful in giving the teachers a degree of self-confidence (as defined and measured in the study) in their knowledge of the music. Most of the participants successfully followed up by implementing the lesson plans dealing with the topic. Moreover, the teachers who received only the lessons were also successful in teaching the music.[11]

While a single study utilizing a specific style constitutes limited evidence, it allows some reasonable assumptions: assuming philosophical acceptance, teachers can obtain an adequate degree of familiarity through traditional short-term workshops and accessibility to thoroughly developed teaching materials provided at workshops or in publications dealing with world musics. However, this expectation should be limited to situations in which Western-related world musics are used. There are such vast differences in musical expressions around the world that it does not seem appropriate to assume that short-term training in musics outside the Western tradition would be equally effective in giving music teachers the degree of readiness required to teach any of these styles. Such an assumption would underestimate the complexity of some of these musics and overestimate the readiness that a European-based training would provide in approaching the myriad of styles found in our musical universe.

A number of presentations dealing with styles based on different music systems (other than Western) have been visible at national conventions and professional meetings since the study with the Puerto Rican styles took place ten years ago. More significant has been an increased awareness of the need to use authentic examples for the teaching of world musics, regardless of the style, and the increased availability of authentic materials.[12] However, we lack evidence that would indicate if, all things being equal, teachers taking workshops in these musics and teachers taking workshops in Western styles will attain the same degree of competence.

An increased interest in diverse musics can be expected, owing to a steady increase over the last twenty-five years in the population diversity of the United States. We hope that increased efforts to present accurate representations of nonfamiliar styles, along with the availability of more sources that help teachers in the classroom, will have a corresponding effect on teachers' willingness to teach non-Western styles. Because there are so many difficult issues involved in reproducing some of these styles, however, I recommend that training in these areas be given only in conjunction with ethnomusicologists, native masters, and those already thoroughly trained in the area. Although more familiar and perhaps less intimidating, training in the area of Western styles also requires expert trainers, rich workshop experiences, and high-quality materials, as previously discussed. When ethnomusicology courses and courses in world musics are not available to prepare teachers for a diversity of styles, accessibility to the latter constitutes the suggested degree of compromise commensurate with the realities of the situation.

Teaching the Music: Context and Authenticity

Philosophical acceptance of world musics and sufficient familiarity to make teachers feel that they can deal effectively with the style of the music are prerequisites for effectiveness. However, those of us endeavoring to teach world musics know that the total equation is far more complicated—if we want to provide successful experiences for public school students. Issues related to the music styles themselves engender some of the most controversial, complex questions that music educators face. Prominent among these issues are those related to context and authenticity. We need only be reminded of the many existing questions concerning interpretation and performance practices in European art music, even though, up to the twentieth century, a common music system had been shared. It is not difficult to imagine, then, what happens when we attempt to work with a myriad of music systems with different contextual backgrounds and belief systems.

The current transition in music education (i.e., moving from a monocultural system to one that embraces all music styles) entails a concurrent process of re-examination in order to properly deal with present challenges. Even in the quest to be accurate and respectful when dealing with authenticity and context, teachers may reflect their European-based training in aspects ranging from problems in transcriptions to the assuming of an "elements-of-music approach" in cases where this may be inappropriate for the music culture. Conversely, teachers may be so aware of limiting factors (including their own limitations) that they totally reject the challenge of dealing with certain styles.

A balanced perspective should be assumed when dealing with these complex issues. Considerations of authenticity and context do not apply to the same degree to different expressions of world musics styles.

For example, tone color may be so crucial for certain styles that substituting instruments when the original instruments are not available would be totally inappropriate—but this is certainly not true for other styles. Similarly, taking certain styles out of context, particularly those of ritual musics, may completely destroy the essence and significance of the music for the people who created it—for other styles, the context is not as crucial. Different degrees of difficulty, therefore, will be encountered in re-creating these musics in the classroom. No less significant is the consideration that, even among experts in specific world music styles, there may be differences of opinion concerning issues of authenticity and context. In the field of ethnomusicology, where individuality of approach is common, such differences are not at all unusual.

Issues of Authenticity

Authenticity is particularly critical in dealing with music systems outside Western traditions when performance is involved. Transcription of musical examples to Western notation for pedagogical purposes constitutes a preliminary obstacle, because this system of notation expresses a hierarchy of musical elements particular to Western music. People from different parts of the world may conceptualize music differently, and these differences are expressed in the structure of the music itself. Even while trying to be true to the musics, adapting them to a system that reflects different musical values will result in distortions and inaccuracies. As a result, the meanings and values that the music expresses can be partially or completely lost. Expressing this concern, Kazadi Wa

Mukuna calls the transcription of music from different cultures into Western notation an error and argues for the creation of new methods that avoid this distortion.[13]

Creating new approaches to transcription almost inevitably entails working with ethnomusicologists' systems for transcribing different musics by adapting them for use in the music education field; but such conjectures only suggest efforts still in the future. In the meantime, music teachers use approximate notations that are distributed during workshops and in-service training sessions with the best intention of helping teachers implement world musics in their classrooms. For some musics, these notation systems may work, particularly for those that emphasize melody and do not use tuning systems that are drastically different from Western music. But for musics not conceived metrically or characterized by a high degree of ornamentation, slides, tone-bending and other effects, these systems may prove useless. Many teachers can testify to the difficulty of trying to transcribe complex African rhythms to conventional Western notation. The use of recorded examples and oral teaching, which is the authentic method of transmission, is the appropriate alternative when dealing with complex rhythms and melodies from other music cultures.

Authenticity is also an issue in music cultures where musical elements may be valued differently than in Western music. Tone color, for example, may be a highly valued music element, as in Japanese aesthetics. Consequently, reproducing the mediums of performance may be a critical issue. In such cases, the availability of instruments that very closely reproduce timbral characteristics—if not the original instruments—should be the main concern. When there is doubt about proper adaptation or substitution of instruments, consultation with a native musician or ethnomusicologist is recommended. In cases where the teacher has had to substitute instruments for performance purposes, recorded excerpts in which the authentic instruments are used should always be played for the students. This will complement the performance experience by providing an authentic aural model.

The best perception about how much compromise in performance practices is permissible before seriously hampering authenticity is obtained from master native musicians, who might be surprisingly flexible. Their deep knowledge and understanding of their music lets them determine how far they can deviate from the ideal, something that an outsider cannot do. Panya Roongruang, Thai music master and ethnomusicologist, gives teachers who include Thai music styles in their (elementary) classrooms the following advice:

> Regarding the use of instruments, while Thai music can be played on re-tuned Orff instruments, this may be complicated for some teachers. Thai musical idioms, tunes and styles can also show characteristics of Thai music, and not just the instruments or the tuning.[14]

In this particular case, the use of Orff instruments in their natural tuning can be an adequate medium to reproduce Thai melodies and to accompany Thai songs that are appropriate for the elementary classroom. In Roongruang's views, Western symphonic instruments may be used for Thai classical styles, but, in that case, the instru-

ments should be re-tuned to Thai tuning.

While it may be self-evident that issues of authenticity in approaching children's songs may, indeed, be less constraining in instances such as the one described above, music styles should be approached individually when introducing them into the classroom. Consequently, experts should be consulted for each particular style to avoid undue generalizations or inaccuracies about what constitute authentic interpretations of different music styles within a particular cultural area. Without expert guidance, a host of potential problems are likely to arise, such as inaccurate information about origins of the music and adaptation or alteration of rhythmic and melodic characteristics to fit stereotypes or to simplify the music for teaching purposes. In vocal forms, problems may also be present in the use of translations that do not reflect the true meanings or intentions of the song. These alterations of melody, rhythm, and lyrics may render a song unrecognizable to the people with whom it originated. (Brooks and Brown long ago warned of this problem of authenticity in songs used for teaching purposes.[15]) While there may be different versions of a song that are equally authentic, as verified by insiders, practitioners of a style, and scholars, it is best to respect the identity of the particular version as expressed in its arrangement of the musical elements. In addition, singing the songs in the original language should be the goal, and the translations should only be used to transmit the meaning of the text. For this reason, a literal translation of the lyrics is preferable.

If a style of music cannot be performed in the classroom without seriously compromising its integrity, carefully guided live or recorded listening experiences can be used instead to help the students perceive the uniqueness of the style. This should be preceded or accompanied by as much information about the context, performance practices, and the general culture as possible.

In dealing with authenticity of world music cultures within the United States, the following considerations apply. People create the kind of music that they need to serve their purposes and to reflect their values; music is, indeed, dynamic and subject to change. According to Philip Bohlman, the interaction among groups from different cultures in this country is less likely to create hybrid styles than to bring about changes within the musics, reaffirming the groups' identity at all costs:

> Music that is ethnic, therefore, reflects patterns of organization within the group and reveals the ways in which the group understands and maintains its identity. Because the overriding concerns for organization and identity are products of the New World, ethnic music itself becomes connected even more to the group after it has immigrated to the New World.[16]

The implications of Bohlman's words concern the reaffirmation of an immigrant group's identity through music. Caution must be observed when presenting "transplanted" musics in the classroom. As previously stated, ideas and information about styles of music given by people within the United States are shaped by this people's particular experience outside their country of origin. So are interpretations and transmission of traditional songs and different types of musical expression. While a certain

model may represent a particular immigrant group, it may not constitute a typical example of the style outside the context of this group (i.e., in the country of the group's origin). Awareness of this distinction is necessary when teaching these musics. For example, dealing with Korean-American musics in the classroom may not be the same as dealing with Korean musics; in matters of context and authenticity, there may be substantial differences between the two.

Dealing with Context

Ethnomusicologists study particular musics in their original contexts and in their customary venues by living among the society that created the music. Any other re-created situations, including stage presentations, take the music out of context— if the music was not originally intended for such venues. But following this line of reasoning, all presentations of world musics in the classroom, with the exception of songs intended to be sung in schools, imply music taken out of context. In its most extreme form, this position argues against any re-created performance of world musics. But, notwithstanding the degree of built-in artificiality in classroom or stage presentations of traditional music styles, the general consensus is that, as long as the students (or audience, for that matter) are led to understand the cultural context within which the music was produced, it is acceptable to reproduce music removed from its original context.

In some Oriental musics, such as Japanese or Chinese, the added philosophical dimension to some styles or instruments implies an inherent limitation to their presentation in a classroom situation. The

Chinese *quin,* for example, is related to an ideological system that fuses philosophical and mystical associations. The instrument should be played in private as an act of contemplation, or in a peaceful, natural environment. It would be difficult to isolate this and other musics from their philosophical associations and still transmit their meanings. The musics that derive their meaning from religious associations are also difficult to approach in terms of context and yet may be the most important musical expressions in some cultures.

An honest evaluation of the particular music style involved, including consultation with experts, seems like a reasonable alternative to dealing with the contextual limitations just described. If the teacher is the only "expert," he or she must have a high degree of knowledge about the style and must use respect and common sense in determining if a style will retain its integrity after taking it out of its normal context. Sacred ritual music especially should be approached with caution and with due consideration of the role that this music plays in the lives of its creators. Musics that are not intended for outsiders or are intended to be secret should not be considered at all, for ethical reasons.

A serious commitment to present world musics within their contexts, as ethical considerations and circumstances dictated by the styles themselves allow, should always be demonstrated. Careful explanation about a style's usual venue and intention should precede or accompany its introduction to the students.

Methods of Transmission

Many styles of world musics are transmitted by oral tradition, and, consequently,

a system of notation may not have been developed by the practitioners of the style. Other musics have notation systems that are very different from Western notation and express a different hierarchy of musical elements. In general, it is always better to learn the music using the same transmission method used in the culture of origin. However, in some cases, modifications may be acceptable without serious detriment to the style or the meaning of the music. In Thai classical music, for example, students learn by ear regardless of the fact that a system of notation exists. Students customarily receive a lesson every day. Because of the complexity of the music, oral teaching is usually very difficult for Westerners limited to one lesson a week. My Thai teacher Panya Roongruang believes that learning by ear permits a more subtle perception of the style's nuances and idioms. But for the Thai ensemble that he conducted at Kent State University, constituted mostly of non-Thai students and faculty, he transcribed the music to Western notation, followed by score memorization for performance. Still, from the enthusiastic response its performances received during a tour of Thailand, this group evidently reached a high level of authenticity. A critical factor, of course, was the teacher, a master with extensive years of teaching both native and international students, but the example still demonstrates that there are instances in which flexibility in the approach to context and authenticity are allowable and have positive results.

In adapting methods of transmission to the classroom situation, individual styles must be considered. Some styles of music, such as some Middle Eastern styles, may be unmeasured or have rhythms that are not organized into metrical groupings. With these, as with many complex African styles, adaptations to Western notation result in frustration and misrepresentation. In teaching some musical styles, therefore, an oral-aural approach is the only alternative. This individualized approach to style is no different from the approach suggested for authenticity and context, entailing the same degree of knowledge and respect on the part of the teacher.

Implications and Practical Applications

The "Which Musics to Teach" section discusses the teachers' importance, including the factors of training and degree of willingness to teach unfamiliar musics, with the conclusion that teachers are inclined to accept those styles that they consider important, for which they have philosophical acceptance, and in which they feel comfortable and capable. If teachers are key factors in implementing curricula, the implications are clear: our collective efforts should be directed at expanding teacher-training programs in world musics at all levels.

I am concerned that, outside the circle of world musics educators, the clamor for materials is present without a corresponding call for training. Possibly, some still feel that that traditional training in European art music is sufficient to teach any style. But the persistent errors of transcribing non-Western musics into Western notation for teaching purposes, and the resultant "Westernized" versions of these musics, prove that this is not the case.

Which Musics to Teach

The question of how many kinds of world musics need to be presented in the classroom is consistently raised by teachers who are concerned about these styles. Assuming a belief in the inherent value of the musics, how many kinds of world musics does the teacher feel comfortable with in terms of training? How accessible are materials in these styles? These are the factors that ultimately determine what styles of musics will be taught in the classroom.

Training in world musics should include introductory courses in ethnomusicology and, as in the traditional training of music teachers, different areas of specialization or the possibility of concentrating on specific geographical areas. However, practical considerations dictate that music teachers should strive to feel comfortable with at least two world music styles other than Western musics. One style could be determined by the teacher's own cultural background, while the other could be a style outside Western music traditions. If these two coincide, a Western or another style outside the Western system is suggested.

In my experience with teacher training, I have noticed that many teachers seek training in musics from the dominant cultural background of their students. This is, indeed, a pedagogically sound strategy and consistent with the democratic aims of world musics in music education. However, providing the students with a variety of experiences that will expand their own experiential references is also consistent with the aims of teaching world musics. Although there is no magic number, "two" still seems like a practical minimum. This position appears to be well-accepted by music educators.

While training in world musics should be centered on ethnomusicology courses, there are strategies that provide experiences similar to those offered in introductory ethnomusicology courses. For example, teachers in training or in practice can establish contact with ensembles or individual practitioners of a style, not only to request classroom presentations but also to re-create field experiences with this person (or persons) as the informant or source of information. Interviews can be scheduled and prepared with carefully selected questions. If dealing with an ensemble, permission to attend rehearsals or presentations in their normal venues can be sought, followed by prepared interviews. This should not be difficult to coordinate; depending on the area in the United States, there are native musicians from different cultures who are very eager to share their music and knowledge. The firsthand knowledge that is gained this way is invaluable and perhaps constitutes the closest practicable alternative to field experience.

While methodologies from ethnomusicology can be adapted to approach the study of world musics, it is a reality that our generation is faced with the task of creating models and pedagogical approaches that are both appropriate for the musics and specifically suited for public school music teaching. To future generations of music teachers we owe undergraduate courses in strategies, methodologies, and related materials, courses that are designed in collaboration with ethnomusicologists or expert consultants and taught by music educators with a high degree of expertise in world musics. By providing background in strategies specifically

designed for a variety of world musics styles, an increase in the range of offerings at the public-school level would be ensured. If music teachers feel comfortable in a variety of music styles, they are likely to teach them. Moreover, teachers will be better prepared to create their own materials; with the exception of some MENC publications, materials currently available to teachers deal only with a limited number of world music styles.

Until institutions of higher learning update their offerings to accommodate the growing needs of world music programs, seminars and workshops have the function of the courses just described. Consequently, the number, content, and design of workshops and seminars, as well as the degrees of expertise of those giving them, are crucial factors in spreading world musics into school curricula.

The Need for "Reasonable Adaptivity" to Issues of Context and Authenticity

In an interview, the Thai master Panya Roongruang noted that we tend to be too concerned with context, referring mainly to music teaching situations in the elementary classroom. Small children, according to this master, respond to music itself and may not be ready to assimilate too much contextual information (i.e., concerning the music's culture and original venues).[17] Moreover, children's songs from different cultures, commonly used at the elementary level, are associated with activities common to most children in the world. This should alleviate many contextual concerns for the use of various children's songs in the classroom.

The ethnomusicologist, scholar, and

African music master Kazadi Wa Mukuna, while stressing that teaching about cultural context is indispensable when teaching any music, concurs with the notion that it is possible to study and understand musics outside their contexts, provided that instruction about context is always present.[18] Because context is one way to create meaning, calling students' attention to the culture and particular circumstances in which the music is used and re-creating the music as closely as possible to the original is the proper approach, provided it is also adapted to the age of the students being taught.

In presenting Hispanic styles for both teachers and students, I have sometimes introduced variations from the original practice (changes in context) in order to call attention to elements of music organization that reveal more about the music. For example, in teaching song-dances, I have structured changes in steps to coincide with significant changes in the music. In specific examples where call-and-response elements are stylistically important, I have the students change the direction of the steps to underline the alternation between call and response or between soloist and group. Similarly, steps are introduced by tapping and counting, so as to highlight the duple meter and strong rhythmic drive of the music. These musical characteristics are among significant indicators of the music's cultural origin and give us information about the people's past and present. In this particular case, it indicates the presence of the African element in the people's past and the manner of adaptation to the present, so that the style is no longer "African," but

a unique expression that is different from others of similar backgrounds. While in the natural context dancers would most likely change directions randomly, this small pedagogical adaptation does not change meanings and yet proves to be very effective in introducing these styles to middle school students.

Sara Miller, a music educator with extensive experience in ethnomusicology and in Thai music and dance, and I have used a strategy similar to the one just described when teaching certain Thai village styles that include dance. Contextual information including purpose and social meaning of the dances precedes the actual teaching. In presenting this music, the main difficulty lies in the fact that in Thai music the accent is perceived at the last beat of the metric grouping, something quite foreign to Western ears. Unless steps are counted, it is difficult to get an initial overall structure of the dance. Even when learning the dance from Waraporn Roongruang, a professional classical dancer, I had to resort to this counting technique in order to help the students grasp the step sequence. In this particular experience, which I frequently re-create in my own teaching, the worth of an experience with Thai village dancing far outweighs the possible infraction committed by learning the dance by Western-style counting.

In both the Hispanic and Thai examples, the music was taught by applying techniques that work in a classroom. However, in both cases, contextual information—including purpose and social meanings of the styles—was carefully dealt with. Any possible infractions to context were not considered a detraction from the integrity of the music by persons who were both practitioners of the style and cultural insiders.

A common concern among music teaches is not only what strategies are adequate to approach the teaching of world musics, but also what methods encourage respectful attitudes in students. As discussed earlier, music may be defined differently by diverse societies. Consequently, a relativistic stance is characteristically assumed in the field of ethnomusicology when pursuing the understanding of values expressed in the different musics. The music teacher is expected to assume and encourage this attitude by discouraging inappropriate value judgments and promoting understanding and respect for the music.

While it is not always easy to convey this message to young students, focusing on both the particularities and commonalities of musical expression around the world may help. For example, explaining to the students that music in other societies may be integrated into various life activities in ways sometimes similar, but sometimes different from ours, may discourage disrespectful attitudes toward the musics. Conversely, there are some things about music that are shared by all or most cultures and that ethnomusicologists call "universals." I have seen the interest of college nonmusic majors awakened when, after dwelling on particularities, I tell them that all or most societies sing and use instruments and that all or most cultures that we know use music in religious rites to transform ordinary experience. I am careful to explain that this transformation may refer both to the exhilaration felt during a concert, as well as to the music-induced trance

that may occur during the celebration of a rite. Sharing this information even with younger students has proven to be an effective introduction to many of the world musics experiences in my classes. Underlying the unfamiliar variety of sounds and timbres that students hear defined as music, the commonality of music as a human experience comes across.

Final Considerations and Conclusion

Throughout this discussion, I have attempted to maintain a balance between what I consider the most relevant issues, the directions that we should follow, and the realities of our times, basically assuming a practical stance. A recurrent theme, however, has been the need for teacher training, an implicit acknowledgment that the teacher is a key factor in the educational process. In addition, limitations have been acknowledged, and compromises suggested. But this in no way detracts from my firm conviction that we should have the highest possible aims in pursuing the implementation of world musics in the school curriculum, particularly as it concerns teacher training. We must set high expectations for the teachers responsible for its dissemination.

I have also emphasized the importance of adopting methodologies and approaches closer to those used in ethnomusicology. This includes focusing on music as a common human experience with both unique and similar musical expressions and manifestations and preserving the integrity of the musics so that their meanings remain intact—because it is precisely at the level of meaning that music communicates, where "captivating" experiences happen, and, I believe, where the strong bond of our common humanity emerges loud and clear.

All the truly moving, captivating experiences that changed and expanded my own perspectives about musical expression had a common element: All those who provided those experiences, whether outsiders or insiders, were highly knowledgeable and deeply connected to the musics and their cultures. That perception is shared by many of my colleagues. Our responsibility and challenge, then, is to nurture music teachers by offering them deep and thorough experiences with world musics, so that they, in turn, will be able to provide such experiences for their students.

Notes

1. Terese Volk, *Music, Education, and Multiculturalism* (New York: Oxford Univ. Press, 1998), 4.

2. Milagros Agostini Quesada and Terese M. Volk, "World Musics and Music Education: A Review of Research, 1973–1993," *Bulletin of the Council for Research in Music Education,* No. 131 (Winter 1997): 44–66.

3. Standards 1 and 2 include, respectively, "Singing alone and with others, a varied repertoire of music" and "Performing on instruments, alone and with others, a varied repertoire of music." Standard 9, "Understanding music in relation to history and culture," refers specifically to world musics and includes listening to or aural identification of these. For more information on content standards, see Consortium of Arts Education Associations, *National Standards for Arts Education* (Reston, VA: MENC, 1994).

4. For this particular view of ethnomusicology, see Kazadi Wa Mukuna, in the preface to *African Urban Studies,* 6 (Winter 1979–80), vii. For an anthropological perspective on music, see Alan Merriam, *The Anthropology of Music* (Evanston, IL: Northwestern Univ. Press, 1964).

5. Bruno Nettl, "Recent Directions in Ethnomusicology," in *Ethnomusicology: An Introduction,* ed. Helen Myers (New York: W. W. Norton, 1992), 393.

6. Gerhard Kubick, "Interconnectedness in Ethnomusicological Research (Charles Seeger Lecture at the annual meeting of the Society for Ethnomusicology, Bloomington, IN, 1998)," *Ethnomusicology* 44, no. 1 (Winter 2000).

7. For introductory books on ethnomusicology, see Mantle Hood, *The Ethnomusicologist* (Kent, OH: Kent State Univ. Press, 1982); Helen Myers, ed., *Ethnomusicology: An Introduction;* and Kay Kaufman Shelemay, ed., *Ethnomusicology* (New York: Garland Publishing, 1992).

8. "The Housewright Declaration," *Vision 2020: The Housewright Symposium on the Future of Music Education,* ed. Clifford K. Madsen (Reston, VA: MENC, 2000), 219. To a greater or lesser degree, the movement toward the use of world musics in music education has been present in the United States throughout this century (albeit not always expressed by accurate representation of the musics). The Tanglewood Declaration explicitly gave it legitimacy.

9. Robert Glidden, past president of the National Association of Schools of Music, expressed concern that the 1973 recommendations by the Association on the inclusion of non-Western musics was actually carried out by few schools. See "Finding the Balance," *Arts in Education* 91 (1990), 5.

10. Milagros Agostini Quesada, "The Effects of Providing Teaching Materials and an In-Service Workshop Concerning Puerto Rican Music on Music Teachers' Self-Efficacy and Willingness to Teach Puerto Rican Music" (Ph.D. diss., Kent State University, 1992).

11. Ibid.

12. A CD-ROM series entitled "Global Voices," being developed by Mary Goetze and Jay Fern, will include information about cultures, contextual information, a video model of the included songs performed by native musicians, and pronunciation and translations.

13. Kazadi Wa Mukuna, "The Universal Language of All Times?" *International Journal of Music Education,* 29 (1997): 49.

14. Panya Roongruang, professor of Thai Music, Chulalongkorn University, Bangkok, Thailand, and director of the Thai Music

Ensemble at Kent State University in Kent, Ohio, interview by author, February 10, 1998, Kent. Videotape and cassette in author's files.

15. Marian Brooks and Harry Brown, *Music Education in the Elementary School* (New York: American Book Company, 1946).

16. Philip Bohlman, "Ethnic North America," in *Excursions in World Music*, 2nd ed., ed. Bruno Nettl et al. (Upper Saddle River, NJ: Prentice Hall, 1997), 273.

17. Roongruang, interview.

18. Mukuna, "The Universal Language of All Times?" 47–48.

MILAGROS AGOSTINI QUESADA, who has lectured and published on world musics in the United States, Puerto Rico, and Canada, is associate professor of music at Kent State University, Tuscarawas Campus, and a past member of MENC's *Music Educators Journal* editorial committee and the National Education Committee of the Society for Ethnomusicology.

9

Weaving the Tapestry of World Musics

Bryan Burton

*M*y standard biographical statement contains the usual account of educational background and professional history, roster of publications, workshops and papers presented, service to the profession and honors earned, and the requisite roll call of professional memberships—but sheds little light on my gradual transformation from a public school instrumental director (and, sometimes, choral and general music instructor as well) with traditional training in musical arts and pedagogical techniques to a person recognized for some small degree of expertise in the field of world musics. The road map for that journey is found neither in the catalogs and curricula of formal institutions nor in the various job descriptions that I have sought to fill in the earlier stages of my career in music education. The roadway has run parallel to more formal aspects of my education and teaching, converging only in the past decade.

A case might arguably be made that my journey into the world of multicultural musics began in 1736, when the first Burton to immigrate to America became frustrated with failing crops on his northeastern Georgia farm and angry that his neighbors' hogs had once again ruined his garden fence and eaten the family vegetables. He abandoned his acreage and fled across the Savannah River "into the Carolines and there dwelt amongst the savages," thus taking the first steps along the pathway to my Native American cultural connections and interests. Early in the next century, another ancestor, Jacob Wolf (of the North Carolina Wolfs, as his more pretentious relations would remind all within hearing), worked for nearly half a century as friend and teacher among Cherokee, Choctaw, and Shawnee who had been "relocated" to lands in northern Arkansas. Also, during the nineteenth century, branches of my family tree acquired a reddish hue through the addition of a Native American or two whose tribal origins were never clearly identified by my "good Southern family."

I was born and raised in the cultural mosaic of Texas, the home of many vibrant cultures from across the world, including many that added their flavor to the ethnic mix in the days when immigrants were recruited to homestead the vast expanses of the Republic of Texas. The resulting patchwork of ethnic enclaves and languages and cultures was a continual influence upon my interests in music, as I experienced songs, dances, festivals, and more. When I visited German relatives in central Texas, I also heard musics of the Czechs, Poles, and others whose small communities maintained the sights and sounds of "the old country." The sounds of mariachi and norteno music drifted into my bedroom window from the Mexican dance hall a few blocks away. Highland gatherings offered the sounds of pipes and drums, and pow wows and tribal fairs brought Native American sounds into my life.

As a student earning tuition in an assortment of clubs, school dances, and studios, I quickly learned that a successful band played a varied repertoire that always included a few ethnic specialties—and that there are, indeed, differences between German, Czech, and Mexican polkas that the audience knew even if we didn't! In a more formal setting, I was exposed to folk and traditional musics through high school band performances of the works of Grainger, and Holst, and a host of Spanish pasa dobles. Unfortunately, other than these few performance examples, my formal education in music contained little training in musics of the world—I was too busy being trained to be "the world's greatest band director."

As an adult, I continued to explore and experience a rich variety of musics at every opportunity, with my only forays into teaching these cultures coming with performances of transcriptions and occasional opportunities to share cultural information with social studies and home economics classes (I cook a mean enchilada!). Over the years, I began to incorporate elements of the teaching/learning styles that I had observed in other cultures into my pedagogical approach to music education and to participate more actively in folk festivals and concerts. My travels to learn musics from more cultures increased steadily, with explorations of music in Mexico, China, Japan and, of course, more and more time spent on reservations learning about my own heritage. I began to accumulate a substantial library of field tapes, recordings, books, and cultural artifacts.

After entering the field of higher education, I was able to devote more formal research time to the study of world musics and to develop campus connections among cultures through concerts and festivals, including the performance of several all-multicultural-repertoire wind ensemble programs. To teach the nuances of such music, I employed the assistance of a variety of community resource people, including Appalachian fiddlers, Japanese drummers, and Native American dancers. With the encouragement of the Dean of Arts and Humanities at the small college where I taught, I developed an introductory course in world musics to be offered as an elective. The inevitable round of workshops and lightweight articles began in the late 1980s, and I awoke one day to realize I had become a specialist in world musics well on the way to producing the books, recordings, and workshops that now fill my curriculum vitae. In 1991, I accepted my current teaching position, with its focus on developing courses and materials in world musics and their applications in music education at all levels. I have never looked back.

Although I would have scoffed had anyone predicted this career path when I crossed the stage to collect my baccalaureate degree, I now see this journey as having been inevitable. I hope the path and the musical experiences that remain ahead are never-ending.

Philosophical Issues
In Search of Terminology:
An Exercise in Futility?

As an essential step in any debate or scholarly discussion, terms must be defined, parameters established, and directions charted. At a meeting in June 1998 on the campus of Northwestern University to examine issues revolving around the various musical traditions of the world and their relation to music education, a select group of scholars sought to define and label the elusive genre of music known variously in music education circles as "multicultural," "ethnic," "folk," "traditional," "non-Western," or "world music."

What, at first, was expected to be a simple task soon proved complex and, in some minds, an exercise in futility. Each term in common usage, though strongly endorsed by scholar-educators from different nations or backgrounds, carried with it negative or politically loaded connotations often unknown to the other scholars participating in the discussion. Elizabeth Oehrle, from the University of Natal, explained that "multicultural" was a term used by the apartheid government of South Africa to rationalize keeping races and cultures separate rather than joined in a single nation representing a rainbow of cultures. "Ethnic" was viewed by some as implying an inherent inferiority due to decades of use of this term to describe "exotic" sounds from "other" cultures. Peter Dunbar-Hall, Sydney Conservatorium of Music, labeled "world music" as a commercial recording industry category that describes music created through artificial combinations of instruments, vocal styles, and melodic patterns from an assortment of cultural influences.

Several present felt that "folk" and "traditional" music failed to recognize the classical traditions of such cultures as China, India, Indonesia, and Japan. "Non-Western" also failed to provide the inclusivity sought by this assemblage of scholars because it omitted the nonclassical musics of Europe and the Americas. Bennett Reimer, host of the seminar, offered "multimusical cultures" as an alternative to the more familiar terms.

Turning to commonly used classroom resources as a guide, seminar participants discovered that "multicultural" is frequently used by United States publishers and professional organizations. For example, Music Educators National Conference (MENC) publications include *Teaching Music with a*

Multicultural Approach,[1] *Multicultural Perspectives in Music Education*[2] and *Making Connections: Multicultural Music and the National Standards.*[3] The Organization of American Kodály Educators provides a volume titled *The OAKE Collection: Multicultural Songs, Games, and Dances.*[4] Macmillan/McGraw-Hill's basal series *Share the Music* uses "multicultural" as a major subject heading in its index and as instructional focuses.[5] However, "multicultural" is by no means the sole term used in American publications. Silver Burdett Ginn's *The Music Connection,* for just one example, prefers "Folk, Traditional, and Regional Selections" for the same category of music and instructional activities.[6] Once again, the scholars felt a strong kinship with those blind men who sought to describe the proverbial elephant. Each nation, each publisher, and each scholar seemed to prefer one term to the other, yet a consensus proved elusive, even as the seminar ended.

As a consequence, we appear to have a definition without a term. While participants in the second Northwestern University Music Education Leadership Seminar (NUMELS II), held in 1998, agreed upon what we were examining, a single term for the genre eluded our grasp. Thus, an assortment of terms are used in this book by the contributors, each of whom clearly understands the genre yet passionately endorses a specific label that may not meet with the unanimous approval of other authors.

For myself, I choose "world musics" as an appropriate label. World musics implies that there are multiple musics existing in multiple cultures throughout the world and that the discussion will be as all-encompassing as time and space allow. World musics include both folk and classical traditions from each culture. The term "world musics" is a broad umbrella covering all musical genres and practices from all cultures. Is world musics *the* solution for a single label describing the many musics of the world? Of course not! After all, this is a discussion of diversity and respect—I choose to respect the diversity of terminology chosen by different authors and their rationales for choice of a specific label.

Authenticity:
Does the "A-Word" Truly Exist?

Providing a universally accepted definition of "authenticity" proves as elusive as the search for a single term to describe the musics of all the cultures of the world. Definitions offered through scholarly (and, sometimes, not so scholarly) debate range from very narrow parameters establishing dates, genres, and styles of performance for "acceptably authentic" music from a given culture, to broad definitions encompassing any musics created or performed by any member of the culture regardless of style, form, and genre. In his remarks at the NUMELS seminar, Anthony Seeger indicated his beliefs that "authenticity" is no longer a valid concept, due to continual, inevitable evolutions of the musics of the world.

Perhaps the terms "reliability" and "trustworthiness" would be better yardsticks for measuring musical materials to establish the degree of linkage between a music and its culture. Is the source reliable? Can the source be trusted to transmit the music of that culture?

Others may debate more fully the issue

of authenticity as it applies to musics of the world. Personally, I prefer to use the following questions to establish the accuracy of the link between a music and its culture and thereby its acceptability for use in a music classroom:

■ Is the source person (culture-bearer) a recognized performer/creator of music within the culture? This creator/performer need not be "the best," but his or her performances must be considered acceptable by a reasonably representative element within the culture.

■ Is the music and the performance of the music representative of an identifiable segment of the culture's musical mosaic? Again, this need not be a vast majority of the culture's repertoire, nor does the size of the music's "following" need to be a majority of the culture's population. But neither should the music, performance, or performer be a fringe cult with little following and unlikely "shelf life" within the culture.

■ Does the music hold a niche from the past, from the present, or is it just being established within the life of the culture? Music has clearly defined roles within any culture; this is even more true when considering the musics from many cultures outside the West. If the music no longer has a meaningful role in the culture or is not establishing a role within the culture, the meaningfulness of the music may be suspect.

Once the reliability and trustworthiness of the musical materials offered as representative of a specific culture have been established, the music educator may then apply guidelines for establishing the reliability and trustworthiness of educational materials intended for classroom use. These guidelines, listed below, will be more fully defined in the section on educational applications of world musics:

- Materials must be prepared with the involvement of a culture-bearer or a serious student of the culture.
- Each selection must be set within its cultural context.
- The original language should be used for the primary lyrics, along with a pronunciation guide, explanation of subject matter, and recorded example of the performance.
- Where possible, photographs, videotapes/films, and illustrations that show members of the culture engaging in musical activities should be provided.
- Any transcriptions provided should be prepared under the guidance of a culture-bearer or a serious student of the culture.
- Recordings of the musical materials should be provided as models for performance.
- Clear instructions for games and dances should be included when appropriate.
- Sacred or ritual materials should seldom, if ever, be used in a casual classroom setting.

A similar set of criteria may be explored on the Internet at the Web site for World Music Press at www.worldmusicpress.com.

Cultural Connections and Fusions

Whenever the musics of two or more cultures come into contact, an exchange of melodies, rhythms, and instruments seems inevitable. Songs, dances, and instrumental pieces exchanged in this way frequently find a home in the new culture, being adapted to various extents to the musical styles and genres of this home. In some instances, borrowed or acquired songs become so closely identified, over time, with the new culture that they become accepted as "traditional" to that culture. For example, the wedding dance performed by the Nanticoke Native Americans in Delaware is actually a Lakota courting song thought to have been learned at the turn of the twentieth century from Lakotas performing with Buffalo Bill's *Wild West Show*. This music has been passed down through intervening Nanticoke generations through the oral process and is now an integral part of their tribal repertoire.[7]

In other instances, new styles and genres are fused with the music of a particular culture, creating a hybrid with identifiable elements of both cultures clearly preserved in the "new" music. In the latter half of the twentieth century, rock music from Western culture has been fused with indigenous musics throughout the world. Some examples of such fusions include "Indian Rock," performed by Tom Bee and XIT, which combines traditional Native American melodies, instruments, and subject matter with the instruments, forms, and performance techniques of Native American music; and the Aboriginal rock performed by Yothu Yindi in Australia, combining Aboriginal music, instruments, and dances with elements of rock music. Other examples may be found on every continent. The mixture of styles varies considerably from group to group, with many performers continuing to perform music from their traditions alongside newly fused genres. These performers and their audiences may appear to travel on a middle ground, with no single clear cultural identity.

In other cases, indigenous elements become almost completely lost in the mixture of sounds (Western and indigenous in this discussion), with the result that the original music of the culture seems to have been replaced by Western styles. In eastern Canada, for example, some scholars and Native Americans claim that "traditional" Native American music has been usurped by a type of country-western music performed by Native American musicians.

To what extent does this fusion of styles and genres among cultures represent a deterioration of the original culture of each party in the exchange? To what extent does the new musical style represent simply a natural evolution of the culture's music? This question is the topic of much scholarly debate among ethnomusicologists and multiculturalists, but it is unanswerable and far beyond the scope of this chapter to examine fully.

My strong belief is that this process represents an evolution of style within the culture not unlike the evolution of a classical genre or Western popular style. The musical elements of two or more cultures join to create new genres and styles within each culture.[8] In many, if not most, cases, performers maintain a close connection with their original culture, with their musics retaining a clear connection to those musical traditions. For example, in the fusions of Native American music of the rock group Red Thunder, Native American melodic curves, instruments, languages,

and subject matter clearly identify the music as Native American despite the presence of electronic keyboards, guitars, harmonies, and format. Mixed in among the fusion songs are traditional songs performed in a strictly traditional manner. Similar examples of musics and performers clearly maintaining traditional elements as an integral part of newly evolving forms may be found throughout the world.

More challenging to define are the orchestral and choral works of indigenous composers that claim to be "Native American," "African," and so forth. By transporting ethnic musics to orchestra and chorus—ensembles in the Western music tradition—the material becomes far removed from its origins, being made subject to the compositional conventions and performance techniques of Western instruments and vocal styles.

Louis Ballard, a Cherokee-Quapaw composer, conductor, and educator, has written in all Western genres, incorporating Native American melodies and instruments into his orchestrations. However, the overall effect remains a Western symphonic work, cantata, chamber piece, or the like. Ballard cites Zoltán Kodály and Béla Bartók as his models for the integration of "folk" materials within "classical" venues; he clearly follows their lead, except that he does use more ethnic instruments within his works than these earlier composers. Ballard wrote a classic textbook for the use of Native American musics in the classroom and remains a strong advocate for Native American music and musicians.[9] Again, similar models from cultures throughout the world may also be cited.

Examination of these fusions, and the

newer genres created by such interactions, is but one element to be considered when attempting to define the "authenticity" of any song or piece from the musics of the world:

> One truth does emerge from this discussion: musical culture evolves with time and these evolutions reflect the influences of cross-cultural contact. Another truth is that, regardless of such evolutions, older styles continue—and will continue to exist—alongside new musical traditions.[10]

A Rationale for Teaching World Musics

Many rationales have been offered for the teaching and learning of world musics. William Anderson and Patricia Shehan Campbell present solid educational benefits of teaching with a multicultural approach in the introductory chapter of *Multicultural Perspectives in Music Education*.[11] Readers are encouraged to examine their discussion from that text in full. Other basal series and articles offer similar rationales. Perhaps one of the most comprehensive rationales for the teaching and learning of world musics, applicable to both classroom and less formal learning settings, is the one given by Bennett Reimer in 1994 at the twenty-first world conference of the International Society for Music Education (ISME):

> To help our students understand that the creation of musical meaning is a universal need of human beings; that such meaning is created within the culture from which it rises; and that each individual can find both soul in the music of his or her culture and share soul to some extent with those of other cultures, is to have helped them experience musically the paradoxical—and fundamental—nature of the human condition.[12]

The importance of learning and understanding world musics (to whatever extent that may be possible), then, goes beyond academic exercise. To explore, examine, and understand these musics is to explore, examine, and, hopefully, begin to understand ourselves as humans engaged in the diverse human practice known as music.

As our society has become increasingly diverse, so, too, must our music education curriculum become equally diverse, serving as an accurate reflection of who we were, are, and will become musically. Writing in *Riding the Waves of Culture,* Fons Trompenaars states:

> We need a certain amount of humility and a sense of humor to discover cultures other than our own; a readiness to enter a room in the dark and stumble over unfamiliar furniture until the pain in our shins reminds us of where things are.[13]

In the late twentieth century, the diverse musical culture found within American society has become that room in the dark. The new sounds, instruments, forms, and styles are the unfamiliar furniture. A multicultural approach to teaching music should serve as our guide through that room; to minimize the pain in our shins, we discover "where things are." After many decades, the words of Carl Seashore still ring true: "When you listen, you hear what you are."[14] Entering the twenty-first century, when we listen, we still hear what we are—a remarkably rich and diverse mosaic of multimusical cultures.

Teaching from the Inside Out

Should musics of world cultures be performed and taught in Western schools in the original vocal and instrumental styles, or are "Westernized" versions of the music acceptable as representative of these styles and genres? Referred to by the NUMELS II seminar participants as the "Mike and Pete" dichotomy (from the different educational practices advocated by Mike Seeger—a more purely ethnomusicological style—and by Pete Seeger—a "just-sing-it-and-enjoy" style popular among American folk singers in the 1950s and 1960s), these opposing views are at the center of the debate regarding the appropriate use of world musics in music classrooms.

For many decades, examples of music from all cultures were frequently presented in the public school classroom through basal series transcriptions and records that were frequently "corrected" to match Western tonalities and performed using Western vocal styles and Western instruments. Even American cowboy songs were often performed in an operatic style rather than in hillbilly style (the predecessor of today's country-western). This practice is well documented in Terese Volk's *Music, Education, and Multiculturalism.*[15] The most recent generation of classroom basal series and culture-specific texts advocates use of singers and musicians from the culture performing selections as they would be performed within the culture. The Macmillan and Silver Burdett publications cited above and the catalog of publications by World Music Press offer clear examples of this contemporary approach to presenting world musics to American audiences. Listeners hear the timbres and tonal nuances associated with the specific culture, expanding their aural repertoire of sound and text rather than ethnocentric "corrections" of earlier generations.

Musics of the world should be presented as nearly as possible as they would be performed within the home culture, preferably under the guidance of a culture-bearer or a serious student of the culture. (This approach is strongly advocated by such educators as Mary Goetze and Fay Fern,[16] Maria Pondish Kreiter and Bryan Burton,[17] and Patricia Shehan Campbell,[18] among others.) Where possible, students' total immersion into the culture—music, dance, art, language, religion, literature, food, and clothing—should be attempted in order to replicate the cultural experience to the greatest degree possible, considering educational circumstances. One must realize, of course, that any performance or presentation of musics from world cultures in a classroom setting removes the music from its cultural context and is, at best, a mere shadow of the original.

In some cases, it may be possible for students to observe indigenous performers making music in the original cultural setting. For example, students may attend Native American fairs and pow wows, cultural events hosted by immigrant groups within the community, or special cultural tours abroad specifically targeting musical performances. Again, inserting groups of observers from outside the culture will modify the context, but participating in such a performance/event provides a rich experience of sound, sight, feeling, and aroma with an ambience that cannot be duplicated by any classroom experience, however complete the recording and video library, instrumental inventory, or experience of the instructor. As Ballard explains,

You cannot understand the music of my people until you come to our homes and experience our music in its natural state and see how intertwined our lives and music are. You must hear the music, smell the campfire, move with our dancers, feel the energy, taste our food, experience the emotions.[19]

Musics of any culture, including the Western art traditions, should be taught from the inside out. Teach from within the cultural context—when would the music be performed in the culture? who would perform it? under what circumstances would it be performed? what role is played by the music within the culture? Finding the answers to these questions through experiencing the musics as sung, danced, played, and told by members of the cultures leads to deeper understandings and appreciation of the musics of all cultures. Through these cultural explorations, we may discover that we are all truly more alike than we are different.

Applications
Preparing Music Educators to Teach World Musics

During the past decade, there has been an increasing emphasis on cultural diversity in the music curriculum for elementary and secondary schools in the United States. Educational mandates and voluntary standards in many countries now require instruction in world musics as part of each child's music education, necessitating changes in teacher preservice and in-service education programs to prepare educators to teach these "new" musics in the music classroom. For many educators whose music training has been solely in the Western art tradition (often colloquially referred to as "classical music"), this new direction in music education has created "a world turned upside down."

Conferences and symposia sponsored by music education organizations including Music Educators National Conference and the International Society for Music Education, as well as Orff-Schulwerk and Kodály affiliates, have regularly scheduled workshops and demonstrations focusing on the teaching of world musics. In addition, many universities have included units on world musics within pedagogical methods courses and newly created world musics courses. Publishers of music education texts and sheet music have increased world musics offerings in their catalogs of publications.

How well, however, have in-service music educators been prepared through existing teacher education programs to select appropriate multicultural materials, design learning experiences based upon these selected materials, and effectively present such learning experiences in an appropriate cultural and performance style? To identify strengths and weaknesses in teacher preparation to teach world musics, I asked music educators attending selected multicultural music education sessions at three national music education conferences in the United States to respond to a questionnaire inserted in session handouts.[20]

Music educators identified three broad areas of knowledge in which more thorough preparation is desirable: (1) world musics literature (a repertoire of songs, dances, singing games, and instrumental works representative of a wide range of cultures); (2) effective performance techniques for both instrumental and vocal works from diverse cultures (tone quality, timbre, embellishments, etc.); (3) cultural context of materials (background information on appropriate use of specific musical examples, including who usually performs the music, when the music is performed, and under what circumstances the music is performed). In addition, music educators commented that (1) world musics are frequently not encountered until music education courses in the third year of study (even in these courses, the above three areas of concern are infrequently addressed, the world music lessons being presented merely as demonstrations of teaching technique); and (2) resource persons, including performers in ethnic traditions, are seldom available within an academic environment, necessitating a search for such culture-bearers in the general population. The lack of exposure to world musics outside of the music education class and the limited access to culture-bearers from world cultures were cited as probable cause for major weaknesses in preparation to teach world musics.

World Music Repertoire. Classroom textbook series, such as those published in 1995 by Silver Burdett Ginn and Macmillan/McGraw-Hill, have made major strides in integrating world musics into published curricula, and specialized, small-press publishers and major music publishing houses have increased world musics titles in their catalogs. However, music educators report that they do not have knowledge of an adequate number of resources for supplemental materials from which they may create original lessons. Despite the increase in published titles, some offerings contain little more than a relatively authentic melody and

simple identification of its ethnic source. What follows are some specific examples of world musics experiences for preservice music educators that focus upon repertoire.

Music Education Methods Classes

In addition to the model lessons presented in methods courses, preservice music educators should be exposed to representative literature from world cultures in all aspects of the music curriculum. In addition to participating in model lessons using ethnic music and dance, students should review published educational materials incorporating or featuring multicultural songs, dances, singing games, and stories (both materials within classroom basal series and specialty publications). Specialty publications should include both texts containing information on multiple cultures (e.g., *Multicultural Perspectives in Music Education*[21] and *Roots and Branches*[22]) and texts that focus upon a single musical culture (e.g., *Let Your Voice Be Heard! Songs from Ghana and Zimbabwe*[23] and *Moving within the Circle: Contemporary Native American Music and Dance*[24]). In reviewing these texts, music education students should note the cultural validity of primary materials and supplemental materials (recordings, workbooks, video materials) and the ease of application to the music classroom setting.

Music Theory. Theory and aural skills courses should include non-Western scale and melodic forms as an integral part of both written and laboratory learning experiences. For example, an aural skills class might listen to the Native American "Quiltmaker's Song"[25] and determine at what points the sung version differs from notated versions; listen to a Chinese folk song and identify how the tonality of the language affects the pitch of the melody; or listen to a performance by Ravi Shankar and identify the use of *raga* as a structural element. Composition classes should include assignments using non-Western scales and forms based on models examined in theory and history courses.

Music History and Literature. Music history and literature courses should include surveys of world musics styles, forms, and historical traditions to further familiarize students with representative styles and literature from other cultures. Addition of world musics to theory and music history curricula would both increase familiarity with such musical sounds and help eliminate the impression too often implied in these courses that non-Western musics are somehow inherently inferior to Western art music. Examples of lessons using these materials in music history and literature classes include the following: (1) compare and contrast an English madrigal such as "My Bonnie Lass" with the South African song "Gabi Gabi" to identify similarities and differences in structures (alternation of sections using imitative writing with sections in homophonic style); (2) compare and contrast an example of Western opera with Beijing opera, exploring the use of visual art, drama, music, and dance in each; (3) examine the different forms of a Schubert art song, a popular song of the 1960s, and a folk song from a non-Western culture to identify similarities in form (many will be AB, ABA, or theme and variations); and (4) examine the roles that musics and musicians play in diverse cultures around the world (to establish the cultural validity of diverse musics and arts).

Performance—Individual and Group Instruction. Performance instruction (including private studio and ensembles) should introduce materials that incorporate elements of world musics. This may include settings of ethnic materials for Western ensembles and voicings—the works of numerous twentieth-century composers contain folk melodies and/or utilize the sounds of ethnic instruments. Educators should take care, however, to avoid materials that do not contain authentic melodies but rely, instead, upon musical clichés and stereotypes. Lists of works for various performance ensembles have been published in the *Journal of the Conductors Guild*[26] and in Volk's *Music, Education, and Multiculturalism.*[27] Such repertoire lists should not only be made available in conducting classes and ensembles, but representative examples from these lists should be used as an integral part of the course of study in performance and conducting experiences for the preservice music educator. Conductors and studio teachers should seek to perform at least one world-musics-derived work on each program.

Performance Techniques. Performance skills in world musics, whether producing a correct vocal style or playing an ethnic instrument, present special problems to music educators thoroughly trained in "classical" techniques yet lacking exposure to techniques common to various ethnic musics. Unfortunately, studio instructors still fear that performing in culturally correct styles will "ruin" vocal or instrumental techniques learned during lessons. (Some university instructors reported instances in which studio instructors forbade their students from participating in multicultural performance activities. Fortunately, these conflicts appear to be diminishing in number.) A significant development in teaching a variety of vocal and choral techniques has come with Mary Goetze's world music choral ensemble at Indiana University, in which culture-bearers from throughout the world teach students repertoire, vocal techniques, and appropriate movements. Goetze's work along these lines reinforces the importance of seeking guidance from performers and culture-bearers beyond the bounds of the academic environment.

Vocalists should be allowed to experiment with various techniques of tone production from world cultures—indeed, many contemporary vocal and choral works call for a greater variety of sounds other than those produced by the bel canto voice. It may be argued that various vocal and tone-production techniques found in the different genres and historical periods of Western arts music require greater differences in use of the vocal instrument than may be the case between "classical" and ethnic styles. Some performance schools already offer training in musical-theater vocal techniques and encourage students to develop a repertoire of vocal styles ranging from bel canto to various popular styles in order to allow greater 'employability' in studio performance. Guest recitals, demonstrations, and workshops featuring performers from varied vocal traditions should become a standard component of vocal training for the future music educator.

In order to teach songs effectively in non-Western languages, preservice music educators must learn pronunciation guides far beyond the general introduction to Latin, Italian, French, and German provided in voice classes and studio lessons. Basal series, specialized music collections, and choral works now include languages as diverse as Zulu, Apache, Shona, Khmer, Korean, various Chinese dialects, Eastern European languages, and others. Although many publications offer a pronunciation guide for the language used, many of these guides are "cobbled-together" efforts that lack a consistent basis for pronunciation. Fortunately, an increasing number of publications are providing guides written in a modified international phonetic alphabet.[28] Perhaps this modified international alphabet should be taught in studio and class voice instruction, and publishers should be *strongly* encouraged to make the use of this tool a standard practice for all multicultural publications.

Opportunities to perform on representative instruments from a variety of cultures must form part of each music educator's preservice experience. Each teacher education institution should purchase and maintain an adequate quantity of ethnic instruments to form ensembles typical of selected ethnic cultures (Mariachi band, Chinese and African percussion ensembles, Irish folk ensembles, etc.). Due to the expense of obtaining ethnic instruments, institutions should target specific cultures for initial ensembles, expanding their offerings as finances allow. Preservice music educators should be offered instruction in instrumental performance techniques through several means, including (1) instruction in proper performance techniques on selected ethnic instruments in model lessons presented in music education methods classes, (2) workshops/recitals/demonstrations by guest performers specializing in ethnic instruments, and (3) opportunities to perform on ethnic instruments in instrumental ensembles (including accompanying groups for choral performance). One should note that performers on instruments from world cultures may be found in many settings beyond the academic classroom. For example, skilled performers from Asia, South America and elsewhere—often highly trained and respected within their cultures—have come to the United States as immigrants. Because of many factors, including language skills and lack of academic credentials, these culture-bearers are unable to find employment in the field of music and are "lost to view" of academe. Exceptional teachers and performers from world traditions have been discovered working as clerks in convenience stores, waiters in restaurants, and custodians in schools!

As with choral literature, an increasing number of instrumental works, from chamber ensembles to orchestras and concert bands, incorporate ethnic instruments—particularly in the percussion section. Movie scores and musical theater productions in particular are calling for performers on various ethnic instruments. *Uilleann pipes, didjeridu,* assorted string instruments (*balalaika, erhu, charrango,* etc.), and *kena* are only a few of the ethnic sounds now commonplace in contemporary instrumental musical scores. Performers, as well as educators, must become familiar with these "new" sound sources. Those educators who have experimented with performing on such instruments have discovered that these are not "simple" folk instruments; on the contrary, they demand high levels of

skill to produce authentic tone quality and stylistic performance.

Cultural Context. At present, cultural context is addressed primarily in specialized texts that focus on a single culture (or a limited number of cultures) and in workshops at music education conferences. (These conference workshops also appear to focus on a single culture or a limited number of cultures.) Many of these texts and workshops are usually written and/or presented by educators who are serious students of the culture(s) and who rely upon the assistance of a culture-bearer from within the cultures. Most of the authors/presenters offer well-researched lessons with supporting information on cultural context, authenticity, and so forth. Although specialized texts and workshops provide sorely needed cultural information to music educators, dissemination of this information is limited to conference attendees and those who become aware of specialized texts through workshops and journal reviews. (Surveyed music educators identified such workshops and specialized texts as their primary source of materials for developing multicultural learning experiences.)

Cultural context should be addressed to varying degrees in all courses within the teacher education curriculum. Logically, music history and literature courses should address such issues for world musics in addition to the music of the Western art tradition. Such instruction is simply an extension of current practice in such courses in which cultural and historical contexts are established for the works of Western composers, style periods, genres, and so forth. For example, Ludwig van Beethoven is frequently discussed within the context of the revolutionary era in Europe; Claude Debussy is linked with visual art movements of his era and Dmitri Shostakovich and Sergei Prokofiev are discussed within the framework of the Soviet era in Russia and/or government control of the arts. Medieval and Renaissance music is discussed within the context of Church and political history. Few educators presenting Wolfgang Amadeus Mozart's *Requiem* fail to relate the story of the "mysterious visitor," Mozart's obsession with his own death, the theories about Mozart's death, and so forth.

Contextual information about world musics selections used in lessons or performances should be presented through similar means to explain the role that the music and musicians play within the specific culture. For example, when general music teachers present a Cherokee or Ute bear dance, they should include an explanation of the importance of the bear within Native American culture and, perhaps, include a brief legend about bears and humans. Choral conductors preparing "Wonfa Nyem" (a mourning song from Ghana) should explain the layers of meaning behind this funeral song and compare the slow-fast contrasting sections with the early Dixieland jazz funeral music. Presenting the cultural context for each selection used in the music classroom validates the music within its home culture.

Model lessons presented in pedagogical courses should include references to the cultural context of all musics rather than merely providing isolated examples of songs, games, and dances for the sole purpose of demonstrating technical presentation skills. As preservice music educators come to understand the role of music and musicians in a variety of cultures, they will be less likely to use music in an inappropriate context or add teacher-created activities in which cultural faux pas occur (e.g., adding drones on classroom instruments to music that does not have such harmonizations, adding movement activities to materials for which movement is inappropriate or using a ceremonial song for a social dance).

Recent educational publications such as *Multicultural Perspectives in Music Education*[29] and *Making Connections: Multicultural Music and the National Standards*[30] clearly provide appropriate contextual information. Even newer texts for beginning instrumental instruction are providing brief contextual notes in the teacher's edition for the numerous folk tunes contained in these texts.[31]

Summary. During the past decade of increasing emphasis on the use of culturally diverse songs, dances, singing games, and instrumental works in the music curriculum, many positive steps have been made in the training of music educators, preparation and publication of authentic/appropriate multicultural materials designed for classroom use, and availability of instruction covering appropriate/authentic multicultural materials whether in teacher education programs or music education conferences. Teacher education programs at many universities have instituted new courses focusing upon teaching the musics of diverse cultures and/or have inserted special units on multicultural musics into existing pedagogical courses. University/school sponsored performances by ethnic music and dance ensembles are becoming more commonplace. National and international music education conferences offer numerous workshops, demonstrations, and performances focusing on diverse ethnic musics.

Several areas of weakness remain, however, in the ways that music educators are prepared to make multicultural materials selections, design learning experiences based on the selected materials, and present such learning experiences effectively in appropriate cultural and performance formats. Some of these perceived weaknesses were identified through a survey of preservice and in-service music educators attending selected sessions at national music education conferences in the United States during the 1995–1996 academic year. Three primary areas of concern—world music repertoire, performance techniques, and cultural context—have been briefly discussed here.

To further strengthen music educators' understandings of diverse music materials and enhance their presentations of these materials to new generations of music students, I offer several suggested revisions to existing courses and several new instructional and performance opportunities for world musics. These suggestions include the following:

■ Integrating scales, harmonic structures, and forms from world musics into music theory and the music history/literature components of the music education curriculum—familiarity with the basic building blocks of a culture's music is essential to understanding.

■ Expanding vocal instruction to include vocal techniques and styles of world musics and to offer instruction in a modified international phonetic alphabet to facilitate performance of world musics—familiarity with

the performance techniques of a culture's music leads to greater understanding and appreciation.

■ Expanding instrumental instruction to include basic performance techniques on selected instruments from world musics—familiarity with the performance techniques of a culture's music leads to greater understanding and appreciation.

■ Incorporating cultural contextual information as an integral part of world musics instruction in all courses in the music education curriculum—familiarity with the "who, what, when, where, and why" of a culture's music is essential to give meaning to the sounds.

■ Seeking out performers and culture-bearers from outside the academic environment and recognizing the validity of such resources within the greater community—these guides are essential to provide not only nuances of performance and pronunciation, but also a living link between the culture and the classroom.

Getting Started with World Musics in the Elementary and Secondary Curriculum

Is the culture I wish to study accessible for teaching?

"Accessibility" as used here refers to the quantity and quality of teaching materials and cultural background information available to the music teacher at grade-appropriate levels, as well as the availability of instruments and live performers from the culture. If such resources are not easily obtained, pursuing study of the specific culture may not be a viable learning activity. Music educators have reported this particular problem in selecting cultures for study in situations where a school curriculum has identified a culture for school-wide study without considering the availability of materials for all disciplines. Music teachers have also reported instances where classroom teachers (or teachers from other disciplines) request musical support for projects, without considering the availability of musical resources for the culture. One humorous example occurred when an art teacher required students to relate the art of a period or culture with the music of the same period or culture—a worthwhile effort within a related arts curriculum. The problem? That semester, the art students were studying Cro-Magnon cave art. The music teacher briefly considered suggesting Igor Stravinsky's *Rite of Spring* but decided that the humor would be a wasted effort.

Music educators should follow a set of criteria to determine the accessibility of a given culture that may be useful in designing useable learning experiences for students throughout the curriculum:

■ Recordings: A variety of high-quality recordings of musical examples from the culture should be available. They should feature respected musicians performing in an appropriate style and provide liner notes with detailed discussions of cultural contexts and identification of instruments. Lyrics in the original language, along with a translation or extended meaning, should preserve the specific message associated with the music.

■ Music transcriptions: Any transcriptions of the music should be at levels appropriate to class skills. Translations, pronunciation guides, and guides to proper performance styles should be provided. A companion recording of the music should be available

as a further guide because Western notation is an inadequate medium for representing the music of non-Western cultures, and pronunciation guides may not be readily understandable to students. A growing number of educators advocate learning the music in the same manner as it would be learned by the culture—often this process is aural, not visual.

■ Instruments: Authentic instruments or reasonable reproductions should be readily available at reasonable prices. Instructions for proper performance techniques should be provided as well. Fortunately, music education suppliers have an ever-growing catalog of ethnic instruments available for classroom use. Remo, Inc., for example, now produces a high-quality line of reproductions of ethnic drums that have been embraced by both musicians from various cultures and knowledgeable music educators specializing in those cultures.

■ Live performers: The ultimate classroom enrichment is always live performance, which allows students to witness the sonorities, sights, movement of hands and feet, facial expressions of a performer, and the immediacy of his or her joy in sharing music with others. To young students, recorded performances seem to lack reality. After all, the sounds are detached from any physical or visual sense. The presence of a live performer focuses the child's attention more completely. Add to these sensations the "exotic" elements of unfamiliar clothing, instruments, and, perhaps, physical appearance of the musician from another culture, and the intensity of the learning experience increases dramatically.

These performers need not be members of a professional touring ensemble. In fact, the impact of the learning experience is greater if the performers are members of the community in which the school is located: businessmen, laborers, housewives, teachers, or religious leaders. Often, highly skilled musicians and dancers from many cultures may be found in every walk of life—with the number of cultures represented within a given community being far greater than one might suspect.

One Pennsylvania school engaged in a project in which students, whose parents/grandparents had been born in another country, learned songs/dances/ stories from relatives and shared these materials with classmates in music classes; thirty-seven nationalities were represented in the small area of the community served by the school.[32] When creating a multicultural festival, a small college in the Allegheny Mountains of western Maryland discovered numerous skilled performers from many cultures in a small town of 5,000—medical workers, chefs in restaurants, custodians, parents of students, and so forth.[33]

The value of students observing practitioners of the music and dance of a culture is increasingly recognized as among the most effective teaching tools to enhance understanding and respect for that culture. Among those advocating this approach are Kay Edwards,[34] Louis Ballard,[35] Goetze,[36] and Burton.[37] Discovering these resources within a community takes only a little detective work by the creative music teacher.

■ Cultural context: Much of the meaning of the music is lost if a sense of the role that music plays within the culture is not presented. When using older texts or song anthologies that do not include such information, the music educator may be able to provide this information for a specific learning activity by researching the culture in newer publications or contacting members of the culture for background information.

Is it the "real thing?"

Music educators are rightfully concerned whether the materials available for use in the music classroom are a reliable representation of the culture selected for study. They should approach each new source with such questions as: are the materials really from the identified culture? is the translation correct? is the recorded performance in the correct style? are the instruments used authentic? are instructions for games, dances, and other activities accurate? will members of the culture be offended by presentation of these materials?

Unfortunately, songs, dances, instrumental pieces, and stories have sometimes been misidentified. One recent publication for young band, for example, used a title implying that all songs used in the medley were Scottish in origin while, in fact, these songs were Irish. Older basal series are filled with generically labeled selections— "traditional," "folk song," "ancient melody," "an old favorite"—that provide no clue as to the origin of the music. Worse yet, examples may be found in which the editors have "corrected" melodies, imposed Western harmonies and accompaniment patterns on music of other cultures, created sets of singable lyrics that may not be remotely related to the actual meaning of the original text, or added texts to instrumental pieces. Volk explores the history of

177

such practices;[38] these practices have been addressed by other authors in texts on specific cultures.

Recent classroom textbook series (such as *Share the Music* by Macmillan and *The Music Connection* by Silver Burdett Ginn) have made great strides toward providing accurate and appropriate materials under the guidance of culture-bearers and serious students of each culture. Recent individual texts as well have sought to carefully document sources, origins, and the cultural accuracy of melodies, dances, stories, and other materials, thus providing reliable and trustworthy resources focussed on selected ethnic groups and prepared under the guidance of culture-bearers and serious students of the cultures. MENC publications in multicultural music (cited previously) also offer models of accessible and accurate teaching materials. However, recent vintage does not guarantee the reliability of materials, nor are major publishers immune to the occasional faux pas—a recent text focusing upon South African music included a number of cultural errors, including west-African-style percussion accompaniment for a South-African style piece that is usually performed a cappella, misidentification of the genre of some songs, and misunderstanding of some texts. One of the more humorous errors concerned a photograph of what the author identified as a sacred hut of a specific tribe—the building turned out to be a public restroom at Kruger National Park in South Africa.

How does the music teacher determine whether resources for teaching world musics are reliable and trustworthy? Perhaps this task can be made somewhat less daunting through the application of the following guidelines, which may be useful in determining the degree of reliability of educational materials for teaching world musics in the music classroom:[39]

■ Materials should be prepared with the involvement of a culture-bearer (one raised within the culture who is a recognized practitioner of the culture's music and dance) or of a student who has worked under the guidance of such a culture-bearer. This is essential to provide accuracy in performance technique, language skills, and cultural context.

■ Each selection, whether song, instrumental piece, dance, game, or story should be set clearly within its cultural context. This context should include source, circumstances under which it is performed, by whom within the culture it is most appropriately performed, historical and geographical information, maps, and so forth.

■ The original language should be used as the primary lyrics, along with a pronunciation guide, literal translation and extended interpretation, and, wherever possible, a recorded pronunciation track by a native speaker of the language. Any effort at creating a "singable translation" must be done with the guidance and approval of a culture-bearer. One cannot overly stress the importance of the original language to the music. After all, not all languages readily adapt well to English translation; subtle shades of meaning are inevitably lost when one creates a contrived translation for singing purposes; full immersion into the culture is impossible when the song is performed in translation. Teachers are noting that young children often pick up pronunciations and performance subtleties rapidly and accurately.[40]

■ Photographs, films/videotapes, drawings, and illustrations showing musical activities of the culture should be used whenever possible. Visual images of the culture in action bring the educational experience to life in the classroom and provide models for student performances.

■ Musical transcriptions of songs that have been approved by a culture-bearer should be available. However, musics of many cultures are not readily transcribed into Western-style notation; such efforts will, at best, be compromises—this should be stressed when transcriptions are used, particularly if a recording is also used as a model for performance.[41] The transcription should be reviewed and approved by a culture-bearer; any derivative arrangements must retain the original style traits unless approved by the culture-bearer.[42]

■ Recordings of the materials by native singers or their longtime students should be provided as a model for melody, style, performance techniques, and pronunciation. Authentic instruments or accurate reproductions should be used in companion recordings.

■ Any games, dances, or stories should have clear directions and diagrams for performance. Filmed versions of these activities are more beneficial but often not readily available. Games, dances, and/or stories must be appropriate for use with the provided song or instrumental piece.

■ Sacred or ritual materials should not be included in a collection intended for use in a casual classroom or community setting.

By applying these guidelines to music and educational materials proposed for use in the music classroom, the creative music educator will be able to determine the trustworthiness of such material and whether it may be learned from a basal series, textbook, song collection, another teacher, or musician. Lists and reviews of multicultural educational resources in a variety of publications can further assist music educators in selecting materials that reliably represent specific musical cultures. Some easily accessible examples include the following: an annotated bibliography in the appendix of Patricia Shehan Campbell's *Music in Cultural Context* that offers texts, videos, and an introduction to resources commonly used in public school and university classes;[43] a listing of band, orchestral, and choral works based on melodies from world cultures published in *Journal of the Conductors Guild* that provides a repertoire of selections for use in ensemble performance classes;[44] and a series of articles in *General Music Today* from 1998 to 2000 that reviews current books, book/recording sets, and book/video sets intended for use in the general music classroom (each article focuses upon a cultural area such as Africa, Native America, Asia/Pacific Rim, Latin America, Europe, and the Middle East, as well as a review of texts covering multiple cultures).[45]

Music educators, regardless of their selected program within the music curriculum, do not lack for well-researched, well-written teaching resources that are reliable and trustworthy representations of the culture being explored. Of course, older, less reliable resources remain in pre-1995 basal series, individual publications, and so on, but judicious application of the guidelines offered above will allow music educators to separate the good from the bad.

University/Public School/ Community Partnerships

Beginning with the 1997–98 school year, the general music teacher at Media Elementary School in Media, Pennsylvania, and the multicultural music specialist at West Chester University of Pennsylvania formed a partnership for the purpose of developing creative instructional units that would both meet specific school district goals and address the National Standards for Music Education. Their work provides a model music curriculum that combines elements of the applications principles described above. World musics have been fully integrated into the music curriculum; music has joined with other disciplines to bring world cultures into all disciplines; and the school has joined with a teacher education institution and community members to bring world cultures into a meaningful community setting. Students, educators, and parents joined in a teaching-learning project that had an impact far beyond the music classroom.

This partnership between a classroom teacher and a university professor specializing in multicultural music combines the strengths of two worlds, joining the elementary classroom teaching expertise of one with the research and writing strengths of the other. Also, students have access to materials, such as world musics instruments, recordings, and video materials by the multicultural specialist, that normally may not be available in the classroom. Another advantage of this type of partner-

ship is the creation of a unique teaching team that includes the elementary classroom teacher, the university professor, and music student-teachers assigned to Media Elementary (these student-teachers observe the interaction of the two instructors, as well as take part in research, planning, and instruction).

The primary objectives of this partnership during the 1997–98 year were to (1) develop instructional units focusing upon the Rosetree-Media School in Media, Pennsylvania, and its goals addressing cultural diversity and developing crosscurricular instructional projects; (2) develop instructional goals focusing upon the National Standards, stressing creative activities such as improvising, arranging, and composing (Standards 3 and 4) and historical, cultural, and interdisciplinary facets of instruction (Standards 8 and 9); (3) meet specific curricular expectations in the areas of Pennsylvania history, Native American culture, and African-American culture; (4) explore projects to include members of the community as resources for information and materials; and (5) cosponsor, if possible, special events such as workshops and performances. These objectives were selected in an effort to expand the scope of music instruction in the school and to add balance to instructional activities within the music program as a whole.

All grade levels in the school were included in various ways during this partnership. This report, however, focuses on two specific projects for fourth- and fifth-grade students: a semester-long project linking Native American culture with Pennsylvania history through music, history, and related arts, and a special project in

African-American culture that included a public school-university cosponsored workshop featuring Margaret Campbell DuGard (in Pennsylvania, these grades are required to study local Pennsylvania history and Native American culture).

The Native American project was based upon "Quiltmaker's Song" created by Dakota-Maricopa flute player, composer, singer, and dancer Robert Tree Cody. This song (on his *White Buffalo* album), described by Cody as "a song such as might be sung when making a quilt,"[46] was written in memory of Cody's aunt, a well-known maker of star quilts. On the recording used in class, the song is presented as a "theme and variations" opening with a simple rendition of the melody presented vocally by Cody's wife Marlene, followed by settings for Native American flute and synthesized orchestra, and ultimately combining Marlene's vocal performance with the flute and synthesizer.

A three-tiered approach was used to teach the musical component of this project. Listening lessons allowed students to discover form, tonality, cultural style traits, and instrument timbre. Performance-based instruction ranged from singing the melody to performing simple drum-and-rattle accompaniment modeled upon the recording to performing the melody on recorders and Native American flutes. Creativity-based instruction included performing improvisations on the melody using Native American ornamentations and improvisational style, as well as composing sets of themes and variations.

In crosscurricular activities, students in the classroom studied the Amish, Mennonite, and Quaker cultures in Pennsylvania, the Lakota culture in North

and South Dakota, and the connection between these cultures through quiltmaking. (Quaker and Mennonite missionaries carried quiltmaking to Lakota reservations during the late nineteenth century, where it became a popular craft among Lakota women and gradually a part of ceremonial, as well as social, life.) Class trips to nearby Lancaster County displayed Pennsylvania cultures firsthand, and students viewed quilts displayed in museums and stores. Parents from the community visited classes to display family quilts and demonstrate quilting techniques. Quilt patterns from Amish, Quaker, Mennonite, and Native American traditions were studied as an art project. Stories about quilts and quiltmaking were read as a literature component of the project. In the music classroom, students made quilt squares based upon models provided by community members, made by the music instructors, and seen in books on these cultures. To pull all these components together, students were given the traditional Native American story "The Legend of Starwoman"[47] to develop into a musical play for their spring concert. Students wrote a script based on the story and incorporated appropriate songs and dances from previously learned Native American materials.

The African-American project grew from the Native American project through the common element of quiltmaking traditions. Students discovered that African-American quiltmaking was distinguished by brighter color combinations, smaller bits of material in irregular patterns (i.e., the "crazy quilt" technique—due to poorer quality clothing scraps), and the frequent use of pictorial quilt panels to record family histories. In addition, guest instructor Margaret Campbell DuGard passed on the oral tradition that certain quilting patterns were used as signals on the underground railroad, providing indications of safe houses, dangers ahead, and so forth. The fifth-grade chorus chose to perform DuGard's "Hand Me Down My Mother's Work," which contains references to patchwork quilting (this song is dedicated to DuGard's grandmother, who decorated clothing with tatted lace). Students' attention was drawn to the similarities in thought and concept between "Quiltmaker's Song" and "Hand Me Down My Mother's Work." Students also created an African-style polyrhythmic accompaniment, harmony parts, and an improvisatory introduction for the work. DuGard presented a workshop on African-American music and creativity as a part of this partnership project.

The creative partnership formed for these projects continues to develop ideas and new projects. In the spring of 1999, Mary Goetze (University of Indiana) and Sheasby Matiure (University of Zimbabwe) presented workshops at West Chester University, Penncrest High School (RTM Schools), and the Pennsylvania Music Educators Association State In-Service. In October 1999, workshops on secondary level Orff-Schulwerk were presented by Carol Richards (then at the University of Newcastle, Australia). Workshops on this partnership process have been presented at state, national, and international music education conferences. A description of this partnership forms the basis of a chapter in the MENC publication *Music Makes the Difference*.[48]

Summary and Conclusions

In attempting to discover a single term to describe the various music repertoires of world cultures, participants in NUMELS II found that each of the many terms in circulation has some undercurrent of meaning that diminished its usefulness as a universal label. Many of these undercurrents were political, while others failed to be adequately inclusive to satisfy all needs, and still others appeared to be of commercial origin. I choose to designate this repertoire as "world musics," indicating that there are many musics of many cultures throughout the world.

"Authenticity" proved as elusive to define as finding a universal label for world musics. Because each culture's music is in a perpetual state of evolution, any example is merely a snapshot of a single aspect for but a moment of the culture's history. The terms "reliability" and "trustworthiness" may prove to be more effective guides to the appropriateness of a given song, instrumental piece, or dance. The fusion of styles and genres among world cultures likewise obscures any effort to determine "authenticity." I view this process of fusion as an evolution of style and genre, with benefits to each culture incorporated into the mix.

Two philosophical aspects regarding the teaching of world musics are important: (1) *What rationale may be offered for the inclusion of world musics in the music curriculum?* The importance of learning and understanding world musics goes beyond mere academic exercises. To explore, examine, and understand these musics is to explore, examine, and, hopefully, begin to understand ourselves as human beings engaged in the diverse human practice known as music. (2) *What approach should be used to present world musics within the curriculum?* The music should be presented "from the inside out." Musics of the world should be presented as closely as possible in the ways that they would be performed within the home culture—with the greatest degree of total immersion into the culture possible (considering educational circumstances). Such an effort to replicate many aspects of the culture will lead to a greater understanding of music's role in the culture.

Moving on to practical classroom applications, here are questions concerning world musics' curricular role at university and K–12 levels and suggested answers based on the arguments presented above:

Can world musics be fully integrated into the music curriculum from kindergarten to graduate school? Suggestions in the opening section of this chapter hopefully provide practical guidelines for bringing the full spectrum of musical sounds into the university curriculum, while the suggestions for selecting cultural resources for the elementary and secondary music program provide insights into curriculum building appropriate for those levels.

Can world musics serve as a bridge between university and public school classrooms and between schools and the community? The model offered above shows how a simple song and the cooperation among a classroom teacher, university professor, student teachers, and community members have had far-reaching effects on teaching and on attitudes toward music in not only the original school, but, hopefully, in schools and teachers in many other communities.

Whether the answers offered here are definitive is not as important as the fact

that the questions have been asked and answers sought by a gathering of scholars, each of whom brings unique experiences and perspectives to the discussion. These questions will continue to be asked and the answers debated, perhaps in perpetuity.

There is currently one point of agreement in American music education programs: We recognize that we are an incredibly diverse people with many cultural backgrounds and many tastes. All of us benefit when music education wholeheartedly accepts, reflects, and enriches this diversity.

Notes

1. William M. Anderson, *Teaching Music with a Multicultural Approach* (Reston, VA: MENC, 1991).

2. William M. Anderson and Patricia Shehan Campbell, eds., *Multicultural Perspectives in Music Education,* 2nd ed. (Reston, VA: MENC, 1996).

3. William M. Anderson and Marvelene C. Moore, eds., *Making Connections: Multicultural Music and the National Standards* (Reston, VA: MENC, 1997).

4. Ruth Boshkoff and Kathy Sorenson, eds., *The OAKE Collection of Multicultural Songs, Games, and Dances* (Fargo, ND: Organization of American Kodály Educators, 1994).

5. *Share the Music* (New York: Macmillan/McGraw-Hill, Inc., 1995).

6. *The Music Connection* (Morristown, NJ: Silver Burdett Ginn, 1995).

7. Bryan Burton, *Moving within the Circle: Contemporary Native American Music and Dance* (Danbury, CT: World Music Press, 1993).

8. This viewpoint is defended by David McAllester in his discussion of the music of Navajo-Ute musician R. Carlos Nakai in Nakai's *The Art of the Native American Flute* (Phoenix, AZ: Canyon Records Productions, 1996).

9. Louis Ballard, *American Indian Music for the Classroom* (Phoenix, AZ: Canyon Records Productions, 1973).

10. Bryan Burton, "Preservation, Evolution or Destruction? The Impact of Technology on Traditional Native American Musics" (paper presented at the ISME World Conference, Tampa, Florida, July 1994), 44.

11. Anderson and Campbell, eds., *Multicultural Perspectives.*

12. Bennett Reimer, "Can We Understand Music of Foreign Cultures?" in *Musical Connections: Tradition and Change,* ed. Heath Lees (Auckland, NZ: University of Auckland Press for ISME, 1994).

13. Fons Trompenaars, *Riding the Waves of Culture* (Burr Ridge, IL: Irwin Professional Publications, 1994).

14. Carl Seashore, *In Search of Beauty in Music* (New York: Ronald Press, 1947).

15. Terese Volk, *Music, Education, and Multiculturalism: Foundations and Principles* (London: Oxford Univ. Press, 1997).

16. Mary Goetze and Jay Fern, "Performing Choral Music of Diverse Traditions with Integrity: Issues and Methods for Classrooms and Rehearsals" (paper presented at the ISME World Conference, Pretoria, South Africa, July 1998).

17. Maria Pondish Kreiter and Bryan Burton, "The Multicultural Musical Quilt" in *Music Makes the Difference: Programs and Partnerships* (Reston, VA: MENC, 1999), 55–60.

18. Patricia Shehan Campbell, *Lessons from the World: A Cross-Cultural Guide to Music Teaching and Learning* (New York: Wadsworth Publishing, 1991).

19. Ballard, telephone conversation with the author, April 1997.

20. These conferences were American Orff-Schulwerk Association, Dallas, Texas, November 1995; Organization of American Kodály Educators, Provo, Utah, April 1996; Music Educators National Conference, Kansas City, Missouri, April 1996.

21. Anderson and Campbell, eds., *Multicultural Perspectives.*

22. Patricia Shehan Campbell, Ellen McCullough-Brabson, and Judith Cook Tucker, *Roots and Branches: A Legacy of Multicultural Music for Children* (Danbury, CT: World Music Press, 1994).

23. Abraham Kobena Adzenyah, Dumisani Maraire, and Judith Cook Tucker, *Let Your Voice Be Heard! Songs from Ghana and Zimbabwe* (Danbury, CT: World Music Press, 1986; rpt. 1997).

24. Burton, *Moving within the Circle.*

25. Performed by Robert Tree Cody on *White Buffalo,* Canyon Records CR 555.

26. Bryan Burton, "A Survey of World Folk Music Literature," *Journal of the Conductors Guild* 16, no. 2 (Summer/Fall 1995): 110–15.

27. Volk, *Music, Education, and Multiculturalism.*

28. For example, Kathy Sorenson has provided pronunciation guides using a modified phonetic alphabet combining the vowel sounds of the International Phonetic Alphabet and English consonant sounds for both Macmillan's *Share the Music* basal series and Kodály Educators' *The OAKE Collection of Multicultural Songs, Games, and Dances.*

29. Anderson and Campbell, eds., *Multicultural Perspectives.*

30. Anderson and Moore, eds., *Making Connections.*

31. Two examples are *Essential Elements 2000* published by Hal Leonard (Milwaukee, WI: 1999) and *Standard of Excellence Music Theory and History Book* published by Neil A. Kjos (San Diego, CA: 1996).

32. Documented in Bryan Burton, "Connecting Cultures, Communities, and Classrooms" (paper presented for the ISME Commission on Community Music Activities, Durban, South Africa, July 1998).

33. Bryan Burton, "Multicultural Festivals: Extensions of General Music," *General Music Today* 5, no. 3 (Spring 1992): 17–18.

34. Kay Edwards, "North American Indian Instruction: Influences upon Attitudes, Cultural Perceptions, and Achievement" (Ph.D. diss., Arizona State University, 1994).

35. Ballard, conversation with the author, April 1997.

36. Mary Goetze, "The Challenges of Performing Choral Music of the World" (paper presented at the ISME World Conference, Pretoria, South Africa, July 1998).

37. Bryan Burton, "Preparing Educators to Teach World Music" (paper presented at the ISME World Conference, Amsterdam, The Netherlands, July 1996).

38. Volk, *Music, Education, and Multiculturalism.*

39. These guidelines, originally developed by Judith Cook Tucker for use in assessing submissions to World Music Press, have been updated and adapted.

40. Bryan Burton and Maria Pondish Kreiter, "A Musical Quilt: Connecting Cultures and Classrooms through World Musics" (paper presented at the Pennsylvania Music Educators Association State In-Service, Valley Forge, PA, April 1999).

41. Once again the work of Goetze in this field is of prime importance.

42. There is a trend toward the creation of collaborative works by culture-bearers and contemporary composers, for example, R. Carlos Nakai and James Demars or Chesley Goseyun Wilson and Brent Michael Davids.

43. Patricia Shehan Campbell, ed., *Music in Cultural Context: Eight Views on World Music Education* (Reston, VA: MENC, 1996).

44. Burton, "A Survey of World Folk Music Literature."

45. These articles include Bryan Burton, "Multicultural Resources," *General Music Today* 11, no. 2 (Winter 1998): 24–27; Bryan Burton and Maria Pondish Kreiter, "Resources for Teaching Native American Music, *General Music Today* 11, no. 3 (Spring 1998): 25–29; Bryan Burton and Maria Pondish Kreiter, "Resources for Teaching: Music of Asia and the Pacific Rim," *General Music Today* 12, no. 2 (Winter 1999): 28–32; Bryan Burton and Rosella DiLiberto, "Resources for Teaching: Music of Africa," *General Music Today* 12, no. 3 (Spring 1999): 24–30; Bryan Burton, "Resources for Teaching: Latin American Music, Part 1," *General Music Today* 13, no. 1 (Fall 1999): 23–26; Bryan Burton, "Resources for Teaching: Latin American Music, Part 2," *General Music Today* 13, no. 2 (Winter 2000): 22–25; Bryan Burton, "Resources for Teaching: Music of Europe and the Middle East," *General Music Today* 13, no. 3 (Spring 2000): 23–28; Bryan Burton, "Resources for Teaching: A North American Sampler," unpublished.

46. Robert Tree Cody, *White Buffalo,* Canyon Record CR 555.

47. Researched by the author in three years of field work with various East Coast tribes.

48. Bryan Burton and Maria Pondish Kreiter, "The Multicultural Musical Quilt."

BRYAN BURTON, professor of music education and coordinator of graduate studies at West Chester University in West Chester, Pennsylvania, has authored several texts on Native American music and presented papers and workshops for music education organizations in the United States, Canada, Europe, Africa, Asia, and Australia.

10
Experiencing World Musics in Schools: From Fundamental Positions to Strategic Guidelines

C. Victor Fung

I am a native of Hong Kong and have lived in Indiana, Minnesota, Ohio, and Texas. I also have visited about two dozen different states within the United States and more than a dozen different countries. The experiences that I have had with people and places within and across continental boundaries have opened my eyes to cultural differences. My experiences in different cultures have helped me discover the cultural treasures that humans have. Not only capable of creative and artistic thinking, humans also possess diverse cultural resources that have made possible unlimited ways of thinking, feeling, living, and music making. With fascination and curiosity, humans have fashioned infinite variations out of their musical creativity, expressions, behaviors, and beliefs. The more I learn about music from different cultures, the more I am convinced that all humans are different but connected. As I live and travel across cultural boundaries, I find myself enlightened and enriched. My hope is to share these experiences to enrich all people's lives, and be enriched myself, in a world of musics.

The Treasure of Cultural Differences

The multiplicity of approaches to music education and their interconnectedness with other aspects of life have played a major role in attracting me to music education. I regard music education as a high-order activity that occurs in a great number of ways. Music education can be carried out in various settings, such as school, family, apprenticeship, and the mass media, in all geographic locations. Some speak of music made by animals (not human), and some speak of the cosmic music of the spheres. This chapter, however, focuses on music made by humans.

John Blacking defines music as humanly organized sound.[1] There are whole spectrums of aesthetic, social, and philosophical thought upon which to ground the ways to organize these sounds. I suggest that the plural form of the word music—musics—is appropriate to describe the variety of grounds and systems upon which musical sound is based. Musics represent a range of musical systems that differ in their fundamental frameworks and aesthetic perspectives. World musics are musics that can be found anywhere and anytime in the world. World musics include the spectrum of structures and behaviors in sounds from Western to non-Western, from popular to art, from vocal to instrumental, and from ancient to modern. World musics entail a collage of musical beliefs and practices, each with distinctive values, norms, and expectations.[2] The task of identifying a common ground among these distinctive values, norms, and expectations presents a challenge to music educators.

Within the United States, world musics from outside the Western art tradition in music education could be a response to two aspects of American culture: (1) global and encompassing, and (2) national and diverse. Because the United States is positioned as a world leader in politics, economy, military, sciences, and the arts, one might expect that its music educators would include a variety of world musics in their music curricula, in response to the need for global awareness and America's global understanding and leadership. Second, because the United States is a nation with many cultures that contribute to its unique character,[3] one might also expect that its music educators would use a variety of musics from within the United States as exemplified by its component cultures, almost all of which originated outside the United States. Whether to reflect the United States' status as a global leader or as a composite of component cultures, the use of world musics in American schools should demonstrate both the distinctions between and connections among indigenous musics from various world regions and diverse musics found in the United States. The use of "indigenous musics" from various world regions implies an examination of world musics in their indigenous settings. The use of "diverse musics" found in the

United States implies an examination of world musics in American settings. Musical migration, change, and relationships should be included to show their distinctions and connections.

The use of world musics in American schools, especially those of non-Western traditions, is now a strong current within mainstream curricula. The movement began like a strong but slow-moving weather system with the clouds gathering between the 1960s and 80s. During the 1990s, the storm hit hard as a result of changing demographics and diversity awareness. Many writers and researchers have written about the theories and practices of world musics in education. Many lesson plans and teaching materials involving world musics have been developed and published. Workshops and professional conferences are filled with topics in world musics. Scholars and educators intermingle and discuss issues such as world musics, multicultural music education, ethnomusicology, and their relationships to each other. However, many of the fundamental issues remain murky, leading to a multitude of positions supported by a wide range of philosophical tenets, some clearly articulated and others not so well expressed.

The purpose of this chapter is threefold. First, in the midst of the storm of materials, discussions, and philosophical debates, I will attempt to clarify my fundamental positions on the inclusion of world musics in American schools. These positions are not rationales[4] but are points of departure from my worldwide perspective, based on the proposition that "music is best comprehended and even introduced with reference to a world context."[5]

Second, I will discuss types of experiences that I believe are appropriate and educative in school settings. It is my intention to exclude certain musical experiences that are debatable, including those with stringent religious, sacred, and ritualistic practices that cannot be appropriately re-created in classroom settings. Such musical experiences, when re-created in the classroom, may be disrespectful to the original meaning of the musics and the people who created them.

Third, I will provide some broad strategic guidelines for music teachers who aspire to include world musics in their practice. I should emphasize that these are broad guidelines and are not exhaustive. Creative and inspiring music teachers will be able to generate further guidelines. In sum, this chapter begins with some fundamental positions as points of departure, followed by a discussion of appropriate musical experiences for use in school settings, and culminating with some broad strategic guidelines for music educators who aspire to include world musics in their curricula.

Fundamental Positions

This section elucidates four fundamental positions for the inclusion of world musics in American schools. These positions propose that (1) musics have a cultural context, (2) musics provide experiences beyond sound, (3) musics are changeable and fluid, and (4) diversity is a valuable resource in the society. These positions are my starting points for discussing many educational implications.

1. Musics Have a Cultural Context

Humans make music, and they make music in social and cultural contexts. One cannot properly understand and appreciate music without some knowledge of its social and cultural context. Most importantly, context is not just something that comes with music; it is part of the music. Oftentimes, it is the reason for the music's existence. Context is central to all musical events. Every musical event is contextually situated, whether a Buddhist chant, a Brahms symphony, an Indonesian *kecak*, or an African-American work song. Specific types of music are expected in various contextual settings, be they an opera theater, a church, a discothèque, or a Native American pow wow. No one expects to hear a Buddhist chant in a Christian church nor a Brahms symphony at a disco, because music's meaning depends upon its context. However, in the United States and many Westernized societies, the concert setting and listening to recordings seem to be acceptable contexts regardless of the origin and nature of the music. This is why these settings are considered apart from the other types of musical experiences in the next section of this chapter. The concert setting has built-in distinctive roles for both performers and listeners. Listening to a recording involves the performer's "frozen" actions, a set of technological devices, and the commercial practices and behaviors of listeners. Both of these settings present unique social and cultural contexts that are acceptable within many traditions, especially the Western art and Western popular traditions.

The social and cultural context of music and the music itself can be perceived from two general perspectives—insider and outsider—depending on the vantage point and identity of the individual. Some may term this dialectic as "insider and outsider,"[6] "self-ness and otherness,"[7] or "emic and etic."[8] Connotations of "emic" and "etic" have evolved in the last few decades, and they have striking parallels with insider and outsider in the contemporary literature. A crude description of the first of each pair (insider, selfness, and emic) is that it takes the vantage point of native members or members being initiated into the culture. The second of each pair (outsider, other-ness, and etic) takes the vantage point of an observer who does not belong to the culture. However, this distinction is not always clear-cut because an "outsider can learn to act like an insider," and an "insider can learn to analyze like an outsider."[9] Ethnomusicologists often view these two vantage points as complementary and mutually beneficial. One can learn from both vantage points and can learn to become a person having the other vantage point. Thus one can better understand the music, its process, and its concept, when the study is approached from both vantage points.

Regardless of the vantage point, however-er, all human senses (seeing, hearing, smelling, tasting, and touching) may poten-tially be implicated when music is perceived in its context, which entails a rich amalgam of stimuli within the musical event. From the psychological literature in music and music education, topics on the senses of sight and sound, naturally, exceed those of smell, taste, and touch. Although all senses are potential sources of contextual percep-tion, evidence suggests that the senses of sight and sound account for major differ-ences in an individual's musical experi-ences. Therefore, the senses of sight and sound, naturally, deserve more attention

from music educators, because they often help humans to receive cues in musical events. For example, eye contacts among jazz ensemble musicians provide important visual cues to the musicians. A group of singers responds to the soloist's call in call-and-response songs (i.e., aural cue). Thus, the context provides all sorts of sensual cues and momentum for musical behaviors.

2. Musics Provide Experiences beyond Sound

Americans and others who have been trained in the Western art tradition often believe that musical sound is the center of the music. Since the early part of the twen-tieth century, recording technology has accelerated the efficiency of isolating sound elements in musics. With a simple touch of a button, near perfect musical sound can flow from two or more speakers. One needs no muscular movement and skill in playing an instrument to experience music, nor need one be in the location where the musical sound is created or re-created. One needs neither composition nor improvisation skills. One does not even need to know how the musical instrument looks or the original context in which the music was performed or created.

In this regard, listening to the musical sound alone is certainly not a full musical experience. For example, one who listens intently to the recording of Mozart's K. 313 Flute Concerto in G, performed by Jean-Pierre Rampal with the Vienna Symphony Orchestra conducted by Theodor Guschlbauer (released by RCA) with eyes closed, can have a full listening experience, but I would argue that this is not a full musical experience. This act of intense listening offers no guarantee of the listener's knowledge of how a flute looks or how the posture and movement of the flutist looks. The listener may or may not appreciate the techniques or fingerings that Rampal uses to produce the melody, the phrasing, the tone color, or the dynamics. Listening intently does not presume that the listener understands sonata form or motivic development. Furthermore, this act of intense listening cannot guarantee the listener's understanding of the cultural context in which Mozart composed the piece in the late eighteenth century. Certainly, the listeners may form a unique perception, or mental process, about the musical sound, but this perception or mental process can be either abstract or concrete and is highly symbolic and individualistic.

Whereas all of these factors contribute to the fullness of the listening experience, a full musical experience requires more. A full musical experience engages one's body and mind simultaneously with sensual faculties within a cultural context. Only if one has had experiences in sight (e.g., the look of the flute, the movement of playing the flute, the score, and the live performance), physical action (e.g., blowing and fingering the flute), mental action (e.g., imagining the musical patterns, analyzing the music's structures, remembering the music's themes and tracking their development, and making mental connections with the composer's affect and intent), and context (e.g., the culture in which Mozart composed the music), can one have a full musical experience. The act of intense listening is an experience in sound at the time of listening, or, at best, a full listening experience. If one can experience a re-created

context of music in the late eighteenth-century European tradition (e.g., a concert) embracing the sight, sound, physical action, and mental action, then a full musical experience may be possible.

There is no doubt that sound plays a major role in musical experiences. Sound, however, is not the only sensation offered by music. If people experience only sound in relation to their musical life, their musical experience is incomplete. Those ethnomusicologists who cognize the triangular model proposed by Alan Merriam in 1964 have begun to rediscover and value the non-sound aspects of musical experiences. This triangular model suggests that sound, behavior, and concept are equally important in the study of music. A comprehensive understanding of music includes an understanding of sound, physical behavior, and mental concepts. As such, sound is only one aspect of a musical event.[10] This leads me to believe that one who understands music has fully experienced what musics have to offer through having experienced musics within their context.

Furthermore, musicians trained in the Western art tradition may feel perfectly comfortable with a paradigm of musical experience stemming from the Western art tradition; one such approach was presented in Roger Sessions' book *The Musical Experience of Composer, Performer, Listener.* As Sessions put it, composer, performer, and listener are regarded as "three successive stages of specialization," and "in the beginning, no doubt, the three were one."[11] These statements suggest that musical experiences in the Western art tradition may be linear and distinctively compartmentalized. To the contrary, I believe that the successive stages of composing, performing, and listening may not be applicable to understanding musical experiences in non-Western art traditions. In other words, a new kind of paradigm may be needed to describe, discuss, and understand musical experiences in a wide range of traditions. To be more inclusive, I consider composing to be a kind of mental action, performing to be a kind of physical action, and listening to be an experience in sound, and I see composing, performing, and listening as simultaneous in many non-Western art traditions. For example, Ghanaians often tell Americans that "there is no audience in our musical tradition; everyone is a participant." This means that no one merely listens to the sound in the Ghanaian musical tradition. Listeners are active participants involved physically by playing the drum, dancing, and/or singing, where drumming, singing, and dancing are all part of the music. Playing the drum, dancing, and singing are what I call physical actions. Improvisation is a manifestation of a mental impulse to create and, as such, is a mental action that may include any mental impulse, imagination, memory, or reflection. Thus, physical action goes beyond performing to include dancing and any muscular or psychomotor activities that are considered part of the music.

Phenomenologists, especially Thomas Clifton, have helped us understand the nature of musical experiences, providing fresh insights into the fullness and richness of the lived experiences we have with music. Phenomenology concerns the essence of experiences. Thomas Clifton suggests that the essential constituents of musical experiences are time, space, play[fulness], and feeling.[12] All four constituents are essential in musical experiences, and these experiences must be received through the human body and mind. Wayne D. Bowman summarizes this view: "Music is a bodily experience in the fullest sense: a richly corporeal mode of being that integrates mind, emotion, all the senses, an entire person."[13] Musical experiences occur in a multidimensional field of action, motion, and senses embodied in the human body and mind. Phenomenologists would agree that musical experiences occupy the entire human body and mind through multiple senses and human faculties, to include context, sound, sight, physical action, and mental action. These five musical parameters form the basis for my discussion of types of musical experiences. The fullest of musical experiences would embrace all five parameters simultaneously.

3. Musics Are Changeable and Fluid

As a function of the creative spirit, musics are fluid and changeable. Musical change is a subject of research for many ethnomusicologists. Musical changes occur as musics travel through time and space and are subject to artistic interpretations. Bruno Nettl suggests that all cultures and all musics involve change and that "the musics of the world have combined with each other—combined elements of melody, rhythm, harmony, performance practice, instruments—to produce new kinds of music appealing to a large, multicultural audience."[14] Parallel views are expressed by many. Margaret Kartomi discusses the pluralistic coexistence of musics and writes that "some musicians may combine and transform the elements of two or more musical sources, thus creating a new synthesis."[15] In discussing the overall context of world musical systems, Mark Slobin writes, "World music looks like a fluid, interlocking set of styles, repertoires, and practices which can expand or contract across wide or narrow stretches of the landscape. It no longer appears to be a catalogue of bounded entities of single, solid historical and geographical origins."[16] Music, therefore, is non-static, and its boundaries cut across time, space, and musical structures.

The issue of musical change is becoming more apparent and important for educators and ethnomusicologists alike, because musical and cultural changes have accelerated throughout the world in the twentieth century. When musics are being re-created in American schools, are these school experiences themselves considered part of the musical change? The schooling enterprise is relatively young compared to the enterprise of music, and it has become part of contemporary civilization. Admitting the institution "school" into our society is a change in itself. Musics that occur in schools, then, are inevitably part of the changing nature of music. When dealing with world musics that originated outside of the United States, what changes are legitimate and what changes are too far-fetched, making the experience inauthentic in the classroom? Music teachers are often forced to make changes and adjustments in the music to match students' abilities or to re-create the musical experience in a way that is different from that of the primary musical tradition. Good and legitimate changes must be based on a thorough understanding of the musical tradition and must have good reasons for change. Changes that do not ground students in a good understanding of the musical tradition are at best distortions. A good indicator of legitimacy for musical changes would be consulting a cultural insider, because such an opinion would likely be based upon a firm understanding of the acceptable aesthetic frame within that musical tradition. Well-trained outsiders, such as expert ethnomusicologists, can be of great assistance in this regard, too.

4. Diversity Is a Valuable Resource in the Society

There is no doubt that the United States is one of the most diverse nations in the world, in which immigration plays a major role in the formation and development of the society, bringing tremendous cultural diversity to the nation. At the same time, American citizens, by and large, live by the premises of freedom and democracy. Freedom and diversity, however, present an American paradox. In discussing the pluralistic context of American society, Maxine Greene suggests that "education for freedom must clearly focus on the range of human intelligences, the multiple languages and symbol systems available for ordering experience and making sense of the lived world."[17] I suggest that world musics are among the richest symbol systems available to human beings and that world musics are among the most sophisticated manifestations of intelligence. For these reasons, world musics should be part of the education system in order to fulfill a mission to educate for freedom in a culturally diverse society. Furthermore, I view our cultural diversity, including musics, as an array of rich resources that many other nations do not have, generating an array of challenges that provide a unique opportunity for American music educators to share these resources and to use them constructively. Given the nature of American society, we must celebrate diversity as a resource that adds to freedom and offers citizens expressive opportunities. There is a need to build communities that allow diverse constituents to prosper and be complementary to one another.

Types of Musical Experience

Anthropologists, psychologists, and philosophers have informed us in many ways about the richness and complexity of experiences available in world musics. An understanding of these experiences may help music educators who wish to provide educative world music experiences in their classrooms. Understanding various types of musical experiences may help educators to plan their teaching strategies.

Based on the premise that musical experiences are multidimensional, I present eight types of musical experiences in relation to five primary musical parameters mentioned earlier: context, sight, sound, physical action, and mental action. This categorization of musical experience is by no means hierarchical. This section shows the different types of human involvement and their characteristics in experiencing musics with reference to the five musical parameters. Each type of experience can be active or passive, depending on one's ability, determination, and social role and setting.

The eight types of musical experiences discussed in this section can be incorporated by music educators in all educational settings. Types 1 and 2 involve participants

on-site, where the musical event occurs in the primary setting: (1) be-there-and-do-it and (2) be-there. Types 3 to 8 are most likely to occur in a transformed location such as the music classroom: (3) do-it-someplace-else, (4) multimedia, (5) attend a live concert, (6) listen to a recording, (7) view a photo, a relevant object, or music notation, and (8) verbalize.

1. Be-There-and-Do-It. The first type of musical experience is the "be-there-and-do-it" experience. To have this experience, an individual must be physically transported to the location where the music is occurring, be it a pow wow, a jazz club, or a church. The participants' sensual faculties receive and react within a context. In particular, they see the event, including its actions, and listen to the sounds. The "do-it" portion of this experience requires that the body, with movements such as performing or dancing, be part of the musical experience through actual participation. The mind is actively involved in thinking, imagining, analyzing, or reflecting on the music. At the same time, participants use multiple senses and the body and mind to experience the full context, sight, sound, physical action, and mental action. In some musics, only insiders who have been trained, enculturated, or acculturated in the tradition can achieve this (e.g., Beijing opera); while in other musics, this can be achieved by all. For example, many Native American social dance songs are designed for full participation by all without extended periods of training, enculturation, and acculturation.

2. Be-There. The second type of musical experience is the "be-there" experience. This type of musical experience involves transporting the participants to the location where the musical event occurs, such as a Chinese tea house or an African village celebration. Through virtual participation, the "be-there" experience includes the use of all senses to receive and respond to the context. The participants listen to the sound, are involved in mental actions (such as thinking, analyzing, memorizing, and imagining), and see the instruments and motions of the event. One who has the "be-there" experience is a listener, thinker, viewer (of the visual stimuli of the music), and observer and receiver (of the larger context), but not an actual performer or dancer. Although the body is essential in listening to musical sounds, I distinguish the use of the body in listening from the use of body in large muscular movements, such as performing and dancing, by labeling the former "sound" and the latter "physical action." In the "be-there" experience, the lack of physical action directly associated with the making of musical sounds (i.e., performing or dancing) may be due to the individual's choice, ability, or other social and physical limitations such as group membership and social role.

3. Do-It-Someplace-Else. The "do-it-some-place-else" experience is one that involves large muscular physical actions directly associated with making the musical sound, such as playing an instrument, singing vocables, and dancing. Participants "do" the music but in a context and location different from that of the primary one, that is, not in a Chinese teahouse for *sizhu* music, not in a Christian church for a Christian hymn, and not at a New Orleans funeral for jazz funeral music. The music is being recreated "someplace-else." In this experience, one can actively listen to the musical sound, and

the experience can be substantially as good as that in the actual setting if participants understand the context and are capable musicians. Although the context is transformed, the sound aspect of the music tends to be comparable to that in the primary setting. For example, a master drummer from Ghana playing for an elementary school music class, rather than playing in Ghana with other drummers and dancers, suggests that this drummer is "doing" the music "someplace-else." Similar incidents are often found in classrooms, where the music making has been transformed to the classroom context. The "do-it-someplace-else" experience also provides the opportunity for mental actions, such as thinking, creative impulse, analyzing, imagining, recalling, and reflecting, for those who "do" the music.

4. Multimedia. The "multimedia" experience includes any type of multimedia presentation in world musics that is a recording from the primary setting. Multimedia presentations include video, CD-ROM, DVD, and some URL addresses on the Internet. Note that all forms of multimedia presentation incorporate more than one form of sensual stimulation, namely both visual and aural. Single-medium, such as audio CD, will be discussed below. The multimedia experience generally presents the primary sight and sound and some of the primary contexts. The better the production of the multimedia product, the better the context is presented. However, the context is never complete due to elements that are not transmittable through current multimedia technology such as certain sound effects, objects, and social and cultural events not captured by the camera lens: the wind, the

195

temperature, the humidity, and the social and cultural climate of the primary setting. The quality of this type of experience can vary a great deal. Nevertheless, multimedia experience in world musics can evoke very active mental actions, such as imagination, thinking, analysis, and reflection.

5. Attend-a-Live-Concert. "Attend-a-live-concert" is similar to the multimedia experience in many ways. Attendees of the concert may receive very similar types of information in sight, sound, and context, but there is generally no large muscular physical action being done by the concert attendees as part of the planned and desirable musical sound. The sound element may be comparable to that of the primary setting, but the sight and context elements may be altered or incomplete due to the concert setting. If the concert setting is the primary setting of the music (e.g., music in the Western art tradition), then, for the sake of this categorization, it coincides with the "be-there" experience for the audience and the "be-there-and-do-it" experience for the musicians, as discussed above. Attending a live concert in a type of music in which the concert setting is not the primary setting, such as Inuit throat-games, makes the experience incomplete in sight and context when compared with primary ones. Mental actions, such as thinking, analyzing, memorizing, and imagining, can still be very active in attendees of a live concert.

6. Listen-to-a-Recording. "Listen-to-a-recording" of the music may provide comparable sound (to a reasonable degree) as in a primary setting, but there is no visual information. This type of experience helps participants to focus on the sound elements in

mental actions.[18] Little or no contextual information is provided in this type of musical experience. Physical actions such as dancing or head nodding may be the only physical reactions to the music, and they need not be integrally connected to the music. Therefore, no large muscular physical action is required to complete this type of experience. Mental actions, such as thinking, analyzing, memorizing, and imagining, can be as active as those of the "attend-a-live-concert" experience.

7. View-a-Photo, -a-Relevant-Object, or -Music-Notation. "View-a-photo, -a-relevant-object, or -music-notation" can provide visual information and evoke active mental actions, such as thinking and imagining. Participants see photos of the music-making process or objects involved in the music-making process, such as musical instruments and relevant artifacts. These visual stimuli can provide some contextual information. Viewing the music notation may evoke inner listening, provided that the receiver is trained in reading it. No primary sound or physical action is involved in this type of musical experience. Therefore, this type of experience is best used as a supplement to other musical experiences.

8. Verbalize. Finally, to "verbalize" the music provides neither visual nor aural information. This type of experience involves a different symbol system—language. One may verbalize some or all of the above types of musical experiences. One may read, write, and talk about the music itself or the experiences that they have had with the music (i.e., 1 to 7 above). This experience can still evoke active mental actions. Mental actions based on verbalization could be about the musical sound

Table 1. Types of Musical Experience and Involvement of Primary Parameters

Types of Musical Experience	Context	Sight	Sound	Physical Action	Mental Action
1. Be-there-and-do-it	x	x	x	x	x
2. Be-there	x	x	x		x
3. Do-it-someplace-else		some	x	x	x
4. Multimedia	some	x	x		x
5. Attend-a-live-concert	some	some	x		x
6. Listen-to-a-recording			x		x
7. View-a-photo, -a-relevant-object, or -music-notation	some	x			x
8. Verbalize (read, write, talk)	secondary				x

Note. x = Involves primary parameter

but without the actual presence of the sound. Contextual and other information in this type of experience may become secondary due to the transformation of musical experience to a linguistic one (i.e., verbalization). No visual information, other than visual imagination, of the music's setting is involved. Therefore, this type of experience is often presented in combination with other types of experiences, such as photos (i.e., 7 above) in books (verbalization) and/or program notes (verbalization) in concerts (i.e., 5 above).

Table 1 shows a summary of the eight types of musical experiences discussed above with the involvement of the primary parameters (context, sight, sound, physical action, and mental action). It is important to acknowledge that the "be-there-and-do-it" experience involves the reception of all primary parameters. This suggests that the "be-there-and-do-it" experience is the fullest of all types of musical experiences,

as it involves all relevant senses and utilizes all relevant human capacities, from playing to thinking and from seeing to hearing. Taking full advantage of this experience depends on the participant's determination, ability, and social role and identity.

Table 1 also shows that mental action, which is divergent, flexible, and cross-functional, can occur in all types of musical experiences. Any type of musical experience may involve thinking, analyzing, imagining, memorizing, recalling, reflecting, creating, or a combination of these.

Strategic Guidelines for Music Teachers

The discussion above describes the types of musical experiences and their characteristics with reference to the five primary parameters (context, sight, sound, physical action, and mental action). That discussion, in conjunction with the four fundamental positions, leads to several broad strategic guidelines for music teachers who aspire to include all musics (especially musics from non-Western art traditions) in their curricula. These guidelines are not grade-specific or program-specific (choral, general, or instrumental).[19] They should be considered relevant regardless of grade level and program context. These guidelines may help teachers design their curricula and derive their lesson plans using world musics in educative and respectful manners.

Guideline 1. Music teachers should strive to include as many types of musical experiences as possible. All eight types of musical experiences could be included in the study of world musics. The above discussion suggests that "be-there-and-do-it" provides the highest potential for the fullest musical experience. All other types of experience seem to have some missing parameters. It is understandable that music teachers seldom have control over transporting students to a primary musical setting to provide a "be-there-and-do-it" or "be-there" experience. Teachers may consider building in more exchange or field opportunities, allowing students to be transported to the primary setting of the music. Experiencing the music firsthand in its primary context is far more rewarding than experiencing the same music elsewhere in a re-created context.

If the "be-there-and-do-it" and "be-there" experiences are not possible, music teachers should maintain a balanced diet of experiences by exposing students to all five primary parameters of musics (i.e., context, sight, sound, physical action, and mental action). This can be achieved by providing students with a profile of musical experiences that involves as many as possible of the five parameters. A profile of musical experiences can be established through time (i.e., through the period of a music education program). For example, a combination of "do-it-someplace-else" experiences and high quality "multimedia" experiences can cover all five primary parameters. Similarly, a combination of "do-it-someplace-else" experiences and "be-there" experiences can also cover experiences in all five parameters. This suggests that music teachers must not rely on only one type of musical experience. Any single type, except for the "be-there-and-do-it" experience, is lacking one or more of the musical parameters.

Guideline 2. Music teachers should be aware of the insider-outsider effect—the understanding of musics from different vantage points—and design their curricula and teaching strategies accordingly. Teaching and learning always involve interactions between the teacher and the learner, and these interactions vary depending on the type of teacher, the type of learner, and the subject matter involved. I believe that four scenarios are possible in teaching and learning world musics, due to the insider-outsider roles and identity of the teacher and of the learner.

Scenario 1 suggests a specific type of interaction between the teacher and the learner when both are insiders or culture-bearers of the music involved, such as when both the teacher and the learner are born and raised in Japan. In this scenario, certain conventional cultural practices, such as the reason for *gagaku* actors to sit on the floor instead of sitting on a chair, may not need explanation, but there is certainly a need for learners to develop a heightened awareness of these conventional practices. When learners are from within the culture, they may not be aware of practices that are uniquely their own. If both the teacher and learner have never been exposed to a non-Japanese culture, they may not be aware of the widespread use of chairs in other cultures. The learner may practice these conventions for a long time before becoming aware of the cultural contexts in such conventions. Awareness of such conventions should lead to a better understanding of their own conventional practices and those of other cultures.

Scenario 2 suggests a type of interaction between a teacher who is an outsider of the music and a learner who is an insider or culture-bearer, such as when the teacher, teaching Native-American music, is a Caucasian-American and the learner is a Native-American singer and drummer growing up in a reservation. In this scenario, the learner can significantly contribute to the learning experience, while the teacher serves as a facilitator for the learner's deeper awareness and understanding. At the same time, the teacher should learn from the learner with an open mind. Although the teacher is an outsider, the teacher should take advantage of the opportunity to benefit from the knowledge of the learner, while guiding the learner to a higher level of awareness of the conventional practices in the music. In a class setting, the teacher should allow the learner to take pride and contribute to the learning experience of the whole class. The teacher should also reinforce the learner's identity and cultural affiliation with positive attitudes.

Scenario 3 represents an interaction where the teacher is an insider or culture bearer of the music, but the learner is an outsider, such as when the teacher is an African-American gospel singer and the learner is a Caucasian-American who has had no experience in gospel music. The teacher's role as a model and an authority figure is reinforced; learners are likely to perceive the teacher as an authority. The teacher should not be shy in identifying an insider's perspectives. Being a bearer of the culture, the teacher has the obligation to present the music authoritatively, using all the knowledge and skills at his or her disposal in order to present the music truthfully and to make the learning experience educative, rather than miseducative.

Scenario 4 is very common in relatively homogeneous communities in the United States, where both the teacher and the learner are outsiders of the music. This scenario can be found in diverse communities also, where neither the teacher nor the learners are insiders of a certain music, such as in a class of African-American, Latin-American, and Caucasian-American learners, none of whom have had experience in Chinese music. In this scenario, the teaching and learning process may be presented as an exploratory process, and the teacher's role is a leader in the exploration. It is important that both the teacher and the learner recognize their outsider's views and agree to explore the new musical terrain together. The teacher should make use of available resources, such as books, recordings, and musicians in the community, to ensure musical truth. It is also the teacher's responsibility to attend workshops and seminars to keep up with current practices and to learn about unfamiliar types of musics. I believe that being willing to admit one's limitations and being open to explore new terrain are some of the most essential qualities found in good teachers. Such teachers model a musical open-mindedness for students and an adventurer's attitude in the search for diverse musical pleasures and meanings.

In all four scenarios, the teacher should be flexible in serving such various roles as guide, mentor, counselor, tutor, leader, and model. In addition, the teacher should not be afraid to learn from students; the teacher should be glad to gain by interacting with them and should make this apparent by being truthful to oneself and to students. Teaching and learning should complement each other.

One should be cautious about the possible ambiguity between the insider-outsider roles. I admit that vantage points taken by insiders and outsiders can be ambiguous (as discussed in the first fundamental position above), and therefore I have to admit that there are chances for ambiguity among the four scenarios. The ambiguity becomes more complicated when multiple learners are involved. A class of learners may contain a mixture of both insiders and outsiders. Therefore, when examining the four scenarios, the insider-outsider vantage points should be seen as general characteristics of learners rather than distinct demarcations.

All four scenarios suggest very different types of teaching-learning interaction. They imply that the practice of teaching world musics, from design and teaching approach to materials, may differ, due to variations among the four scenarios. Therefore, there is no "one-size-fits-all" approach to curriculum planning, lesson planning, or creating teaching materials in teaching world musics.

Guideline 3. Music teachers should include musics to which students in the class are able to relate. This has two implications for music teachers. One implication is to include musics that learners like. Music teachers should include musical styles and characteristics with which students are familiar. Students generally prefer world musical excerpts that are fast, loud, tonal-centered, with regular rhythm and many different pitches, consonant, moderately embellished, smooth sounding, moderate or complex in texture, instrumental, with bright timbre, and similar to Western music.[20] When videos are being used, students also tend to like those excerpts that have active visible movements and bright visual colors.[21] Teachers should add to what learners already like by guiding students toward experience of various musical parameters (context, sight, sound, physical action, and mental action) and to deeper levels of experience. If students already like the music, they can be led to explore a wide range of issues, such as what they like about it, what the context of the music is, and how to make a piece of music like that.

Another implication is to include existing resources that can be drawn from component cultures of the class and of the school community. Music teachers can utilize musical insiders in class to broaden the teaching and learning experience. They can also invite parent musicians or local musicians to their music classes. The main idea behind these suggestions is that learners can make connections with music within their community and among their friends. Learners come to realize that their community represents a wide range of cultural heritages.

Guideline 4. When providing musical experiences in American classrooms, music teachers should be faithful to the nature of the musics involved. Certain musics consider certain elements as being essential to the experience, and each type of music is based on a different musical belief and practice, with distinctive values, norms, and expectations. For some musics, improvisation may be the essence; for others, notation may be essential. For some musics, the perfection of sound may be the essence, while some others may have certain social behaviors as the essence. Some may be cooperative, while others may be individualistic. Some may involve quiet contemplation, while others may involve body movement. The list continues indefinitely. The key is that the music teacher should have a basic understanding of the essence of the musics involved so that musical experiences that are re-created in the classroom are faithful to their natures. If lyrics are involved, the proper language should be used. If notation is involved, the proper form of notation should be used also. Thus, musical experiences provided by teachers should follow whatever tradition is faithful to the music. Teachers will learn a great deal as well through the process.

Guideline 5. Music teachers are often constrained by a fixed-size classroom with traditional furniture and equipment, but opportunities should be taken to adapt to particular stylistic needs. Teachers can uti-lize good quality multimedia materials or the flexibility of classroom furniture. If at all possible, teachers should bring in authentic musical instruments and relevant artifacts to provide culturally related visual and contextual experiences for learners. And, of course, all possible field trips to live performances should be undertaken.

Guideline 6. Music teachers should emphasize the qualities of individual pieces rather than stereotyping certain types of musics. Each piece of music presents itself with unique qualities, even when allied to other pieces in the same style. A few pieces of music can hardly represent a musical style, but each piece of music is a sample of a musical style. It is important to recognize that another sample of the same musical style can be very different.

In addition, musical and cultural boundaries in the world were dissolving quickly in the twentieth century. The teaching of music according to geographic boundaries, for example, is an extremely dangerous enterprise. The fluidity of musical culture transforms musical genres and musical experiences around the globe. Musics and musical experiences have broken through the boundaries of geography, time periods, and musical structures. Musics from the other side of the globe can be created, performed, and heard here. Musics from centuries ago can be re-experienced today. Contemporary musics may incorporate structures of various types of world musics. To develop deeper musical sensitivity, examinations of the qualities of individual pieces are necessary to avoid a stereotypical pigeonholing of musical styles.

Guideline 7. In light of the constant musical change occurring around the world, music teachers have the responsibility to educate the younger generation to deal with musical change by instilling the habit of creative thinking based on a genuine understanding of and respect for various musical traditions. I would encourage musically creative activities to use world musics as an array of rich resources. For example, a class may create musical patterns and musical pieces using percussion instruments from China, Cuba, Ghana, and Indonesia. A class may also create musical pieces based on the sonata form incorporating the heterophonic texture of the Chinese *sizhu* music. In order to utilize the range of resources available in world musics, one must, of course, understand the natures and properties of these resources. Such strategies help to introduce future composers and other musicians to a global perspective.

Guideline 8. Music teachers need to maintain verbalization modes (read, write, and talk) in the teaching and learning process. These will assist learners to understand, cognize, and communicate about world musics. Learners may describe, discuss, compare, and contrast the essences of the music and the influences of diverse cultures on various musics. Learners can also express their feelings about world musics through words. Certain types of musical understanding may be available only through verbal modes, and teachers must utilize this mode of instruction. In conjunction with mental actions (e.g., think, imagine, and analyze), verbalization allows a complex but valuable web of communications among learners and between teachers and learners.

Guideline 9. Music teachers need to recognize their needs to participate in continuous professional development activities. No one can fully experience and understand all types of world musics. Music teachers may want to become at least bi-musical so that they can experience at least one different musical framework. Hopefully, bi-musical music teachers devoted to using world musics would become multi-musical and inspire others to become bi-musical and then multi-musical.

Toward the Future

The use of world musics, especially those from non-Western art traditions, has been a strong current in the United States in the 1990s and will no doubt continue in the new millennium. We need all types of research to put the ideas in this book to the test. We need to be able to speak with more research support in the future. In addition, diverse musics are created by diverse people in diverse contexts. Walls between peoples are becoming transparent; boundaries between cultures are becoming diffused, as world intercommunication increases dramatically. As the world becomes more connected, boundaries between "world musics" and "music" are becoming less clear. This blend of terms is healthy and necessary. The term "world musics" may disappear in the future. The meaning of "music" may be expanded to include what we know as "world musics" today. Whether it will be "music" or "world musics," the enterprise of music education is constantly facing refinements and re-definitions of terms, theories, and practices. The forward motion of this enterprise relies on contributions and cooperation among music educators, (ethno)musicologists, and communities around the world.

Notes

1. John Blacking, *How Musical is Man?* (Seattle, WA: University of Washington Press, 1973).

2. This is what Estelle R. Jorgensen calls "spheres of musical validity." See Jorgensen, *In Search of Music Education* (Urbana: University of Illinois Press, 1997).

3. Michael L. Mark suggested that music educators should be involved in discussing the position of the United States as a nation of nations or a single nation with many cultures that contribute to its character. See Mark, "Some Thoughts on William Billings," *The Bulletin of Historical Research in Music Education* 18, no. 3 (1997): 188–91.

4. For rationales, see C. Victor Fung, "Rationales for Teaching World Music," *Music Educators Journal* 82, no. 1 (1995): 36–40.

5. Barbara Lundquist and C. K. Szego, eds., *Musics of the World's Cultures: A Source Book for Music Educators* (Reading, UK: International Society for Music Education, 1998), 18.

6. Marcia Herndon, "Insiders, Outsiders: Knowing Our Limits, Limiting Our Knowing," *The World of Music* 35, no. 1 (1993): 63–80.

7. Bennett Reimer, "Selfness and Otherness in Experiencing Music of Foreign Cultures," *The Quarterly Journal of Music Teaching and Learning* 2, no. 3 (1991): 4–13.

8. Frank Alvarez-Pereyre and Simha Arom, "Ethnomusicology and the Emic/Etic Issue," *The World of Music* 35, no. 1 (1993): 7–33; Max Peter Baumann, "Listening as an Emic/Etic Process in the Context of Observation and Inquiry," *The World of Music* 35, no. 1 (1993): 34–62; Gerhard Kubik, "Emics and Etics: Theoretical Considerations," *The World of Music* 7, no. 3 (1996): 3–10.

9. Kenneth L. Pike, "On the Emics and Etic of Pike and Harris," in *Emics and Etics: The Insider/Outsider Debate*, ed. T. N. Headland, K. L. Pike, and M. Harris (London: Sage, 1990), 34.

10. Alan P. Merriam, *The Anthropology of Music* (Evanston, IL: Northwestern Univ. Press, 1964).

11. Roger Sessions, *The Musical Experience of Composer, Performer, Listener* (Princeton, NJ: Princeton Univ. Press, 1950), 4.

12. Thomas Clifton, *Music as Heard: A Study in Applied Phenomenology* (New Haven, CT: Yale Univ. Press, 1983).

13. Wayne D. Bowman, *Philosophical Perspectives on Music* (New York: Oxford Univ. Press, 1998), 268.

14. Bruno Nettl, "An Ethnomusicological Perspective," in *Musics of the World's Cultures: A Source Book for Music Educators*, ed. B. Lundquist and C. K. Szego (Reading, UK: International Society for Music Education, 1998), 23. See also Bruno Nettl, *The Western Impact on World Music: Change, Adaptation, and Survival* (New York: Schirmer Books, 1985).

15. Margaret J. Kartomi, "The Processes and Results of Musical Culture Contact: A Discussion of Terminology and Concepts," in *The Garland Library of Readings in Ethnomusicology,* Vol. 3: *Music as Culture,* ed. Kay Kaufman Shelemay (New York: Garland Publishing, 1990) 275–97.

16. Mark Slobin, "Micromusics of the West: A Comparative Approach," *Ethnomusicology* 36, no. 1 (1992): 9, 10.

17. Maxine Greene, *The Dialectic of Freedom* (New York: Teachers College Press, 1988), 125.

18. John M. Geringer, Jane W. Cassidy, and James L. Byo, "Effects of Music with Video on Responses of Non-Music Majors: An Exploratory Study," *Journal of Research in Music Education* 44, no. 3 (1996): 240–51; and John. M. Geringer, Jane W. Cassidy, and James L. Byo, "Non-Music Majors' Cognitive and Affective Responses to Performance and Programmatic Videos," *Journal of Research in Music Education* 45, no. 2 (1997): 221–33.

19. Choral, general, and instrumental are the three basic types of programs offered in American school systems. Choral and instrumental programs are ensemble-oriented programs. All nonensemble-oriented music programs tend to be categorized as "general," including history, theory, keyboard, and composition.

20. C. Victor Fung, "College Students' Preferences for World Musics," *Contributions to Music Education* 21 (1994): 46–63; C. Victor Fung, "Music Preference as a Function of Musical Characteristics," *The Quarterly Journal of Music Teaching and Learning* 6, no. 3 (1995): 30–45; C. Victor Fung, "Musicians' and Non-

Musicians' Preferences for World Musics:
Relation to Musical Characteristics and
Familiarity," *Journal of Research in Music Education*
44, no. 1 (1996): 60–83.
    21. C. Victor Fung, "Effect of Video
Presentation of Asian Music Perceptual
Dimensions," *Psychology of Music* 26, no. 1
(1998): 61–77.

C. VICTOR FUNG, author of about thirty
articles and research studies presented in
Asia, Australia, Europe, and North
America, is associate professor of music
education at the College of Musical Arts at
Bowling Green State University in Bowling
Green, Ohio, where he teaches multicultural issues, psychology of music, and applications of technology in music education.

11
A Materials Girl in Search of the Genuine Article

Rita Klinger

My journey to world music is multifaceted. I was brought up in an Irish-Italian neighborhood on Long Island by Jewish parents who had been subliminally taught to hide their "Jewishness" in order to fit into American society. My mother, the daughter of Lithuanian Jews living in England, was a post-World-War-II immigrant to the United States, where she met my Brooklyn-born father. My father was the son of a turn-of-the-century Jewish immigrant from the Austro-Hungarian empire and a German-Jewish third-generation American mother. Upon his arrival in New York at the age of 14, my paternal grandfather promptly cropped his Orthodox sidecurls and set forth on a journey that was typical of Jewish immigrants of his day—to become an American. To him, this meant that he should rid himself of all traces of his European Jewishness. My paternal grandmother was very proud of being a third-generation American, which further encouraged my grandfather to lose every trace of his European accent. My mother was quick to adopt the ways of her new American husband and home, so by the time I came along, the only thing Jewish in our lives was the family seder at Passover and the Chanukah menorah I lit each year while all of my neighborhood and school friends were celebrating Christmas.

Like all typically rebellious teens, I wanted to be different from my parents. Fortunately, this led me to learn about my Jewish roots. In doing so, I also discovered the world of Jewish and Israeli music. At the age of 15, I unwittingly began making "multicultural" music at Jewish youth group gatherings. Over the years, I continued learning, singing, and teaching this music at Jewish functions. Until more recently, however, the multicultural music that was part of my cultural heritage remained quite separate from the music that I learned and eventually taught as an elementary vocal–general music specialist in public school.

During and after my undergraduate studies, I developed an increasing interest in the Kodály approach to music education. Some of what captured my interest was Kodály's emphasis on indigenous folk music in the curriculum for both its intrinsic beauty and its relationship to (Western) art music. I learned that one of the key principles of the Kodály approach is that musical literacy skills be derived from music of the "mother tongue." In other words, repertoire drives the teaching sequence that is the basis of the music curriculum. I wholeheartedly adopted the mother tongue principle and began to teach accordingly, looking for musical materials from which I could derive melodic and rhythmic patterns that would lead my students to musical literacy. I accepted Kodály's notion of teaching from a musical mother tongue and went in search of the authentic American musical mother tongue.

These Kodály experiences opened my ears and mind to the variety of musical styles and genres that are "American." There was no singular music that could be called "American." I learned that American music included Mississippi and Chicago blues, work songs from the fields and jailhouses, hollers, cowboy songs, spirituals and gospel, songs from playgrounds and jazz from nightclubs and ballads from Appalachia that are very different in vocal timbre, instrumentation, and metrical feel from Mississippi blues or New England sea chanteys. All became part of my teaching repertoire. I also began to understand more fully that American music was much more varied than the folk, composed, and contrived songs that were plentiful in the series books upon which I had come to rely.

Yet the classroom performances of these very distinct musics were essentially homogenous. Field recordings provided information about the primary musical elements: melody, rhythm, form, and harmony. The "expressive qualities" that made the music musical were often demoted to the nonessential, and the extramusical context that brought the musical culture to life may be something interesting to know about but was not a necessary part of the curriculum. My search for what I later began to call "trustworthy" materials that represent various musics fairly and genuinely has shaped my career.

I'm a Materials Girl

Materials have always been at the core of my music teaching. Long before my formal training in Kodály pedagogy that led to a master's degree, I taught musical concepts and skills from the song and listening repertoire I introduced into my classes. My Kodály training emphasized the symbiotic relationship between personal musicianship and pedagogical skills with the study and analysis of folk songs and art music for use in the classroom. At the very center of this training was the notion of a musical mother tongue as the basis for musicianship training leading to literacy in the Western sense.

My knowledge and love of Jewish and Israeli music had little to do with the K–6 music lessons I carefully planned each week for my first teaching job in Vermont in 1975. I recall that I reluctantly included a Hebrew round in a 1976 fifth-grade choral concert. The song had little to do with my students or the literacy-based curriculum that I had mapped out for them. The children made fun of the guttural sounds that I attempted to teach. What was my purpose in including that song? I was conflicted about the purpose of that music (or any music that was "different") in my music program.

The result of all my teaching and learning was a split musical personality. I was a general music teacher with a fondness for "American" music, and I was also a Jewish woman who wanted to know more about Jewish and Israeli music and how Hebrew might fit Kodály's concept of a musical mother tongue. In 1977, I traveled to Israel where I lived, worked, sang, and collected children's songs for three years. Music from Israel, music for Jewish holidays, Jewish camp songs, and the music of Ashkenazic and Sephardic Jews became part of my personal repertoire. My years in Israel and my time spent collecting and dabbling in Jewish music became intertwined with my years of being part of the Kodály movement and examining American music. The more I examined music that is "Jewish," the more I realized that, just as there is no single definition of American music, there is no one Jewish music.

The Danger of the "A" Word

Early on in my teaching career, while many of my teaching colleagues were seeking songs that were specifically composed to teach melodic contour or rhythmic durations, I was seeking "quality" folk materials, which I equated with "authentic" materials. I fully believed there was one true, primary source for any given song. One version or variant of a song must be "better" to use in the classroom than another because it was the first one. I thought that it was my responsibility to seek the most historically accurate musical representation I could find of the repertoire I selected for my curriculum. I was drawn to researching song material to find a song's familial roots. I sought the real thing!

During the early 1980s, I distrusted songs printed in basal series books. Information about songs was rare, citations were uncommon, and the recordings, all sounding virtually the same, featured beautifully in-tune, light, high, Anglo-sounding children's voices always backed up by a variety of instrumentation that may or may not have had anything to do with the "authenticity" of the song.

Today, basal series and volumes by numerous individual publishers provide increasing amounts of information about music from cultures perceived to be less familiar to teachers than the "norm." Gone are the days when a footnote stating "Song from Africa" sufficed on the bottom of the page, or singable English was the only option for "foreign" materials. Most songs come with translations, transliterations, and/or International Phonetic Alphabet pronunciations. A few even print characters in the original language. All this is in addition to facts that are furnished about the song, the country of origin, and the people.

The more information provided about a song, the more music educators still search for "authentic" music for their students. In the 1990s, there remained a tendency among music educators to believe in music as being a stagnant item that, once found and preserved on paper, could be re-created in classroom settings.

It took years for me to recognize that paper re-creations are merely a reflection of the musical transcription skills of one listener and, perhaps, the contributions of a score of editors. I also came to understand that all versions and variants of a song from a variety of time periods are in some way authentic. People evolve and music evolves. Musical traditions are not static, but rather live, grow, and change as people's environments change. Performances, interpretations, and arrangements may vary, but performances, interpretations, and arrangements are not necessarily related to a song's legitimacy. A historical artifact is not necessarily more or less authentic than a contemporary arrangement of the same song.

The Test for Trustworthiness

Rather than use the term "authentic," I prefer to look at the *trustworthiness* of a song. Authentic musical experiences depend more on the trustworthiness of the source than the time, place, or particular arrangement. From where does the printed material originate? Who transcribed it? Is there an accompanying video or a recording? Is the recording accurate according to whatever information is known about music of that culture?

The key to determining the trustworthiness of a piece of music is somewhat personal and requires some patience and perseverance on the part of the teacher. Some sources are intrinsically more "trustworthy" than others.

A musician from a particular ethnic or cultural group presenting a song that is considered typical of that ethnic group would be a very trustworthy source. Take note of the word "musician." This level of trustworthiness can only be true of someone who is recognized as a musician within his or her ethnic community. Someone who is from Java, for example, but is not a musician might still be a trustworthy source for contextual usage and the circumstances of a song, but may or may not be capable of performing the song according to cultural musical norms. Someone not familiar with Javanese music wouldn't know if this person was singing with acceptable rhythmic or pitch accuracy according to Javanese standards.

Another trustworthy source is an ethnomusicologist who has studied, recorded, and sometimes transcribed the music of particular ethnic groups. From ethnomusicologists, school music teachers can learn about the people who make the music and the circumstances in which the music is made. If there is notation, the transcriptions would be an accurate representation of musical performances. Ethnomusicologists can also lead us to valuable recorded sources of the music that they study.

Audio and video recordings of music performed by indigenous musicians are other notable trustworthy sources. For most music teachers, it would be ideal if these recordings are accompanied by musical transcriptions, but it isn't necessary in order to consider the source trustworthy. Collections distributed by Smithsonian Folkways, Rounder, or World Music Press are typical of such trustworthy sources.

Unfortunately, I am often told that music teachers have neither the time nor inclination to gather and "translate" even most of the readily available trustworthy materials for their students. Rather than researching music, teachers often prefer music that has been transcribed into what they consider to be a singable key and arranged for immediate classroom consumption. If the materials are accompanied by teaching strategies, all the better.

But if the material has been arranged to be accompanied by classroom percussion instruments, or the words have been altered in translation, then what? Is such material automatically less trustworthy than music in an unaltered state? Should it be used or tossed aside solely in favor of the more trustworthy sources? The answer to this question is a bit ambiguous and depends on the teacher's preferences, comfort level with such materials, and goals for using the material in the classroom. A teacher is likely to use any material that is found to be appealing, regardless of the trustworthiness of the source.

How should music educators determine the trustworthiness of materials? In the end, you must trust something! If you are to trust your source, you should be able to trust that the translation and pronunciation guide are accurate. If you are to trust your source, you should feel certain that no one from within the culture will be offended by your use of the song in the classroom. If you are to trust your source, you should be confident that the music is at least from the culture that the publisher claims, if not representative of music from that culture.

Selecting music that truly represents a particular culture or ethnic group is extremely difficult. Once a music teacher came to me at the end of an Israeli music conference presentation and asked me the following question: "If you only had room in your curriculum for one song from Israel, which one would you choose?" In reply, I asked her which American song she would choose if she only had room for one. I don't believe any one song can truly be the sole musical ambassador of a particular culture. If we had to choose only one song from each country or ethnic group, we might wind up with a repertoire of international national anthems, and I certainly don't believe "Hatikvah" to be any more representative of Israeli music than the "Star-Spangled Banner" is of American music.

The Who, What, When, Where, and Why of Materials

Finding trustworthy source materials is a big hurdle, but determining which of these materials to actually select for use in the curriculum may present an even bigger obstacle. Selecting materials for the curriculum requires that the following questions be addressed:

Who? For whom are the materials? Who are the teachers, students, parents, and members of the school and larger community?

What? What materials do we tend to select? What materials should we select?

Why? Why do we choose what we choose *when* we choose it? Why at all? Are our selections influenced by our audience? Should we allow this?

When? and *Where?* When and where in the curriculum do our selections occur?

The choice of any musical materials is personal and often delicate. There are music teachers who choose musical materials because they are readily available in textbooks that their schools have adopted, or because teachers received the material from a class, colleague, or workshop. Other teachers choose materials because of the music's perceived curricular value; these teachers look for specific materials to fit a carefully constructed teaching sequence of musical skill development. There are still others who choose materials because, for whatever reason, they find the materials appealing and believe that their students will, too.

When it comes to multicultural or world musics choices, the criteria for selection are to some extent the same. Teachers choose world music materials because they are available, fit into their curriculum, and/or because they simply like them. In the case of world musics, however, there are often additional reasons for selections. These reasons are often related to a school district's or individual teacher's goals for multicultural music education.

Sometimes individual school districts require that specific geographic areas or ethnic groups be studied in particular grade levels. The music teacher is often asked to supplement or enhance the general curriculum by including repertoire from those countries in the music program.

Some music teachers choose multicultural materials because the materials coincide with calendar themes. African and African-American materials appear in their curriculum for a Martin Luther King celebration or Black History Month; an Asian song is taught for the Chinese New Year; and an Israeli song surfaces around Chanukah.

Sometimes music teachers choose materials because of the diversity in their school's student population. These teachers frequently see it as their responsibility to bolster self-esteem in their students, and they view music as the vehicle for achieving this end. Some music teachers in urban settings see it as their duty to use African and African-American music as the core of the music curriculum, often making the curriculum "Afrocentric" as opposed to "Eurocentric." This reinforces the belief that multicultural education can be achieved through using music representative of school and community populations.

Conversely, there are music teachers who choose to teach the music of particular cultures because their school population is homogenous. When there are no students of a particular ethnic background in a school, some teachers regard music as a way to broaden their students' views. This often coincides with the perceived goal that multicultural music education teaches understanding and acceptance through the inclusion of music representing a variety of American ethnic groups and subgroups.

Some teachers choose multicultural materials because they are most similar in language, form, timbre, rhythm, melody, and/or harmony to the music with which the teacher is already familiar. Some are afraid of the unknown, and most haven't

been trained to use anything other than the limited materials they were taught in school and university. For most teachers, this translates to Anglo-American songs and Western art music.

With each choice comes a consequence. If music is chosen primarily to fit a school calendar or holiday theme, music may gain importance in the general curriculum, but the intrinsic value of the music might become secondary to extramusical goals. This approach may reduce music to fulfilling a stereotypical calendar need at the expense of learning the music for its musical value.

If music is chosen primarily to reflect the school and community population, a wealth of material will be lost to students simply because of the community in which they live. This approach may or may not enhance students' self-image; there is no guarantee. It is probable, however, that such an approach will not open the door to diverse cultural or musical experiences. Similarly, music that is chosen primarily because it seems familiar or has similar characteristics to familiar music will not necessarily generate varied musical experiences.

Of these reasons, music that is chosen to counter homogeneity in the school and community appears to have the most noble place in the curriculum. However, this approach does not ensure that students who are exposed to such music will automatically gain respect and understanding of the culture from which the music originates.

A combination of approaches is probably the best solution. If teachers are comfortable with a particular music because it has familiar musical characteristics, it stands to reason that students might also be comfortable with that music. Music that seems familiar might be used as a springboard to study less familiar music. Music should be selected primarily for its intrinsic value but also analyzed for its potential extramusical value. Musical choices should not limit African-American music to Black History Month, for example, or designate one Chinese song in the curriculum for use on the Chinese New Year. Care should be taken not to teach only, or even primarily, the music of the main ethnic group in the school community. Musical choices should both reflect and expand upon the diversity (or lack of diversity) in the school and community population.

Teacher Education

For 20 years, I have been involved in various aspects of teacher education, and I have observed the music education pendulum swing from Western art music to world musics. There was a time when a solid knowledge of Western art music was all that was necessary to be a music educator. Now it is considered the norm for music educators to have at least one world musics course on their college transcripts. This change has required music education departments in colleges and universities to examine existing curricular requirements and make program adjustments that have been hard for some university music educators to come to terms with.

Whereas departments and schools of education have readily revised their curriculum to include courses in diversity in the classroom, diversity in approaches to curriculum, and varied curricular content, schools of music and departments of music education

have been slower to respond. It is true that there are numerous music departments that require students to take world musics classes, but it is rare that the materials from those classes become part of the student's teaching repertoire. There are other institutions that require courses specifically designed for future music educators to write curriculum and plan lessons using world musics materials as the basis. But if this type of curriculum is not valued by all members of a music faculty contributing to the education of future music teachers, the desired result of the single class might not come to fruition. Unless the departments themselves are "multicultural" in their approach to producing music and musicians, single class offerings will have little impact on future generations of music teachers.

Although one might expect preservice teachers to be more receptive to world musics than their collegiate music departments, this is not inevitably the case. Preservice music teachers may be as slow to accept change as some of their university professors. Holding onto familiar musical materials and pedagogical approaches seems to be a need among present and future music educators at every level of instruction. In this respect, future music teachers seem to differ significantly from their general classroom teacher counterparts.

The distinction between these two groups of students is clearly in evidence in the following two scenarios. Both classes consist of future teachers. The difference is that the first group represents future music teachers and the second group represents future elementary classroom teachers.

Scenario 1. These students are being trained to conduct wind ensembles and orchestras and to develop musical reading and writing skills in young students. Almost everything these future music educators learn is geared toward the understanding and performance of Western art music. They may have to take an obligatory course in world musics or classroom diversity, but they are still uncomfortable with what they consider to be "other" music. In their elementary general music methods class, these future music educators don't want to hear that their conservatory-style, Eurocentric training is not the only path to understanding music or becoming a musician; they seem indifferent to the fact that it is linked to one specific musical tradition. When they are introduced to, for example, a lullaby from Mexico, they lose interest.

Scenario 2. In their state-mandated music methods class, future elementary classroom teachers are excited at the prospect of using music of various cultures to enhance their social studies and language arts curriculum. To their eyes, music helps to build confidence and self-esteem through the use of various urban musics to which students can easily relate. These students are not intimidated at the notion of "other music" because they have little formal musical training and their objective is utilitarian— using music to serve the general curriculum. They are delighted at the opportunity to learn a lullaby from Mexico.

These two scenarios are very real to me; I have experienced them often. I find the difference between these two groups of students quite disturbing. Music students often want to become music teachers because they were inspired by a high school band or choir director. These students want to emulate their music teachers, who were

likely to have known little of world musics, nor could they conceive of a place for it in their school music curriculum. This approach to music curriculum has long been intensified at the college level. University music departments typically devote most of the curriculum to reinforcing the value of the Western art music tradition with which undergraduate music students already have some familiarity. The very nature and mission of most collegiate music departments makes this a difficult cycle to break. When music departments begin to integrate world musics into all curricular offerings with the same enthusiasm as many elementary schools, music students will begin to see that there are many paths to musicianship and many diverse musics to consider along the way.

Being "Politically Correct"

Regardless of the world musics offerings and requirements of college and university music departments, future teachers seem most influenced by diversity or multicultural course requirements in departments of education. In contrast to the Eurocentric flavor of many music courses, the goal of these education courses often seems to be to sensitize future educators to issues they can resolve proactively, to use a very "politically correct" ("PC") term, if they know what to anticipate. In the case of music education, I have discovered that sometimes being PC comes at the price of discarding musical materials that might be deemed offensive.

Musical materials that were acceptable in the past may no longer be considered PC. A consequence of being proactively PC in the classroom might mean neglecting a wealth of material because it is not PC. A treasury of song material would not be acceptable if we should be forced to discard it due to perceived offensive texts. In response to this problem, some advocate altering words to eliminate any questionable sections, omitting verses that might offend, or even discounting entire genres, such as choosing games or counting-out rhymes, because they aren't inclusive or multicultural enough. Below are only some of the personal encounters that I have experienced on this issue:

I have been admonished for singing songs like "Ida Red" in which rhyming words have a suitor buying mink for his gal dressed in pink: "Mink!" said a California student teacher when I introduced the song in an elementary methods class. "How can we teach our young students that it is acceptable to kill mink for fashion?" I have been chastised for teaching "'Oh,' said the Blackbird," a New England variant of a song describing how birds got to have different colored heads, because it deals with fickle women leaving the nest: "This song would be very insensitive to children of divorced or separated parents," said one undergraduate student newly indoctrinated to multicultural awareness. I have been cautioned by a school principal not to sing the word "amen" as it occurred at the end of a Thanksgiving canon that a classroom teacher had asked me to introduce for a school Thanksgiving luncheon: "Instead of 'We give thanks, amen,' can't you sing 'We give thanks, again?'" he asked. I have been questioned by future classroom teachers on the use of the playground game "Pizza Pizza Daddio" because the words force children to choose someone of the opposite sex to be

"it" by chanting, "Johnny has a girlfriend" or "Sally has a boyfriend." A very serious graduate education student asked one day: "What if Johnny is a homosexual and would rather have a boyfriend? By playing this game you are imposing a societal notion of correct sexual preferences on these children. That is not very multicultural."

Even the traditional "Farmer in the Dell" has been called into question because of the selection of children for traditional roles. I was told: "Children need to know that boys can choose boys for wives **if** they like!" It had never before occurred to me that my first-grade students would be thinking of anything other than being chosen, or the motions they would get to make up should they be chosen, to be "it"!

It could be that the pendulum has swung too far in the name of multicultural education. I am not at all sure about what we have accomplished by producing future educators who are oversensitized to multicultural issues. If we are to be held to increasing community and classroom standards that claim music teaches or preaches specific moral values or religious beliefs, our teaching repertoire would be greatly reduced.

Although I am not generally in favor of altering words, there cannot help but be a certain amount of time-related subjectivity involved. That which is considered PC now might not be PC in ten years and may not have mattered at all ten years ago. We can and should take a few moments to separate the song text from the contextual values that the song text might support. In the case of "Ida Red," for example, I can easily explain to my students that mink was at the time a treasured, valuable possession.

However, it never occurred to me to con-textualize the text to the song about a doll made of china when I used it as part of an open house to which parents were invited. The lesson, which I thought went very well, ended with me being called a racist for teaching the Appalachian song "Mammy, Buy Me a Chiney Doll" about a little girl who would give anything to own a porcelain doll: "You are the most bigoted person I have ever seen and should not be allowed around children," said an irate African-American man whose daughter sang the song as part of my classroom demonstration.

The offending word was "mammy," which in the context of this Appalachian song was a perfectly acceptable way for a child to address her mother but provoked images of a racist South to this parent. If I have been proactive, this scene might not have occurred. But in this instance, I didn't believe that I should be proactive. The only word in the song that I thought might be problematic was "chiney," and I usually introduce the song to children by explain-ing that "chiney" was slang for "china" and that the girl in the song wants a doll made of fine china. It did not occur to me that other words to this otherwise-innocent chil-dren's song would illicit such a reaction from a parent. Rather than take time to worry about all the words in this song, I now teach an altered version song known as "Mama, Buy Me a China Doll."

Perhaps I should continue to alter the original words when I teach a song like "Chiney Doll," but I am not sure the battle is worth the result. Over the years, I have found myself resisting some of the pres-sures of being PC. However, I am not sure that all PC changes are intrinsically bad.

They may be part of the natural process of change that occurs in any musical tradition. Music is, after all, influenced by the social, political, technological, and environmental issues of the time. Music is influenced by the times and, therefore, changes over time. The "Chiney Doll" song, altered to conform to the pressures of the day, might represent such change.

All musical materials, without regard for country of origin or ethnic affiliation, must be held to the same standard for accept-ance into the classroom music repertoire. For all the years I spent searching for "authentic, quality" material, I now believe that this standard can be expressed as the "trustworthiness" of the material source. In contrast to the increasing quantities of musical and contextual information provid-ed about materials perceived by some pub-lishers to be unfamiliar, the accuracy of information about what has long been the basis of classroom song repertoire—Anglo-American folk songs—is often ignored. We don't generally seem to be concerned with contextualizing Western art music, yet we want to give tons of information about a song if it comes from another culture. Teachers should be just as interested in the origins and circumstances of what has become a standard Halloween song, "Skin and Bones," introduced into the classroom repertoire by Jean Ritchie of Kentucky, as they are in the origins and circumstances of a Haydn Symphony or a stone game from West Africa.

Although the scenarios described above are clearly related to multicultural issues, they primarily reflect the same political dilemmas faced by music teachers when selecting material that *isn't* necessarily perceived to be multicultural. When the material choices are broadened to include world musics, the criteria for political correctness in many cases seem to become less stringent. The mere fact that "exotic" or "multicultural" music is in the picture sometimes makes the material choice acceptable, without questions and without regard for the "who, what, when, where, or why" of the material. To some, that same traditional game with traditional roles for boys and girls becomes acceptable if it is from a "different" culture. In fact, there are those who equate including world materials with being politically correct, no matter what the source, context, or meaning.

Individual teachers will accept different acceptable criteria for their choice of material. Once material choices are made, the materials can be analyzed according to musical categories such as instrumentation, timbre, form, tuning, and the use of melody and rhythm. Then it may be possible to broaden the base of our musical experiences to investigate the who, what, when, where, and why of the people and culture from which the materials come. We can then begin to go beyond the sound to know who the people are, where they live, what the context of music is within their society, under what circumstances music is transmitted in their society, whether they use or value notation, and not only what the music sounds like, but what the music makers look like. All of these things comprise the context that brings the student into the musical culture of the "other." Perhaps by doing so, music educators can help to create musical environments in which the "other" becomes less "other" and more the norm.

That leaves only one more big question: How? How can music of less familiar cultures be introduced into the classroom? How can teachers transmit to their students what they know about a musical culture? Once we accept that we can't learn everything about all the music to which we wish to expose our students, that the classroom environment is never going to be as "authentic" (dare I use the word?) as traveling with the students to the culture, and that there are a variety of musics from a variety of genres (American and otherwise) that we want to have as part of our repertoire, then we will be freer to explore a variety of ways to introduce and teach music.

What about the "Dead White Guys"?

Over the past several years, I have come to be untroubled by my multifaceted musical self. I realize that I am, to a certain extent, "pluri-musical." My repertoire includes some (though not all!) American musical forms, some (though not all!) Israeli and Jewish musical forms, and a smattering of songs, games, and instrumental musics from a variety of different world cultures. Importantly, I am comfortable re-creating my repertoire in my music classes, and I have begun to integrate much of my repertoire into all of my teaching.

I thought I had a grip on what it meant to teach from a "multicultural" perspective. I became comfortable balancing the PC problems of song text with the trustworthiness and diversity of materials. I was on a mission, and it became my responsibility to pass this on to my college students. I concerned myself not only with the notes and rhythms but also with the vocal timbres, variations in tunings, and expressive qualities any musical materials might present. I long ago stopped confining my song analysis to musical parameters and began to explore extramusical uses that would appeal to classroom and music teachers alike.

I thought I had all the answers when the following incident made me reconsider my course of action. The only student with prior musical training in my class of twenty-eight elementary education students had heard enough from her peers (and the teacher!) about musical diversity. When it came time for her end-of-the-year teaching presentation (a listening lesson as part of a unit integrating anything musical into the general curriculum), she presented a music and language arts unit on Holst's *The Planets* and proudly said to the class, "Someone has to stand up for the dead white guys!"

The comment stopped me cold. Had I gone too far? I had introduced the students to a multitude of ways in which they could use world musics to integrate the curriculum. We had discussed American ethnic groups and immigrant groups and experienced the music they brought with them. We had played African-American playground games and Native American flute songs. We had heard blues and Broadway and danced play parties and polkas. Among the world lullabies, rock-passing games, *gamelan* tunings, and Israeli folk dances, where had I placed the Western art music tradition that was my first musical love? Was I shortchanging Western music by neglecting the fact that it, too, is a "world" music with a particular ethnic identity?

I haven't yet come to terms with this delicate balancing act. And there is so much to balance: formal with informal musical traditions in the West and around the world; musical qualities with extramusical qualities; Western notation with non-notated, aural musical experiences; trustworthy sources with expedience; authentic performance practices with classroom resources; and being true to a particular tradition with being PC. A difficult balancing act indeed!

Conclusion

American music, I believe, has always been multicultural. American music is music of the symphony hall and Broadway stage; it is music of the playgrounds, streets, and garages; it is cowboy songs and country dances, New Orleans jazz and Chicago blues, Polish polkas in Cleveland and Cajun dances in Louisiana, the Appalachian "Chiney Doll," and the New England variant of "'Oh,' said the Blackbird." These musical forms each represent a different ethnic or cultural facet of American life, hence making the amalgam of these musics multicultural.

Music educators, however, have been slow to embrace all the music that falls under the American umbrella. Although there are now many trustworthy material sources readily available, the goal of many music educators has not been to expose children to the worlds of music in America and beyond, but rather to continue to train students to relish European art music. We can (and should) still teach Western notation and aesthetics as one of the many world music perspectives. By all means, we should teach and use notation, but we should also teach music without the use of notation. We should teach from a broader perspective the music of cultures that are not readily performed in concert halls. We should not be fearful of music that requires us to "bend our ears," as my teacher Barbara Lundquist would say, and forces us to listen to scales, vocal timbres, tunings, instruments, and forms that are unfamiliar.

We may not have come to any agreement as to how we should label the trend in music education to teach world musics. It has been assigned names such as multicultural music education, multiethnic music education, world music education, and global music education, each accompanied by a somewhat distinct meaning and goal. Everything from teaching tolerance and building self-esteem to understanding cultural differences through music has been attributed to one or more of these various labels. Goals both musical and utilitarian have been associated with world musics in the classroom.

To me, however, the label is not as important as the musical content it represents. And regardless of what we call it—multicultural, multiethnic, global, or world musics—the materials are the major means through which we acquaint students with musical cultures. Through materials, we introduce our students to a variety of musics and provide multiple exposures and musical experiences that will lead to familiarity, understanding, and, hopefully, ownership and valuing. We choose musical materials for our classrooms every day that reflect what we believe should be musically valued by our students. It is our job to take music that is unfamiliar to our students and bring it to life. It is our job to make that unfamiliar music not only familiar, but meaningful.

RITA KLINGER, associate professor and coordinator of music education at Cleveland State University, has taught music from preschool through college in the United States and Israel, where she spent three years collecting children's songs and singing games. Klinger specializes in the Kodály method.

12
Teacher Education for a New World of Musics

Kathy Robinson

*A*s a biracial child growing up in the heart of Pennsylvania's conservative Dutch country, the teachings of Martin Luther, German Baroque music traditions, and a loving, caring family laid the foundation for who I have come to be. God blessed me with a powerful voice and gifted fingers that allowed me to master the organ, piano, clarinet, and accordion. My musical talents carried me through the awkward teen years—the tumultuous 1960s and 1970s—into an outstanding music teacher education program at Lebanon Valley College, a small liberal arts college in the heart of the Dutch country. But what I learned from this rich background and what I could share with my students in Central Pennsylvania was not all I was—personally and professionally.

Who I was extended beyond my Dutch interior to include the songs, stories, and feelings of those who shared my blackness—a part of me to which I had little access during my first two decades. When African-American perspectives, culture, and musics did find a way into my world, they were so marginalized that I was reluctant to claim them. The desire for advanced schooling took me out of the Dutch country to the big city of Chicago, where I met people and communities who valued and validated African-American culture—there I began to grow into my blackness.

To put my newfound personal and intellectual understandings into practice, I took a teaching position at Willard Elementary School— a center for Evanston's English as a Second Language Program and "home" to children who spoke more than twenty-six different languages. As I was preparing my students for the sights and sounds they would encounter in an upcoming theater presentation, I began to sing the Japanese rain song "Ame ame fure fure" to my first graders. One budding musician's eyes became wide as saucers—"That's my song," she said. I remember her beaming face as she sang the song for us; she told us about its meaning and how she had learned it in her native Japan. The passage of ten years has not faded the power of that moment. Daily I strive to teach in a way that honors a multiplicity of voices—including my own—and that roots music education in the reality of people's lives.

What Does Multicultural Music Education Look Like in the Elementary General Music Classroom?

Multicultural music education means many things to many people. Many educators disagree on its nature and value but do agree that in some form its curricula include "many" musics. Should these musics be studied on a daily basis or occasionally, such as during May Day, Black History Month, Hispanic Heritage Month, or the months of the Chinese, Vietnamese, and Korean New Years? Should the world's musics promote a connection to the lives of people from various cultures (like my Japanese student) or be studied in isolation for their pitch relationships, form, rhythmic content, and so forth? In U.S. schools, should these musics be sung in their indigenous language and learned as people of the culture would learn them, or sung in English from the printed page?

My recent study[1] of the practice of multicultural music education in public elementary schools was centered in Michigan—a state that mirrors the rest of the United States in many ways, including population distribution, ethnic breakdown, and teacher age, education, and experience. Based on self-reported data from elementary general music teachers in public schools, I determined that Michigan's most exemplary programs had at their core effective teachers with strong democratic attitudes, beliefs, and values, who have made a personal commitment to increasing competence in the teaching of multicultural music through continuing education, concern for authenticity, and understanding of the various uses and functions of music and its strong connections to culture. The following four profiles demonstrate four exemplary multicultural music education programs (the schools' names have been changed for purposes of confidentiality).

Washington Street Elementary (School A) is a PreK–5 elementary school in a diverse lower-class to lower-middle-class community in Detroit (Michigan's largest city) with a student population that is 65 percent Arabic, 20 percent African-American, and 15 percent Caucasian and an equally diverse teaching staff. Both the principal (in her late fifties) and music teacher (in her late twenties) are African-American female musicians with master's degrees who are committed personally and professionally to multiculturalism. The music teacher, in her sixth year at the school, is extremely well-organized; through her elegant teaching style and personal commitment to multiculturalism, she demonstrates great respect for each child she teaches.

Mitchell Bay (School B) is a K–5 elementary school in an upper-middle-class to upper-class monocultural suburb of Kalamazoo (Michigan's second largest city). The school's veteran music teacher is a European-American woman with more than twenty years' experience, a master's degree, and a dedication to continually gaining competence in world musics. The principal, a former vocal music teacher with ten years' administrative experience, believes that it is critical for Mitchell Bay students to develop global awareness and an understanding of and tolerance for others in this "small" world.

Kingwood Elementary (School C) is a K–5 elementary school in a middle-class to upper-middle-class suburban neighborhood bordering Detroit. The school community is very diverse—consisting of nearly equal numbers of Chaldean, Caucasian, and African-American students, plus students of other backgrounds. This diversity, however, is not reflected in Kingwood's teaching staff, which is 94% Caucasian. Multicultural education is critical to Kingwood School. The principal, an African-American woman and former music teacher, feels that the importance of and commitment to multicultural education should be communicated through her leadership. Of Middle Eastern heritage, the general music teacher holds a master's degree and has nearly twenty years' teaching experience. Interest in multiculturalism comes from her ethnicity, which she believes gives her a special sensitivity; she often thinks about her pride in her own background and wants that for her students.

Easterville Elementary (School D) is a PreK–6 elementary school with an attached special education center in a blue-collar, union-oriented suburban Detroit community. The school population and teaching staff are overwhelmingly Caucasian. Multicultural education is very important to the school; the European-American principal believes it to be the primary issue at Easterville. The African-American music teacher, with a master's degree in vocal performance, emphasizes singing, listening, theory, and music fundamentals in her classroom.

These exemplary programs vary greatly in location, school ethnicity, and classroom resources, yet they are closely aligned in their school and music-education philosophies. While of differing ethnicities, each of the teachers possesses a master's degree and a personal commitment to multiculturalism. While none of the teachers had multicultural content or perspectives in their preservice methods courses, they each enjoy and feel effective in teaching world musics in the classroom. To increase world musics competence, each teacher regularly

seeks out workshops, conference presentations, multicultural music experts, and published materials. Two of the teachers have taken an ethnomusicology course, and two regularly consult teachers, students, parents, and community musicians in their quest to learn more about world musics.

Each of the teachers works in a school climate where multicultural education is very important and their work is supported by curricula that have specific multicultural goals. Musics from a wide variety of cultures are used in their classrooms; however, which musics are studied varies according to teacher preference, the heritages of students attending the schools, classroom teacher units, school themes, and proximity of each music to Western structure and function.

The "common elements" approach, in addition to separate multicultural units/lessons, is the primary means of multicultural music inclusion in each school. Singing and listening activities predominate, and teaching procedures usually involve the native language, English translation, and aural examples of authentic musics from the culture being studied. Teacher C notes that singing songs in their indigenous languages has become "second nature" for students whom she has taught since kindergarten.

These teachers identified the greatest challenges to multicultural music education: finding good quality materials that are interesting to the children; accurate pronunciation and translation of foreign language texts, developing curricula; and increasing world-musics performance skills, particularly in African rhythm patterns and the scale patterns of Asian musics.

Ultimate decisions regarding the musical content and perspectives taught in the classroom rest with the teacher—decisions for which a teacher often has had little training or support. While these teachers have administrative and curricular support and the motivation to seek out some world musics knowledge and skill, they have had limited opportunities to question individual beliefs and values and to develop musical and cultural competence beyond the Western European perspective. Without these opportunities, teachers continue to transmit what has been taught to them— the narrow lens and perspective of the Western-European-art tradition—even when teaching a variety of world musics. Their background and education have not provided them with a full knowledge of the range of issues surrounding teaching music with multicultural content and perspectives.

The following seven questions and challenges are at the core of today's music education practice.[2] Each music teacher makes decisions about these issues on a daily basis. While there are no easy solutions to these challenges, a comprehensive understanding of each is central to moving the practice of multicultural music education forward.

Musical content (form) and context: which to emphasize and when? how to balance the time available while resisting superficiality and tokenism in each area?

Folk and classical traditions: which to begin with? which to emphasize? how to achieve balance and resist superficiality? how to sequence experiences? how to honor both aural and written traditions?

Transmission and transformation: how to transmit musics of the past, present, and future? how to build bridges between tradi-

tions while removing barriers to understanding?

In-school and out-of-school music (continuity and interaction): how to connect the in-school and out-of-school musical lives of students? how to move from the student's world to another's world?

Making and receiving music: which to emphasize and when? how to balance the roles of composer, performer, and listener? how to embrace technology while experiencing music as a vehicle of personal expression?

Understanding and pleasure: how to relate understanding the structure and meaning of music to its pleasurable, sensual, and emotional dimensions?

Philosophy and practice: how to balance the ideas, tools, and methods that are inherent in each musical system with teacher and students' personal philosophical belief systems and with curricular goals? how to honor multiple beliefs and perspectives about music-making?

While these exemplary teachers struggle daily to balance musical content and context, folk and classical traditions, and in-school and out-of-school musics, the challenge of synthesizing philosophy and practice often proves most difficult. A substantially wide gulf existed between Teacher D's self-reported beliefs and her classroom practices. If Michigan's most exemplary teachers are struggling to understand some of these questions and to translate their beliefs into classroom practice, what does this mean for the majority of teachers?

Difficulties encountered by teachers in exemplary programs (e.g., deficits in education in world musics, language skills, clear-cut multicultural classroom goals, support, instructional techniques and strategies, and awareness of published world musics materials and of the full range of multicultural music education issues) were magnified in other Michigan elementary programs. The quality most noticeably absent from other teacher reports was the willingness to actively seek out world music resources (print and personal) and thus increase teacher competence.

In general, the interpretations and practices of multicultural music education in Michigan were "widely varied," ranging from curricular inclusion of multicultural content during holidays or month-long celebrations, to year-long infusion of diverse musics in a variety of instructional strategies, with concern for issues of authenticity and representativeness, inter/intracultural understanding, and context. Most Michigan teachers' commitment to multicultural music education tended toward the narrow, interpretive end, and thus their practice was superficial. Understanding the issues and challenges of teaching music with multicultural content and perspectives is crucial to moving the practice of multicultural music education forward. The key to improving the practice is music teacher education.

School-Level Issues in Teaching Elementary General Music with Multicultural Content and Perspectives

Superficial treatment of multicultural content and perspectives pervades our nation's public school music programs, as evidenced in the widespread use of the "heroes and holiday" curricular approach. Using musics similar to Western music,

rejecting indigenous languages in favor of English, teaching aural traditions by note-reading, and favoring Western tone colors are practices typically used in a superficial program.

While many teachers truly believe in the value of multicultural experiences for their students and in teaching from a multicultural perspective, a wide gulf exists between what teachers say they believe and the manifestation of those beliefs in their curricula and instructional practices. For the most part, the gulf between philosophy and practice is probably unintentional but may be the result of several factors: lack of training in multicultural education and multicultural music education; lack of opportunity and guidance to fully explore beliefs, values, and attitudes about multiculturalism; lack of time in an already crowded curriculum (coupled with reduced contact hours); lack of appropriate instructional materials, and of guidance and support from school administration; and confusion regarding the goals and possible strategies of implementing multicultural music education.[3]

Goals and Definition

Lack of agreement on the definition of multicultural music education, its goals, and strategies for implementation is a major obstacle to effective practice. Most music educators and scholars agree that multicultural music education in its various forms involves curricular inclusion of "foreign" or non-Western music materials. The term "multicultural" (i.e., many cultures) is one that characterizes U.S. society, often used interchangeably with the term "culturally pluralistic." According to Horace Kallen, however, a culturally pluralistic society has many cultures whose members enjoy *equal* access to the wealth of that society.[4]

In the United States, the Western European ideas and ideals upon which our country was founded still radiate from the country's every pore. Those people whose heritage falls outside of Western European strains may have some degree of limitation placed on their access to the "American dream." To fully embrace "cultural pluralism," those of Western European heritage who have traditionally enjoyed U.S. political, social, economic, and educational opportunities and resources need to make room for those of other cultural heritages who have not. What might a nation that wholeheartedly embraces and celebrates diversity look like?

"Culture" in almost every concept of multicultural music education has tended to refer to ethnicity (i.e., the music of a specific ethnic group or country). In general education, a much broader definition of culture exists—a definition that includes ethnicity but also encompasses gender, race, social class, religion, lifestyle, exceptionality, and age—all dimensions of multiculturalism that are beginning to garner more attention in music education. Gender issues involving women composers, performers, and conductors have found a louder voice in music education within the last ten years; however, their consideration has been primarily in the context of equity rather than multicultural music education as we now know it. What might a musical education that embraces diversity and the multiplicity of musics found in the U.S. look like?

The cornerstone upon which U.S. formal music education is built was note reading and singing—the study of which aided Protestant forebearers to more fully worship God. From these beginnings, music education grew into a way to elevate (and standardize) the "culture" of students whose heritages lay outside the influence of Western Europe. Does teaching multicultural music education or music from a multicultural perspective imply giving up curricular inclusion of Western art music? Does it imply, rather, that Western art music is one of many musics that should be included in the musical education of our nation's children? If the latter is true, and multiple musics are to be present in curricula, then we must also: (1) recognize the pervasiveness of the Western lens and develop other lenses allowing us to "see" clearly in a variety of contexts; (2) emphasize musical and contextual qualities that are critical to and valued by the culture being studied rather than those relevant to Western contexts; (3) respect the means of transmission of each music; (4) judge each music tradition on its own terms from an in-depth understanding of that specific tradition; and (5) understand that the role of music in people's lives varies greatly across cultures and that the ways people interact with music are rooted in the ways that their culture functions (e.g., means of socialization into society, symbolic representation, aesthetic enjoyment, etc.). Consideration of these issues requires a depth of understanding not adequately present in Michigan's exemplary music educators nor the majority of U.S. music teachers.

If one goal of education is to transmit the heritages of a society's peoples, our music education curriculum needs to reflect the reality of our diverse society.

How do we honor music and the music-making of the past, present, and future in our music curricula? Honoring the past means continuing the presence of Bach, Beethoven, and Mozart, as well as offering singing, reading notation, guided listening, and performance opportunities in wind ensembles, choirs, and string orchestras in U.S. music curricula.

This Western European tradition is part of who we are but not *all* of who we have been or are today. "We" includes peoples whose roots or heritage lies in Africa, Eastern Europe, Latin and South America, Asia and Southeast Asia, and other corners of the world. Honoring the past and present means honoring, valuing, and giving voice to multiple traditions rooted in geographical regions, gender, age, and styles, such as popular, classical and folk musics. Music education must be transformed and must encompass a broader way of viewing music—its transmittal, roles, and uses—using a new structure born of this new perspective. This is the challenge. To transform requires fundamental change—not just adding onto or adjusting existing curricula—but new ways of thinking and acting.

Issues at the heart of curricular transformation include selecting and balancing the variety of music traditions, which fall into two main categories—classical ("art") and folk—both found throughout the world. Most of the world's musics are transmitted orally (by watching, listening, and/or imitating, both formally and informally). Western classical music and many other classical traditions are not; these require specialized training and performance, often by professionals, and sometimes specialized notation as well. Works within this tradition are most often "set" and beloved of those within and outside the culture. Folk traditions, which may not be as well-known outside their regional base, are of the people (not elitist), perhaps "simpler" in structure, and transmitted orally. As such, one would think that classical and folk traditions are natural complements, but in U.S. society, they are very separate, as is their study.

Their separation is mirrored in our society, where the "cultural capital" (e.g., behaviors, skills, language, and meaning) of Western Europe has prevailed since our country's inception. What does the predominance of this "cultural capital" mean for the arts—for music in particular? The Western European art tradition is so strong that it has almost become an international musical "language," cutting across continents, languages, ethnicities, and social classes. What it has meant to be musically literate has been firmly grounded in the classical tradition: the ability to read and write music within the Western European tradition, the emphasis on the re-creation of music, and the entire Western European aesthetic have been highly legitimized and have long been thought of as the "right" way. It is only in the last thirty years that our African-American-rooted jazz tradition (an "aural" tradition) has been deemed appropriate for curricular inclusion. This incredibly strong legacy of Western European cultural domination makes curricular transformation quite challenging for music educators.

Conceptual approaches to multicultural teaching that place musics in the broadest possible context are known as "music-as-culture" approaches. Some scholars believe that a concept of multicultural music education that includes gender and other facets of culture is too broad, unwieldy, and confusing. Can we ignore issues such as age, gender, and race in the teaching of world musics? Should we teach world musics from a "music-as-culture" approach or with a musical, rather than cultural, focus?

While the "music-as-culture" curricular approach focuses on rooting music in context, comparative approaches, such as the "world musics education" approach of Anthony Palmer[5] and Jacqueline Yudkin,[6] focus on musical understanding and, as such, include a wider range of musical styles than the former. The "world-musics" approach isolates specific qualities of music and music making. However, the intent is to view those qualities through the eyes of the culture. While the practice of multicultural music education in Michigan does include a music-as-culture approach, the "common elements" approach is the most predominant; it isolates musical qualities but views them through a Western lens, placing a high value on analysis and structure and little value on context. The widespread popularity of this "conceptual" approach calls into question a teacher's depth of understanding of musics presented in "music-as-culture" units.

Beyond an emphasis on the "musical" or "cultural" approaches, there are few clear objectives to any concept of multicultural music education. To further obscure seemingly clear goals, teachers at times blend these two approaches in their classrooms. Should students "know about" world musics, or "know" the music itself, of which the latter seems to indicate some degree of

multimusicality? Do music educators emphasize skill or appreciation when teaching multicultural content and perspectives? Each teacher will probably have a different response to the question, "What do we want our students to know and be able to do regarding the world's musics?" This language—"know and be able to do"—is reminiscent of the National Standards for Music Education, which were crafted to "guide reform of PreK–12 music as America moves toward the 21st century."[7] The National Standards advocate the classroom use of musics of diverse genres and styles in order to reflect the multimusical diversity of America's pluralistic culture, avoid musical stereotyping, cultivate understandings about relationships between music and other subjects, equalize opportunities to learn music, and increase utilization of community resources to enhance and strengthen the music program. Specifically, the National Standards call for students to sing, play, listen to, and describe musics of diverse cultures, in addition to distinguishing different characteristics of a variety of musics and recognizing the functions, roles, and contexts in which music-making occurs in different cultures.[8]

Most teachers successfully pass on what they themselves know or are able to do; while these broad goals are excellent for focus, their realization in the classroom will be filtered through the teacher's lens, which is often Western. Until teachers are provided with opportunities to understand and affirm multiple traditions and perspectives, our nation's music curricula will change only minimally. Multicultural music education's definitions, goals, and strategies for implementation are of utmost importance to successful practice. Michigan's four exemplary teachers each had different curricular goals and objectives with differing degrees of clarity in the teaching of multicultural music education. Many teachers around the United States, unfortunately, are less focused on what the outcomes of their teaching with multicultural content and perspectives should or could be.

Lack of Time

In addition to the confusion surrounding definitions and goals, another barrier to the successful practice of multicultural music education is limited student contact time. Many of our nation's schoolchildren have music classes only once a week. Some elementary general music teachers in my Michigan study reported seeing each child in their school(s) as little as eleven times in one year.[9] While lack of instructional time is any educator's nemesis, its widespread citation among these teachers also illustrates that they view multicultural music education as a content "add on"—an extra that is not valued as an integral part of the curriculum and thus not infused, along with perspectives, on a day-to-day basis within the music classroom. An add-on, content-driven multicultural music education, often approached through a Western lens, is likely to produce incomplete and inadequate understandings about music.

Materials

The exemplary teachers profiled at the beginning of this chapter indicated that finding quality multicultural materials was a challenge; for many others, it is a primary barrier to teaching multicultural music.

Instructional materials are essential tools for incorporating world musics in the elementary general music classroom. At no time in our history as a profession have there been more world musics materials (e.g., books, recordings, films, videos, CD-ROMs) available to music teachers. This proliferation of materials brings new and often unfamiliar traditions to music educators.

In addition to culture-specific materials, current music series textbooks, such as those published by Silver Burdett Ginn and Macmillan, include more songs and instrumental pieces of various world cultures presented in a more authentic manner than ever before. Many of these publications feature pieces to sing, dance, or play, with explicit directions, pronunciation, recordings of indigenous music-makers, and contextual information. While these materials are fine "starters," moving deeper musically into the culture requires additional education and experience.

Herein lies another challenge. How do teachers with little to no experience with world musics determine what is critical and valued by multiple cultures? Should not the qualities and characteristics of a culture's music and its role and transmission determine how we must teach the music of that culture? Attendance at world musics workshops and seminars; listening to recordings and performances; studying books, articles, videos, and films; attending festivals and celebrations; taking lessons, dance instruction, or college coursework; and going into communities to meet and talk with people are various means that increase knowledge and skills in multiple traditions. While these vital experiences require much time and effort, teachers must value others' music enough to seek out these cultures and then thoughtfully transmit what they learn to their students.

Several guidelines (including Tucker's checklist[10] for world musics choral literature) and annotated bibliographies and reviews (including those found in *Music in Cultural Context*[11] and *General Music Today*[12]) have been published to aid teachers in choosing appropriate materials for classroom use. While a proliferation of materials and a support system that helps identify appropriate materials exists, accessibility to the full range of instructional materials still depends on the mindset, experience, and perspective of the individual teacher.

This "lack of materials" barrier suggests that one of the greatest challenges to the successful practice of multicultural music education is not *what* is taught but *how*— the teacher's perspectives and instructional strategies. We do not adequately prepare teachers to relate to their students the combined social and cultural values that surround and underpin different musics in the course of instruction, yet this is an essential component of multicultural music education. Musical knowledge without cultural competence is ineffective and incomplete. Perhaps music teachers are charged with doing more than their education allows.

Teacher Beliefs and Attitudes

Teachers' beliefs, values, and attitudes about multiculturalism and diversity affect curricular content and perspective and also have a major impact on their students. The Michigan teachers indicated a strong value for multiculturalism. However, in interpreting their statement, we must remember that teachers, like the children that they

teach, have been reared in a climate that places varying significances on racial, ethnic, linguistic, religious, gender, and socioeconomic differences. Teachers are human beings who bring their own cultural perspectives, values, hopes, and dreams to the classroom. They also bring their prejudices, stereotypes, and misconceptions to the classroom, despite any disclaimer to the contrary.[13]

"Teachers' values and perspectives mediate and interact with what they teach and influence the way that messages are communicated and perceived by their students."[14] Because students in teacher education programs often receive knowledge without time to analyze concomitant assumptions and/or values or engage in the construction of their own knowledge, they often leave teacher education programs with many misconceptions about people of diverse cultural, ethnic, and racial groups.[15] Current and prospective teachers need opportunities to explore their attitudes and biases in order to gain knowledge about people who are different from themselves.

Teacher Training

Lack of instructional time and/or quality materials, confusion surrounding definitions and goals, and other barriers contribute to a wide gulf between what teachers say they believe and the manifestation of those beliefs in classroom multicultural music education practices. The presence of these barriers also reveals a teacher's inability to fully grapple with the seven interrelated issues listed above. The key to increasing understanding of these interrelated issues, and thus fostering improvement in the practice, lies in music teacher education.

Many of today's teachers completed music education degree programs prior to the current emphasis on teaching multicultural content and perspectives. U.S. public school teachers are overwhelmingly female, in their early forties, have taught for approximately ten years, and are of a Western European background.[16] They are products of their home environments, schooling, and formal college and university training. Teachers with this background—predominantly monocultural education and heavily Western European socialization—may create a learning environment far removed from the students' world, where public schools are increasingly minority dominated.

Today, while many acknowledge the importance of moving beyond Eurocentric curricula and Western art music in college music education programs, many teacher education institutions still do not embrace that initiative. If twenty-first-century teachers are to adopt a broader perspective about music and music-making, how will they balance folk and classical traditions in their curricula? How will they reconcile note-reading and a certain level of technical proficiency in Western classical music with the languages, scales, and rhythmic/harmonic/textural qualities found in other musics? How do they teach using perspectives that they may not know? How do they obliterate class distinctions in music—distinctions that marginalize some musics and allow others to be emphasized by assuming they are of more value? Many music teacher education programs do not prepare teachers to answer these questions at more than a superficial level, if at all.

Until recently, few music teacher education programs required students to take coursework in world musics, or even popular music or jazz. When multicultural content and perspectives were present in music teacher education programs, Michigan teachers often indicated that what they did learn was overgeneralized, inaccurate, and not of much use in today's music classrooms. Poor quality or inadequate multicultural music instruction in teacher education curricula was also coupled with the presence of few in-service models or mentors in student teaching and initial teaching positions. Little value for multicultural content and perspectives in teacher education programs may translate to little value in teachers' classrooms.

The barriers to effective multicultural music education practice are substantial. The most powerful and pervasive barrier is that of teacher education. Music educators are expected to teach musical and cultural content and perspectives for which they have little to no education. What it means to be musically educated and prepared to teach our nation's children has clearly changed as we begin the twenty-first century.

Vehicles of Teacher Preparation

Western European musics and perspectives comprise ninety-eight percent of the courses and eighty percent of the scholarships found in U.S. public university schools of music, according to a recent *Chronicle of Education* article.[17] American music and jazz typically comprise less than four percent of course offerings, and ethnomusicology offerings, while present, seem to propagate elite foreign classical musics (e.g., traditions from India, Japan, and Indonesia) rather than folk traditions. The majority of the world's music traditions are currently left out in the training of musicians and music teachers, providing a monocultural music education in a multicultural world.

While most of these institutions of music learning were founded to propagate the Western European canon, that singular body of principles, standards, and norms is no longer solely valid in our multimusical nation. American music education curricula have changed little since the early 1900s. Prior to 1930, music education's guiding concept was to promote music literacy, performance competency, and educated taste through Western art music. Ethnic, folk, and popular musics were rejected in favor of music which would "elevate" and "uplift" all students—including students of color and immigrants whose heritage was not Western European. Music from "exotic" lands began to appear in the late 1930s, but the strongest support for curricular inclusion of music representing a broad range of genres, styles, periods, and cultures came in the final declaration of the 1967 Tanglewood Symposium report.[18] More than thirty years later, American music educators have only begun to heed the call. The musics and concomitant perspectives studied in most of our nation's music classrooms do not reflect the multimusical diversity in our multicultural society; music education is daily moving farther away from the worlds of our students. What it means to be musically educated in colleges and public schools has clearly changed since the 1930s; the institutions of musical learning have not kept pace.

What does it mean to be musically educated as we enter the twenty-first century? I believe that it means to view music as a universal human expression. The world of musical styles and genres and their creators who used to be found in the far corners of the world are now found in the centers of our communities. These diverse traditions and the ones that were always present in our communities have a voice that can no longer be muted, a voice that calls for us to view them as valuable forms of human musical expression that are valid in their own right. Barbara Reeder Lundquist calls this the "ethnomusicological perspective" about music and music-making.[19] In a nation where the musical traditions valued by an ever-increasing segment of society lie outside Western European traditions, we can no longer afford to invalidate or devalue multiple perspectives of music and music-making. When diverse musics and perspectives are not present in institutions of higher learning, these musics appear to be devalued and invalidated; this practice sends the message to people whose roots are not Western European that their music and their voice are not valued on the same level.

The celebration of our multiplicity of voices has taken many forms in our society. On just one weekend in the greater Philadelphia community, people were keeping their traditions alive and sharing with others through music and dance at a Native American Indian Arts Festival, Ecuadorian Andes music at local gardens, Brazilian Pop music at a downtown club, a Latin fiesta, a reggae festival, international folk and country line-dancing parties, the Gospel Jam at the year's first riverfront festival, and various orchestral and choral concerts in more traditional venues. In our multicultural society, music of nearly every region of the world is easily available, providing a fertile ground for rich musical exchanges and boundless new creations.

Earlier in the year, I witnessed such a creation—a piece by African-American composer Hannibal—that fused a symphony orchestra, West African *griot*, jazz trio, gospel choir, and Caribbean drummers. Tuxedoed string players and brightly clad, barefoot drummers sitting next to them on the stage of Philadelphia's Academy of Music all applauded the composer at the end of this extraordinary offering. However, the collaboration of a British madrigal ensemble, I Fagiolini, and Sadasa, a South African gospel choir from Soweto, which I witnessed at the 1998 International Society for Music Education (ISME) conference in Pretoria, was the most incredible. I cannot put into words the visual and sonic beauty created by the intertwining of these two disparate traditions, as two worlds became one. How much richer and more real a musical education would be if this multiplicity of voices were heard in our school music classrooms.

The vast array of musics resulting from the mixing of stylistic and conceptual elements found in traditional and Western cultures constitutes the bulk of most people's non-Western music experiences. Music teachers, who are almost universally concerned with issues of authenticity, have difficulty conceptualizing these musical hybrids. Authentic music refers to music that is "real" or "true." Traditional music is not the only vehicle of this. Whatever a group says is their music—the music practiced within their society—is their music and, as such, is authentic. Authentic music, then, can be traditional, a hybrid, or more

popular—"world beat" musics. Interestingly enough, authenticity appears to be an issue of much greater concern for the music educator than for the indigenous musician.[20]

A musical education for today's U.S. society should consider technological advancements, along with burgeoning diversity. With the aid of technology, we can bring people and music together more rapidly and easily than ever before. The world's people and their musics are only the turn of a dial, a voice command, or a "mouse-click" away. With growing diversity and technological advancements, the learning needs of our nation's children have also changed. In our world, students have an unprecedented variety of stimulating activities and experiences from which to choose on a daily basis. Students' inability to differentiate between work, play, and learning, coupled with the need for instant gratification and a lack of focus and study skills, requires more and different teacher knowledge and skills than ever before.

How do we craft a musical education for the children of this century? Wherein does its value lie? The cultural, social, economic, technological, and political changes in our society warrant a change in philosophical position. Music must be taught from the perspective that music is a powerful factor in human society and cultural practice, a fact that *all* teachers must respect and represent. To "respect and represent" the teaching of a South African folk tune means to transmit it orally in the indigenous language with movement; a wide open vocal sound; limited involvement of the conductor; the large half-steps found in indigenous scales; an understanding of the text, meaning, and context; and an omnipresent vision of honoring those to whom the song "belongs." A twenty-first-century musical education should employ a multiplicity of musics presented through strategies that, according to James Standifer, "intellectualize and humanize."[21] Preservice music education should provide the necessary experiences, foci, perspectives, and possible processes to start student teachers on the path to giving such a musical education to today's children in today's world.

Prospective teachers should be prepared to respond to varied teaching situations— urban or rural, monocultural or multicultural, empowered or impoverished, oral or written, popular or classical, and countless others. To do so, they need a firsthand knowledge of several musical styles and systems and need to assimilate multiple approaches to music teaching and learning. Development of skills for effective crosscultural communication, whether face-to-face, written, or on-line, is essential. Teachers need the ability to look beyond their personal "cultural packages" and to develop strategies to connect with people, communities, and social and educational institutions that are different from their own points of reference. Technological skills to facilitate on-line learning, compositional and creative activity, and personal record-keeping must also be a required component of preservice teacher training. Computer and multimedia skills that are used in creating instructional materials and strategies are also primary.

A broad understanding of the various conceptions of "education," formal and informal, and the roles that they play in the lives of their students is essential for prospective teachers. Twenty-first-century teachers must learn how to honor the child whose musical knowledge and skills has developed in a variety of ways, from hearing and singing childhood songs that introduce fictional characters or instruct them how to "be" and act within their society, to singing plagal Amen cadences or gospel tunes every week in church, to watching and imitating family members who play the fiddle or congas at weekly dance parties, to spending time with grandparents enamored of Nelson Eddy and Jeanette McDonald, to imitating adult musicians with friends, to taking weekly private lessons in addition to participating in general music classes, band, orchestra, and/or chorus in school.

Prospective teachers must also be prepared to make daily decisions regarding the seven questions listed above and regarding challenges inherent in current music education practice: musical content (form) and context, folk and classical traditions, transmission and transformation, in-school and out-of-school music (continuity and interaction), making and receiving music, understanding and pleasure, and philosophy and practice.

The challenges to the teaching of world or multicultural musics are not easily solved; they need to be continually revisited. These and other dialectics surrounding the teaching of world musics are discussed in greater depth in Estelle Jorgensen's *In Search of Music Education.*[22] Many of these challenges, however, can be addressed within music teacher education programs in our colleges and universities. The following section offers some suggestions to help equip our future teachers with more skills, knowledge, and broader perspectives for teaching multicultural music in our nation's schools.

Music Teacher Education for Our Multimusical World: Experiences to Gain

While addressing the many challenges surrounding teaching multicultural content and perspectives may not bring immediate gains, it may be the best avenue for long-term growth. Giving prospective teachers the knowledge and skills of multiple traditions, along with opportunities to develop broader perspectives, are excellent ways to start addressing these challenges. Pre-service teachers need experiences that lead them to understand the impact of their background and biases on the classroom: teach *with* culture, not *about* it; know culturally specific dimensions of music with attention to representativeness; develop strategies to deal effectively with languages; soften the boundaries between student and teacher to develop a community of learners; experience the power of music-making and -receiving across cultures; and use technology to connect with people and their musical traditions.

Prospective teachers need to understand the powerful impact that their own backgrounds—socialization and formal schooling—have on all that they do and understand. The ability to question, look beyond the norm, and acknowledge the existence of diverse ways of seeing, hearing, and making music is essential to teaching music with multicultural content and perspectives. When linked with knowledge about a variety of peoples, this ability becomes a powerful tool in the classroom, which

affords more opportunities to connect with and respect diverse students and school communities.

Knowing culture-specific and universal dimensions of multiple traditions offers a warehouse of possibilities for teaching multicultural content and perspectives. Understanding the various roles, functions, and compositional processes of musics broadens possibilities for creative/compositional classroom experiences. The ability to link to scholars, ethnomusicologists, and indigenous musicians in person, on-line, in communities, and through writings and music-making can foster continual growth long after an undergraduate music education program ends.

The fastest and perhaps most critical way to move into a significant understanding of a tradition is through direct involvement. Performance opportunities in non-Western traditions bring students face-to-face with issues of authenticity. Building a repertoire of pieces and experiences will allow prospective teachers to share from their own knowledge bases, giving more power to their instruction. Experiences in receiving aurally transmitted music can strengthen and broaden aural skills and provide models upon which to base classroom instruction. The power of learning another tradition firsthand is undeniable.

Skills for effective interaction across cultural and ethnic boundaries can be developed through participating in performance ensembles and community music/cultural events and through making personal contacts with "culture-bearers" in familiar and unfamiliar settings. Knowing how to access resources available through social and educational institutions at the community,

---

Table 1. A Twenty-First-Century Undergraduate Music Education Curriculum

1. Social Foundations of Education, Psychology, and Sociology
   A. Exploration of the realities of multicultural society and education for twenty-first-century America
   B. Examination of cultural specifics and universals and the magnitude and pervasiveness of the Western lens

2. Foreign Language
   A. Minimum of two years of study, including exploration of cultural/linguistic differences among peoples
   B. Learning the International Phonetic Alphabet (IPA)
   C. Complement-to-Diction classes for singers

3. Music History: Multicourse sequence that includes a variety of styles, forms, and traditions and that links music to culture

4. Ethnomusicology
   A. Two courses: Survey of World Musics and a culture-specific class for in-depth knowledge
   B. Emphasis on listening, performing, creating
   C. Required attendance at non-Western music events

5. Music Theory and Composition
   A. Inclusion of non-Western scales, melodies, rhythms, harmonies (textures), and forms in aural, written, and creative experiences

6. Performance groups
   A. Western and non-Western groups utilizing aural and written transmission
   B. Western groups incorporating world musics repertoire, voicings, instruments, and melodies; variety of timbres (instrumental and vocal); and associations with traditional musicians

7. Music Technology
   A. Combination of classes (Notation, Sequencing, Multimedia, Web Page Construction, etc.) and Competencies (Word Processing, CD-ROM, Spreadsheets, etc.)
   B. Opportunities to use skills in preparing instructional materials and in instructing students

8. Music Education Classes (Methods and Instrument Skill Classes)
   A. Inclusion of diverse content and perspectives, including model lessons in all classes
   B. Inclusion of multicultural instructional materials and means for their evaluation as representations of specific tradition
   C. Inclusion of opportunities to become facilitators and approach differences as opportunities and challenges
   D. Capitalization on learnings in other coursework (language, education theory, etc.)
   E. Non-Western instrumental competency in skill classes
   F. Field experiences including observation and pre-student teaching that culminate in student teaching with a cooperative teacher who models strategies for curricular inclusion of multicultural content and perspectives
   G. Coursework in or extended experiences with teaching world musics in the schools

9. World Musics Workshops/Demonstrations/Concerts: Attendance at a prescribed number of events for edification beyond what the school or university offers in world musics

---

regional, and national levels is also an invaluable skill. Developing skills in on-line communication and linking through the Internet to communities and schools the world over can bring world musics to one's doorstep. Thus, the development of technological skills is critical to multicultural teaching and learning.

In order to access the information/resources necessary for multicultural teaching, the boundaries between teacher and student/culture-bearer need to be de-emphasized in order to foster a sense of the class as a community of learners. Knowing how to set the stage for students or outside-of-school culture-bearers to share their musics and cultures firsthand is critical to multicultural teaching and learning. Teachers must learn how, and when, to be the "guide on the side" as well as the "sage on the stage."

The experiences put forth in this section are more powerful if suffused into every facet of the undergraduate music education curriculum, including coursework in music (theory, history, and composition), foreign languages, and education. How do these experiences translate into undergraduate teacher-training curricula? Table 1 includes the aforementioned experiences and forms the basis for a twenty-first-century undergraduate music education curriculum that, while not a complete list, serves as an example of some ways to provide these experiences. Coursework that includes these experiences will greatly enhance the knowledge, skill, and mindset that music educators must develop for effective multicultural music teaching in the twenty-first century. Had the teachers mentioned above been privy to these experiences, they could be bringing a more real, more powerful world of musics and music-making to their students. Teacher education is the key.

Notes

1. Kathy M. Robinson, "Multicultural General Music Education: An Investigation and Analysis in Michigan's Public Elementary Schools, K–6" (Ph.D. diss., University of Michigan, 1996).
2. Estelle R. Jorgensen, *In Search of Music Education* (Urbana, IL: University of Illinois Press, 1997).
3. Robinson, "Multicultural General Music Education."
4. Horace Kallen, *Culture and Democracy in the United States* (New York: Boni and Liveright, 1928).
5. Anthony J. Palmer, "World Musics in

Elementary and Secondary Music Education: A Critical Analysis" (Ph.D. diss., University of California–Los Angeles, 1975).
6. Jacqueline J. Yudkin, "An Investigation and Analysis of World Music Education in California's Public Schools, K–6" (Ph. D. diss., University of California–Los Angeles, 1990).
7. MENC, *The School Music Program: A New Vision, The K–12 National Standards, PreK Standards, and What They Mean to Music Educators* (Reston, VA: MENC, 1994), 3.
8. Ibid.
9. Robinson, "Multicultural General Music Education."
10. Judith Cook Tucker, "Circling the Globe: Multicultural Resources," *Music Educators Journal* 78, no. 9 (May 1992): 37–40.
11. Patricia Shehan Campbell, *Music in Cultural Context: Eight Views on World Music Education* (Reston, VA: MENC, 1996).
12. Bryan Burton and Rosella DiLiberto, "Resources for Teaching: Music of Africa," *General Music Today* 12, no. 3 (Spring 1999): 24–30.
13. Donna M. Gollnick, "Multicultural Education," *Viewpoints in Teaching and Learning* 56 (Winter 1980): 1–17.
14. James A. Banks, "A Curriculum for Empowerment, Action and Change," in *Empowerment through Multicultural Education*, ed. Christine E. Sleeter (Albany, NY: State University of New York Press, 1991), 139.
15. Ibid., 125–41.
16. National Education Association, *Status of the American Public School Teacher, 1990–91* (Washington, DC: National Education Association, 1992).
17. Sammie A. Wicks, "The Monocultural Perspective of Music Education," *The Chronicle of Education* (January 9, 1998): A72.
18. Robert A. Choate, *Music in American Society: Documentary Report of the Tanglewood Symposium* (Washington, DC: MENC, 1968).
19. Barbara Reeder Lundquist, "A Music Education Perspective," in *Musics of the World's Cultures: A Source Book for Music Educators*, ed. Barbara Reeder Lundquist and C. K. Szego (Nedlands, Australia: Callaway International Resource Centre for Music Education, 1998): 38–46.
20. Anthony J. Palmer, "World Musics in Music Education: The Matter of Authenticity," *International Journal of Music Education* 19 (1992):

32–40. See this article for a more detailed discussion of the issues of authenticity.

21. James A. Standifer, "Multicultural Education in Action" (unpublished paper, 1982). Photocopy.

22. Jorgensen, *In Search of Music Education*.

Kathy Robinson, assistant professor of music education at the Eastman School of Music in Rochester, New York, and co-director of Umculo: The Kimberley Project (a music teaching/learning/cultural exchange program sending experienced educators to teach in Kimberley, South Africa, schools), presents workshops frequently throughout the United States and abroad on the topics of world musics and general music education.

A Life in World Musics

13

In Study of Expressive Cultures: The Pathway of a White Middle-Class Music Teacher

Patricia Shehan Campbell

*M*y resume portrays me as a music teacher with an inclination toward "the academic" through involvement in research, publications, and projects that are about the curricular inclusion of musical cultures in classes for children. Through books, essays, research, and research-based articles, I have been working to bring teachers in touch with music that they may not have known before and with issues of cultural diversity that are not typically a part of most music teacher education programs. When I'm not teaching, it may appear that I'm writing, always writing—for that is my professional profile.

But as is true of music teachers across the globe, I am first and foremost a maker of music. My formal musical studies began with piano, soon centered on voice (covering the music of the common practice period, 1650–1900), and then moved on to other instruments and traditions, including *Japanese* koto, *Indian* mridingam *(drum), Lao* kaen, *Celtic harp, Bulgarian* kaval, *instruments of the Javanese* gamelan, *and Thai* mahori, *Filipino* kulintang, *and vocal music of Bulgaria and Macedonia, Karnatic India, Pakistan, Turkey, Venezuela, and Vietnam. While musical mastery of one or more traditions*

beyond Western art music could have been my aim, I chose instead to study a year of this and a year of that, sampling rather than mastering these traditions—knowing just enough to come to grips with the fact that I know very little.

But I am a teacher, and so it has been critical for me to experience these musics as an applied student (I regard music more highly as performance than as academic study), to experience the ways and means of its transmission (the teaching-learning process is as important as the repertoire itself), and to enter into dialogues with musicians from these cultures (their teaching method, as well as their music, binds me to them). As an "academic," I have converted my experiences into words on paper (and also into my teaching), and from this have come such works as Lessons from the World *(1990),* Multicultural Perspectives in Music Education *(1989, 1996),* From Rice Paddies and Temple Yards: Traditional Music of Vietnam *(1990),* Silent Temples, Songful Hearts: Traditional Music of Cambodia *(1991),* The Lion's Roar: Chinese Luogu Percussion Ensembles *(1992),* Roots and Branches *(1994),* Music in Childhood

(1995), Music in Cultural Context *(1996),* Songs in Their Heads: Music and Its Meaning in Children's Lives *(1998), and* Canciones de America Latina: de Sus Origenes a la Escuela *(2001). I am now engaged in co-editing with Bonnie Wade (University of California–Berkeley) a book/CD series called* Global Musics *for Oxford University Press. I continue my work as professor of music and head of the program of "Music, Education, and Culture" at the University of Washington.*

Growing Up Catholic, Caucasian, and Middle Class

Since the middle of the twentieth century, post-modern scholarship has been predicated on the tenet that a direct relationship exists between an individual's private and public life. Musicologist Kofi Agawu questioned the devalued place of experiential knowledge in the world of traditional scholarship, pointing to the conventions that encourage us "to value fieldwork paid for by others and knowledge acquired during relatively short periods of intentional search for knowledge over knowledge and experience gained as part of an informal and extended musical education."[1]

For Agawu, who grew up Ewe in Ghana, the question emanated from his return to his home culture to conduct research as a fieldworker on the nature of rhythm in the lives of Ewe people that he already knew. Following Agawu's lead, teachers intent on understanding issues of music, education, and culture may benefit from looking first to their own experiences as student musicians, more expert performers, and then teachers, and to review and interpret experiences in light of the challenges that are surfacing and surrounding them in their classrooms and studios. I believe that there are rich revelations to be had in looking critically—each of us—at our "informal and extended" musical lives.

Feminist writers in particular have been keen to place the writer's specific social location and perspective explicitly within the text. Political scientist Naomi Black claimed that scholarship should "insist on the value of subjectivity and personal experience."[2] Sociologist Judy Long recognized the effective approach of studying ideas through the use of autobiography; she asserts that "first person accounts are required to understand the subjectivity of a social group."[3] Alma M. Garcia wrote in "Voices of Women of Color" that she found her writing effective when it encompassed autobiographical discovery and self-reflection.[4] Thus, I am inspired and encouraged to write in a reflective style and with a personal tone so as to illuminate the thoughts and behaviors of a "social group" of music teachers who are looking to facilitate the learning of music in its multiple splendors in classrooms of children that are more culturally varied than ever before. I will shift between current issues, historical streams, social and cultural themes, and first-person accounts and scenarios, all with the intention of coming to grips with an understanding of the complexities of teaching music today as inspired by global and multicultural influences.

As per the advice of Socrates to "know thyself," this is the launch for us all in determining our course. Knowledge of self may require contemplation of our origins or "roots"—our first family and home—and the path of development in our early years, and since then. My own roots aren't dead for me, either. I knew as a young child in Cleveland that my ancestors had come from elsewhere, because I saw it and heard it. Dad's family was in the phase of shifting from Irish immigrant laborers to blue-collar workers, and he himself was caught up with his family's plan to Americanize even while it retained the old world: Irish soda bread with butter, carved glass candy bowls straight out of Waterford, dainty handmade linen-lace doilies hanging on the arms of velvet chairs, and coats-of-arms for the family names and clans hanging on white-washed walls in simple wood-frame houses. I often heard the sounds of button-box accordions, fiddles, and the rather rickety baby grand at my grandfather's place. Moreover, I recall the men toasting their ales and shots of whiskey at wakes, weddings, and communion and graduation parties, and breaking into a repertoire of songs that were neither here nor there, not quite Ireland anymore and yet surely not all-American: "Rakes of Mallow," "The Low-Backed Car," "Peg o' My Heart," and "I'll Take You Home Again, Kathleen." When I hear those melodies today, I often gasp, tingle, and shut down all serious thought just to drift back in time and place to one of my first two musical communities.

My mother's family was also in transition to American ways, with both parents coming from Austria and settling into a generic German-speaking network of foundry workers, housekeepers, day laborers, and Sunday social clubs that thrived in Cleveland in the 1920s. From this side, I learned a darker, deeper brand of Catholicism and developed a contemplative self. Because my mother had spoken only German at home, I too learned to speak all of the familiar, affectionate, and bedtime banter in her Austrian (and motherese) dialect. We sang little nursery songs together in German, with rhymes and clapping chants—songs that she, as the eldest child of eight, had often sung to her younger siblings as she helped to raise them. Sunday picnics and weddings were occasions for baked chicken, potato salad (with vinegar rather than mayonnaise), *nussrol* and *strudel,* and polka bands. The bands played as many waltzes as polkas, and I remember the Serbian-American accordionist Frankie Yankovic guest-starring onstage at some of these Austrian weddings, squeezing away as he danced his fingers up and down the sideways keyboard. We kids slid across the slick sawdust floors and hopped to the oom-pahs of accordion, violin, a trumpet or two, and drum set. Grandpa still read his Innsbruck newspaper, Grandma swore in (very) Low German, and we sang "O Kommt Kleine Kinder" and "O Tannenbaum" every Christmas.

I was "ethnic" then (all people are), and I remain linked by these early experiences to things Irish and Austrian. But these ethnic identities are what Herbert Gans calls "symbolic ethnicities,"[5] in that they are individualistic in nature and without real social cost for the individual. They are essentially leisure-time activities, rooted in nuclear family traditions and reinforced by the voluntary enjoyable aspects of being ethnic. For many later-generation Caucasian ethnics like myself, ethnicity is not something that influences our lives unless we want it to. The danger of creating a symbolic ethnicity is that it may be equated with the socially enforced identities of non-White Americans, which may thus obscure the fact that the experiences of Whites and non-Whites have been qualitatively different in the United States. As a White American, I can choose by the hour whether I wish to "go White" or "go ethnic," and, unless I celebrate my ethnicity and underscore it by word and action, I will pass as a member of the mainstream population—with all privileges of that status offered to me. My colleagues of African-, Asian-, Latin-, and Native-American ancestry may not have such choices, and their own personal and family histories are likely to be filled with unfortunate and "unequal" incidents. I am aware of this, even as I make my pilgrimages to Ireland, play my Celtic harp, and sing my son to sleep with German-language lullabies.

Life is fairly closed to anything beyond family in our earliest years, and, although my parents believed that they were raising us as Americans, we were in fact a particular flavor of American children growing up in the 1950s. Not only were there the family's ethnic-cultural experiences that shaped us, but there were also the beginnings of mediated influences on our thoughts of ourselves and cultural others. Aunt Jemima appeared in her full frontal portrait on the pancake box that stood on the stove on weekends, smiling warmly at us. I often thought that Mrs. Butterworth, the figure on the brown syrup bottle, might be somehow related to Aunt Jemima, each of them teaming up to offer us a taste of the meals they fed their families in city neighborhoods that I never knew.

There were no African-Americans in our tract-house neighborhood, which was, in fact, just like so many self-styled ghettos of white European-American families who had pulled out of the cities to forge safe surroundings in the homogenized world of the suburbs. We watched *Amos 'n' Andy,* read with curiosity the conversational style of Br'er Rabbit in the *Uncle Remus* stories, and on the radio heard Mahalia Jackson sing her heart out with "How Great Thou Art." The mighty Jackie Robinson was just breaking the color line in baseball, but Joe DiMaggio and Mickey Mantle were still the real stars of White middle-class children of mid-twentieth-century America. Through the new media of television, Mexicans were parodied as gun-toting banditos through Looney Tunes' misadventures; Native Americans were all enemies with feathers and bare chests (except for the *Lone Ranger*'s Tonto), and the only Asians we knew of were the pigtailed cartoon characters of befuddled cooks and tailors who bowed as they walked in very small steps. Chalk it up to the media to provide lingering stereotypical images of the way "other people" outside our family might be.

It was no wonder, then, that I found myself intrigued with the boy in front of me on my first day of school. One of my mother's oft-told tales was of that day when I ran home excited to tell her that a "colored" boy was sitting in front of me. He was indeed "colorful," much healthier in skin color than my own pale complexion. Frank Giallombardo was the handsome olive-skinned son of the Sicilian family two blocks away—he was the furthest stretch afield from "my own people" that I'd seen in all my six years. I recall my initial disappointment, however, that he could not answer any of my questions about what "chitlins" were and why little colored girls didn't need bobby pins in their hair at night to make curls in the morning. But Frank was rather interesting anyway; his friendship was, in fact, as exotic to me as Italian spaghetti and lasagna were as dinner fare to my meat-and-potatoes family. I simply had had no exposure to the world beyond the White, middle-class, Beaver-Cleaver view. And when young Frank brought his accordion to school that Christmas, he gave my ears their first treat of the sound of the *tarantella,* the national dance of Italy, when previously I had known only jigs, reels, and polkas.

It was not until high school that my Caucasian, Catholic, middle-class view was seriously challenged. In the late 1960s, the Black Power and Black Pride movements were sweeping American cities, secondary schools, and college campuses. I was enrolled in a Catholic school within the boundaries of a Northern city teeming with racial strife that blew up into violent confrontations between Blacks and Whites, and I watched the neighborhood change colors as Whites fled to the outer fringes of the metropolis. The classmates I had known in the ninth grade were mostly gone by the eleventh grade, and my senior year was spent adapting to a new role as a White minority student. Before and after "the change," the school's music program was regarded as one of the best in the city, and it mattered not to Sister Cecilia what her students' "backgrounds" were: we would still play her favorite Haydn and Mozart symphonies, and we would still sing all the best of Bach's chorales and Brahms' German folksong arrangements. "Only the best music for my girls," she would say, and we took top honors all four years at festivals. But at lunch, on the way to track meets, and

at weekend dances, we grooved to Smokey Robinson and the Miracles, the Supremes, and the Temptations on the radio, as played by Black-American cover bands with fuzzy bass tones and funky *wah-wah* pedals.

Though weaned on Gregorian chant and all-Latin Masses while growing up, I had heard on Sunday morning radio the worship services of Mt. Lebanon Baptist Church. But it took my friendship with Janeese Boyer to bring me up-front and personal with the gospel sound. Janeese and I had begun to hang out together in the choir room after school when we were in the tenth grade. We sang Italian art songs, and she joined me in a duet of "Blowin' in the Wind" for an all-school variety show, but she could produce amazing renditions of "Were You There?," "Summertime," and "Motherless Child" that had me rethinking my own musical identity. Janeese taught me when to slide my voice across—rather than leap over— the pitches between two points, when to sit on the minor third, and when to take my time on a climax or at the end of a phrase. Janeese was as bimusical as she was bicultural: she spoke one mainstream dialect in class but would drop syllables left and right, and even whole words, out of class. I was fascinated that she could live in two cultures, home and school, and that she could switch musical styles on call. Even as I continued my formal study of piano and composition in the community school every Saturday morning, Janeese had sparked my interest in figuring out what other musical capacities I might have had within me to be realized—all the way to the development of a multiple musicality. The sums of my background had always equaled "American" to me, but Janeese had challenged me to think beyond my music lessons to what other musical styles I could perform—and how to perform them.

Seeking Musical Relevance

Student life during the period of one's university training can seem to a visiting outsider like all calm-and-repose on bucolic greens and in worn but cozy practice rooms, but to those in late adolescence and emergent adulthood, it is often a time of searching for "the self," of *sturm und drang,* of emotional roller coaster rides, and of wanting to "fix things" that aren't right about the world. In the early 1970s, when campuses were hotbeds of revolutionary causes like "the war" (Vietnam) and "rights" (Black, Chicano, Native American, women's, and gay/lesbian), we could barely keep our concentration on our studies, so militant were some of the efforts to call attention to injustices. Marches to Washington, sit-ins outside the courthouse, rallies in front of the university's administration building, and finally clouds of teargas to squelch and silence the voices—these activities surrounded and enveloped us and had even the most studious among us questioning what was relevant and where to direct our efforts. We who were largely middle-class and White were catching the messages of racial inequities in works like Ralph J. Ellison's *Invisible Man,* Eldridge Cleaver's *Soul on Ice,* and Dee Brown's *Bury My Heart at Wounded Knee* and through the songs of James Brown, Odetta, Ritchie Havens, Joan Baez, and Buffy Ste.-Marie. I felt compelled to contribute to the movement and the marches as a singer of songs, and I spent a good many evenings at the

university's War Memorial with my guitar, singing and leading others to sing "Where Have All the Flowers Gone?," "We Shall Overcome," "Kumbaya," and "Four Dead in Ohio." There was little calm-and-repose in these works, where the challenges of war and civil rights were expressed through words and melodies of writers and singers with multicolored lenses.

For music majors who performed the music of "dead, White, male" composers, it took going beyond the School of Music to hear or to perform much of what the rest of the world offered by way of musical expression. By 1970, ethnomusicology was still involved in defining itself as a scholarly discipline and distinguishing itself from musicology (and anthropology), and there were few ethnomusicologists on faculties of North American universities, other than those with graduate programs like the University of California–Berkeley, Indiana University, and the University of California–Los Angeles.[6] The standard training of music majors in smaller state universities and liberal arts colleges was centered on the repertoire and performance techniques of Western European art music, and there was no room in the schedule for the study of world musics—nor were there faculty members to teach such courses. Not only were Indonesian *gamelans* and Trinidadian steel drum bands uncommon then, but even jazz studies programs were still marginalized (or disguised by the use of the term "stage band" in lieu of the loaded "j" word).[7] While ethnic studies programs had begun to be instituted on campuses, it would be several decades before courses on American traditional and vernacular musics would be widely offered.

One year, a visiting "fellow" from Ghana came to our campus. It was 1972, and he had been invited by the university to teach in the newly evolved African Studies program. He was a singer, dancer, and drummer, and he was marginally admitted to the music faculty to teach just one course. We music students were neither advised to take the course nor notified of the presence of this artist on campus, and his sparse enrollment consisted of eight African-American students and myself. I had overloaded my schedule that quarter to register for the class, and I found myself listening, struggling with the lack of words and notation in the class sessions, listening more, and being drawn to the constant possibilities for musical participation. The 1970s was an era of "musical happenings" and post-Cageian chance music, but this music of the Ghanaian instructor was something else. In the Akan music he led us in making, there was a careful balance of structure and freedom and of individual skill and sensitivity to the sounds of others in the group. The drumming and dancing allowed those of us trained in structured music a chance to develop "engendered feeling,"[8] for this music demanded motor involvement, improvisation, and vital musical drives. When I would return to the practice room to play my Chopin études and sing my Bach arias, I felt some new sense of time kicking in, and I liked what the drumming and dancing was doing to me, musically. No other visiting faculty came during the time of my undergraduate training, but this single experience with a tradition-bearer in a music far from my experience had made its impact on me.

For musicians-turning-teachers, the methods books we trained in were monocultural in nature, and the third edition of *Music in the Elementary School* by Robert and Vernice Nye,[9] while rich with songs and instructions for instrumental play, did little to prepare us for classes of children in urban centers and the growing multicultural populations we would teach. One paragraph took note of the trend toward developing intercultural understanding through music, mentioning that "depth studies dealing with comparative treatment of musical elements (rhythm, texture, melody) in both our culture and a non-Western culture are possible with children possessing a mental age of from nine years upward."[10] Antiquated language aside ("depth studies," "non-Western," and "mental age"), we cannot help but ask these questions today: Which culture is "our culture"? Is the study of "musical elements" a Eurocentric approach to musical study? Why is there no mention of the importance of studying cultural context in order to develop musical (and intercultural) understanding? Why would there be a need to delay the study of the traditions of world musics until "a mental age of from nine years upward"?

Later in Nye and Nye's text, in a paragraph on "the Negro child," the reader is forewarned that "many deprived children seem lazy, inactive, and appear to have little concept of … the value of time," all of which results from "a home environment where there is no reason to hurry, meet appointments, or to compete with anyone."[11] Beyond the uneasy sense we have in reading a label we no longer use, we may wonder why there was not a more careful discussion of "deprived children" as emanating from many (rather than only one) ethnic-cultural backgrounds. More importantly, we no doubt question the generalized, negative portrayal of African-American homes and their influences on children's learning styles. As this volume was, unfortunately, the principle text in general music methods for a generation of teachers, little further attention was given to world and multicultural issues, beyond descriptions of Latin and Hawaiian percussion instruments.[12] While the authors contributed in important ways to the development of music instructional practices, they also reflected the pervasive professional position some thirty years ago of insularity and myopia relevant to music and the cultural communities of American children.[13]

Taking on the Teacher's Role

The teaching experiences that I faced did not match my musical training. The junior high school site of my student-teaching internship was two-thirds African-American, with a smaller percentage of first-generation Puerto Rican students, and a smattering of students of Polish, Hungarian, Irish, and German backgrounds. Nearly all were from families of lower socioeconomic backgrounds, where color TV, stereos, and transistor radios (rather than pianos) were the focal points of their homes. I felt then that I was straddling two worlds—that of the university and that of my students' home-and-school lives. The longer I was removed from the art music world of my university training, the wider the gap appeared between there and where the children were. The feeling was one of watching the earth quake and then crack below me, one side pulling away from the other—until it seemed that I had to

finally "jump" to one side to save myself—the side of the "real world" of my children, their families, and the community. So I began my training in the trenches, watching the master teacher (a fine African-American gospel singer and pianist herself) model lessons on blues, spirituals, and the gospel song.

It was not a smooth road. I did not know blues and could not play jazz piano or figure out how to make Beethoven work in a middle-school general music class. Moreover, I was no match for my mentor, whose ethnicity was reason enough for many young African-American students to be attracted to her as their role model—particularly as she was the only non-White teacher on a staff of forty teachers. She sent me home with dozens of records to listen to, telling me that the key to learning the blues was to listen. She introduced me to several "gigging" musicians, and she took me to jazz and blues clubs in African-American neighborhoods that would have felt off-limits had I gone there myself. She assigned me "riffs" to practice at the piano, underscoring that I would not "get it" within the duration of student teaching and that I needed the summer, the next year, and a lifetime to grow into the style.

She was my entry-point, my informant, a culture-bearer, and gatekeeper who opened my ears to yet another musical world.[14] That spring, however, teaching the music that I could not perform to the children that I did not know sputtered along in an arhythmic manner. I lost most of the students almost immediately and could not lure them back with my dull lectures, inactive listening lessons, and plodding piano style. At the sound of the final bell on the last day of school, over half of them literally jumped out of the first-story classroom window—a certain sign that this student teacher had not connected—musically or otherwise—to her students.

My first full-time teaching experience lasted a year and a half at a church-based school in a neighborhood of Polish-immigrant and first-generation steelworkers. The post was described as a "general music and choral music teacher" for 200 students from kindergarten through eighth grade, but, in the end, I taught beginning strings, a guitar class, a recorder group, and a host of hymns in Polish for weekend Masses. I was entering into another community I did not know, where accordion—not piano—was the instrument of choice by the younger children and where Bruce Springsteen's "Born in the U.S.A." reigned as the musical signifier of the millworkers' sons and daughters, whose lives were still partly linked to Poland. When if ever could I use the choral works of Ralph Vaughn Williams and Randall Thompson? I wondered. Early on, I realized that the parish council—not the teachers—were in control of curricular content. Music had its uses in this Polish-American working-class community,[15] and it was clearly used to serve functional and not purely aesthetic purposes during my stay there. Instead, as the music teacher for the parish as much as for the school, I was needed to rehearse the young accordionists in ensemble with a drummer for parish dances, to play the pedal organ in the musty old church for the High Masses given by visiting monsignors from Crackow and Warsaw (pronounced "varsarva"), and to co-direct with the local polka impresario the seventh and eighth graders in a junior "polka choir." The music

of my training and even the jazz and blues genres toward which I had been drifting were put on the back burner as I struggled with the needs of this musical community.

For three years following, I taught at three schools located in two decidedly low-income neighborhoods. It was a mad race between two elementary schools (one in an all-Black district and another in a mostly poor White community) and a junior high school fed by the two schools—three trips a day into and out of their varied settings. Series books and their recordings, some dating from the 1950s, lined the walls of the music rooms of the elementary schools. At first, I was religiously fashioning lessons that progressed through page after page of songs and recording after recording of listening selections. I led children from the piano in singing what was available in print—songs from Japan, France, Argentina, and Africa (often no specific country or culture on that vast continent was named). There was within these sources a complement of European orchestral masterworks and "songs from many lands" (with recordings), and I saw that I could feature a sung canon attributed to Mozart and then a step-by-step guided listening tour of one of his symphonic movements.

We cannot help but teach what we know well.[16] However, the music with which we are familiar "bleeds" into the musical experiences we design for our students. Thus, I was playing blues-style piano and had students learning to play the chordal progressions on guitar. My fourth, fifth, and sixth graders could play three chords in two keys, and that was enough to get them through most of the repertoire of folk songs I had acquired as a university student. My children were playing polyrhythmic percussion patterns on hand drums, maracas, and wooden sticks—shades of the Ghanian music course I had taken, as well as transcriptions I was making from UNESCO and Nonesuch recordings. We danced the Balkan dances I was learning at weekend workshops connected to the international folk dance association I had joined. In the junior high where I had taught, I found groups of young adolescent students who would sing the Weelkes and Wilbye madrigals I had retrieved from my own experience as a chorister. At the elementary schools where I taught, children would play my prized Renaissance pieces on recorder and would go-with-the-flow of my directed listening lessons and compositional projects. I had arrived as a teacher and could finally put my musical training (and growing experience) to practice.

There were misses, too. My elective choirs were small, and over sixty percent of the junior high population chose sketching, painting, photography, or drama over music for their fine arts requirement. I saw how ineffective many of my lessons were, particularly when I did not really know the music well enough to teach it and could not possibly have my heart (or soul) in performing it. I didn't know the languages of the songs I was teaching and too often relied on the recordings (alone) to deliver the pronunciations and stylistic nuances. Some of the children were not connecting to the classroom-styled percussion of the "rhythm band" variety, where clicking sticks together was neither authentic to Akan tradition nor rhythmically grounded. I felt the kids slipping away from me from time to time and woke to nightmares of them

jumping out of windows again. I struggled with the White kids who scoffed at the films and recordings of the music from Africa and anguished over the Black kids who mimicked and laughed at the nasal voices of the lessons on bluegrass I had so carefully developed. I was uncertain of my teaching of African-American music and became even more insecure when told by my African-American students that my spirituals were too "Joan-Baez-ed" and "Joni-Mitchell-ed." They advised me: "Stick to the stuff you can do, Mizz Shehan." Above all, I worried that we were going through the motions of music lessons that in the end were leaving little impression upon the musical thinking and doing of my children in their lives beyond the classroom.

Turning Points

As we teach, we yearn for further study to stimulate us and to provide answers to questions our students raise. Like so many others, I sought help through enrollment in graduate school, and one thing led to another. The master's in voice performance was its own unique (and musically necessary) journey, culminating in recitals of Schubert, Schumann, Debussy, Granados, Rossini, and Puccini. But there was also my compulsive drive to know pedagogical processes better, and so my intention was to layer atop my performance studies a full load of courses in instructional theories and practices. I never imagined that studies in ethnomusicology and world musics performance practices lay ahead of me, studies that would forever bend my ear and turn me toward other cultures.

My worldview changed in a flash through a course on Asian Music. We were led by William M. Anderson, educator and ethnomusicologist, through encounters with the musics of India, China, Japan, Indonesia, and the Middle East. We listened analytically, kept *talas,* sang *drones,* chanted *gong* cycles and drum patterns, and watched the films of fieldworkers. The virtuosity of Indian *tabla* performance and the complex mathematical permutations of rhythm on the South Indian *mridingam* drum were revealed to us, and the aesthetic principles of the music of the Japanese theater forms (*noh* and *kabuki*) were presented to us in a carefully crafted manner so as to compel our further independent listening and study beyond the course itself.

By summer's end, it was clear that we had been led by a master teacher to step into other musical worlds far beyond the Western one in which we were steeped. Coincidentally, I was also enrolled that summer in a Baroque music course, and I could quite literally feel a perceptual "tilt" occur as I puzzled out a thematic analysis of a Bach chorale alongside the tracking of a melody in a Balinese *gamelan* piece. My experience in a single summer course had rocked my perceptual world, and, as a result of knowing something of these Asian musical traditions, the music of my earlier training made more sense to me. In similar fashion, John Blacking, an anthropologist working in southern Africa in the later 1950s and 1960s, observed his own transformation as a result of his fieldwork: "I have come to understand my own society more clearly and I have learned to appreciate my own music better."[17] For me, the great "aha" musical (and pedagogical) experience had happened, and there was no turning back.

In a matter of months, I was racking up graduate courses on African music, Chinese theatre music, musics of Southeast Asia, Indian music, and traditional music of Europe. Halim El-Dabh offered drumming and dancing classes of West and Northern Africa, and Terry Miller delivered specialized studies in the musical traditions of East and Southeast Asia. I was determined to balance academic seminars with performance studies, and I learned music from culture-bearers by ear and by observing them. My teacher of Indian *kriti* (vocal music) and *mridingam* drum banned my tape recorder from his basement studio and would not allow any note-taking during my two-hour weekly lessons with him. I had to relearn the value of learning by listening and to grow in my appreciation of the importance of rote-learning and of having rhythms and melodies imprinted in the ear and in the body through repeated observation and imitation.[18] Kovit Kantasiri approached his teaching of *ranat* (xylophone) and *kim* (hammer dulcimer) in the Thai ensemble in a similarly aurally-based way, and Jarenchai Chonpairot and Terry Miller taught the free-reed *khaen* instrument of Laos and northeast Thailand by leading students to listen and feel for the groups of fingering patterns on and off the holes of the bamboo tubes, thereby developing a kinetic memory for tunes.

This oral and aural learning process was not the way that I had formally learned music; it was in direct conflict with the goals of American music education. I was teaching children notational literacy in my classes at school, even as I began to learn these new instruments in this unfamiliar manner. I struggled with this non-notation process and longed for a staff, letters, or numbers—any visual cue to help me along. I watched the flying hands, mallets, and fingers of my teachers and heard their repeated patterns and variations. I struggled with playing in imitation of them, of "doing what they do," as they seldom broke the music down into the smaller units for which I yearned. We never talked about what the music contained, either; in fact, my questions along those lines were directly discouraged. The acquisition of performance skills was deemed to be beyond verbalization by my teachers, and so I went with an "automatic pilot" approach to feeling the music.

There was a point, I began to realize, when mental attention to the musical task to be learned clicked off and a motor response took over. As Pierre Bourdieu had reasoned, I was graduating into a "habitus" phase of learning from which the strategies of practice emerge.[19] I was losing myself in a connection between the ear and the physical movement of the body, such that what I heard I also physically felt and what movements I made as I played reinforced my listening comprehension.[20] When fully engaged in this process of listening, I had accelerated the speed by which I could acquire musical knowledge and repertoire on the instruments. My teaching was evolving as a result of these experiences, and only in retrospect did I fully recognize the change, so fully immersed had I become in a process that put me in direct contact with the new musical sounds. In the end, I came away from this new-to-me music not only with repertoire and technique but with a learning-and-teaching process that would work for many of the world's musical traditions.[21]

Flashing Forward

The rest is history—my personal history of study and experience in musical cultures different from those of my family and training. There are tales to be told of musicians, teachers, and students from whom I have learned, but they are far too numerous to mention here. Suffice it to say that now, at the present state of my journey to know music more globally, there have been moderate musical successes: Euclides Aparacio would judge my Venezuelan maracas-playing to be yet "un-crisp" ("*no quebradizo*") but "coming along" (he frequently announced that it was "okay"), Nusrat Fateh Mi Khan would politely accept my performance of Pakistani *qawwali* (praise songs) as passable but not provocative, and Phong Nguyen would smile and thank me for my enthusiastic attempts to sing his songs with the flavor of his southern Vietnamese accents. It is no surprise that a year (or less) in the study of a musical culture certainly is insufficient; performers of any musical tradition understand that mastery requires long-term, highly disciplined study. Still, teachers like me striving for a musical democracy within school programs recognize the critical need to experience multiple musical cultures and, in a limited lifetime, that may mean sacrificing depth for breadth. Master musicians have admitted to me that it has been worth their time to teach me what little I could learn and that learning is a two-way channel of person-to-person interactions. Importantly, they agree that teachers are links in the chain of cultural transmission; they play a vital part in mediating music and culture to young people whose worldviews can be expanded through exposure, experience, and education.

Flashing forward from the turning points of my professional development, I see the blur of teaching moments and music-making events pass quickly by. As an assistant professor at Washington University in St. Louis, I developed courses in ethnomusicology and survey classes on Asian Music and European traditional musics. With faculty in dance, theatre, and comparative literature, I co-created a course on Japanese *noh* theatre, patterning my own lectures after the engaging classes of William Malm (with whom I studied during his NEH-sponsored seminar at the University of Michigan on the subject). My doctoral students wrote theses on teaching children to dance to Balkan music[22] and to experience the expressive culture of the Huichol Indians of Mexico.[23] A local school allowed me to teach intermediate-grade children every Wednesday afternoon, and I modified some of the participatory listening lessons that I had delivered to university students. These were rich learning times for me, and I was "at the right place at the right time" to reap the many benefits of working as an educator at the fringes of ethnomusicology.

At Butler University in Indianapolis, the department was in the midst of redesigning its undergraduate music education program, so the music-culture units that I developed were easily incorporated within methods classes. On a broader scope, the Lilly Endowment funded my proposal for the "Butler World Music Project" to undertake a renewal and restructuring of the core courses for music majors at large. The project proceeded through two phases: a campuswide "Symposium on the Teaching of World Musics in the Undergraduate

Curriculum" and a series of ten campus residencies of scholars and performers of musical cultures ranging from "Black America" to the Blackfoot Indians and from Romania to Indonesia. The principal intention of the project was to expand students' awareness of music as an international cultural phenomenon. The students were mostly White, middle class, and clinging to the belief that the world revolved around Western European art music.

In a relatively brief span of time, several curricular modifications resulted from the project: new courses in music and music education, broader content in traditional music history and general music courses, and new repertoire choices for three choral ensembles (including the Indianapolis Children's Choir, based at Butler University), which was an almost immediate reflection of the influences of campus visitors. Through the unfolding of the Butler World Music Project, I came to understand that in university settings the music educator's task extends beyond the classes that they teach to include the wider spectrum of academic and applied music. The content of a multifaceted degree program should reflect what teachers need to learn in order to represent musics responsibly in their diverse forms of expression.[24]

My most recent academic post at the University of Washington in Seattle is also the longest of my professional record. I continue to remove myself from the treadmill of teaching, service, and research to study more—a habit of professional students everywhere. Running down the stairs to ethnomusicology class, I sit with my students and stumble along with them in learning the instruments and vocal styles of visiting artists. I am privileged to have had first-rate teaching colleagues. The styles of three in particular have influenced me the most: ethnomusicologist Chris Waterman's holistic way of situating music at the core of a culture's identity, Barbara Reeder Lundquist's riveting approach to teaching the world's musics through engaging and all-inclusive participatory experiences, and musicologist Larry Starr's method of weaving his own live performances into a set of recorded selections and colorful lectures that lead students to a thorough grasp of the musical essence of a work, a genre, or a culture. They are models for their colleagues, as well as their students, to emulate.

Here in Seattle, we have an arrangement at the state's "Research One" institution[25] allowing prospective teachers to enroll in ethnomusicology or world musics studies for nearly 10 percent of their undergraduate program in music education. Students are as likely to graduate with applied music studies in Thai classical court music or Ghana's Ashanti drumming as in orchestral instruments. One recent graduate, a saxophonist trained in the repertoire and technique of "legit" and jazz music genres, characterized the year he performed Korean *kayagum* (zither) and *chhango* (drum) in a chamber music recital as "a transformative experience." For master's students in music education, a popular stream of studies allows them to enroll in equal parts of ethnomusicology, applied Western art music, conducting, and education studies. Doctoral students blend studies in education and ethnomusicology with courses in anthropology, sociology, and American ethnic studies. The fusion of these disciplines emerges in theses about Samoan song text translations;[26] the training of high school

students in African, Brazilian, and Afro-Caribbean rhythmic percussion music;[27] the collection, analysis, and application of traditional Korean children's songs;[28] the realities of culture-bearers in elementary music classrooms;[29] and the influence of master teachers and societal forces in shaping Seattle's urban school music program in its zenith period from 1960 to 1975.[30]

Through my ongoing interactions with students of every age, I have come to realize that the dynamic process of understanding music as artistic cultural expression is a learning experience for the teacher as well. The input of my students and their reactions to my teaching have had major influences on views of music, education, and culture today. When a young child returning from a museum trip talks excitedly about the use of animal skins on musical instruments in Nigeria, there are lessons to be learned about children's curiosities, the museum as a community resource, and the material culture of the Yoruba people of Nigeria. When a graduate student (and experienced teacher) enthusiastically learns Khmer-language songs but then raises concerns about teaching them to Vietnamese students (whose cultural history predisposes some of them to repudiate Cambodia, its people, and its American descendents), the gains are a greater awareness of cultural attitudes and opportunities for collective problem-solving on issues of bias reduction. In these cases, students inform us of classroom realities we cannot anticipate but which subsequently guide our instructional thoughts and actions. It is intriguing to consider the frequent tribute that is paid to "elders" and to those who are hierarchically at a high level of institutional achievement, but students also bring important teaching—and learning—moments and are, in fact, catalysts for greater understanding of music and culture.

Still Catholic after All These Years

My approach to this essay has been autobiographical in nature and has been aimed at presenting a chronology of events with which other teachers "cut from a similar cloth" might identify. *Plus ça change, plus c'est la même chose*—so say the French ("The more things change, the more they remain the same"). In all these years, my Whiteness has not gone away, nor does a teacher's lifestyle ever completely allow her to remove herself from a middle-class status. Living through a period of ethnic angst, I am nostalgic for my family's past—and thus the jigs and the polkas, and even *Riverdance,* the post-modern version of Irish step-dancing, still get my blood up. Furthermore, I remain after all these years a practicing Catholic drawn by the rituals of the religion as much as its orientation toward family and community. But based upon my personal journey, there are musical and teaching convictions that have evolved and can be distinguished from my earlier stance on music, education, and culture. These tenets upon which I am currently basing my multimusical (and multicultural) teaching are worked out in print over the course of the last decade and are reviewed below in light of their practical payoffs to teachers.

Lessons from the World appeared in 1991,[31] when it began to occur to me in my own "ethno-performance" experiences that there might be crosscultural practices in the acquisition of repertoire and techniques and that the cultivation of attentive listening and creative expression were central aims in the making of musicians across time and distance. I organized the book in three sections: music learning in the West, music learning in the world, and classroom and studio applications. While the first two sections of the book surveyed the extent to which aural learning, improvisation, notation, vocalization, solmization, and memory strategies were evident, the final section offered specific recommendations for developing aural and improvisational skills in young musicians through crosscultural techniques. In retrospect, it fascinates me that the thrust of this book has had a stronger appeal to musicians and educators in Europe, the United Kingdom, and countries whose histories are still strongly linked to the U.K. (Australia, Canada, New Zealand, and South Africa) than in the United States. Perhaps the American penchant for the development of music literacy and standard performance practices over creativity is what brought the book lukewarm acceptance stateside. Or perhaps American music teachers were more focused on the search for world musics teaching materials rather than the "universals" of musical and pedagogical processes that this book addressed. Still, *Lessons from the World* prompts questions of learning and transmission that are increasingly being sought out by ethnomusicologists and educators. I am afraid that the progress on this front has been slow and may be halted due to Japan's economic downturn.

As a result of my presentation to participants in a Colloquium for Elementary Music Methods at Mountain Lake, Virginia,

253

I was invited to publish my thoughts on "multiculturalism and the raising of music teachers for the twenty-first century."[32] I focused on ways to frame the world's musical cultures in a revision of teacher education programs, including how to lead students from their musical competence to a development of their bimusical or even multimusical sensibilities. Subtitles like "the sensation of overwhelm," "no competence, no teaching?" "the Big 'A'" (for authenticity), and "the real vs. the ideal" denoted the challenges of raising musicians and teachers who are multicultural and international in perspective. The substance of the essay emanates from my own "Ethnomusicology in the Schools" course lectures, which are peppered with personal stories of filmsong-singing rickshaw drivers in India and encounters with teachers whose state "American Heritage" song-list in the mid-1990s was still lacking a broad cultural representation. The concluding section recommended a review of repertoire and instructional strategies in teacher education programs to ensure their musical, pedagogical, and cultural validity in American classrooms of children of mixed ancestries.

Manny Brand, editor of *The Quarterly Journal of Music Teaching and Learning*,[33] noted in his introduction to the special MENC issue that I had spoken "frankly and directly about MENC's successes and failures in multicultural and world music initiatives" in the critique "Musica Exotica, Multiculturalism, and School Music."[34] Something needed to be said, I sensed, about the force and frequency of multiculturalism's influence in shaping school music programs—as it was promoted by the principal umbrella group of music educa-

tors in the United States. The article commenced with an objective tracing of the organization's efforts to become inclusive and international, from the formation of the Committee on International Relations in 1929 through the 1967 Tanglewood proclamation of "musics of all periods, styles, forms, and cultures" and all the way to the proliferation of MENC publications and symposia on multicultural music education in the 1980s and 1990s. The critique unfolds in a section called "missing the mark," and a call is raised for MENC to attend to neglected professional activity in defining goals in the name of multicultural music education, recommending a diverse musical repertoire, advancing the development of teachers' musical and cultural competence, and providing the means for assessing multicultural-musical objectives. Some of these points have been attended to, while others are yet "waiting in the wings" to be realized.

In 1995, Marie McCarthy edited *Cross Currents,* the proceedings of the Charles Fowler conference at the University of Maryland at which I presented a keynote address on "Music, Education, and Community in a Multicultural Society."[35] Growing out of my earlier writings, I sought to present various political, ethical, and musical issues confronting music teachers who present musics of the world's cultures to students. Once again, I landed on matters of curricular goals, problems related to the choice and use of musical repertoire, teacher competence, and assessment. I attempted to distinguish between multicultural music education as culture-driven and world musics education as musically grounded by way of illustrations of curricular programs in the United States and abroad. All of this leads to the presentation of a Concentric Circles Music Model that stresses the importance of the teacher's personal and familial musical heritage, his or her extended musical training, and the cultures of the communities in which the school is located. This rational, pragmatic response by teachers answers the demand for increased, additional repertoire that can be confidently and competently taught—an approach that focuses concretely on teachers as transmitters of musical knowledge.

As a member of the Council of the Society for Ethnomusicology (1989–1992, 1997–1999) and chair of its Education Committee (1989–1995), I have been long interested in ethnomusicological perspectives on issues of teaching and learning. With the approval of the Education Committee, I conducted a series of eight interviews with ethnomusicologists for the 1994–95 volumes of the *Music Educators Journal,* which were later published as *Music in Cultural Context: Eight Views on World Music Education.*[36] The eight views represented older and younger generations of scholars whose expertise was in the music of a discrete culture in Africa, Asia, and the Americas; several were "culture-bearers" (persons whose personal/family culture is the same as that of their scholarly expertise). All responded to questions about authenticity, acculturation, traditional and contemporary "popular" styles, transmission (teaching and learning), and general concerns about ways in which musical cultures of the world could be best presented to elementary and secondary school students. The collected views of these eth-

nomusicologists show both unified stances (on authenticity as a "non-issue" in that music is never static nor stabilized but is always in flux) and diversified views (on culturally representative music, which ranged from one culture's turn-of-the-century social dances to another's elitist opera and narrative song genres to still another's electro-pop music, which nonetheless utilized traditional instruments and was played at traditional functions). The collaboration of ethnomusicologists with educators, I learned, was not just about scholars-giving-teachers-traditional-musics-to-teach but also about attaining understanding regarding the challenges to the mutual aims of musical transmission (and preservation) on a very broad scale.

I shifted the focus of my interests in music, education, and culture in 1998 back to the recipients of all curricular and instructional efforts—the children. Again, partly as a result of interactions with ethnomusicologists, I was growing into ethnomusicological fieldwork as a prime modus operandi for understanding children and the meaning of music in their lives. *Songs in Their Heads* (1998)[37] spirals out of the work of John Blacking, whose anthropological study of children's music in *Venda Children's Songs* (1967)[38] was one of first cases of an ethnomusicologist attending to children for the music they made and their reasons for making it. Inspired by Blacking, I observed American children on playgrounds, in school cafeterias, on buses, in toy stores, and at the periphery of a music class and interviewed them in a wide span of schools, all in an attempt to determine what their expressed thoughts and actual "musicking" behaviors were. I came to know children who were bicultural and bimusical and whose family heritages, religious backgrounds, and socioeconomic class influenced their intentional and natural music values and behaviors.

Importantly, I learned that there is an endless variety of individual children, a spectrum of children's subcultures that define them, and a large set of similarities that bind them to their own "big" culture. A teacher's knowledge of children from multiple perspectives is the best guide for teaching the world's musics to them.

Following the ethnomusicological model of "developing understanding ... through the lived experience of people making music,"[39] it has become of central importance to me to find ways for university students to do this within music education programs. Thus has arisen the "Cultural Immersion Project," a week-long music-making and teaching residency for undergraduate students at the Yakama reservation school. With funds from the university's Office of Minority Affairs, the project has provided students with opportunities for growth in pedagogical content and delivery systems appropriate for teaching children in elementary schools, while giving them a deepening understanding of learning styles that may be unique to Native American children whose lives have been wholly spent within the realm of their tribal culture. Now, after three years in operation, university students participating in this project have demonstrated growth well beyond teaching strategies; they have come to know the children themselves, including those with insufficient diets, poor housing, extended familes that include grandparents, aunts, uncles, cousins, and

friends, and community practices that do not include parental monitoring of homework assignments nor driving children to piano lessons or soccer practice. These prospective teachers are learning that they will, in fact, share responsibility for the welfare of the young people that they teach. They are learning how musical training may provide an outlet for these students' social needs, personal expression, and even solace from the difficult situations that they may face. This field experience is hooking theoretical principles to the reality of teaching practice in less-than-ideal settings and has me re-thinking university courses that assume without question students' sensitivities to issues of musical and cultural diversity.[40]

The insights shared in this essay are drawn from the experiences I have had, similar in many ways to the experiences of other music teachers. Because teachers are the composites of their past experiences and the reflective thinking they have had on these experiences, they fit each thought and deed like pieces of a puzzle into the current picture of the work they do in multicultural classrooms. They teach with the confidence of having become skilled performers and analytical listeners (and maybe composers and improvisers as well) of one of the world's great musical traditions. For those teachers who have taken on the study of musical cultures beyond their first training, they are rewarded with increased sensitivity toward their cultures and with greater receptivity to still other musical expressions that come their way. They enter unfamiliar cultures through their musical studies and are informed of the music by the people that they come to know. This is as it should be, I think, with teachers continuing their professional quest for multimusical teaching in American schools through the meaningful encounters they have with musicians—with people and their musics.

From one Caucasian, Catholic, and middle-class teacher to others who will identify with me (by way of race, religion, socioeconomic class—or, most certainly, occupation), the responsibility for nurturing children who are more broadly musical and culturally sensitive rests largely on how we ourselves plan our pathways. Developing the musical worlds of students—as well as their worldviews through the musical cultures they encounter—requires teachers who continue to seek and thrive on new knowledge that they themselves acquire.

Notes

1. Kofi Agawu, *African Rhythm: A Northern Ewe Perspective* (Cambridge: Cambridge Univ. Press, 1995), xiii.

2. Naomi Black, *Social Feminisim* (Ithaca, NY: Cornell Univ. Press, 1987), 75.

3. Judy Long, "Telling Women's Lives: The New Sociobiography" (paper presented at the annual meeting of the American Sociological Association, New York, January 1987), 5.

4. Alma Garcia, "Voices of Women of Color: Redefining Women's Studies," *Race, Gender & Class* 4, no. 2 (1997): 11–28.

5. Herbert Gans, "Symbolic Ethnicity: The Future of Ethnic Groups and Cultures in America," *Ethnic and Racial Studies* 2 (1979): 1–20.

6. Helen Myers, *Ethnomusicology: Historical and Regional Studies* (New York: W. W. Norton, 1993).

7. Allen Scott, "Jazz Is Alive and Well on the College Campus, Thank You," *National Association of Jazz Educators Journal* 2, no. 5 (1970).

8. Charles Keil, "Motion and Feeling through Music," in *Music Grooves,* by Charles Keil and Steve Feld (Chicago, IL: University of Chicago Press, 1994).

9. Robert Evans Nye and Vernice Trousdale Nye, *Music in the Elementary School,* 3rd ed. (Englewood Cliffs, NJ: Prentice Hall, 1970).

10. Ibid., 13.

11. Ibid., 560.

12. Ibid., 223–25.

13. Max Kaplan, "We Have Much to Learn from the Inner City," *Music Educators Journal* 56, no. 5 (1970): 39–42.

14. Timothy Rice, "Toward Mediation of Field Methods and Field Experience in Ethnomusicology," in *Shadows in the Field,* ed. Gregory Barz and Tim Cooley (New York: Oxford Univ. Press, 1997).

15. Charles Keil, Angeliki Keil, and Dick Blau, *Polka Happiness* (Philadelphia, PA: Temple Univ. Press, 1992).

16. Linda Gohlke, "The Music Methods Class: Acquisition of Pedagogical Content Knowledge by Pre-Service Music Teachers" (Ph.D. diss., University of Washington, 1994).

17. John Blacking, *How Musical Is Man?* (Seattle: University of Washington Press, 1973), 35.

18. Emile Jaques-Dalcroze, *Rhythm, Music, and Education* (Geneva: The Dalcroze Society, 1921).

19. Pierre Bourdieu, *Outline of a Theory of Practice* (Cambridge: Cambridge Univ. Press, 1977).

20. John Blacking, *Venda Children's Songs* (1967; reprint, Chicago, IL: University of Chicago Press, 1995). See also Jaques-Dalcroze, *Rhythm, Music,* for similar sentiments.

21. Patricia Shehan Campbell, *Lessons from the World* (New York: Schirmer Books, 1991).

22. Frances Irwin, "Comparative Methods for Teaching Meter Using Dance Music of Southeastern Europe" (Ed.D. diss., Washington University in St. Louis, 1984).

23. Linda Boyer Johnson, "Indigenous Music of Mexico: Rationale, Method, and Content in the Middle School" (Ed.D. diss., Washington University in St. Louis, 1982).

24. Patricia Shehan Campbell, *The Butler World Musics Project* (Indianapolis, IN: Franklin Printing, 1989).

25. One of about 75 doctoral-granting universities nationwide whose mission is as much research as teaching. The term "Research One" is based upon the Carnegie Classification of Institutions of Higher Learning. For further information, see www.carnegiefoundation.org/ Classification/index.htm.

26. Robert Engle, "Song Text Translation, Cultural Priority, and Implications for Vocal Music in Education: An English-to-Samoan Model" (Ph.D. diss., University of Washington, 1994).

27. Christopher Della Pietra, "The Effects of a Three-Phase Constructivist Instructional Model for Improvisation on High School Students' Perception and Reproduction of Musical Rhythm" (Ph.D. diss., University of Washington, 1997).

28. Young-Youn Kim, "Traditional Korean Children's Songs: Collection, Analysis, and Application" (Ph.D. diss., University of Washington, 1998).

29. Rita Klinger, "Matters of Compromise: An Ethnographic Study of Culture-Bearers in Elementary Music Education" (Ph.D. diss., University of Washington, 1996).

30. Patricia Costa Kim, "Making Music Their Own: School Music, Community, and Standards of Excellence in Seattle, 1960–75" (Ph.D. diss., University of Washington, 1999).

31. Patricia Shehan Campbell, *Lessons from the World* (New York: Schirmer Books, 1991).

32. Patricia Shehan Campbell, "Multiculturalism and the Raising of Music Teachers for the Twenty-First Century," *Journal of Music Teacher Education* 3, no. 2 (1994): 21–29.

33. Manny Brand, "MENC: A Meaningful Analysis," *The Quarterly Journal of Music Teaching and Learning* 5, no. 2 (1994): 3–4.

34. Patricia Shehan Campbell, "Musica Exotica, Multiculturalism, and School Music," *The Quarterly Journal of Music Teaching and Learning* 5, no. 2 (1994): 65–75.

35. Patricia Shehan Campbell, "Music, Education, and Community in a Multicultural Society," *Cross Currents: Setting an Agenda for Music Education in Community Culture*, ed. Marie McCarthy (College Park, MD: University of Maryland Press, 1996), 4–33.

36. Patricia Shehan Campbell, *Music in Cultural Context: Eight Views on World Music Education* (Reston, VA: MENC, 1996).

37. Patricia Shehan Campbell, *Songs in Their Heads: Music and Its Meaning in Children's Lives* (New York: Oxford Univ. Press, 1998).

38. Blacking, *Venda Children's Songs*.

39. J. T. Titon, "Knowing Fieldwork," *Shadows in the Field*, ed. G. Barz and T. Cooley (New York: Oxford Univ. Press, 1997), 87–100.

40. Patricia Shehan Campbell, "Lessons from the Yakama," *The Mountain Lake Reader* (2001): 46–51.

PATRICIA SHEHAN CAMPBELL is Donald E. Peterson Professor of Music at the University of Washington, where she has developed children's curricula in music and cultural studies that benefit from her background in music, education, ethnomusicology, and multicultural studies.

MENC Resources on Music and Arts Education Standards

Bringing Multicultural Music to Children (video). 1992. #3075.

Multicultural Songs, Games, and Dances, an OAKE research collection of 24 selections, with pronunciation guides. 1995. #1702.

Multicultural Perspectives in Music Education (2nd ed.), edited by William M. Anderson and Patricia Shehan Campbell. 1996. #1509.

Music in Cultural Context: Eight Views on World Music Education, by Patricia Shehan Campbell. 1996. #1634.

Music Resources for Multicultural Perspectives (CDs), selected by William M. Anderson and Patricia Shehan Campbell. 1998. #3017.

World Musics and Music Education: Facing the Issues, edited by Bennett Reimer. 2002. #1512.

Making Connections Series

Making Connections: Multicultural Music and the National Standards (Book and CD), edited by Willliam M. Anderson and Marvelene C. Moore. 1997. #3020.

Making Connections: Multicultural Music and the National Standards (Book). 1997. #1510.

Making Connections: Multicultural Music and the National Standards Companion Recording (CD). 1997. #3000.

Sounds of the World Series

Music of Eastern Europe: Albanian, Greek, and South Slavic, with a teacher's guide by Patricia Shehan Campbell. 1990. #3038.

Music of Latin America: Mexico, Ecuador, Brazil, with a teacher's guide by Dale Olsen, Charles Perrone, and Daniel Sheehy. 1987. #3032.

Music of East Asia: Chinese, Korean, and Japanese, with a teacher's guide by William M. Anderson, with Terry Liu and Ann Prescott. 1989. #3036.

Music of the Middle East: Arab, Persian/Iranian, and Turkish, with a teacher's guide by Sally Monsour, with Pamela Dorn. 1990. #3040.

Music of Southeast Asia: Lao, Hmong, Vietnamese with a teacher's guide by Patricia K. Shehan. 1986. #3030.

Teaching Music with a Multicultural Approach Series

Teaching the Music of African Americans (video). 1991. #3070.

Teaching the Music of Hispanic Americans (video). 1991. #3071.

Teaching the Music of Asian Americans (video). 1991. #3073.

Teaching the Music of the American Indian (video). 1991. #3072.

A Tribute to Woody Guthrie and Leadbelly Series

Teacher's Guide by Will Schmid. 1990. #3065.

Student Textbook by Will Schmid. 1990. #3064.

Folkways: The Original Vision, produced by the Smithsonian Office of Folklife Programs. 1988. CD #3062A; Audiocassette #3062B.

Folkways: A Vision Shared, produced by Columbia Records. 1988. VHS #3036A; CD #3036B; Audiocassette #3063C.

For more information on these and other MENC publications, write to MENC Publications Sales, 1806 Robert Fulton Drive, Reston, VA 20191-4348, call 800-828-0229, or visit our Web site at www.MENC.org.